Praise for Cleop

"Angela strives to make the ancient world accessi...
ers . . . [offering] genuine insights."   *—Publishers Weekly*

"[*Cleopatra*] combines scholarship with novelistic detail and character
depth. . . . Alberto Angela effectively draws on previous scholarship,
wading through legend and myth to get at the truth of what actually
occurred. . . . [A] character-rich historical biography."
                                                                                        —Kirkus Reviews

"The political machinations, betrayal, and battles may appeal to those
fans of George R. R. Martin's A Song of Ice and Fire series interested
in a real-world game of thrones."   *—Booklist*

"Maybe we think we know everything about this charming woman,
yet Alberto Angela, with his thirst for art and culture, will tell us
things that will perhaps surprise us and surely remain in our minds
and hearts."   —Roberto Baldini, *Sololibri*

"*Cleopatra* is more than a book; it is like being immersed in a doc-
umentary expertly narrated by the one Italian who can do it best:
Alberto Angela. . . . Written well, in a precise and engaging way, it
reads lightly despite the topics covered."
                                                    —Silvia Capelletto, *Leggere a Colori*

"Its fidelity to historical sources is complimented by its imaginative,
light-on-its-feet narrative style."   *—Il Messaggero*

"*Cleopatra* dismantles falsehoods and stereotypes to reconstruct a
more authentic and reliable portrait of its central figure."
                                                                                        —La Stampa

"A compelling and convincing fresco, full of action and emotion."
                                                                                        —La Repubblica

Cleopatra

Cleopatra

The Queen Who Challenged Rome and Conquered Eternity

Alberto Angela

Translated by Katherine Gregor

HarperVia

An Imprint of HarperCollins*Publishers*

Map designs © 2020, Studio Leksis.

HarperCollins books may be purchased for educational, business, or sales promotional use. For information, please email the Special Markets Department at SPsales@harpercollins.com.

Translation copyright © 2021 by Katherine Desiree Gregor.

Originally published as *Cleopatra: La regina che sfidò Roma e conquistò l'eternità* in Italy in 2018 by HarperCollins Italia.

FIRST HARPERCOLLINS PAPERBACK PUBLISHED IN 2022

Designed by SBI Book Arts, LLC

Library of Congress Cataloging-in-Publication Data is available upon request.

ISBN 978-0-06-298422-7

22 23 24 25 26   LSC   10 9 8 7 6 5 4 3 2 1

To Riccardo, Edoardo, and Alessandro.
To all the boys and girls with the future in their
eyes and all our hopes in their hearts.

Contents

Preface

Cleopatra is a name that summons definite images and feelings in every one of us. In our mind's eye we immediately see the face of a stunning-looking, intelligent, and elegant woman with a deep gaze, and oozing sensuality. We're immediately enveloped by the charm of Ancient Egypt and Rome. We automatically associate her name with Julius Caesar and Mark Antony, and the two greatest love stories of all time. Few figures from the past can arouse such powerful feelings in us, even though they lived a long, long time ago, more than two thousand years ago to be precise.

But how could this have happened? How did a delicate, lone woman, in an ancient world dominated by men, lead the kingdom of Egypt to its greatest expansion ever and become one of history's brightest stars? It's a question I have tried to answer in this book.

I've tried to discover who Cleopatra really was, how she managed to seduce and conquer some of Rome's greatest men, like Caesar and Mark Antony, and to what she owed her extraordinary talent for strategy in the field of geopolitics.

You will see emerge the figure of an amazingly modern woman, one very different from what we expect. It's precisely Cleopatra's "modernity" that allowed her to stand out so powerfully in ancient history. Even now, she would most probably have left her mark on politics, industry, or high finance, but since she lived more than two millennia ago, she had a crucial influence on her world.

One of the driving forces behind this book was to try to discover the importance of her role at one of ancient history's pivotal moments.

Of course, it escapes no one's notice that she lived at a turning point between two great civilizations, Ancient Egypt and Rome. But that's not all: she was present at the exact stage when the long history of the kingdoms of Egypt—including the pharaohs—ended and that of the Roman Empire began through the principate of Augustus. I could summarize the life and times of Cleopatra in just a few words: the twilight of a kingdom and the dawn of an empire.

This book focuses on a crucial passage in history, specifically on the fourteen-year period between March 44 BC and August 30 BC. It comes as a surprise to discover how pivotal these few years were for antiquity and Western history. As a matter of fact, our story begins with six important names connected to power—Caesar, Cassius, Brutus, Mark Antony, Octavian, and Cleopatra—and only one is left at the end: Octavian. It was he, now with no more rivals, who would have the time and wisdom to lay the foundations of one of the greatest empires of all time: Rome.

The question is: How instrumental was Cleopatra in making this process possible and indirectly allowing Octavian to be the only one left in power? As you will see, very much so. Because Cleopatra is not only an alluring woman and a queen very capable of managing power, but also an incredible historical catalyst.

Your journey through this book will take place in the extraordinary framework of classical antiquity, against the backdrop of three continents: Europe, Asia, and Africa, from the river Nile to the mountainous expanses of Armenia, from Cleopatra's palaces to Caesar's home, from the Lighthouse of Alexandria to the Roman Senate, from the Greek coast to the arid areas of the Middle East; and it will transport you for thousands of miles, crossing the Mediterranean many times. You will witness important naval clashes, cruel land battles, explore the splendid home of Cleopatra in Alexandria and those of the Roman authorities, all of this told in a narrative style devised specifically to make you feel as though you are right there, in the places and atmosphere of that time.

This journey has involved the careful consultation of a great number of materials and sources, from essays written by modern historians, experts, and scholars to texts by ancient authors and descriptions of archaeological findings. It has not been easy to reconstruct in full the events and locations you will read about. More than two thousand years later, sometimes all you can rely on is the evidence and writings of the ancients, bearing in mind all their potential limitations, since some were hostile to Cleopatra and Mark Antony or else influenced by pro-Octavian and anti-Cleopatra propaganda. Moreover, in these writings many episodes are incomplete or fail to feature altogether.

In addition, we can't be certain what the buildings visited or lived in by Cleopatra, Caesar, and Mark Antony looked like because hardly any of them are still around. The tables, clothes, marbles, and palaces have disappeared, the legendary lighthouse has collapsed, and entire cities have vanished: the Alexandria of Cleopatra was demolished over the centuries and is now covered by modern buildings, and Antioch, which used to be the third-largest city on the Mediterranean, no longer exists. To make a comparison, it would be as though Paris, Frankfurt, London, New York, or Washington were to disappear two millennia from now, and people would wonder what they were like, relying on books and descriptions.

We don't even know what Cleopatra really looked like . . .

So what can we do? We can take the only possible approach. If reality has gone, we can make *plausible* reconstructions based on what we know about that time, on archaeological data, and by making use of the advice of contemporary historians. All the fictionalized parts in this book are based on faithful historical reconstructions of the locations and customs of the time.

The narrative style helps to breathe life into actual, experienced history, which clings, often in shreds, to these precious ancient texts—provided everything in the storytelling is carried out with precision or, in the absence of information, as plausibly as possible.

The hardest thing was to describe Cleopatra's, Caesar's, Antony's, and Octavian's states of mind. These have sometimes been taken from ancient sources, while at other times it has been necessary to describe a scene, making it clear that it's actually a reconstruction—plausible of course, but nevertheless hypothetical. I don't believe there's any other way to stand beside the protagonists at the very moment when history is being made. There are many books on ancient history, and precious, inexhaustible sources of information, data, and quotations. But these are often rather dry because they lack "life." History is also a story. Is it possible to bring together historical information and story-telling? To combine the pleasure of reading a novel with the rigor of an academic text? I'd like to think so, and have tried to do something different with my book: to breathe life into history and create a piece of work that provides information using a different way, in a style akin to—and certainly not intended to replace—the classic books on ancient history. I take full responsibility for any potential errors, but the opportunity to stand next to Cleopatra during the crucial moments of ancient history was not to be missed . . .

Enjoy the book.

Cleopatra

1

The Twilight of a Republic

March 15, 44 BC

She gazes at the distant horizon, as though trying to re-create the embrace of tender, protective feelings and memories.

A silk scarf, swelled by a gust of wind like a sail, forms a frame around her face. It would have already been blown away were she not holding it firmly in place with her hand. It's the only sign of strength in the naked body of this woman, nestled in the valve of a huge shell. You can't make out her contours in the faint light of dawn. And you couldn't anyway, since her beauty is made up of thousands of small stone tiles that form her curves in the center of a room. This elegant mosaic of Venus in a shell is gradually caressed by a distant rustle, that of a fine gown brushing the floor as it approaches. All of a sudden, it stops and, as softly as a feather, a small, well-cared-for foot steps on Venus's hip. It lingers on the mosaic for a moment, then resumes its walk across the room quietly, accompanied only by the murmur of the gown on the floor. With every step, the snow-white dress sways in tandem with the body, like a dancer clinging to his beloved. This regular movement is conducted by the hips, which surface for a second through the whiteness of the tunic, like dolphins emerging from the water before plunging back and vanishing again, giving the long folds just a few seconds to resume their elegant arrangement. The tunic seems to float in the semi-dark corridor, the obscurity pierced only by a few beams of light, rhythmically projecting the glow of the gown on the frescoes covering the walls, like a luminous caress that touches the paintings as lightly as a cloud. Heading to a remote window, the form is silhouetted against the light. The tunic then seems to dissolve and turn into a luminous halo around the body, that of a twenty-five-year-old woman, small, slender enough, but very curvy. Her every move suggests an indefinable blend of harmony, voluptuousness, and elegance that gives rise to a deep sensuality. She walks slowly, and the pattern traced in the air by her hips does the rest. This woman's allure is as impalpable as the trail of perfume in her wake. And, just like with a scent, her true secret lies not so much in her beauty as in the feelings she arouses in those near her. It's a secret she has learned to dose and use with skill, just like the healing potions and poisons she mastered a long time ago.

She is Cleopatra.

Contrary to popular belief, her name is not Egyptian, but Greek.

It means "father's glory," in the sense of "glorious lineage" (from the Greek κλέος, *kleos*, "glory," and πατρός, *patros*, "of the father"). Cleopatra isn't actually Egyptian, but Greco-Macedonian. She belongs to a dynasty of invaders who have occupied the Egyptian throne for almost three hundred years: the Ptolemaic dynasty, with different customs and a different language, Greek. Her full name is Cleopatra Thea Philopator, literally "Cleopatra, the goddess who loves her father" (from the Greek θεά, *thea*, "goddess," and Φιλοπάτωρα, *philopatora*, "who loves her father"). Although we perceive her name as unique in history and belonging to an equally unique queen, she was not the only one to be called that. We know of six others preceding her, which is why, to avoid any confusion, modern historians refer to her as Cleopatra VII. Why were there so many Cleopatras? The reason is that it was customary among the Ptolemies to use recurring dynastic names (like the French kings did with Louis). Consequently, the princesses invariably had one of these three names: Arsinoe, Berenice, or Cleopatra.

Cleopatra's Egypt was very different from what we all imagine. There are respectively 1,200, 1,300, and more than 1,400 years between her and other famous Egyptian women such as Nefertari (Pharaoh Ramesses II's wife), Nefertiti (Pharaoh Akhenaten's wife), and Hatshepsut. It's like comparing a modern woman with one who lived at the time of Charlemagne or the early-medieval Lombards. Cleopatra lived in a completely different Egypt, a kingdom already invaded and ruled by Persians for quite a few centuries before being conquered by Alexander the Great, who then started the Greco-Macedonian Ptolemaic dynasty that remained on the throne for another three centuries or so.

When Cleopatra was born, Egypt seemed destined to end up in the jaws of Rome, the new world power. She would become a great stateswoman and strategist who would give Egypt a new lease of life and even bring it new lands and new wealth. As a matter of fact, thanks to Cleopatra's shrewd politics and her ability to ensnare first Caesar, then Antony, Egypt would gain control of practically every shore of the eastern Mediterranean, from Turkey to Libya. It was an extraordinary result, owed strictly to her talent. This would be the final great dominion of the kingdom of Egypt before the latter vanished from history forever. Cleopatra would reign for only twenty-one years, but the destiny of the ancient world would be played out through her, making her into one of the most powerful, influential, and determined women of all time. Perhaps no other woman, outside Elizabeth I of England, would achieve as much. And yet she would die before the age of forty.

In a world dominated by men, the fate of the Western world was in the hands of a young woman, at a crucial moment when Rome was turning from a republic to an empire. This would not have been possible without Cleopatra, at least not with the kind of results we see in the pages of our history books, since it's also because of her that the power struggle between Antony and Octavian was unleashed and would end with just one player left on the scene, Octavian, capable of ruling and living for such a long time that he would lay the solid foundations of an empire that would last several centuries.

An endless list of titles trails behind the young woman walking silently through the fresco-walled rooms: Queen of Kings and Queens, Queen of Upper and Lower Egypt, Queen of Cyprus . . . Now, however, two thousand years later, her name mainly summons a woman of irresistible and exotic allure, educated, independent, capable of mastering men and conquering them with overwhelming passion. Can all that come together in this woman who is only twenty-five?

Cleopatra has stepped onto a *pergula*, a kind of balcony with an elegant wooden lattice roof, which separates it from the outside world. Her fingers caress the arabesque pattern of the grating and feel the crisp early morning air, with that typically cool, sharp smell seeping through it. The young woman closes her eyes for a moment and fills her lungs with a deep breath. Then she opens them slowly to reveal a warm, intense, and luminous gaze—like the sun in her native land when it rises in the silence of Egypt's boundless desert.

But now, disturbed only by the fluttering of her long eyelashes, a different land and, above all, a different world is mirrored in her eyes. As we gradually draw closer to her gaze, the image we can make out in her eyes is that of a huge city beyond a wide river. It's Rome, as seen by anyone looking at it from Trastevere, where we have the Horti Caesaris, Julius Caesar's large property that hosts the queen of Egypt, who has come to Rome.

You can sense the vastness of the city, the largest on the Mediterranean and increasingly the absolute protagonist of the world as we then knew it. Just as Egypt was for many centuries. But things have changed now . . .

We are getting closer and closer to Cleopatra's eyes. The city reflected in them now looks sharp, so sharp that we can walk down its streets and start to explore it.

Rome at Dawn

We're in 44 BC, at the end of the Republic. There's still an entire generation to come before the birth and power of the Roman Empire, but for some time already Rome has been the chaotic, cosmopolitan city that would astound ancient writers and archaeologists. It already looks stunning.

A strong wind has swept away the clouds and rain of the past few hours. Day is breaking in the east, and the first, timid rays of the sun are already touching the Capitoline Hill and lighting the Temple of Jupiter Optimus Maximus and its huge pillars. Inside, next to the statues of Juno and Minerva, between which priests walk in silence while preparing the morning ritual, stands the towering effigy of the supreme god, Jupiter, a true masterpiece, probably sculpted from ivory and gold. The whole temple, each side about sixty-six yards long, takes your breath away. According to some sources, the magnificent pillars with Corinthian capitals come from faraway Greece; Sulla actually had them removed from the Temple of Olympian Zeus in Athens in 86 (or 84) BC. A Greek soul in the heart of Rome: evidence of the strength of a new power but also a glimmer of the past for its future. It was what Sulla wanted. As the sun rises, the gilt bronze statues and the pediment reliefs on the temple gradually light up; then, suddenly, they seem to be ablaze, like torches. An awe-inspiring, symbolic display, visible from almost every part of the city.

Dawn pours light on the buildings of the Eternal City, breathing life into its colors. The blue-gray veil that had enveloped it since dawn vanishes little by little, revealing the red rooftops. In this first breath of the day, Rome looks like a rippling sea, an infinite expanse of many waves that correspond to buildings of various heights, with terraces, dormer windows, and authentic roof "staircases" following the line of the hills. And, here and there, like flowers in a field, rise the green, gleaming tops of the temples, made of gilt bronze tiles, now tarnished.

It looks like a keyboard designed by an architect upon which life, like a talented pianist, plays the symphony of awakening. Small pillars of white smoke drift up in the crisp air, a sign that some people have rekindled their hearths in order to cook food, are celebrating a ritual in a temple, lighting the large furnaces in the baths, or simply starting up their workshops.

And then there are the walls. Rome is still a city of bricks . . . It is Octavian, the future Augustus, who will transform it into a city of marble, as he himself liked to say. We assume these brick walls are coated in brilliant-white plaster, which, at that very moment, begins to glow in the sunlight, cloaking the city in light. A glow that descends gradually, like luminous steam, into the alleys still immersed in the half-light. A man is walking down one of these alleys, trying to avoid a rivulet snaking across the surface of beaten earth. You can hear wooden shutters creak open above his head, slamming hard against the wall (glass windows are a rarity, probably unknown to the Roman plebs). The man picks up the pace. He knows only too well that opening windows often heralds the emptying of chamber pots. For centuries to come, a toilet at home would be a luxury throughout the Western world, except for the wealthy, who, in Rome, live on the lower stories, the main stories, where there is even water, a precious possession that exists only in the homes of the fortunate few (usually aristocratic families, wealthy men, or those with important connections in local government).

The rabble, however, crowds the upper stories, which have no facilities or running water, living in small rented apartments and, as so often seen in Suburra, the most working-class district in Rome, even subletting rooms (sometimes even dividing them up with canvas and inner partitions in order to allow strangers to share their living space).

In Rome, water is hardly ever private property but rather a public asset that is widespread and available. There's never a shortage of it, but for that you have to go down to street level, where you find a multitude of public fountains positioned strategically on the streets. They are never too far apart, so that anybody filling pails or jugs to take home doesn't have to walk far. It's a capillary distribution system aimed at quenching the thirst of the largest city in the Western world.

And quenching the thirst of almost a million people may well be Rome's true secret. The city would be described in different ways throughout history: *Caput Mundi*, Head of the World; the Eternal City; people would say that "all roads lead to Rome"; yet few remember that it was also called *Regina Aquarum*, Queen of the Waters, because there was such an abundance of it in Roman times.

There would come a stage—after our story—when thanks to eleven aqueducts it would receive 264,172 gallons of running water a day! A quantity that only the modern era, 1964, to be exact, would match and surpass. But seeing that the population of the Rome of the Caesars—under the Antonines in particular—barely exceeded one million, while modern-day metropolitan Rome has a little more than double that, we can definitely say that back in the times of the Roman Empire every inhabitant had twice the amount of water *per capita* as they do today.

Our man has reached the end of the alley and stops to drink from a fountain. Then, wiping his mouth with the back of his hand, he resumes his walk while behind him someone screams then swears in Latin. Somebody has been showered with the contents of a chamber pot. In the present day, this may make us smile, but it would not have done so at the time of our story. On the contrary, it was an actual crime: the various laws in the Roman judicial system included this very kind of "aerial" soiling (a crime, to all intents and purposes), complete with penalties according to the degree of damage to tunics, togas, and, of course, the person affected.

Although the sun has been up for only a few minutes, the streets are already teeming with people. Mainly slaves and servants attending to their early morning chores, wrapped figures, numb with cold, walking down the chilly alleys. There are puddles everywhere because it rained again last night, a real storm, as a matter of fact, with thunder, lightning, and a strong wind. The alleys are strewn with items that have fallen off the roofs and balconies: clothes hung out to dry that are now shapeless rags, baskets flown away, and flowerpots (strangely enough, they were already used in Roman times). Spring has yet to arrive. It's a matter of days.

One thing seems clear. At this time, Rome is not yet the splendid, monumental city we see in the movies or read about in novels. It is poorer and simpler, in both its monuments and its architecture, and is still somewhat provincial in comparison with the majesty it will acquire just a few decades from now. It's a crowded, chaotic city, humble and with a rather medieval flavor, since it was built from a maze of narrow alleys, tall and often precarious buildings, colored with a mosaic of washing hanging out to dry. Among these buildings, in the streets of beaten earth, amid rivulets of liquid sewage, there's an effervescence of life, and children run around laughing and shouting. There's much criticism of the state of the Eternal City's streets, of the *clivi* (uphill roads) in particular, a problem so serious that Julius Caesar has ordered them to be paved because they are too dusty in the summer and too muddy in the winter . . . although this will never happen. And today we'll discover why not.

The Coliseum Did Not Exist

You may be surprised to hear that back in Cleopatra's day, Rome did not have many of the monuments and buildings with which we are familiar and that we assume have always existed. Millions of tourists come to Rome every year to admire them, but back then they had not yet been built. You'd be surprised by the list.

Here is what Cleopatra, Mark Antony, and even Julius Caesar, Cicero, and Octavian never saw:

- The Coliseum would be inaugurated more than a century later, 124 years later to be exact. But then, you will ask, where did gladiators fight? Provisional wooden amphitheaters were erected for the *munera gladiatoria*, or gladiatorial combats, in the same way as bleachers are set up for street performances and concerts today.

- The Pantheon would be built 17 years later, by Agrippa, Augustus's son-in-law and loyal commander. Its current appearance, however, dates back to an era even more remote from Cleopatra. Damaged by two fires, it would be rebuilt by Hadrian, in other words, about 160 years after the day we are currently describing, perhaps by Apollodorus of Damascus himself, who was, some say, a kind of Roman Empire Leonardo, and who would eventually perhaps be murdered by Hadrian.

- The Baths of Caracalla would be built more than 250 years later.

- The Baths of Trajan would appear about 150 years later.

- The Baths of Diocletian would open 350 years later.

- The Imperial Fora would be erected between 42 (Forum of Augustus) and 156 (Forum of Trajan) years later.

- In the Roman Forum, the Arch of Titus and the Arch of Septimius Severus, so frequently photographed by tourists, would be built respectively 130 and 246 years later.

- Obviously, there were no Catacombs during the time of Cleopatra and Caesar. They would start sprouting timidly many years later, and gradually turn into a huge maze under Constantine, in the fourth century.

- The Imperial Palaces on the Palatine did not exist yet. There were a few beautiful, frescoed *domus* belonging to the city's most prominent aristocratic families. It wouldn't be until after the famous fire of Rome, 108 years later, that we'd gradually see the appearance of the great palaces of power, where Roman emperors would live and rule.

- The *Domus Aurea* would appear more than a century later, only to disappear again after a few decades.

- There were no obelisks in the circuses and squares. They were still in Egypt, and Augustus would bring the first two to Rome, on huge, purpose-built ships.

On the other hand, on this March 15, 44 BC, the day of Julius Caesar's death, there are monuments and public events that Cleopatra may well have seen (although we are not sure to what extent a foreign queen could go about the *pomerium*, or "sacred" heart of Rome), but which, in the modern era, no longer exist:

- An anaumachia, built by Caesar in Campus Martius a few years earlier.

- The Temple of Venus Genetrix and the attached sacred area (with, inside, a statue of Cleopatra standing opposite the statue of the goddess).

- The Basilica Julia, although it had not been entirely completed yet.

- You can admire a large number of bronze statues looted from Greece—of a beauty comparable to that of the Riace Bronzes—of which only a few splendid later Roman copies, often damaged, are at present kept in museums. In particular, there is in the Portico Metelli (subsequently called Porticus Octaviae in honor of Augustus's sister), a splendid group representing Alexander the Great galloping with twenty-five of his horsemen, killed during the Battle of the Granicus in 334 BC, which will later be destroyed and recast in the early Middle Ages.

- A huge collection of carved gemstones and sculpted, hard stone goblets that have been brought to Rome by Pompey and even Caesar, for example, the Farnese Cup (or Ptolemies' Cup).

The Rome that Caesar, Mark Antony, and Cleopatra knew still exists, however, and you can admire its buildings, temples, and monuments that still stand centuries later (albeit slightly altered by Romans themselves throughout the generations):

- The Circus Maximus (though not as large and imposing in 44 BC).

- The Roman Forum and many of its temples, including the Temple of Vesta, where Rome's sacred fire is preserved.

- The Forum of Caesar, recently inaugurated by the dictator.

- The Capitoline Hill with its Temple of Jupiter Optimus Maximus.

In other words, the Rome where we are is different from the one we have in mind when we think of the Classical era, and this is an important distinction, because the events we are about to witness in our story are set during what we can call a formative period of Rome. Rome has not yet bloomed in history, nor generated an empire even though it has already subjugated large geographical areas and turned them into provinces. Although it is already the political center of the Mediterranean, it does not yet have the role of cultural, economic, and social mover with which everyone would identify it. This it will acquire at the end of our story: from that point will begin the process that, going through Augustus's principate, will give birth to the

Roman Empire. However, without the pages that lead to it, history would have turned out very differently. It's a critical and essential moment for the entire Western world, and there's no knowing what the present world would be like without the protagonists of this book: Julius Caesar, Octavian, Mark Antony, and, of course, Cleopatra—the woman who weaved their destinies together and determined the fate of Rome. And of the world.

The City Is Awakening

Let us continue along the streets of Rome, as we follow the man who emerged from the alley. He's just come across a group of people having a heated discussion at a crossroads. Two wagons are trying to get through but obstructing each other. It's no more than an ordinary matter of priority, but the carters' tempers are high and there are shouts and insults flying. A small crowd has gathered around them, enjoying the show. This is a classic street scene in modern life, but also one you could witness in Cleopatra's time. And no wonder. Because Rome is so crowded, Caesar has forbidden carts from passing through during the day, and effectively turned the Eternal City into a huge pedestrian area. All the vehicles that deliver supplies to workshops, stores, houses, etc., have to travel the streets at night, the creaking of the wheels and the cursing of the drivers disturbing the slumber of those who sleep on the lower stories. Which is what is happening right now: neither carter wants to back down, because they are trying to rush out of the city before the light of day in order to avoid fines and penalties.

Our man bypasses the crowd, furtively skirts the wall of a building, and walks away. He is tall, slim, with a gaunt face, deep-set eyes, and a penetrating gaze. The thick black beard that comes down to his chest suggests he is a philosopher. A Greek philosopher, to be precise, whose name is Artemidorus Knidos. He has been teaching the language, philosophy, and literature of his country of origin in Rome for many years. We know from the historian Appian, also a Greek, that this anonymous-looking man is actually a close friend of Julius Caesar. We know of his presence in these streets partly thanks to another Ancient Greek writer and philosopher, Plutarch. This man walking down a city street that may look like an anthill from above is no ordinary resident. Even though we don't have the sources, it's very probable that at this precise moment he is holding in his hand a papyrus with a few lines that could change the history of the ancient world and the entire Western world over the coming centuries . . .

It's like a novel about international intrigue: Can that thin roll really contain one of the most significant "sliding doors" of human history? Let's keep following Artemidorus.

Around him, the city is awakening. It's like witnessing a performance being prepared, with workers setting up the stage. Here is a store opening its shutters. Yes, shutters. There are no glass fronts or metal blinds. Every shop (or *taberna*) is closed from within by means of wooden planks placed vertically and secured with a long bolt. The squeak of the rusty bolt is now a familiar sound to anyone living nearby, as is that of the planks being lifted then propped heavily against the wall on the side of the store. A sound that turns into a small cloud of dust.

Artemidorus glances inside as he walks past, and sees in the darkness a father and his two sons starting to display their goods—in this case brightly colored fabrics—outside the *taberna*. With impressive agility, the youngest boy scrambles up a long bronze pole to hang cushions from the ceiling. This is clearly a cloth seller's shop, able to provide all kinds of fabrics, covers, cushions, and ". . . even the rarest, finest silks from the East," as the owner, who is currently at the back of the store, likes to say. You can just about glimpse his face, illuminated by the light of an oil lamp. He is saying his morning prayers while making an offering of wine and food to small, bronze statuettes arranged in an alcove. This alcove, adorned with small wooden pillars, is a lararium, a kind of little home temple that has crucial importance in Roman daily life. The offerings guarantee the protection of the lares against theft, fire, disease, and negativity.

It's no coincidence that you often see outside a shop, either hanging or painted, or even carved in the cobbles, an erect phallus. These are not directions to a brothel, as some people say, but simple amulets to protect health, bring vital energy, attract good profits, and especially act as "lightning rods" to repel invectives on the part of passersby or other, envious shopkeepers. Sometimes, as in this case, one of the statuettes in the lararium represents Mercury, the divine patron of shopkeepers—and thieves. On these streets, the difference is often very subtle.

Artemidorus continues on his way. The next shop is that of a potter, with amphorae, painted dishes, and jugs delicately displayed on wooden tables and stalls near the entrance. What stands out among the various items is that splendid type of ceramic called *terra sigillata*, goblets and dishes decorated so as to get a shiny coat and the typical bright red color. This elegant crockery, mass-produced with pottery molds, is adorned with subtle relief patterns thanks to a technique we now call *barbotine*, which consists of applying diluted clay with a brush or spatula so as to form small lumps or ripples, the ancient Roman equivalent of Capodimonte and Sèvres porcelain. Every respectable family owned some: it was the fine dinner set you showed off to your guests. Did Cleopatra ever use them? She probably did, although considering them very common, seeing how she was used to silver dishes, alabaster and glass goblets and glasses, as well as an even higher, more luxurious standard of living.

A sudden crash makes Artemidorus turn to look. A slave has carelessly dropped a jug. The owner's reaction is brutal: a volley of untranslatable words seconds before a hail of blows and kicks, reminding us how much more violent this society is in comparison with ours. We call it "civilization" (however ancient) because never in the history of humanity has anybody reached such a high level of social organization, as well as artistic and cultural refinement. But in comparison with ours, so many sectors, especially those connected with freedom and people's rights, are still very coarse and cruel toward those who are at the bottom of society—slaves. And not just toward them. In these times, pedophilia, slavery, the death penalty, and massacres at the borders are everyday events and are in no way outrageous or newsworthy . . .

Artemidorus picks up the pace and continues his journey in the atmosphere of Caesar and Cleopatra's Rome, which is waking up to a new day. A few yards farther on, he is greeted by a hollow thud. Then another and another. A butcher has just given a series of blows with his cleaver to a three-legged wooden block to separate an ox's ribs. Every strike of the gleaming cleaver is accompanied by the frightened flutter of hens tied up near the man. Perhaps they can sense the fate that awaits them. At the back of the store, past a collection of pigs' heads, a host of flies, and hanging lambs, sits a woman. She's the butcher's wife and is cleaning a large abacus while waiting for the first customer. In ancient Rome, it's women who generally keep the books in the shops and man the cash desk, no doubt because they are much shrewder at calculations and especially more reliable at managing the pennies.

Artemidorus pulls a face and waves away the flies from the butcher's shop before crossing the street. Now he is enveloped in the strong scent of spices on display in the *taberna* in front of him, caressing his senses . . . but not as much as the smell of freshly baked bread that drifts from the shop next door. It's a *popina*, the typical Roman-era café. You can see them in archaeological sites such as Ostia and Pompeii, with their characteristic L-shaped brick counters and large holes on the top. Many people will tell you that they were for vessels containing wine, but that's not the case. Wine—and Artemidorus could confirm this even now—is stored in amphorae lined up on the counter. The shopkeeper uses these holes to access dried vegetables, grain, spelt, and other foods sold to customers. Back then, cafés were also grocery stores where one could have a drink and buy food.

There are patrons sipping hot wine and eating hard-boiled eggs and *focaccia* with honey. It's a kind of ancient Roman Continental breakfast. We must remember that Romans always had a very large breakfast, which, depending on their means, included milk, meat or cheese, wine, and fruit—ingredients that gave you the required energy to start the day. A day that begins early, at dawn, so as to take advantage of all the available daylight.

This Man Can Change History

Artemidorus does not stop at the *popina* but continues. He's not hungry but very tense and focused on his purpose. His hands are sweaty, his throat dry, his senses on maximum alert. He takes alleys and shortcuts, avoiding places that are too crowded. He often turns to check that he's not being followed before slipping briskly into side passages. He has just one aim: he must absolutely deliver the message as soon as possible without being intercepted. It's a matter of life and death. But to whom must he give this message? And what is written in the sealed scroll that is so important? If it's so urgent, why not give it to a trusted, quick slave? Because there's the risk that the slave may be caught and the message read, and that would spell the death of Artemidorus and, especially, of the person to whom it is addressed.

We said that these lines could change history, but what is written there that is so important?

The message, which, according to Appian, not only really existed but was in the hands of Artemidorus on that morning of March 15, 44 BC, has a single objective: to save Caius Julius Caesar.

In those few lines, the philosopher warns his friend that someone is plotting against him and will try to kill him during the meeting at the Senate. Maybe it also mentions the names of some of the conspirators, hoping that Caesar may prevent them from approaching him, or perhaps it simply begs him not to attend the assembly. We will never know that. What we do know is that if this message reaches its destination and Caesar reads it, the assassination of the Ides of March could be foiled, with incalculable and crucial consequences for the centuries to come.

Throughout the millennia, seldom has a single man held in his hand so important a turning point for the history and fate of so many people for centuries to come . . . This scroll is like a key that can unlock two different kinds of scenario: history without Caesar, as we know it, or else history with Caesar and, consequently, without the clash between Octavian and Antony, without the love affair between Antony and Cleopatra, who would have continued to be Caesar's partner and then definitely obtained the respect of the Romans toward the kingdom of Egypt, which would then not have become a province of Rome. There would not have been, at least not so soon, the rise of Octavian, no given name of Augustus, no birth of an empire, created with patience and wisdom, with the development of the *cursus publicus* (the most efficient postal service set up during the imperial era), a network of fifty thousand miles of roads we still use today, or its laws and reforms. Could someone else have done it instead of Augustus? Perhaps, but not in the way he did, since his extraordinary longevity (he died at the age of seventy-seven, a rare occurrence if not exceptional back then) gave him enough time to build it with care.

Caesar, on the other hand, already advanced in years, would not have had that much time available. Besides this detail, had he lived, his would have been a different world anyway, forged by his reforms and his strength.

Who knows where we would be today?

What's certain is that in the forthcoming hours, a powerful historical catalyst is about to trigger a "domino effect" that will sculpt the centuries to come, future generations, and ultimately, even each and everyone's life at present . . . Because if, on March 15, 44 BC, things had turned out differently, you and I probably would never have been born . . .

It beggars belief that this Greek philosopher should be holding in his sweaty hands the fate of billions of unborn people—simply mind-boggling.

We know from history books how things turned out, and considering the twenty-three stab wounds inflicted just a few hours later, we must conclude that Caesar never did receive this message. And yet that's not exactly what happened. On the contrary, Artemidorus did accomplish his mission and hand Caesar this scroll. What will occur next, however, is unbelievable.

Cleopatra Gets Ready

Cleopatra's eyes are closed. Her eyelids contract only very slightly when Eiras, her stylist, gently presses the golden rod against them to trace that long black kohl line from the eyes to the temples, perhaps the most famous and distinctive trait of Egyptian makeup. It is a slow but confident, almost harmonious movement. The rod slides along the lower lid, then continues along the skin. She repeats the act several times until she achieves a perfect dark line with no smears. Eiras is one of Cleopatra's trump cards: lengthened with kohl, which has eliminated or concealed any imperfection, her eyes now look embedded in black, like full moons in a night sky. And when she opens them again, her gaze, which is already alluring, has acquired extraordinary power.

It's been said that had Cleopatra had a shorter nose, the face of the earth would have been different (its history, that is). We shall discover the truth about the queen's nose further on in our story. The fact is that this Egyptian makeup, so heavy and intriguing, is a silent (and not often mentioned) secret that is perhaps even more significant in Cleopatra's allure and sex appeal, which are legendary.

Eiras is the best makeup artist at the Egyptian court, and given her daily contact with Cleopatra, perhaps even something more. She's probably a good listener in whom the queen confides and someone who can keep secrets. We know that Cleopatra will always want her at her side. A few years later, she will be present at the famous Battle of Actium and remain silently at her side until the end: Cleopatra will die in her arms. It is therefore highly probable that she is also with her here in Rome.

But what makeup does a queen use? What's her beauty regime?

It's not all that different from that of all other Egyptian women (except for the quality of the cosmetics, perfumes, and accessories, the finest and most costly at the time). In Egypt, women use face cream made of natural oils to which natural pigment (an equivalent of earth) is added to give a touch of color to the skin. Unlike our current trends, they try to have untanned skin: it must be very fair. But this involves the use of white "foundation" based on specific kinds of clay. It is said that oily substances are the main ingredient of their cosmetics. They can come from vegetables (based on castor, linseed, or olive oil) but are very expensive, or else from animals, which are more affordable to everyone. Natural pigments, almost always from minerals, are used for making colors: blue comes from azurite, green from malachite, black from burned substances or minerals, and yellow and red from ocher, etc. These are crumbled, pulverized, and blended with the oil on small palettes made of wood or ivory. Which is what Eiras does every morning. The mixture is then delicately applied with small spatulas. Ocher is normally used on the cheeks because it brings warmth and vitality to the face, as well as the lips. As a matter of fact, what was Cleopatra's and Egyptian women's lipstick like? Forget the small screw-on cylindrical container we are familiar with. The "erotic papyrus" at the Museo Egizio in Turin shows a woman in the process of applying lipstick: she uses a long stylus, perhaps a long brush, to moisten her lips.

Makeup is not for carrying in your purse (which does not exist). It's a lot less handy than what we have in modern times because it's applied at home, in the morning. The vanity case is a wooden casket, painted and decorated on the outside so it's personalized, and inside there are compartments for glass bottles with ointments, oils, various cosmetics, and perfumes.

Cleopatra is sitting motionless while Eiras, assisted by a few handmaidens, is getting her ready for this day that seems like any other; nobody knows that today the history of the world will change forever . . . Meanwhile, they are getting on with their preparations, which are laborious. Cleopatra's hand is lying on a small table: a servant is gently painting her fingernails. An Egyptian woman wears nail polish like modern women, but what substance does she use? You'd be surprised: henna.

There are so many interesting details about Egyptian cosmetics. Their aim is in fact not just aesthetic but protective. Creams are used primarily to protect the skin from Egypt's powerful sun and dry climate.

A good example of this is kohl: it's probably made from burnt wood, fat, and antimony—a disinfectant and natural antiseptic that shields the eyes from bacterial infections, mycosis, and parasites, as well as protecting them from irritation caused by the sun and the wind that carries sand from the desert.

For Egyptians, beauty treatments are therefore first and foremost a protection for the body.

This helps us to understand another issue concerning personal care. If you're wondering how Cleopatra appeared before Caesar on their first night together, we can be sure—even though no ancient author has written this—that her body was totally depilated. The custom of removing every hair from the body (except for that on the head, including eyebrows and eyelashes) stems from trying to achieve the best possible hygiene by removing fertile ground for all kinds of parasites. Small combs with tiny teeth found in Egyptian tombs as well as in Pompeii tell us that in antiquity (and even in the present day) there was a constant fight against lice. The existence of small and large blades and small, elaborate tweezers, like those discovered in the famous Tomb of Kha, whose extraordinary contents are on display at the Museo Egizio in Turin, clearly demonstrates that this custom was widespread among all social classes. The presence of a small jar that still contains wax suggests that emollients were applied to the body after shaving.

Roman women also used to remove their body hair, while men usually did not (even though they shaved every morning), except for Octavian. Suetonius recalls his habit of burning body hair off with red-hot walnuts in order to have smooth skin. A strange custom for a man who, for a time, was used to the rough life of a soldier.

What's interesting is that makeup and beauty treatments in Egypt are unisex: both men and women wear makeup, remove their body hair, and use wigs.

It's precisely what is happening with Cleopatra now. This long, elaborate makeup session (even more so since she is a queen) ends with the donning of the wig. As a Greco-Macedonian, she usually doesn't wear the typical Egyptian wig, but in this case, out of respect for tradition, religion, and (equally) the powerful caste of the priests, she will, since she's about to celebrate a ritual. Of all the Ptolemaic queens, Cleopatra is the one closest to the Egyptian people and culture, albeit more out of calculation than conviction.

A handmaiden brings a large wooden chest that, once opened, reveals a voluminous black wig, which is lifted out gently as a strong perfume of scented oils wafts through the room. It's made of real hair, jet black and glossy, carefully gathered in slender, wavy strands that cascade down the sides like water from a fountain and end in small, tight, almost solid plaits that weigh the wig down, preventing it from fluttering in the wind.

The wig is styled in such a way as to form three large sections: one comes down the back of the neck as far as the shoulder blades; the other two go along the sides of the head, behind the ears, and stop just above the breasts. It is precisely this three-section arrangement that gives it stability. For centuries, everybody in Egypt—both men and women—has been wearing wigs like this, although the quality depends on financial means. It conceals the person's real hair, which you can imagine being straight, curly, long, very short (a widespread style), or completely shaved. Naturally, in everyday life people wear their hair loose, styled in various ways and always treated with oil packs.

Here we are. The wig has been gently placed on the queen's head and retouched with ivory combs and gold pins.

There's a final moment devoted to perfumes, sprinkled on her head and clothes, as well as a few drops on her neck. And so the lengthy process, which began with her trusted servants choosing her clothes, and has been repeated on a daily basis for years, comes to a close.

Cleopatra peers into the polished bronze mirror Eiras holds up to her. An involuntary, crafty little smile appears on her face . . . She's ready. She can face the day.

A Likable Rogue

Cleopatra gets up and walks to a portico but her gait is different than it was this morning: it's more regal, and all who meet her bow silently. The queen has vanished through the door and left us, just beyond the portico arches she's passed under, with a splendid view of the majestic Capitoline Hill in the distance. At its foot stands the Forum and, to the side, a large *domus* where at this very moment a slave is waiting for his master to come out of the bedroom. The master has snored noisily all night after spending the evening at a banquet, with laughter and wine flowing. He enjoys being surrounded by people of ill repute who enjoy the good life, and with whom he sometimes spends the entire night. He must certainly have had sex with a woman, any woman. Although he's married, it's a lifestyle he has led for some time.

In the past, one of his love affairs aroused scandal. It was with a much-gossiped-about "showgirl," Licorys, a mime artist also known as Cytheris, a sex bomb who frequents salons and, above all, the men who matter . . . We'll talk about this later, but he did lose his head over her completely: they were even seen around Rome in a litter preceded by lictors. Julius Caesar personally asked him to mend his ways in consideration of his position as consul. Which he did.

Cicero calls him "the gladiator" because he is of the opinion that his muscle development absorbed much of the energy intended for his brain. He does, as a matter of fact, exploit his robust good looks by showing off his broad, muscular chest and his sunny, disarming smile with charming wrinkles, which makes women and his friends forgive him anything. We could describe him as a "likable rogue."

His name is Marcus Antonius, Mark Antony. We will refer to him as both Antony and Mark Antony.

The slave outside his door lowers and shakes his head and leaves, downhearted. The consul has a very large house, more than 22,500 square feet, located next to that of Caesar, on the Velian Hill, a small elevation that no longer exists in modern times, between the Palatine and the Oppian Hills (it's no longer there because it gave way to the building of Via dei Fori Imperiali). According to Andrea Carandini, "it was a substantial house if compared to other average-size houses on the Palatine at the time, which would have been between 9,000 and 13,500 square feet." And yet its owner, Antony, complained about its size no sooner than he had bought it, saying it wasn't "large enough for him," and had it expanded.

It has a large internal garden surrounded by an elegant portico with pillars (the peristyle) a whole 280 feet long: a proper royal palace in the heart of Rome. Revealing a side to Antony's personality, the middle section of this garden has been turned into a gymnasium for physical exercise. And that's not all.

The quadriporticus leads to the part of the *domus* reserved for body care, with a large *balneum* complete with private sauna (*laconicum*).

This beautiful home once belonged to Julius Caesar's great opponent, Pompey the Great, and before him to his father, Gnaeus Pompeius Strabo. So how did Antony come to own it? Not very elegantly but as the result of Caesar's victory. When Pompey died, in 48 BC, his estate was seized and sold at auction. It was an immense estate: according to Cicero, more than 700 million sestertii were made from the sale of Pompey the Great's possessions. Caesar put Antony in charge of the auction, so he obviously managed to acquire the house at a very low price (along with other properties in Campus Martius). It's therefore a house that has traveled through history, and still does.

A Roman Festival

As the minutes go by, Rome fills with people trickling out of the *insulae*, the enormous clusters of houses towering everywhere. There are men with bags full of food, others carrying small wine amphorae on their shoulders, laughing with their friends, then women with canvas, blankets, and cushions. Even before we are surrounded by crowds, we are enveloped by their impalpable presence: feminine scents, the smells of food, the fragrance of spices, and voices punctuated by witty remarks and laughter. But where are all these people going? The answer is very simple. It's the Ides of March (Romans referred to the middle of the month as the "ides" and the first day of the month as the "calends"), and for Romans this means only one thing: the feast of Anna Perenna. People celebrate this occasion by going to a specific place—a small green valley framed by hills covered in sacred forest, where cutting down trees, picking up wood, and hunting animals is forbidden. This valley is just a few miles outside the city and is easily accessible on foot, by Via Flaminia. In the center of this little valley there is a sacred spring, dedicated to the actual Anna Perenna. The name, which doesn't mean much to us (it almost sounds like the name of a 1960s actress), belongs to an important Roman divinity who oversees the perpetual renewal of the year. We may not be aware of this, but we do refer to her when we use words like *perennial* and *perennially*. So on March 15, this valley fills with people and becomes a kind of festival for Roman times. People celebrate religious rites, drink water from the sacred spring, and, most importantly, wine flows and they feast until dawn, lying on the ground. And that's not all.

Tradition demands that a woman should make love for the first time right here, since it's good luck. Whether this actually happens is impossible to say but many take advantage of the night to put up small makeshift tents with ordinary sheets in order to get some privacy with the help of the darkness and the few oil lamps. The next morning, these survivors of a night of passion and excess stagger back into town.

The sacred spring still exists and you can still visit. Its almost unrecognizable remains, made up of a huge mass of bricks still securely bound together, and marble plaques with perfectly legible inscriptions, can be found a few yards deep, next to a restaurant. It was rediscovered by chance, as often happens in Rome, while an underground parking lot was being built. The wooded hills are not there anymore, however, replaced by a forest of modern buildings and, in the place of the fields, there's a road on which thousands of cars travel every day. What for Romans two thousand years ago was an unforgettable sacred site is for modern Romans just a square with a large church, where you can arrange to meet amid the chaotic traffic: Piazza Euclide. How many people know that on this spot where a big church stands today a Roman-era Woodstock took place, with all its stories and people that time has forgotten?

But let us return to that day . . .

Artemidorus has not considered that everybody would set off so early this morning, so when he emerges from an alley to take a larger street he comes up against a huge crowd. He can't avoid people, is surrounded, and gets lost in the throng, holding on to his papyrus scroll even tighter. We can make him out by his lanky but determined gait . . . Will he find Julius Caesar in time?

The Nile on the Tiber

As you can see, in this city, during these hours, history is taking place. Artemidorus is just a pawn in an important game that will decide not only the destiny of Rome but that of entire nations (some of which are yet to be born). And he's not the only one. Somewhere, not far from him, there's Julius Caesar. A little farther, Mark Antony. And then Brutus, Cassius, and even Cicero. As though drawn by a gigantic magnet, they're all converging on the same spot, the same crucial moment in history. There are only a couple of hours to go.

And what about Cleopatra?

Although she's in the city, she will not be involved in these events, but what is going to occur will make her into the main protagonist in the years to come. For the time being, however, she is physically excluded from what is about to happen, partly because she's across the Tiber (*trans Tiberim*, the modern Trastevere), in Caesar's golden residence outside the city bounds. It's a district where many *peregrini*, i.e., non-citizens of Rome, traditionally live. People like her. She cannot live in Rome itself. Roman law forbids any foreign ruler, unless formally invited as a "friend and ally" of Rome, from entering the sacred perimeter that surrounds and defines the city, the *pomerium* (perhaps from *post moerium*, "beyond the wall"). Everything within is the true city, with its temples, the Senate, the Forum—and its chaos. Beyond that, there are, of course, other districts but they are not the actual *urbs*, from which the word *Urbe* derives and which is still used in modern Italian to refer to Rome. Although they are part of it, they have, so to speak, another sacred "prefix."

Even though present-day Trastevere is one of modern Rome's most traditional areas, at the heart of the city's nightlife, in 44 BC it's considered a somewhat run-down district. It's a low-lying area, at least partly built on marsh, where in both winter and summer the air is humid and heavy, with many mosquitoes, and subject to frequent flooding. But if we go past the houses beyond the river and start climbing the hill that overlooks it, the Janiculum, things radically change. No floods, no mugginess, and the air is refreshed by a breeze. Moreover, there's a spectacular view of Rome from up there. This is precisely why Julius Caesar has one of his wonderful properties there, the Horti Caesaris, on Via Portuensis, one mile up. Unfortunately, no description of the Horti Caesaris survives, but from what we know about Roman gardens, we can easily imagine the place where Cleopatra has taken up residence: elegant gardens, avenues, fountains, statues, and small temples.

The song of the nightingale that echoed at the first light of dawn has now given way to the songs of many other birds and turned Caesar's gardens into a nature concert. Here, we are far removed from the chaos of the city streets, the voices in the shops, and the shouts of carters. We are in a wood, surrounded by unadulterated nature, enveloped by the powerful scent of resin from the many very tall pine trees and the essence of herbs still moist with dew.

Ahead of us, there's a row of cypresses beyond which everything changes. The greenery is suddenly no longer free to grow as it pleases and is literally tamed by man. We see trees and bushes with foliage sculpted into elegant shapes, and long hedges surrounding fragrant plants. We glimpse myrtle and box bushes and, a little farther, perfectly manicured lawns with, in the center, huge Italian stone pines with the characteristic parasol shape, real giants and the only ones not to have yielded to man's will. We venture into a small maze of well-groomed miniature lanes with low fences. Gilt bronze statues stand at regular intervals, as well as small temples, altars with a brilliant array of color from flower garlands, and there's no shortage of porticos where you can pause and chat in the shade. In other words, a true miniature Eden.

According to Suetonius, Julius Caesar bought this property in 49 BC in order to let the horses—now considered sacred—with which he had crossed the Rubicon roam freely. There was already a splendid *domus* in the middle of the estate, although it had nothing to do with what Cleopatra is admiring now. The building has been transformed, expanded with new colonnades and porticos, frescoes and mosaics, and become a royal residence, with everything immersed in a small pine forest. There is also a preexisting sanctuary devoted to the goddess Fortuna. A little farther, beyond some elaborate hedges, we notice another temple where a woman is ending a ritual in honor of Isis, an Egyptian goddess. She's surrounded by priests with totally shaved heads, bare chests, and long robes that touch the ground. Some are singing prayers, others beat time with *sistra*, which produce a regular and obsessive sound like that of a metallic rattle. There are other instruments accompanying the ceremony, like every morning. The woman is now bowing before the statue of the goddess and uttering ritualistic formulae. The strands of her black wig, secured with a diadem, fall over her face. Her white, multipleated gown looks familiar . . . It clings like a glove to parts of her body, such as her chest, her belly, and her hips. Then the woman raises her head, her eyes still shut, and opens her arms upward while saying loud phrases in the Egyptian language. It's a solemn moment. These are the final words in the ceremony. For a short time, everything is silent. Finally, she stands up and turns around: it's Cleopatra.

The queen leaves swiftly, triggering, as she walks, a wave of bows on the part of the priests. Her gait is back to what we saw this morning: light, impalpable, and sensual. She's practically flying above the ground.

She is followed, a few yards away, by two of her most faithful servants and, more discreetly, by three armed guards. Cleopatra is a queen on foreign soil, and many in Rome view her with suspicion, especially because of her love affair with Julius Caesar. It's not surprising that even Caesar has allocated an entire guard to protect her and, as well as watch the villa, to keep him informed of whom the queen meets. Naturally, it's her personal bodyguards, from Alexandria, who follow her so closely.

Roman Holiday

As we follow the regular swaying of Cleopatra's tunic down the alleys, we discover that this is not just a villa with a park but a piece of Egypt transported to Rome.

The queen came to live in this luxurious residence two years ago, in 46 BC, after Caesar, who had been back in Rome for some time following his triumphant campaign in Africa, sent for her.

We don't know if Cleopatra has been in Rome for two years in a row until today, the Ides of March. She probably went back to Egypt while Caesar traveled to Spain, and returned in the fall of 45 BC, a few months before the assassination of the dictator in perpetuity.

She didn't come back just for the love of Caesar but out of calculation. Egypt is going to play a strategic role in Rome's imminent expedition against the Parthians, in the east, by supplying ships and men. A small detail that illustrates Cleopatra's intelligence. She's a woman and a queen but above all a politician who wants to play a leading role for the good of her land.

As a matter of fact, after restoring stability to the economy and administration of the country, she prepared her trip to Rome with care, telling her people that she was going to defend and promote the interests of the kingdom. It was a delicate procedure, and it wasn't easy to leave an Egypt that had recently been ripped apart by numerous feuds and tackle a 1,200-mile journey (a huge distance then). But Cleopatra played her cards well: she has bound Caesar to her with an "official" son (despite all the doubts we are about to see), and he has guaranteed the stability of her country with his troops, thus allowing her to come to Rome. Maybe Caesar, too, harbors suspicions about the real paternity, but he doesn't make an issue out of it: primarily because being the son of a foreigner, the child has no legal rights or inheritance in the Roman world, and also because Egypt is a very wealthy kingdom, a coffer for Rome, for Caesar, and his ambitions. And, finally, a hostile or unreliable Egypt is not in his interests either, and Cleopatra is Rome's best guarantee of stability. In other words, as well as having feelings for each other, both are motivated by much more tangible interests.

However, Cleopatra is also a woman, and a twenty-year-old woman at that. Although she is of above-average intelligence, her trip to Rome—as well as being politically motivated—has been prompted by an impulsive desire to experience the life and atmosphere of the greatest and most powerful city of the known world, and perhaps also to live in the heart of the power that by now controls the entire Mediterranean. Not to mention the fact that, as we said, from here she can better protect the fate of Egypt.

This may not be Cleopatra's first visit to Rome. She may have already been here with her father, Ptolemy XII Auletes ("the Flutist"), when he was seeking refuge from a revolt in Alexandria that had been orchestrated by Cleopatra's sister Berenice and her husband, Archelaus of Comana. After a brutal intervention on the part of Roman troops, her father was reinstated on the throne with a Roman garrison to defend him. It was 55 BC.

It's widely believed that during this new trip, Cleopatra followed the model of her father's visit, from the display of wealth and exoticism to traveling by litter. She has certainly enjoyed widespread recognition on the part of Rome, where she is viewed as an ally queen. And Caesar has even had a gilt bronze statue of her made and placed in the Temple of Venus Genetrix, the patron deity of his own *gens*. She and her son, Ptolemy Caesar or Ptolemy XV, known to all as Caesarion—"Little Caesar"—are not here as slaves but as friends and allies. This represents for her a great political success.

Immediately upon arrival, Cleopatra watched Caesar's triumphs, at which her younger sister Arsinoe (who had tried to seize the throne and murder both her and Caesar) was paraded in chains. A strange situation: Cleopatra on a dais as queen, a friend and ally of Rome, while her sister is exhibited before her as an enemy of Rome. Caesar would resolve this impasse by freeing her sister, who would take sanctuary at the Temple of Artemis at Ephesus, a neutral zone, somewhat akin to Switzerland during World War II.

Naturally, the queen has brought something of her land with her. Thanks to Caesar's help, the Horti Caesaris in Trastevere have gradually been turned into an Egyptian court. Cleopatra lives here with her counselors, trusted men, handmaidens, various kinds of slaves, and even eunuchs. That's in addition to physicians, philosophers, dressmakers, cooks . . . and even staff devoted to her son, Caesarion.

We know that she certainly has Ammonius with her in Rome. He is her principal adviser, a wise, shrewd man whom Cicero will hate because he won't give him some precious books (almost definitely from the Library of Alexandria) that the queen promised him, maybe in return for a favor. A delivery that failed because of Caesar's sudden death.

There's Serapion, an old counselor of Cleopatra's father, who was already here in Rome during the journey-exile of Pharaoh Ptolemy XII Auletes. He knows the Eternal City and its dynamic politics better than anyone else at court.

Perhaps there's also Apollodorus the Sicilian, the Herculean servant who secretly carried Cleopatra to her first meeting with Caesar.

And, finally, there's Olympos, Cleopatra's personal physician, who will maybe assist her in her suicide . . .

Cleopatra has requested and obtained dozens of civil servants and persons of rank with her, such as, for instance, the fat, bald scribe now prostrating himself before her and handing her some papyri. However, in addition to the administrative side of things, the members of the court are there especially to keep her company and keep up the Alexandrian lifestyle she misses so much: she is rather worldly and educated.

Cleopatra is not just a woman of power or one who favors the frivolous existence of gilded aristocratic circles. She is a woman who loves culture, has a thirst for knowledge, and loves new insights. Subsequently, this tendency will be shared by Hypatia, Theodora of Byzantium, Elinor of Aquitaine, Caterina Sforza, Isabella d'Este, Caterina de' Medici, Elizabeth I of England, and Catherine II of Russia. In two years, Caesar's house has therefore become a place where you can inhale the delights of culture. What's discussed primarily in the gardens is philosophy, and although we're in Rome, in an Egyptian context, conversations are held in neither Latin nor Egyptian but Greek, the language of wisdom.

During the banquets, you can have a friendly discussion about the chief world systems with Philostratus, one of Alexandria's most famous orators and Cleopatra's tutor, who taught her philosophy, rhetoric, and oratory.

You can also meet and converse with Sosigenes of Alexandria, perhaps the greatest astronomer of the time. Cleopatra introduced him to Caesar during his stay in Egypt, and there's a general belief that he contributed to the new Julian calendar (used until the Renaissance, when it was replaced by the Gregorian).

Strolling in the gardens, sitting under a trellis, and surrounded by people who follow him attentively, you can also come across Didymus, the famous Alexandrian grammarian and one of the most listened-to intellectuals at Cleopatra's court. He belongs to the school founded in Alexandria by Aristarchus, where he taught for a long time.

According to Seneca, he's the author of at least 3,500 books and treatises. This literary "bulimia" earned him the nickname "Chalkenteros" ("bronze guts"), and also another, more affectionate one, "Bibliolathas" ("forget books") because he occasionally contradicted himself, having forgotten what he had stated in his previous books.

The aristocrats who frequent Cleopatra's salon are struck by her good taste and ability to create the right atmosphere, refined aesthetics, and the obviously eastern luxury.

The Egyptian queen starts a new hairstyle trend that Roman women copy, and surprises men with her tight-fitting, white, priestess-like clothes.

Everybody is struck by this young woman who is so different from the uneducated and seldom as charismatic Roman matrons. She talks like a man but with the allure of the most deeply desired woman. Her gentle voice wraps around you and you are trapped by her intelligence.

The villa in which Cleopatra lives is more than a cultured salon; it's an oasis. The food, the music, the conversations, and the ambience take you straight back to Alexandria. To the Nile Delta. To Egypt . . . Even her royal vessel is moored at a private pier. Today, we have no archaeological remains of this incredible world across the Tiber, as is the case with Hadrian's Villa and other luxurious houses. Everything has disappeared over the centuries, making it impossible to describe daily life and architecture with any kind of precision; we can only make a plausible reconstruction.

Caesar and Cleopatra, Both Married but Lovers

And what about Julius Caesar? He is practically part of the household. He brought Cleopatra to Rome as a lover, a queen, and a war trophy, but he is all too aware of the risk he's taking. Rome is not easy, he has many enemies here, and there's a very nasty *vox populi* circulating: the conqueror has been conquered by the foreign queen, a woman he welcomes with the highest honors, and from whom he goes as far as tolerating the claim that she is the incarnation of Isis.

And yet Caesar is no fool, and even in modern times it would be a mistake to call his relationship with Cleopatra a mere love affair. Caesar frequents her above all because she is a queen and therefore has political power. And he has decided to maintain a low profile. He keeps her away from Rome, from the Senate, from the masses, in a gilded court across the river, where he can see her in total privacy. Let us not forget, moreover, that Caesar is a married man . . . Calpurnia, his wife, waits for him every evening at home, in the heart of the Eternal City.

In other words, Caesar has a wife and a lover in the same city, and sees both regularly before everyone's eyes. By the standards of modern morality, this official dual relationship would spell the end of any politician. But not in Republican Rome, and not just because he is Julius Caesar. The Roman man is officially allowed to have a wife and several concubines at the same time. The law permits it. Two wives are not permitted, however. To be honest, Cleopatra's situation is no less complex because she, too, is officially married, and her husband lives in the villa with her. It's her brother, Ptolemy XIV, who became her husband through a peculiar Ptolemaic dynasty tradition that expects brother and sister to marry each other so as not to mix their divine or semi-divine blood. But for Cleopatra, he is more a symbolic than a real husband, since she certainly does not sleep with her brother. Besides, his age hardly makes him a threat to Caesar: he is only thirteen . . .

Cleopatra is shrewd, though, and the fact that she has brought her husband-brother to Rome with her is evidence of her political foresight. Despite Caesar's assurances and the presence of Roman garrisons, leaving a co-reigning husband-brother back home, as well as an empty throne in Alexandria, would be too risky.

There's another person in the villa who is close to Cleopatra's heart. Its youngest occupant, a two-year-old child. Caesarion is Julius Caesar's son, or so Cleopatra has always claimed.

On Caesarion's true paternity, scholars are far from unanimous, however. In its favor is the fact that Ptolemaic queens were not usually promiscuous. Caesar may therefore have been Cleopatra's first man. It's also true that, for all his liaisons, Caesar had only one official daughter, Julia.

Ancient sources do not concur: Plutarch and Suetonius claim that Ceasarion was Caesar's son. Moreover, Suetonius adds that "we know from many Greek accounts that he was very much like him, in looks as well as bearing." Others, like Gaius Oppius and Cassius Dio, refute his paternity, Dio saying, "This son, named Ptolemy, whom she claimed to have borne by Caesar and for that reason called Caesarion."

Just to make things even more complicated, there are ongoing doubts about Caesarion's date of birth. Some scholars put it in 47 BC and others as much as a few years later.

We cannot, however, accept this last theory for the following reasons. Considering the lack and incompleteness of knowledge on a period in history that dates back more than two millennia, calculating months in order to check pregnancies is very risky. Caesar and his people are not naïve. They can, like us, add up the months of a pregnancy, just like their critics, and particularly Cleopatra's enemies. If no one at that time except Cicero (who, however, had a personal hatred of Cleopatra) ever put in question Caesarion's paternity, then we should not really doubt that Caesarion was Caesar's son.

Moreover, the same Octavian would have him killed—a sign that there was no certainty that he was not Caesar's son, and also because—besides Caesar—there are no other plausible theories about the identity of Caesarion's father. Let us also not forget that Caesar embellished his Forum by having a gilt bronze statue cast in Cleopatra's likeness at the end of 45 BC. This collection of observations leads us to not take a definitive stand on the subject. We will accept it as possible that Caesarion may truly have been Caesar's son without going any further.

There's not much more we can do, partly because, as the Latins used to say, *mater semper certa*. We have therefore decided to stick to the most accredited theory, according to which Caesarion was Caesar's son, born on June 23, 47 BC.

And it's this very Caesarion who's running to his mother under a portico, pursued by a female servant trying to ensure he doesn't fall. The hug that follows is long and strong. Caesarion's little hands sink into his mother's tunic, longing for her protective arms. And, for a moment, the most powerful queen in Africa becomes the most loving and attentive of mothers.

A Man Toys with a Dagger

Across the Tiber, far from the light in the gardens of Cleopatra's house, from the smiles and tranquility of that gilded world, a man is struggling with a thousand demons tearing his soul apart. He's shut in a room, sitting at an elegant table with lion-shaped legs. On top of it, an oil lamp illuminates his weary, gaunt face. The surface of the table is a perfect white marble disk. There's a small, almost unnoticeable chip in the middle, into which the man has stuck the point of a dagger, using the indentation as a pivot for turning it. His fingers resting on the pommel, he flicks his thumb abruptly, causing the dagger to spin violently, like a crazed ballerina on pointe shoes. He doesn't take his eye off the glint of light every time the blade turns. It's an obsessive movement that has been going on for some time, the last of a sleepless night. Someone knocks at the door. It's his trusted slave, who wants to know if he should bring him breakfast. The man looks up, stares at the door, but doesn't answer. He is Marcus Junius Brutus.

There's something in the air that you can't make out. Something impalpable, fleeting, and invisible. A poison seeping through the city walls, spreading across the streets, snaking down the alleys, flying on the words whispered into ears in the steam of the baths, hovering over the triclinia of important banquets, sneaking into the minds of senators during private meetings . . . And it carries with it a sinister word: *death*. Death to Julius Caesar.

There's been a conspiracy in the city for some time, one of the most treacherous in history, against a man who is possibly more loved by the people of Rome than anyone else. A man who in the centuries to come will be one of the most admired figures, on a par with Alexander the Great. How can this be possible?

According to Cassius Dio, a historian of the Roman era, the explanation lies in the fact that various men, at various times, conferred such honors on Caesar that he became hated and envied so quickly it rushed him to his death.

In actual fact, the true reasons stem from further back and are much deeper. Caesar has become the new absolute master of Rome, effectively taking away the power from the Senate. He now makes the decisions, not the senators with all their interests.

Since time immemorial, the reins of power and business in Rome have been in the hands of aristocratic families, represented in the Senate by their toga-clad senators. Every decision is obviously dictated by the interests and convenience of these families. According to some historians, the Republic, having reached 44 BC, is no longer the solid aristocracy born with the driving-out of the last king of Rome. By now it has run out of steam, lost its ideals, and no longer includes the enlightened, moderate minds of the past. The few that are left are a distinct minority in what the Senate has become: a place riddled (much more than before) with corruption, profiteering, and abuse of power. A large tree rotting on the inside, as someone said. The greed of the senators (by means of their freedmen, since they are officially not permitted to engage in any kind of vile profit) has plunged the Republic into a crisis, paving the way for strongmen, especially an absolute dictator like Julius Caesar.

He's also from an aristocratic family but belongs to the *populares* faction and has taken the people's needs at heart, so the people reciprocate and, for the most part, support him. And a section of the aristocracy has got it in for him (though not just for that reason).

The goal of the conspirators is simple: to kill Caesar now that he acts like a monarch, in order to trigger a climate of confusion and uncertainty, since there are no charismatic figures capable of taking his place. This way, the Senate would resume its former role, perfect for continuing to manage power without any scruples.

The Smear Campaign

Artemidorus, the man we are following along the streets of Rome, has decided to penetrate once again the maze of alleys. He thinks it's safer than the crowded streets. The buildings around him are so close together, you could shake hands between windows, as Martial likes to say in his *Epigrams*. Even daylight struggles to reach the ground and is no more than a subtle blade hanging high above Artemidorus's head. His pupils are dilated because of the semidarkness but also from fear. It's very dark and he wonders for a moment if it wouldn't be more prudent to turn back. There are frequent attacks and murders in these rough alleys. A body is found every morning, lying in the mud. Murders with no culprits. His senses persuade him to continue. The foul smells are behind him and he is now surrounded by the sugary smell of milk boiling somewhere in a house. He's reassured by the voices coming from different directions—from the windows open above him, from balconies, from doors ajar parading alongside him, and from the ends of the alleys. They are like the caress of invisible veils that tell him he's walking through a true galaxy of parallel lives driving this human hive known as Suburra, perhaps Rome's most working-class district. It's as though his ears are reading a plethora of daily diaries kept by these people. Here, a mother is singing a lullaby, there, a man softly reciting his morning prayers, and there again a slave is at work, muttering a dirge from his distant native land. A woman is lovingly seeing off her husband as he leaves home, while another, in the distance, is arguing at the top of her voice with her man, who is guilty of something or other. Artemidorus smiles and continues. He barely notices a child crying. It's a familiar sound in a working-class district, although the farther he walks, the louder it gets. His suspicion is aroused by the fact that it doesn't seem to be coming from a house but from the end of the alley, where he can see no doors or windows. A few yards farther, the philosopher freezes. At the far end of the alley, a single pillar rises at the intersection. It's just the base of a broken shaft, but at the bottom of it there's a basket with a bundle. That's where the wailing is coming from. It's a newborn baby. There's even a note explaining to whoever finds it how to trace the original family sometime in the future. A child rejected by his family, or rather his father, for some reason. Does he suspect his wife of betrayal? Does the baby have a serious physical disability? Is it yet another child of the same sex as many other brothers or sisters? Are there no means to support it? We don't know. Roman law and traditions allow you to leave a baby in the street so that anybody can pick him up and bring him up as his own. It may be a decent person who feels sorry for him, or else an unscrupulous one who will turn him into a slave. Foundlings are almost always abandoned at well-known locations, like this pillar (the most famous in Rome is the so-called *columna lactaria*, because of its reference to milk, a symbol of newborn babies). A note or personal item can allow whoever picks up the baby to take him back to his lawful parents and ask in return for a sum of money to cover the whole "temporary" adoption period. This is the ancient version of our "foundling wheels" where undesired children were left.

Artemidorus is standing still next to the infant. It's not this abandoned life that's stopping him but an inscription left on the wall next to the pillar for all to see. It's still fresh and two drops are running down the wall, struggling to reach the ground. The inscription is against Julius Caesar, accusing him of being a thief, but worse is the implication that he's about to flee to Alexandria with his lover, Cleopatra, taking with him all Rome's treasures.

Artemidorus shakes his head and picks up the pace. He must absolutely reach Caesar. He is now running down the alley and vanishes in the semidarkness.

Over the past few days, the conspirators have set in motion a true smear campaign to discredit Julius Caesar. This is fake news deliberately spread to outrage the masses, sometimes as inscriptions on walls, more often exploiting the *vox populi*, word of mouth based on the irresistible attraction of whispered rumors. These use as platforms places like barber shops, *popinae*, banquets, baths, and, of course, the Forum.

But what are the rumors circulating about Caesar?

He is accused of weakness, cowardice, all kinds of depravity, and boundless ambition that will end only if he becomes king, a word that triggers old ghosts in the Roman consciousness, when the Eternal City was dominated by sovereigns of Etruscan origin, forced out with great difficulty. Caesar knows this, which is why he prepared a countermove. A month earlier, the day after he was appointed life dictator, during the festival of Lupercalia, he organized, in agreement with Antony, a ceremony in the heart of the Forum, on the Rostra (the orators' podium, named after the *rostra*, chunky bronze rams removed from captured enemy ships). Cassius Dio relates that Caesar was sitting on a golden throne and Antony came up to him with a diadem, a kind of royal crown (some say that it was a strip of white cloth decorated with pearls rather than an actual crown), and said, "This is a gift from the people through me." Just as expected, this was all staged. Caesar expressed a theatrical disdain by declining it and replying, "Jupiter only is the king of the Romans." But did it help to appease minds? Apparently not.

On this important day in history, the principal player, Caesar, has not yet been seen. What has he been doing during the past few hours?

Caesar's Last Supper

A few hours ago, Caesar was lying on a triclinium, relaxed, in the house of a loyal friend, Marcus Aemilus Lepidus, *magister equitum*, at that time during the dictatorship the most important position in the government. We know that Decimus Brutus was also present. No, not the Decimus Junius Brutus who would stab him a few hours later.

He's a highly skilled general whom we will call just Decimus from now on, to avoid any confusion. He is Caesar's trusted friend and ally . . . or so Caesar thinks. He doesn't know that Decimus is one of the conspirators—one of the main ones, in fact. We could say he's dining with the enemy. It's disturbing to think that Caesar is calmly eating next to one of his assassins.

The men talked amid the courses, silent servants pouring them wine, possibly to the accompaniment of a musician in the background. According to the historian Appian, the three of them discussed the political situation in Rome and an imminent military expedition. As a matter of fact, three days from now, Caesar is due to go to war against Rome's sworn enemies, the Parthians. They are a real thorn in the side of the Romans, and their powerful kingdom stretches from Syria to what is now eastern Iran and beyond, including Iraq. What we have all read in *The Gallic Wars* could happen again with new enemies and in a new, Middle Eastern setting. Or rather "could have happened" because, as we know, Caesar would be assassinated a few hours later, which means that scores of history books would never be written and, above all, centuries of a history different from the one we know would have taken place. Another parallel universe of lives, expanding empires, monuments, and feats that never materialized . . . I wonder what the world would be like now.

On the subject of death, at some point during the dinner, the conversation suddenly changes topic. Plutarch writes that "while Caesar was signing some letters, as he was accustomed to do while lying at the table, the discussion turned to the following subject: Which death was best. Before anybody else could answer, Caesar cried, 'An unexpected one!'" Appian claims that it was Caesar himself who brought up this topic. In any case, the coincidence with imminent events is truly eerie. Could he really not have harbored any suspicion? Surely, many rumors must have reached his ears. In that case, why didn't he act? It's a question many historians still ponder.

There have been rumors of possible plots for at least a couple of years. Even Cicero has hinted in one of his letters at a sense of conspiracy in the air. At least one of these plots has been discovered, but oddly, Caesar stopped everything and did not set any enquiries in motion. He just let the conspirators know that he had unearthed their plan through a simple decree in which he stated that he knew everything. No arrests or investigation that would have led to the perpetrators and to the "brains."

All his supporters, friends, and allies (the so-called Caesarians) are worried and say he is too imprudent. He has even dismissed his bodyguard, made up of Iberian soldiers that surround him, swords drawn, wherever he goes. Why? He said that the Senate and the senators have sworn to defend him, so going around with a personal armed guard would be a clear sign of lack of trust in the Senate.

And yet there definitely are signs of an imminent attack. According to Plutarch, only a few days earlier, a few notices appeared, urging Brutus to act. Their content couldn't be clearer: "Oh, Brutus, are you asleep?" and "You are not really a Brutus" (a reference to his ancestor, also called Junius Brutus, who heroically forced out the last king of Rome and became one of Roman history's great men). These inscriptions have been left by slaves sent by senators and aristocrats involved in the plot, in order to prompt Brutus to wake up and act, since he is still undecided.

But then, if Caesar knows (and has known for some time), why did he not react? Some scholars claim that suffering from epilepsy and being of an advanced age (for that time), Caesar decided to die in a kind of scheduled suicide rather than grow weaker and leave the stage anyway. It is, however, hard to believe that a man of action and power like him should have deliberately given up on bringing his own work to completion, concluding his reforms, winning the war against the Parthians, experiencing total success, and breaking off the relationship with Cleopatra. Other scholars, however, have suggested different, historically more plausible theories. Putting it simply, Caesar may not have adopted any countermeasures, and you can understand his viewpoint. To those who point at Brutus as the possible chief of a conspiracy, he replies serenely that he's aging, and that it would be better for Brutus to wait rather than kill him, because it would not benefit him to take power stained with the blood of a murder and the shame of betrayal.

Caesar's explanation does not put the minds of those close to him at rest, however, as they begin to see suspicious behavior everywhere, not only on the part of avowed enemies like Brutus and Cassius but even among the ranks of those who are most loyal to Caesar, like Antony and Dolabella. Plutarch relates that Caesar responds to the panic and fear of his immediate entourage with a remark that illustrates his calm: "He was not worried about fat men with long hair, but about the pale, lean ones." As a matter of fact, Brutus and Cassius matched the latter description, while Antony and Dolabella the former . . .

Finally—and this is crucial—he seems certain, despite repeated warnings, that an attack on him wouldn't make sense and would be "illogical" given the current position of Rome, which would draw no benefit from his death but, on the contrary, as the historian Antony Spinosa says, risk being torn apart by bloody civil wars. In other words, everybody is now benefiting from the stability and power of Rome, which he has created: from the army to the institutions, to commerce, to the people . . . And he is correct. After years of civil wars, stability is perhaps the most precious asset. As such, Caesar has a definite notion that he is the keystone of the entire Roman world. If he were to fall, then everything else would collapse.

Except that he's thinking like a statesman, looking out to the horizon. He does not consider the fact that his enemies and the conspirators are looking much lower down, to much closer, more immediate and personal interests.

Caesar's error is to have overestimated his adversaries and not to have taken into account their narrow-mindedness and stupidity (as a matter of fact, they would all be overwhelmed and killed by his death, as he had foreseen). He would be killed by ignorance and naïveté on the part of the conspirators, who do not realize that the times for an aristocratic regime are over. From now on, debased and devalued, partly because of growing corruption and in particular the spasmodic search for personal power (and Caesar is a leading representative of this), the Senate would, for centuries to come, be nothing more than a minor institution at the service of strongmen: starting with Caesar, continuing with Augustus and his principate, and then with all the future emperors, the real protagonists over almost five centuries of empire.

Caesar's mistake is like his having underestimated danger as a soldier. He fought and defeated the Gauls, Germanic peoples, Egyptians, Britain's Celts, Iberian tribes, and even Roman legions and generals, risking his own life in bloody scrums, and yet he perhaps thought that senators accustomed mainly to luxury and not very inclined toward the *militia* were perhaps incapable even of handling a dagger. That's where he was wrong: these same senators ensnared him and trapped him with what they do best: words and speeches. Never would Caesar have fallen into this kind of ingeniousness on the field, but he's a soldier and as such is used to the enemy facing him, not at his back.

At the end of the dinner, before retiring, Caesar probably vomited. We know from Cicero that for some time now he had been practicing an emetic diet: he would eat in abundance then throw everything up immediately after the meal.

He went to sleep at around 10 or 11 p.m. . . . with a woman. Who was this woman? Cleopatra? No, Plutarch tells us: "As usual, he went to sleep with his wife."

2

The Death of Caesar

Brutus's House, Dawn of March 15: Why Caesar Must Be Killed Today

Marcus Junius Brutus keeps pacing up and down nervously in his room. He is panting, breathless, and has not slept all night. All he can think of is today, and no other plan or thought can enter his mind. Before him, Porcia, his wife, is standing against the door-jamb, watching him intently. She has difficulty being on her feet, one of her legs bandaged because of a nasty injury, a deep cut she inflicted upon herself to prove her loyalty toward Brutus. Seeing her husband so tense, anxious, and distracted, she asked him a few days ago what was upsetting him so deeply but he did not reply. None of the conspirators has ever breathed a word to friends or family, let alone wives. But Porcia is different from the other women. She is deeply principled: the daughter of Cato the Younger, who committed suicide because of Caesar and taught Brutus to fight kings, tyrants, and anyone who holds absolute power.

And that's precisely what Caesar is, says Giovanni Brizzi, professor in Roman history at the University of Bologna and a well-known expert in ancient military history. His own soldiers said so without hesitation. Referring to Caesar's claim that he had fought the civil war in order to defend honor and security, they chanted the slogan "If you comply with the law, you're condemned. If you break it, you become king." As we've said, Caesar could not return to the ranks of the Republic nor, like Sulla, recuse himself from a reconstituted republic. The war waged *pro dignitate* brought him everything but he cannot decide how to manage his position. Rome is now ruled like a subject city he runs as he sees fit. There are still the Senate and magistrates, but they defer to Caesar's will. He lacks a sense for institutions: what he chiefly sees in the Senate are individual senators, many of whom have been appointed by him. The Senate as a whole means nothing to him, and is just an awkward college (it has become huge, with at least nine hundred members) that holds endless, not constructive debates. Since institutions mean nothing to him, the difference between republic and monarchy has no meaning either, whatever his attitude toward the title of king. He uses the consulship as he pleases, conferring it on a whim, and appointing senators at his pleasure. He even gets a consul, Caninius, elected for just one day. Moreover, the powers, prerogatives, and honor tributes he has repeatedly received now break all boundaries. By the end of 45 or the beginning of 44 BC these are, in chronological order:

- Caesar can wear his triumph garments at any time and anywhere.

- He may dedicate so-called *spolia opima* without having earned them (he has never killed an enemy commander).

- The fasces of his lictors will always be wrapped in laurel leaves.

- He obtains the title of *pater patriae.*

- His birthday becomes a public holiday.

- The month of his birth is renamed *Iulius.*

- Statues of him are erected in all the temples in Rome and other Italic cities, as well as temples to the New Concord and to *Felicitas*.

- He obtains tribune immunity.

- He would have a golden seat in the Forum instead of the usual one.

- He would be entitled to wear the gold crown of the Etruscan kings.

- For some time now, as a descendant of Aeneas, he has been wearing the long red boots of the Alban kings.

- All the senators would have to take an oath to defend his life and, every four years, games would be dedicated to him as to a hero.

- Caesar's image as a divinity, already approved and carried in a procession at the circus, would receive a holy place of residence like that of other gods: a pediment would have to be placed over his house as though it were a temple.

- A sanctuary would be consecrated to him and *Clementia*, complete with a flamen, a priest in charge of the cult to a specific deity. (Antony is appointed although the cult would only start after Caesar's death.)

- He would be buried inside the city.

- The decrees of deification would be engraved in gold lettering on silver plaques and placed at the feet of the Capitoline Jupiter.

- His *praefectura morum* and his responsibility over morality would be extended to life.

- And, finally, the dictatorship.

And so there vanishes even a semblance of the temporary nature of his power. It's a *de facto* monarchy, with divine traits that not even the first- and second-century emperors would have. But why does he accept all these honors that put him at risk? Probably because of a desire for immortality in the memory of his fellow citizens; and yet there's a difference with Pompey. Cassius Dio says, "Pompey yearned to be honored by people of their own free will, [. . .] while Caesar did not care if he was at the head of people who hated him, if he had to bestow the honors upon himself." And these were divine honors, like the deified virtues—*Felicitas*, *Concordia*, and *Victoria*—in which he mirrored himself. Something highly dangerous and, in the long run, fatal.

Porcia therefore harbors a deep-rooted hatred toward the life dictator, partly fueled by her first husband, Bibulus, a bitter enemy of Caesar. This information is important for understanding Porcia's role as a woman who exercises a powerful influence on Brutus's decisions. The couple have known each other for a long time, there's genuine love between them—a rare occurrence at a time when marriages were arranged—and they are related, something quite common in the Roman world, however. Cato was Brutus's uncle and Porcia's father, which means Brutus married his cousin.

Moreover, Porcia is a very sensitive and tremendously strong woman, so much so that, faced with Brutus's silence about what had been tormenting him for months, she made an extraordinary decision: to find out if she could withstand pain. She stabbed herself in the thigh with a sharp knife, causing a deep wound. Realizing she could bear it, she went up to Brutus, showed him the gash, and said she deserved his trust because no torture would ever induce her to talk. Faced with this bloody sight, Brutus immediately confided in her the conspiracy but also his fears and doubts. From that moment on, Porcia became more than a support to him. No doubt she would also have contributed her opinion on the time and place of the assassination.

Why *was* it decided to kill Caesar today of all days, March 15, and specifically during a Senate meeting? Would it not have been easier to do it on the street or at a banquet, with just a few close individuals present?

The decision was made very carefully and unanimously at the last meeting of the conspirators. The reasons are evident.

They cannot delay, because Caesar is about to leave Rome to go fight the Parthians. A few days from now he must be in Apollonia, the current Albania, where the army awaits him (among its ranks there's also a young man called Octavian, the future Augustus, unaware of the fate that is about to sweep over him). From there he will go to the Middle East on a campaign that will last nobody knows how long, and if he returns triumphant the people will love him even more, making any reason to kill him obsolete.

Paradoxically, it's the beginning of this war that helps Brutus and the other conspirators: according to the *Sybilline Books*, "only a king can topple the Parthian empire." Except that Caesar is not a king. Which is why the Senate must meet in order to confer upon him the provisional office of king (a "technical" office useful only for this occasion, which would naturally come into force only once he is out of Rome, outside the *pomerium*, the city's sacred perimeter). The senators' worst nightmare—the Senate legally and officially making Caesar a king—is becoming reality.

All this will happen at a specific time: at the Senate assembly scheduled for March 15, the Ides. Everything fits together perfectly, providing the ideal conditions for the time and place of the assassination:

- March 15 is a holiday, so the city will be semi-deserted, with little activity.

- Caesar will come into the chamber unarmed and, above all, alone; he no longer has his bodyguards and, since he trusts the Senate, he will have to leave the throng of supporters, friends, and clients who protect him outside the chamber.

- Afterward, it will be too late.

Brutus stops and stares at the weak flame of an oil lamp on the marble table, illuminating the room. He is practically mesmerized by its light. Then he turns and gives Porcia's pale face one last, meaningful look, deep into her eyes. She responds with a faint smile, exhausted from sleepless nights and weakened by her injury. He silently walks up to her, his warm breath caressing her cold cheeks. Porcia looks up, her gaze clinging to Brutus's eyes. She seems to be pleading for something they have not had in far too many weeks of anguish: the calm of happy days. For a moment, Brutus's long kiss seems to carry them back to that distant time. Then everything suddenly vanishes in Porcia's mind. She feels in her husband's embrace something cold and hard pressing against her belly. She looks down and sees something metallic glinting through the folds of his toga. The pommel of a dagger. Her small, delicate hands descend like angels on this instrument of death pushing against her belly, giver of life. She strokes it, then, with an abrupt gesture, draws it out of her husband's belt. A long blade slowly emerges. She turns the dagger point up, and holds it between their faces. It is a *pugio,* a weapon commonly used by legionaries, slightly longer than a span. The handle is made of bronze and, unusually, ends in a cross rather than a knob (that of the other great conspirator, Cassius, is made of two flat circles, as shown on a coin subsequently minted by Brutus). The blade mirrors the lips of Brutus and Porcia for a long moment. Porcia's eyes travel up and down the sharp edges of both sides. Then she kisses the cold blade and hands it to her husband, who quickly puts it back in his belt without taking his eyes off her. One last kiss and a slow caress to her face. Then Brutus turns and leaves the room with a determined step. All his doubts seem to have suddenly vanished. His shadow grows larger as it draws away from the flame of the oil lamp, devouring the frescoes and dulling their colors. Just like his dark shadow in the colors of history.

The Place Where the World Changed Forever

Where is Brutus going? There would be many legs to his journey but just one destination. On this apparently joyful day like any other, there is a monument in Rome that will act as a giant historical key to unlock the door on a set no one expects. Not even conspirators. The Theater of Pompey. Before the Coliseum was built, it was the most imposing building in the Eternal City, besides the Circus Maximus. For many centuries, Rome did not have theaters made of brick: rigid Republican morality considered them disreputable, promiscuous places, which is why they were erected only temporarily and only next to temples or places of worship, in order to remind everyone of the religious origin of stage shows. However, Rome has been a cosmopolitan city for the past couple of generations and these rules are obsolete and rather "puritanical." There's a more liberal lifestyle and people increasingly like enjoying themselves. The new general theaters attract more and more audiences. This is why ten years earlier, Pompey the Great, Caesar's recently deceased powerful antagonist, had a huge brick theater, worthy of the power and dominion of Rome—which now extends from Spain to the Caspian Sea—built at his own expense. This was actually a skillful political ploy. Using the enormous booty from his triumphant wars in the east, he gave Romans the largest theater ever seen in the city in order to obtain greater consensus and increase his own popularity. So as not to offend the ancient morality and religious traditions, he bypassed the law with a very "modern" trick . . . He erected a large temple dedicated to Venus Genetrix at the top of the bleachers. This way, as you sat down, the stage was before you and the temple on the top, behind you. The bleachers can therefore be seen as a staircase leading to the temple, higher up, or seats for watching the spectacle, lower down. We could call them "two-faced" stalls that keep everyone happy, albeit in a hypocritical fashion.

The theater is a gigantic building, its size never equaled by its successors, a masterpiece of engineering, the fruit of an in-depth knowledge of sophisticated vaults and arches, and the revolutionary use of the concrete (*opus caementicium*) invented by the Romans. It can hold an audience of up to 17,500. At present, its few remains are covered by modern Rome's medieval, Renaissance, and Baroque buildings, and you can get a sense of its shape only from the famous Piazza di Campo de' Fiori.

This theater is not, however, the conspirators' objective. Behind the stage, there's a small paradise in the heart of Rome, almost a huge foyer. An enormous garden framed on all sides by a long portico rich in paintings and sculptures. In the center, there are two plane tree copses with fountains, which flank a central avenue leading from the theater to the place where Julius Caesar will be assassinated: the Curia of Pompey the Great, a large hall accessible via a wide staircase. It contains valuable marbles, pillars decorated in various styles, and tall windows at regular intervals. This is the room where the Senate will meet today.

Why here and not in the Roman Forum, where the Curia Cornelia, its old, natural home, is located? Because building works are currently under way to turn it into a temple. And so pending the completion of the new Curia Iulia commissioned by Caesar, Pompey the Great's Curia has provisionally become the throbbing heart of Rome's decisions. The senators' seats are lined up on both sides. Caesar's chair is on a podium, with its back to an alcove dominated by a giant statue of Pompey the Great, his old enemy. Of course, these are just theories, since archaeological excavations are especially difficult because the area where Pompey's Curia once stood is now beneath a road.

We have called this building a "giant historical key" because of what would happen. True, but during these early hours of the morning, it's something else. It's a huge magnet, a huge attractor, which over the coming minutes and hours would draw all the protagonists like a black hole sucking up stars and galaxies into an ever-speeding vortex. Just as sailboats converge on a single lighthouse at night, so Brutus, Artemidorus, then Antony, Cassius, Cicero, and all the conspiring senators, as well as the sacrificial victim, Caesar, are inevitably approaching this place, some on foot, others in a litter. The actors and spectators of a colossal change of course in history.

Just as a star falls into a black hole (from which even light cannot emerge), changes state, and obliterates itself, their lives will be devastated and shattered from the moment they raise their daggers. Nobody will be able to turn back. Everything will disappear: wealth, dreams, happiness, and in many cases life itself. So let's try to follow them all at the same time, on that morning like no other, on a day that would never again be like the others.

Caesar's House, Dawn on March 15

Caesar has also had a restless night. Where is he now? He lived in a house in the working-class district of Suburra for some time, but at the age of eighteen, since assuming his position in 62 BC, he moved to a more luxurious and important house: the Domus Publica, in the heart of the Roman Forum. It's the official residence of the *pontifex maximus*, which he is. This house also plays a dual role: representative, where public activities take place; and private, where Caesar lives his daily personal life, complete with small baths.

After returning from the banquet with Lepidus and Decimus, Caesar went to bed next to Calpurnia, his wife. It hasn't been a comfortable night. According to what Plutarch subsequently wrote, in the middle of the night, the silence was suddenly shattered by the doors and windows being flung open by the wind. Caesar must have got up to shut them, perhaps joined a few seconds later by a trusted slave, half asleep. Caesar then had a tender gesture for his wife, got close to take her in his arms and hold her, perhaps so he could warm

them both up after the wind had blown the night chill into the bedroom. Only he saw something worrying. Calpurnia was fast asleep,
emitting vague, unintelligible moans. Then she suddenly woke up
upset, almost in a panic. Caesar must have held her and asked what
she had dreamed about, and, like a river bursting its banks, she told
him of her nightmare, experiencing the tragedy once again with her
senses still on alert. Two thousand years later, we have many versions
of this dream, by various authors, all of them terrible. In Plutarch's
take, Calpurnia dreamed that the pinnacle over their house was falling down, crashing onto their bed, while she was screaming for help.
Cassius Dio, on the other hand, says that "the house had collapsed
[. . .] and her husband, wounded by some men, was seeking refuge
in her lap." Appian tells us that Calpurnia saw Caesar's body dripping
with blood in her dream. Finally, Suetonius writes that she "dreamed
that the roof of their house was crashing down and that her husband
was being murdered in her lap."

We can picture the lines on the great general's face contracting for
a moment before relaxing again as he held his wife in his arms in a
long embrace. Calpurnia is weeping, and yet she is not a superstitious
woman. But it was a truly gripping and vivid dream.

It's possible that the loud noise of the wind against the house may
have influenced Calpurnia's slumber, making her feel as though the
roof were collapsing. But details like Caesar's stabbed, bleeding, dying
body in her lap may be a sign of something else. They might indirectly
suggest something we don't know, that over the previous few days she
may have heard rumors of a possible attack on her husband, so was
terrified. Or else he might have confided in her that someone was
plotting to kill him, though not giving much importance to these
rumors.

Once again according to Suetonius, Caesar also then told her his
dream. He'd dreamed that he was flying high, high up, beyond the
clouds, and shaking hands with Jupiter.

Flying in dreams is very common among people about to sit an exam or face a challenge the following day, something Caesar was going to do.

Even so, in both cases, it's startling how these dreams truly seem to herald the tragedy about to strike a few hours later. We have yet to establish whether they were real or "artfully created" after Caesar's death. We will never know. But if they were true, then we can understand Calpurnia's and especially Caesar's state of mind after a steady stream of daily suspicion, conspiracies, as well as negative prophecies and ill omens. They could possibly have been influenced by them. Basically, more than "premonitions," these dreams may have a more rational explanation: that they were "sentinels" alert to an atmosphere of fears and anxieties hovering over their home and their minds during those hours. In other words, they were both very aware of the daily risks.

In any case, there's a surprisingly long list of ill omens that could have influenced Caesar and Calpurnia. Here is a short list, based on what ancient authors have written.

In the days leading up to the Ides, Plutarch talks of "thunder and lightning reverberating in many places at night, and solitary birds flying down into the Forum." This could all be connected to a spring full of thunderstorms, but in the ancients' mindset, used to seeing signs and omens almost everywhere, everything takes on a different significance. Plutarch also reports evidence provided by the geographer Strabo that in the days leading up to the Ides, "many men made of fire were seen fighting, and a soldier's servant had a blaze spurt out of his hand, so much so that those present thought it was burning, but after the flame subsided, they saw that there was no injury to the hand." Today, this would be seen as a classic magic or illusionist trick, but what subsequently happened to Caesar is even more worrying to the mentality of the ancients. Again, Plutarch says that "during a sacrifice, Caesar could not find the victim's

.heart, a terrible sign, because by nature no animal can live without a heart."

According to Suetonius, in accordance with Julian law some veterans and settlers were digging up a few very ancient burial grounds in Campania, in order to build their homes. A bronze slab was discovered in the tomb of Capys, the king and founder of Capua, bearing a Greek inscription predicting the death of Caesar: "When Capys's bones are unearthed, a descendant of Julius will be slain by the hand of his kinsmen, and he will immediately be avenged with great massacres and mourning throughout Italy." Suetonius also tells us that "in the days preceding his death, he heard that the herds of horses he consecrated after crossing the Rubicon, and set free and unattended, had stopped grazing and were weeping incessantly." He then adds that "on the eve of these Ides, a wren, also considered a 'royal bird,' flew into the Curia of Pompey, a laurel twig in its beak; several birds suddenly appeared from the neighboring wood, attacked it, and killed it on that very spot."

Cassius Dio writes that the night before, the sacred shields of Mars, kept in the palace, vibrated and "made [. . .] a lot of noise."

Finally, there is Spurinna, an Etruscan haruspex—a priest who examined entrails during a sacrifice. Romans had profound respect for Etruscan haruspices, so much so that, according to the U.S. historian Barry Strauss, "some leading politicians had personal soothsayers." Spurinna was the *summus haruspex*, the principal priest who had officiated at the sacrifices during the days before the famous Lupercalia, on February 13 and 14, a month before the Ides of March. Since the responses had been especially negative on both the first and the second day, and Caesar appeared unconcerned, on February 15 Spurinna looked into Caesar's eyes and uttered the phrase later immortalized by Shakespeare: "Beware the Ides of March."

Caesar was an unusual Roman. Personally, he didn't believe in signs and ill omens, and went along with these superstitions only in order to follow the customs and make everyone happy. He certainly did take the Etruscan haruspex's warning on board, but quite likely shrugged it off.

Cassius's House, Early Morning

Brutus is not the only one leading the conspiracy. There is another important figure, Cassius, a bad-tempered, abrupt man veering on the arrogant. These traits made him into an excellent general in the Roman legions, albeit much inferior to Caesar in insight and stature. There's some excitement in his house today, with slaves putting the finishing touches to unusually clean and tidy rooms. Some of the slaves, those who have been there for many years, have a twinkle in their eyes. They're getting ready for a celebration . . . but in honor of what? It can't be connected to Caesar's assassination, about which no one knows anything.

By one of those strange coincidences that sometimes occur, today, March 15, Cassius's son comes of age, so to speak: he must wear the man's toga (*toga virilis*). He is named after his father, Gaius Cassius, and is between fourteen and sixteen years old. Last night, before going to bed, he started the ritual that officially marks the start of his adult life. He picked up his boy's toga (*toga praetexta*, trimmed with a crimson strip) and the *bulla*, the necklace containing good-luck charms he has always worn, and placed them on the small house altar with the lares, protective divinities, and the wax death masks of his most illustrious ancestors. Then, in keeping with tradition, he went to bed in an immaculately white tunic (*tunica recta*).

We can imagine his father's state of mind as he's forced to smile and show pride at a time when his thoughts are certainly elsewhere, when he's worried and under tremendous pressure. He had to play the part of the happy father, acting calm, but in his heart he must have been cursing Caesar for having "darkened" a day like that, so important for his family.

His son is now wearing the *toga virilis*, also white, but suitable for a man, and is very excited. At this point, tradition and law expect father and son to go to the Forum, walk across it to the Capitoline, and write the young man's name on the civil list of the Tabularium.

They will not be alone but accompanied by friends, relatives, and his father's *clientes*, and there will also be other people, initially not expected.

They are the people with whom Cassius is currently talking. Everybody thinks they're just friends and fellow senators who've come to celebrate the event as a sign of friendship. Many think this is just proof of the host's fame and power. No one suspects that these senators are actually a few of the conspirators who will escort Cassius to the Senate meeting and change history.

And a little attention would have immediately detected that strange blend of glances and softly spoken half-sentences. Among them, a familiar face: Marcus Junius Brutus, pale and tense, steps out from behind a pillar.

After one last ritual, yet another little sacrifice, and a few appropriate pleasantries from Cassius, the group leaves the house, walking under the flower garlands hanging over the door for good luck. The master of the house smiles next to his son, who is intimidated by this strange day. They are followed by the celebrating group, amid loud comments and jokes. When the last of them comes out, the procession walks down the road, and we can say that the conspiracy has officially been put in motion . . .

Tiber Island, 6:20 a.m.

A slave looks up at the sky as he shuts the door, and notices a dark shadow circling. It's a bird of prey, a buzzard perhaps, flying slowly and majestically. It's on a reconnaissance, searching for possible prey like pigeons, turtledoves, or rodents, of which there's no shortage in the cities. Its presence has not escaped the notice of a haruspex in a nearby temple, and the man watches it, expecting to detect a divine sign in its flight, whether lucky or ominous. He knits his bushy eyebrows when the form of the bird stands out against the brightest part of the sky, in the east, before turning back, still tracing large circles in the air. Where is it going? Why don't the gods "push" the bird of prey in a specific direction, with a definite message for him? The thoughts of this man of religion differ entirely from the animal's instinct. There are no divinities behind its circling but only the search for food. Unable to see anything easy to catch, the bird of prey decides to move. Its wings suddenly flap hard and it heads in the opposite direction to the rising sun, crossing the Tiber and flying to the unspoiled woods and countryside. The haruspex has noticed the abrupt change of course and follows the bird with his eyes for a long time, until it becomes a distant dot, then grimaces and stares down at the ground, lost in thought. The message is clear . . . and nasty. A bird of prey flying to the spot where the sun sets means that something dreadful connected to the authorities is about to happen.

A few minutes later, the bird of prey is flying over the elongated form of Tiber Island. A small army is marching below its wings. Legionaries, complete with their gear, shield on one side, *pilum* on the other, are crossing one of the island's bridges, heading out of Rome. Seen from above, they look like a dark red river because of the hundreds of capes undulating with their every step. The jingling weapons, armor, and so many metal objects accompany the customary rhythmic song of the legionaries, leaving the city through rows of onlookers and passersby. Many windows are suddenly opened, people craning their necks to watch the display. This army represents the power of Rome and will give it the ability to write history for hundreds of years.

It's probably a few centuries rather than an entire legion (too large, with its five thousand soldiers) that have been encamped on Tiber Island. We don't know its name but according to the historian Strauss, these are probably veterans or at least highly experienced soldiers, and definitely not recruits. Men who've marched with Caesar for years and fought in his battles. Just a few of them (perhaps even one, given their ability and experience) would suffice to save him today, but they are leaving, unwittingly bequeathing him to his fate. These men will not go to war against the Parthians. They are Marcus Aemilius Lepidus's soldiers, and just a few hours ago, Caesar has confessed that Lepidus is about to get a new posting: only four days from now he will become the new governor of Gallia Narbonensis and Hispania Citerior. These soldiers will follow him, and he has probably spent the night with them here. At present, they are leaving Rome on a drill outside the capital. Lepidus is probably at the head of the column, riding a white horse, visible to everyone. He, too, is leaving Caesar to his fate.

Caesar's House, About 6:20 a.m.

It is a day full of contrasts. A strong wind keeps buffeting the city, eddying into every alley and house, forcing people to wrap up in thick cloaks and capes and to light braziers. Even the sun cannot warm the air.

In Caesar's Domus Publica, the slaves have already started heating the water and preparing breakfast for the great general. A quick breakfast, as is his custom.

Right now he is sitting with his back to us on a curule, one of those folding seats without a backrest, which you often see in the tents of commanders in military camps. A couple of slaves are carefully grooming his hair, with ointments and small strokes of the comb. He's a tough man, used to life in an encampment, but his appearance is important to him. Although his graying hair is attractive to both men and women, the fact that it's thinning constitutes a real problem.

According to ancient writers, Caesar is very upset by his age-related hair loss. The most effective solution to this is a long, forward comb-over, as you can still see in his statues. And this is just what the two slaves are doing now.

Meanwhile, outside, the brick benches standing against the walls surrounding his house have for some time been crowded with *clientes*, people requesting an audience with Caesar in order to ask for favors, for him to take an interest in their problems, or for recommendations, since he is going to be away for several months. They are silenced by the sudden click of the heavy front-door bolt. A small, bald, and chubby man emerges, a wax tablet in one hand and a pen in the other. He is the *nomenclator*, or slave in charge of identifying clients in order to then "triage" them and speed up the meetings with Caesar. He begins by taking their names.

This is how the last day in Caesar's life has started. Like any other day, but on the wrong footing. According to Suetonius, the great general is exhausted after the restless night. Perhaps he had an epileptic fit. Suetonius claims that Caesar has recently been suffering from fainting, night terrors, and, in at least two cases, attacks of epilepsy, an illness that allegedly first struck him when he was in Africa, at the Battle of Thapsus, where he might not have taken part in the defining attack. We cannot be certain. According to some scholars, including Barry Strauss, news of this condition may even have been invented and circulated by his supporters after the assassination, in order to cover up the evident error in judgment that drove him to his death.

Caesar's Home, About 7 a.m.: More Soothsayers

Calpurnia will not relent. She's truly worried and tries to persuade Caesar not to go out and to postpone the Senate meeting to tomorrow. Maybe her fear of a possible attack runs far deeper than we believe in modern times. This is illustrated by the fact that although Caesar is not a superstitious man, "he hesitates for a long time," as Suetonius tells us. In the end, he gives in to Calpurnia's request and summons the soothsayers. Some believe that the wish to postpone the meeting could be motivated by a true physical malaise, because delaying such an important session at the Senate just for the sake of pandering to his wife's fears would be inconceivable . . . If so, it's safe to assume that he would have called for Antistius, his personal physician, the very man who would examine his lifeless body a few hours hence.

The Curia of Pompey, 7 a.m.: The Gladiators Arrive

A slave is sweeping leaves and rags outside his master's *domus*, blown over by last night's wind. The tight sheaf of twigs that makes up the broom scratches the sidewalk with an almost mesmerizing rhythm, like long brushstrokes. However, their drawn-out, regular lament on the stone slabs blends with another distant sound that's growing increasingly nearer: the regular step of a multitude of male figures who take up the entire street. The slave pauses and watches them in dismay. Their muscular, stout, massive bodies—so similar to one another—immediately tell him that these are people who train every day. Legionaries? Doesn't seem so. Wrestlers? No, their hair is tied in a ponytail at the top of their heads. They all look like . . . gladiators. The slave stares, wide-eyed, then sweeps faster before going back inside the *domus* and shutting the heavy, bronze-studded front door moments before the gladiators arrive. Their eyes look intent, their gait solemn. Many are recognized by the citizens as champions and favorites.

What are gladiators doing on the street at 7 a.m.? They've been hired by Decimus, the other dinner guest from last night. They might belong to his own gladiator school. There are many of them, a hundred or so. They can use weapons at close range like few others. Their task in the conspiracy is therefore to prevent any kind of potential interference on the part of men loyal to Caesar, and even block the doors to the Curia if necessary. They enter the large garden of the Theater of Pompey. Nobody suspects anything. Gladiatoral combats are customary during Senate meetings. Should anybody ask too many questions, the answer would be that they are here to abduct a gladiator who broke the contract with his master . . . Silently, like animals about to pounce on prey, they crouch under the portico. There's an hour to go before the Senate meeting begins at 8 a.m.

Meanwhile, after taking his son to the Capitoline Tabularium in order to add his name to the civil lists, Cassius hugs him and sends him back home with almost the entire party. From there, Cassius, Brutus, and the other senators head to the Theater of Pompey. It is down there, visible from the Capitoline, huge, made of pristine white marble. It seems to be drawing them powerfully, like a challenge.

Caesar's House, 7:45 a.m.: Caesar Decides Not to Go to the Session at the Senate

On their way, the conspirators have no way of knowing that at the very moment they left the Capitoline, Caesar decided not to attend the meeting. The new sacrifices made by the soothsayers have brought a negative response and he's still there, staring at the dead, eviscerated animal, and at the bloodstained knife that slashed open its belly, while Calpurnia gazes at him with imploring eyes. He then smiles and pats her face reassuringly and tells her he will not go.

He turns to his secretary and dictates to him a message for Antony, who lives nearby, asking him to go to the Senate and dismiss it in his role as consul.

Calpurnia is relieved and collapses exhausted on a nearby triclinium. The toll of a sleepless night and several days' worth of anxiety have gotten the better of her.

Caesar rereads the message and signs it. Then, following his peculiar habit, he folds the papyrus to form several pages, like a notepad. Having completed this origami of sorts, he hands the message to his secretary, who heads firmly to the exit of the Domus Publica. Suetonius points out that only Caesar had this odd obsession with folding his messages like bellows, while up to then "consuls and magistrates sent the written papers whole, in their entire width."

The Curia of Pompey, About 8 a.m.: The Conspirators Arrive and Take Their Positions

Nobody among the senators and conspirators is aware of Caesar's decision. In his absence, they start on all the usual administrative chores. As an urban praetor, Brutus, for instance, has to look through petitions and resolve disputes and various legal issues. He does this beneath the porticos surrounding the large garden of the Theater of Pompey, where high-backed chairs have been arranged. He handles this with extreme coolness, smiling at every supplicant, apparently calm and focused. And yet his state of mind is far from this. He harbors a turmoil of emotions, fears, and all kinds of anxieties. Every now and then he glances at the gladiators sitting in silence some distance away, in the semidarkness of the portico. He realizes the deed is now under way, even though it could be aborted at any time. His gaze meets that of Cassius: he, too, seems to have lost the confidence he had earlier this morning. At times he looks lost, often stares at the ground, but by the time he looks up again his eyes have recaptured their lost confidence.

The other senators and conspirators are also tense but feign steely calm. On one side of the portico, in a totally anonymous way, their secretaries are carrying beechwood chests, a little taller than a span, that can contain half a dozen written scrolls, in this case documents that the senators are going to use today. Nobody knows that these boxes also have, concealed among the papers, many of the daggers that will kill Caesar . . . This way, centuries ahead of many espionage movies, the conspirators managed to smuggle weapons into the large chamber of the Curia, using a back door.

Antony's Domus, 8 a.m.:
Antony Receives Caesar's Message

The first impact was from the Gallic slave's green eyes. The Carthaginian servant who opened the door of Mark Antony's *domus* saw before him a huge, muscular form with a ginger beard and very fair skin. He must have immediately gotten an idea of what it would have been like for Caesar's legionaries to fight against these warriors, whose imposing physique instills immediate fear. These are strong, proud people with a history of very ancient traditions. Like his own. A Carthaginian facing a Gaul. These few inches alone summarize the expansion of the Roman dominion over the Mediterranean and Europe. But neither man thinks about history. This is normal for that time. Gauls and Carthaginians also used to have slaves from subjugated peoples who had been conquered or dominated. Caesar's Gallic slave has to deliver a message, and a few seconds later he's standing in the atrium of Antony's large house, immersed in the bright colors of the frescoes on the walls, the powerful smell of the recently redone paneled ceiling of dry timber, and the silence of this elegant home, disrupted only by the sound of a trickle of water from the face of a statue of Hermes, falling into a basin that overflows right into the *impluvium* tub in the middle of the room, creating a series of elegant concentric waves that reflect the sunlight on the walls.

Caesar's slave does not have to wait long for his message to be picked up in person by Antony's secretary, who dismisses him and goes to his master. Let's follow him.

After crossing the large inner garden, the secretary approaches his master. He sits with his back to us, bare-chested, while a slave is putting the finishing touches to his voluminous curls. He waves the slave away and turns around.

The first thing we notice about Antony is his wide, powerful chest, chiseled from exercise. Then his large, dark eyes, with charming wrinkles at the corners that spread to his temples like the rays of the sun. He has full lips, and when he smiles, creases form at the corners of his mouth, giving sensuality to his strong, masculine face with its prominent cheekbones and powerful jaw. When his thick, wavy hair is long, like today, it cascades in curls. It's a strikingly strong, bright face. That of an energetic thirty-nine-year-old.

His large, dark eyes give the secretary a quizzical look. The man bows his head and hands him Caesar's message. Antony smiles as he reads it, and his face lights up with charming new wrinkles. The news that the Senate session is canceled puts him in a good mood. A man he hates, Dolabella, was supposed to be elected to the rank of consul today. And there's no knowing when this is likely to happen now that Caesar is going to be away from Rome for a long time. So the day begins with good news . . .

Domus Across the Tiber, 8:20 a.m.: Cleopatra

A few miles away from Antony, across the Tiber, another hand is clutching a papyrus. Its characters are different, though. These are not sentences written in the Latin alphabet but in Greek. Cleopatra's eyes caress these characters, carefully written by a scribe in Thebes a few weeks ago. It's a letter from a high-ranking civil servant keeping her posted about the administration of a large temple while she's away. Even though a few weeks may seem a very long time to wait for news, back then it was the equivalent of a government conference call, because news had never circulated so swiftly.

Under the Ptolemies, to whom Cleopatra belongs, the official administrative language is Greek, and she is fluent in it, although she would equally have been able to read it had it been in Demotic, the language spoken in the Egyptian hinterland, including Thebes. Since birth,

Cleopatra has been used to daily contact with different languages, cultures, and even alphabets. The same could be the case if Cleopatra were to live in present-day New York, London, Vancouver, Hong Kong, or Dubai.

This is an important aspect of understanding just how modern her mentality is. If she suddenly were to walk through a time portal, she could easily be a top manager at a large multinational, travel on a private plane to overseas meetings, and frequent the jet set. And she would probably be doing better than her male colleagues . . .

Cleopatra is a modern woman in an ancient era. Emancipated, uninhibited, strong, and a key player at a time when other women wear cultural "burqas" and blend into the everyday life of a male chauvinist society.

She pauses for a moment, looks up from the characters written on the papyrus, at a cooing turtledove on a branch beyond the marble balcony. Her gaze travels past the turtledove and loses itself in the skyline of the Eternal City as visible from Trastevere.

As well as Jerusalem, Rome is probably the city in the Mediterranean, Europe, and perhaps the whole world where you can hear the largest number of languages (not to mention dialects, which were much more widespread and important than they are now): those of Gauls, Iberians, Germanic peoples, and Hebrew, Aramaic, Carthaginian, Etruscan, and most probably languages from more distant lands like Nubia, Syria, Armenia, and India, thanks to merchants and sailors.

Naturally, Latin and Greek are very widespread, so much so that the upper classes are often bilingual. However, as you leave the south of the Italian peninsula, the farther east you go, the less Latin is spoken, and Greek becomes the official language, in Greece of course, but also in Turkey, the whole of the Middle East, and all the way to Egypt. This may be the greatest monument bequeathed by Greek culture and Alexander the Great in particular. The eighth wonder of the ancient world exists—Hellenistic culture, which has filled a vast territory that spreads light and openness of mind across continents and very different peoples. It would continue to do so for many centuries. No wonder the Gospels would be written in Greek. And no wonder Cleopatra speaks Greek to those she loves, like Caesar.

The Curia of Pompey, 8:30 a.m.: Tension Among the Conspirators

Meanwhile, at the Curia of Pompey, tension is mounting among the conspirators. Caesar is late and nobody can account for it. The two Casca brothers are among them. According to Plutarch, at some point one of them is approached by a man who takes his arm and says, "You keep it a secret, Casca, but Brutus has told me all." And since Casca is bewildered, the other man smiles and adds, "How did you manage to become so wealthy so quickly, my dear man, that you can compete in the building trade?" Casca stares at him blankly. Taken in by the misunderstanding, he was about to reveal the imminent attack!

But it's not over. This spasmodic wait for Caesar is a stream of coincidences that makes the conspirators even more nervous. A few minutes later, a man comes up to Brutus and Cassius, the leaders of the conspiracy. It is the consul Publius Popillius Laenas. He greets them and seems politer than usual. He then approaches one of them, whispers, "I pray that the gods might grant a successful outcome to what you are planning," and leaves. The two men look into each other's eyes, terrified. What if the plot has been discovered? What if, instead of Caesar, his bodyguards walk in through the door and arrest them? They have taken this possibility into account and are ready for suicide.

One thing is definite. They cannot wait any longer. It's now or never.

The conspirators have arrived in dribs and drabs, some with Cassius, others with Brutus, others under their own steam. The tension is very high. Some are caressing the pommels of their daggers, concealed in the folds of their togas. Others are pacing up and down nervously. But who exactly are these men? And how many are they? It's hard to say, but they're certainly a minority in comparison with the crowd in the room. There were about nine hundred senators in Caesar's time, but there are far fewer present in the room on the Ides of March. Apart from the fact that there's always a high number of absentees at every meeting, we must consider the size of the room (3,600 square feet) and the defections caused by Caesar's delay. Some say there are at least four hundred, while others, such as the historian Barry Strauss, say there were between one hundred and two hundred. What's sure is that the actual assassins are far fewer—more than sixty according to Suetonius; thirty or so, say other sources. In any case, such a large number of conspirators suggests that not only senators were present at the session but also representatives of the aristocracy.

Cicero is also in the room. He knows about the conspiracy but is not involved in the final phase of the plot, that is, the actual murder, perhaps because he's considered unreliable and too much of a talker.

What's most extraordinary is that a large proportion of the assassins owe something, if not everything, to Caesar. Some owe him their lives on the battlefield. There are those who have been his sworn enemies and fought at Pompey's side but were then pardoned by Caesar himself once the war was over, so that they might recover their dignity and political position at the Senate, perhaps even receiving important offices. Humanly speaking, this is the worst possible betrayal.

There are also a few very loyal people who have grown disillusioned, and followers of his old enemy Pompey who want revenge, as well as senators motivated by personal interests, at least in business.

But Brutus's case is truly jaw-dropping. Listen . . .

He comes from one of the most prominent families and is a descendant of a founder of the Republic. Even though his father was killed by Pompey, Brutus joins him against Caesar and together they face him in a famous battle, in Pharsalus. Caesar, however, has always been fond of him . . . perhaps because he's the son of his first great love, Servilia, or maybe because he suspects he's his actual father. We will never know . . .

According to Professor Eva Cantarella, "Servilia's relationship with Caesar wasn't just any of the dictator's many love affairs. She was the only woman to whom Caesar remained attached for decades during which, given his well-known tendency toward love affairs, he certainly did not deprive himself of other distractions. Yet Servilia was the only woman with whom he continued a relationship that wasn't just sexual, and there were quite a few rumors (not unfounded) suggesting Brutus was his son."

And so, before the battle, Caesar orders his generals not to kill him and to let him escape if he resists capture. And this happens. Following the defeat, Brutus flees and from his hiding place (in Larissa, in Thessaly) sends a message to Caesar, who is delighted to hear he's alive and invites him to come to him and be reconciled. When they meet, Brutus intercedes with Caesar for his friend Cassius (who will subsequently become one of the organizers of the conspiracy) and, as confirmation of his esteem for Brutus, Caesar even appoints him governor of Cisalpine Gaul . . . Whereas, a couple of hours from now, he is going to thank Caesar with a stab of the dagger.

One final remark: At first, the conspiracy included the killing of Antony, as one of Caesar's stalwarts. But Brutus objected and thereby saved him to show Romans that the plan was to eliminate only the tyrant Caesar and not his political faction. Moreover, he is confident that Antony will join his side after the murder. This will prove to be a tragic error in calculation for Brutus and all the conspirators . . .

About 9 a.m: Caesar Is Not Coming

The conspirators' voices and thoughts are suddenly halted by the arrival of Antony. Everybody steps toward him. In just a few words, he announces that Caesar is not coming. And the reason? The auspices from the sacrifices performed by the soothsayers are not favorable. After the initial amazement and dismay, there's an outburst of voices, shouts and acclamations. Some walk out briskly, complaining about the waste of time. Others yell and protest. A slave is already taking away Caesar's golden chair since he isn't there. The conspirators huddle together to take stock of what is to be done. We can see them all together for the first time. Who knows? Perhaps the only one who is truly aware of them is Cicero. They decide to send Caesar someone he trusts unconditionally to persuade him to join them. They choose Decimus, his legate, ally, and close longtime friend, but also one of the conspirators. A few minutes later, he's in the streets heaving with people, with an absorbed expression and thoughts racing through his mind. If he can't persuade him, Caesar will go on the expedition against the Parthians unscathed, the conspiracy that's by now on everyone's lips will be discovered, and this will spell the end for them all, including him. As he turns the corner, he doesn't even realize he has bumped into another, equally determined man with an absorbed expression: Artemidorus, the Greek philosopher who wants to warn Caesar of the imminent attack. His throat is dry, his hands sweaty but still clutching the papyrus, ready to change the course of events. The two men look at each other for a fraction of a second. They represent two opposite directions of history: one with Caesar, the other without him. As a freedman, the philosopher casts down his eyes before the powerful Roman politician and gives way. Exactly as history would do shortly.

Caesar's Home, 9:45 a.m.: Decimus Arrives

Decimus has no problem jumping the line of *clientes* waiting to be received by Caesar. As soon as the *nomenclator*, the slave in charge of triaging the supplicants, sees him, he takes him to his master. Now Decimus is before Caesar, who immediately notices that something is amiss in his old friend: he is out of breath, his forehead unusually sweaty, his tone agitated, his every word charged with tension. But instead of being suspicious, he tries to empathize and work out the reason for his friend's unease. "What do you think, Caesar?" Decimus said, according to the ancient writer Nicolaus of Damascus. "Will a man like you lend credence to a woman's dreams and the omens of foolish men?" And so Decimus starts to poke fun at soothsayers and warns Caesar that his decision not to attend will cause offense to the Senate. It's easy to imagine the slander, the invective, and the accusations. Decimus then attacks Caesar's wife, Calpurnia: What would have been the outcome, had she had better dreams? He tells him that this attitude, in addition to his refusal to go to the Senate, could be seen as an unnecessary sign of arrogance and disregard that would also affect all his friends, who might then be unable to defend him. Where is the sense of duty Caesar should feel toward Romans and the Senate?

Caesar notices that the veins on Decimus's neck are swollen like never before as he speaks, and wonders if he has underestimated the consequences of his refusal. As it happens, he would be entirely right not to go to the Senate, but what will let him down is his trust in his close friend. The latter, according to Nicolaus of Damascus, offers him the perfect diplomatic solution on a silver platter: if he really thinks this is an unlucky day, it would be better for him to show up in person to announce that the session is postponed. Behind the door, Calpurnia, short of breath, is listening to everything, hoping her man won't let himself be persuaded . . .

Marcus Brutus's House: About 10:00 a.m.

Porcia, the wife of Marcus Brutus, Caesar's antagonist, is overwhelmed with anxiety. She doesn't know what they are talking about at the Senate. She feels stifled and can barely stand up, but rushes to check the street at every cry she hears. She keeps asking information of anyone coming from the Forum, and sends everyone she can to obtain news of Brutus . . .

No one ever talks about these women, only about their husbands. And yet there's much we can discover about their husbands through their actions and emotions. Porcia is terrified and has now reached breaking point. All the color drains from her face, she tries to say something but her half-open mouth emits no sound and she suddenly collapses on the floor. The handmaidens start screaming and everybody comes running, including the neighbors, who knock at the door. The rumor starts spreading that she is dead—so Plutarch says. But what follows is even more surprising.

A few minutes later, Porcia comes to. Meanwhile, news of her death has started to travel from mouth to mouth and reaches Brutus through a breathless slave. We can imagine his inner turmoil, the impulse to run home and do something and, above all, his desperation to have further news of her . . . Yet he remains impassive, knowing perfectly well that he must now focus only on Caesar's assassination. "Naturally, Brutus was devastated by the news," Plutarch writes, "but he did not abandon the common good and his grief did not turn him toward his personal woe."

Caesar's Home, 10:20 a.m.: Caesar Is Getting Ready to Leave

Caesar stares into his dear friend Decimus's eyes for a moment. Then he looks away and follows a little bird, a tree creeper, as it moves along the branches of a myrtle bush in the garden. His face relaxes and he glances at his friend again. Very well, he agrees to go to the senators.

He does not leave right away, however. Caesar takes great care of his image. He decides to don a woolen tunic (the weather is still cold and windy) and, over it, the crimson toga with golden embroidery, typical of victorious generals at their triumphs, which the Senate has allowed him always to wear, and golden sandals on his feet. He spends several minutes getting his ever-thinning hair done by the slaves.

Then comes the time for the laurel crown he always wears (malicious gossip insists it's only to cover his baldness). Now he is ready.

However, just as Caesar and Decimus are about to step out of the house, something unexpected occurs. Something that will be seen in the centuries to come as one of the most powerful omens. A statue of Caesar in the vestibule suddenly falls and shatters to pieces. The two men turn, startled, and remain silent for a moment. Decimus fears the worst and curses this strange coincidence. But Caesar has made up his mind and heads to the front door of the *domus*. Watching him walk away, Calpurnia feels even more intensely that tragedy is ensnaring her man. All of a sudden, Caesar stops, turns toward her, and looks into her eyes. It's a deep gaze. The last in their lives together, even though neither of them knows it. Then Caesar leaves through the front door, where a litter, as well as a small crowd of escorts, awaits him. Calpurnia stands still, frozen, unable to say or do anything. She watches him leave, and once the door shuts, there's nothing but emptiness in the house. That and the warmth left in her soul by that final, intense look.

Caesar's Home, 10:25 a.m.:
A Slave Tries to Warn Caesar

No sooner has Caesar left the house than a gust of wind almost tears the laurel crown from his head. As he holds it down with his hand, he spots a slave, a curly-haired, dark-skinned young man who tries to approach him by the door and tell him something. Only he is immediately pushed aside by the crowd of people who are here for Caesar. The slave tries again, repeatedly, to edge his way among the bodies and outstretched hands acclaiming the dictator, until the strong arms of a lictor trying to protect Caesar clasp him and wedge him against a wall. His attempt at saying something important fails.

Who is he? What does he want to warn him about? Ancient historians wondered about that for a long time. According to Plutarch, he's a slave from another senator's household. We don't know whether he acted on his own initiative or was sent by his master, perhaps a friendly senator in the chamber who realized what was being plotted when he noticed the conspirators' dismay at the news of Caesar's absence, and in particular Brutus's strange reaction, keeping his position despite the alleged death of his wife. What we can say is that the slave (or whoever sent him) does not know the particulars of the attack. The young man does the only thing he can at this moment, as Plutarch writes: "Pushed away by the crowd gathering around Caesar, he forced his way into the house, appeared before Calpurnia, and begged her to keep him safe until Caesar's return because he had an important message for him."

10:30 a.m.: Caesar Draws Nearer to His Death

Caesar has climbed into the litter and is lying down comfortably, in the same position as when he is at a banquet. He has dismissed his personal bodyguard, made up of loyal Iberian soldiers who were following him with drawn swords, but he's not alone. A large crowd is walking with him, making his trip look like a procession. There are also twenty-four lictors, many magistrates, Caesar's appointed attendants (seeing as he is *pontifex maximus*), and a multitude of citizens, freedmen, slaves, and foreigners.

The litter is gradually lifted by eight slaves and starts moving, its embroidered curtains swaying with every step. The procession starts to travel before the eyes of onlookers who stop in their tracks, and others who acclaim Caesar from their windows and balconies. Everyone, supporters and adversaries alike, already sees him as history's great protagonist.

The litter is above everybody's head, so visible from a distance. Some come out of the *tabernae* so they can see the great general up close, others lift their children to show them the reclining Caesar, and others (few, however) bravely protest against him from afar, but are immediately silenced by the insults and invectives of Caesar's sympathizers. Even though the feast of Anna Perenna is in full swing, there are many people surrounding the procession. These are mainly supporters, although there are also many people asking favors, handing in letters, hoping for a recommendation for a relative, and submitting petitions. We do not know the exact itinerary but we can estimate a distance of about 1,400 or 1,500 yards, which, given the crowds and the hills and slopes, would have taken about three quarters of an hour.

I wonder if Caesar realizes he is seeing Rome parading before him in all her splendor for the last time, like a final salute to the man who made her so great. There's something sinister and prematurely funereal about this cortege.

What can Caesar have seen for the last time? Of all the monuments, temples, and buildings he would have looked at during his journey from the Basilica Julia to the Rostra, two in particular would have moved him deeply because of their link to two key players in his life. Two individuals who have given him, respectively, glory and love: Vercingetorix and Cleopatra.

The Mamertine Prison, which the litter is passing at this very moment, transports him back in time to the wars in Gaul and the surrender of his bitter enemy, the chief of the Gauls, Vercingetorix.

This is where, many years after his victory, the triumphal procession, and a long imprisonment, he had him strangled. He recalls with nostalgia the years of campaigning in Gaul, so impetuous and dramatic, yet so full of life.

A little farther, his heart skips a beat in the Forum of Caesar, which he built (one of the few enterprises he saw completed in his lifetime). He remembers the days of its inauguration well, along with the triumphs over Gaul, Egypt, Pontus, and in Africa. It was on that occasion that Caesar had a large sign inscribed with *VENI VIDI VICI* ("I came, I saw, I conquered") that would accompany the itinerary of booty and the conquered in chains.

At the triumph over Egypt, he paraded a giant painting of the Nile and a model of the Lighthouse of Alexandria. Moreover, a huge naval battle was staged, with four thousand rowers and many Egyptian ships he had captured and ordered to be taken to Rome for the occasion. And how can anyone forget the amazement of the Romans at also seeing giraffes on display? Nobody had ever seen one, and they were renamed "camelopards" because they looked like camels with leopard spots. As we recall, Cleopatra's sister was also paraded in chains that day.

However, he gasps with even more tenderness when he goes past the Temple of Venus Genetrix and thinks about all the many masterpieces kept there, including a statue of which he is very fond—that of Cleopatra. He had it made of gilt bronze, and it's stunning. It stands next to that of Venus and will do so for generations. Nobody will dare touch it because it was ordered by Caesar, in everyone's eyes one of the greatest Romans of all time. We cannot see it but it probably looks like Isis, the goddess Egyptians associate with love, therefore comparable to Venus (and for this reason standing next to her). According to some scholars, she is naked, but not according to others. What we can say for definite is that she represents a beautiful, sensuous woman, so much so that almost two hundred years later, Appian tells us that the statue is still in the temple and that it's "very beautiful." True, there's also war loot in the temple, but this particular sculpture symbolizes more than just a conquest. A conquered heart. Caesar's. Having the image of a foreign queen in a sacred temple in the Forum is an exceptional tribute, and even much more . . .

The Curia of Pompey, About 12 Noon: Julius Caesar Arrives

Caesar's sedan makes its entrance into the large quadriporticum of the Theater of Pompey. The great general's experienced eye immediately notices the assembled gladiators, since their trained bodies stand out. Seeing Caesar frown, Decimus, who has walked beside him all the way, immediately plays down the situation and explains their presence with the hunt for the "deserter" gladiator.

After all the traps Caesar set the Gauls, as reported in *The Gallic Wars*, it's surprising that he should not be suspicious. Maybe he's distracted by the chaos in the porticos, the to-ing and fro-ing of people engaged in lawsuits and in all the activities that take place down here.

Caesar's arrival revives the conspirators' spirits. Here we are. The plan can now be triggered. Many eyes are fixed on the great general as slaves help him down from the litter. Their expression turns to dismay when they see a senator approach Caesar. It's the one who told Brutus and Cassius that he was aware of their plan and that they should hurry up with it: Popillius Laenas. They see him make his way among those present so he can be the first to greet Caesar. He is now speaking to him. Brutus and Cassius look at each other blankly. And so do all the other conspirators. Unable to hear the senator's words, they fear the worst, that he is telling Caesar about the plot. These are endless, confusing seconds. Cassius and a few senators have already placed their hands on the cold pommels of their daggers, ready to commit suicide. Then Brutus notices that Senator Laenas's body language isn't that of an informer but rather a petitioner. Brutus cannot warn the others because there are people around him who are not connected to the conspiracy, but he tries to reassure Cassius and the conspirators with his facial expression, communicating that they must wait.

As a matter of fact, Senator Laenas kisses Caesar's right hand and calmly walks away. He has clearly discussed a personal matter. Perhaps he, too, doesn't realize the attack is taking place today. The conspirators relax and some slump into their seats, looking blank.

Now Caesar is near a small altar where the umpteenth sacrifice is to be performed, as customary before a Senate meeting. Once again, the auspices are not favorable. Annoyed, Caesar looks at his friends, but Decimus persuades him once again to pay no heed, to quote Nicolaus of Damascus, "to the empty chatter" of soothsayers and to get on with state business.

At this very moment, Caesar sees a familiar face in the crowd: Spurinna, the soothsayer who predicted the unfavorable Ides of March. Caesar's face lights up and, as Plutarch writes, he bursts out laughing. "The Ides of March are upon us, Spurinna," he says, and the man replies in a grave, solemn voice, a dark expression under his bushy eyebrows, "Upon us, yes, but not over yet." Does Spurinna know something about the plot but decides not to help Caesar? We will never know.

Caesar resumes his walk along the portico toward the chamber of the Curia, where the meeting is to take place. Picture the scene. There are many people surrounding Caesar to ask him something, give him a parchment to read, petition for something. He's talking, joking, reassuring, moving ahead. The crimson toga with gold trimmings and the laurel crown on his white hair make him visible to all, like a ruby set in a diadem.

One man doesn't lose sight of him for a second as he makes his way with sweaty hands, pushing people away. He is breathless and his heart is throbbing in his temples. He's been looking for him for hours. Annoyed by his smell, a senator with well-groomed, perfumed hair turns abruptly to send him away but is dumbfounded. The man before him is much taller than him, with an intimidating thick beard, tousled, curly hair, and, above all, a distraught, sweat-drenched face. The senator promptly disappears. There's nobody between Caesar and this man now. The great general turns around and their eyes meet. Caesar immediately recognizes him and smiles. It's his friend Artemidorus, the philosopher we've already seen, who's been looking for him for hours to give him the scroll that could change the course of history. He has finally reached his target and is standing before Caesar. Only, he has just a fraction of a second to deliver the message and there's a problem. He's seen the general receiving many notes and rolled papyri, and he isn't reading any of them but passing them to his private secretary. It's essential that his scroll doesn't follow the same fate. Caesar tilts his head, intrigued by his friend's hesitation. Artemidorus has no choice. He slowly stretches his arm like someone about to point an accusing finger and hands him the papyrus. Then he slowly approaches and whispers in his ear, "Caesar, read this yourself alone, immediately; it contains revelations of paramount importance to you." Caesar pulls a surprised face and keeps staring into those dark eyes for a moment. They have always been so definite in explaining life's events and yet they now seem to be pleading. He looks at the sweat-drenched, crumpled papyrus, unrolls it, and begins to read.

But the crowd suddenly interrupts him and demands his attention for new petitions and new compliments. Caesar does not, however, give Artemidorus's papyrus to his secretary but puts it among the papers he's holding in his left hand, so he can read it shortly. This is what Artemidorus sees (and what the ancients, such as Suetonius, report). The Greek philosopher stands still while the crowd shoves past him. He has reached his target. He has delivered the message to Caesar. But will he read it? He sees the crowd swallowing up the great general's crimson robe as his white head crowned with laurel moves away and vanishes through the entrance to the Senate. Artemidorus is exhausted, drained. And so he leaves, exiting history. Did he succeed in changing history? Caesar received the message and he asked him to read it immediately, so why shouldn't that happen?

There remains no answer to this question. It's one of those unfathomable events that have moved in the opposite direction to logic, thus sentencing the great general. And it's not the only one. Let's think about it for a second. There are also the severe doubts raised by the soothsayers and the negative omens (Caesar may have been a skeptic but he was still a man of antiquity, dominated by superstition). In addition, we have Calpurnia's words and anxiety, as well as the fears of his followers. Not to mention the suspicions Caesar was bound to have had but which he did not heed. Why didn't he act on any of these clues, signs, and alarms?

In life as well as in history, tragedies occur through many concentric circles, which, when put together, form a deadly funnel that draws the victim in. All it takes is for just one of these circles not to form for the tragedy to be averted. This happens so often and nobody realizes they've had a brush with disaster. In Caesar's case, there's a perfect alignment caused by the plot, chance, and his underestimating the danger. History's most famous murder is about to take place.

About 12:15 p.m.: Caesar's Assassination

Just a few dozen yards away, outside the chamber, other, faster and more flustered footsteps are treading the marble in the large courtyard—Mark Antony's. He had left, but when he heard that Caesar had agreed to attend the meeting, he rushed back to the Curia, annoyed. He's certain the Senate is about to elect as consul the much-hated Dolabella. He doesn't know that what's about to happen is much more serious and that it will rock his life as well as that of millions of people under Rome's dominion.

He, too, has noticed the gladiators. They are now all standing up, as though waiting for an order. He climbs the steps to the Curia, giving them worried glances. He has sensed something odd in the air. A hand stops him. He looks away from the gladiators and stares at the man holding him. It's Gaius Trebonius. The two men briefly study each other. Antony doesn't even have time to ask him about the gladiators before Trebonius assaults him with a list of requests concerning some unresolved issues. They don't sound all that important, but he knows from Trebonius's determined, loud voice that he has to give him some kind of answer. And so he does, but the man has more queries, insists, holds him tight by the arm, and blocks him on the final steps with what are nothing but excuses. Their purpose is simply to prevent him from being at Caesar's side to defend him. The conspiracy now proceeds like clockwork, with mechanisms set in motion one after the other.

Caesar walks into the Curia of Pompey with a severe expression and a solemn bearing. His golden sandals slowly tread the elegant floor with its colored marble patterns. The assembly of senators stands up and pays the customary homage.

He stops and looks at the chamber. In addition to the senators, there's the usual coming and going of civil servants (*apparitores*) attending to senators and magistrates. It appears to be a meeting like so many others. He resumes his typically regal walk to his seat, which, oddly enough, is located at the foot of the statue of Pompey, his late old rival. Has he noticed that the conspirators have taken position behind his high-backed chair?

Someone sees Cassius look up at Pompey's statue and invoke him. Is it the signal? Meanwhile, Caesar sits down.

The conspirators now slowly gather around him like a pack of wolves. It could be a harmless approach in order to discuss a problem, but many are concealing one hand under their togas, clutching their daggers.

The first to come to him is Senator Tillius Cimber. Caesar has exiled his brother and he wants to discuss this. He begs him to let his brother return to Rome . . . but this is just a pretext, the beginning of the end.

Other conspirators draw nearer, feigning to add their own supplications to his. The circle tightens. Silence falls over the chamber as everybody watches this strange knot of senators surrounding Caesar.

You can clearly hear their voices. Caesar denies their requests but they insist, so he starts to reprimand each and every one of them. His firmness suggests he still harbors no suspicion and doesn't realize this is a trap . . . which suddenly clicks shut.

Tillius Cimber grabs him by the toga with both hands and pulls it down, exposing his neck and part of his chest to make them vulnerable. It's the signal.

According to Plutarch, Caesar shouts, "But this is violence!" His reaction and in particular the intimidation he instills in all those present create uncertainty and hesitation. For a few seconds, nobody has the courage to act. It's not easy to kill a man in cold blood.

Caesar gives them a fierce look. Appian writes that it is Tillius Cimber who puts an end to this moment of general paralysis by shouting, "Friends, what are you waiting for?"

Senator Publius Servilius Casca is the first to draw his dagger and strike. He aims for Caesar's neck but hits his left shoulder instead, just above his collarbone. Caesar's instinct as a former soldier might have helped him to avert the blow—the injury is neither deadly nor deep. He suddenly stands up and grabs Casca's dagger to keep it still. They both start shouting and, according to Plutarch, Caesar cries, "Wicked Casca, what are you doing?" and the latter cries out to his brother, also a senator.

The chamber suddenly falls silent. Everybody is astounded, even the senators involved in the plot, who, as Plutarch says, "suddenly felt a shudder of horror at the attack and did not dare even escape or help Caesar, let alone utter a word."

According to Suetonius, Caesar grabbed his attacker's arm and stabbed him with a stylus (*graphium*), and the fact that he defended himself and struck at least one of his assailants is a little-known re-action and one important to highlight. He tries to lift himself from the seat but receives a second blow on the part of Gaius Servilius Casca, the first attacker's brother. The gleaming blade penetrates his body. It's a devastating wound, right in the chest, the only mortal one of all the wounds that would be inflicted. Blood runs down Caesar's skin.

At this stage, all the conspirators draw their daggers and start attacking Caesar from every side.

"Held in a vise," Plutarch writes, "Caesar encountered blows and blades directed at his face and eyes wherever he turned; he struggled like a wounded animal in his attackers' hands." The first to stab him after the Casca brothers is Cassius, until not long ago the calm father who took his oldest son to the temple. "He strikes him across the face," Nicolaus of Damascus tells us, "and shortly afterward Caesar's close friend Decimus approaches and slashes him across the loins."

Blows are raining on Caesar.

All the conspirators must symbolically stab him with their daggers and, Plutarch then tells us, "taste his blood." But chaos and frenzy reign supreme and some even injure one another.

Trying to stab him again, Cassius accidentally catches Brutus's hand instead. Minucius, too, misses his target and ends up cutting Rubrius's thigh.

Caesar tries to put up as good a fight as he can, pushes his attackers, moves to avert the blows, and screams at every stab. All the senators can see is a messy fluttering of white togas, and through them the occasional glimpse of Caesar's crimson garment and many daggers rising and falling violently.

Caesar feels his strength and consciousness draining as a result of internal and external hemorrhaging, preventing blood and oxygen from reaching the brain. Then, when he sees Brutus also draw his dagger and approach, he knows it's the end. He grimaces, fills his lungs with what's left of his strength, and cries, "You, too, son?" Suetonius writes.

These final words many of us learned in school, "*Tu quoque, Brute, fili mi,*" apparently were uttered by Caesar in Greek: "καὶ σύ, τέκνον?" (*kai sü, teknon?*)

Gasping with this last cry, he collapses, exhausted. Sensing death coming over him, he pulls the toga over his head, perhaps instinctively trying to conceal his body from his assailants or maybe re-creating the gesture performed during a sacrifice to consecrate the victim to the gods, thereby dying as a sacrificial victim. Darkness falls on him.

The senators stop, breathless, their togas smeared with blood, hands clasping the daggers still dripping with Caesar's blood.

Some are pressing on their wounds, making hollow moans, while others stare at Caesar's body shaking in the throes of death.

Slowly, a bright red bloodstain seeps through the crimson toga and spreads over the marble floor, following the gaps between the stone slabs, as though seeking a new horizon, as though his life is abandoning Caesar's body in search of historical immortality.

Above him towers the statue of Pompey, his defeated old rival, like a posthumous revenge. Did the assassination take place at the foot of this statue by chance or intention? We will never know for sure.

Everything happened in a very short space of time, perhaps even less than it took you to read the description of the assassination. Caesar received at least twenty-three stab wounds, of which, as his private physician Antistius would find, only the second was fatal.

Still, how come nobody tried to save him? Although it was all very quick, two senators did try. We know that Caesar raised many of his trusted men, even former centurions, to the rank of senators. Two of them, used to battlefields, tried to intervene, but they were unarmed and the large number of murderers' daggers prevented them from saving him.

Only chaos reigns now. Brutus is trying to address the senators, screaming the reason for the assassination. A few succinct, theatrical words. Of those destined to become part of history, there is something like "Fear not. Caesar was bound to fall and we have given you back your freedom." Except that they would never become part of history because nobody is listening to them. We will never know what he said exactly. In the chamber, there's only a general stampede, with chairs knocked down. Many fear that the daggers will now turn on them. Soon enough, the Curia of Pompey is deserted. All the senators, conspirators or not, have fled screaming in panic. All that is left is Caesar's body, lying alone and growing cold.

3

Rome in Chaos

One Murder . . . Many Murders

The most striking thing is that in these few instants not just one person was murdered but many. As a matter of fact, a large proportion of the main conspirators would die violently within a few months or years. That's not counting the thousands who would lose their lives in land and naval battles or because of proscription lists. It's no surprise: apart from the legends engendered by the brutal fate met by all the conspirators, it was also inevitable that Caesar's death should trigger bloodshed, revenge, and unprecedented violence. Something he had, after all, foreseen.

Just taking a look at how twenty or so of the principal conspirators ended up is disturbing enough:

- **Gaius Trebonius**, who blocked Antony on the steps of the Curia of Pompey, would be the first to die, killed and beheaded by Dolabella's men eleven months later, in February 43 BC, in Smyrna, Asia Minor. A particularly chilling detail—the soldiers played football with his head.

- **Lucius Pontius Aquila**, tribune of the plebs at the time of Caesar's assassination, would die thirteen months later while fighting against Antony's army during the battle of Modena on April 21, 43 BC.

- **Servius Sulpicius Galba**, great-grandfather of the future emperor Galba, would be sentenced and executed seventeen months later, in accordance with *Lex Pedia*, the law approved by Octavian in August 43 BC, which set up a special trial for the conspirators.

- **Decimus (Decimus Junius Brutus Albinus)**, Caesar's loyal friend and "great traitor," would go to his death eighteen months later in a fantastical manner while attempting to flee Italy disguised as a Gallic *eques*. Discovered, executed, and beheaded by a Gallic tribe at the end of September 43 BC, his head would be delivered to Antony.

- **Lucius Minucius Basilus**, another of Caesar's former loyal lieutenants turned enemy, would be murdered eighteen or nineteen months later by his slaves out of personal revenge in the fall of 43 BC.

- **Cicero** (a supporter of the conspirators) would be assassinated in Formia by order of Mark Antony just over twenty months later, on December 7, 43 BC.

- **Cassius (Gaius Cassius Longinus)**, one of the principal leaders of the conspiracy, would command one of his freedmen to kill him at the end of the first Battle of Philippi, just over two and a half years later, on October 3, 42 BC. Plutarch says it was his birthday.

- **Lucius Tillius Cimber**, the man who gave the signal for the conspiracy to begin, would die during the Battle of Philippi in the fall of 42 BC.

- **Publius Servilius Casca**, the first to stab Caesar, would die in Philippi like Tillius Cimber. Similarly to what happened to many conspirators, all his possessions would be auctioned, and a table with his name engraved would be purchased by a wealthy man and displayed in the atrium of his *domus* in the heart of Pompeii (where it can still be seen).

- **Brutus (Marcus Junius Brutus)**, the other leader of the conspiracy, would commit suicide following the defeat of the second and decisive Battle of Philippi, on October 23, 42 BC.

- **Pacuvius Antistius Labeo**, a famous jurist and Caesar's bitter enemy, would commit suicide in Philippi at the end of the battle.

- **Petronius**, who took refuge in the Temple of Artemis at Ephesus after the defeat at Philippi, would be executed on Antony's orders at the beginning of 41 BC, not even three years after Caesar's death.

- **Publius Decimus Turullius**, commander of Brutus and Cassius's fleet, would be killed at Kos after the Battle of Actium by Octavian's men at the start of 30 BC, almost fourteen years after the Ides of March.

- **Gaius Cassius Parmensis**, poet and author of caustic writings against Octavian, would die in Athens, where he would be executed by order of the future Augustus at the end of 30 BC, just under fifteen years after Caesar's death.

We should add to this long list the conspirators about whose end we do not know:

- **Marcus Spurius**, senator or *eques*.

- **Gaius Servilio Casca**, Publius Servilius's brother, the second man who stabbed Caesar, and the one who inflicted the only mortal injury.

- **Rubrius Ruga**, former supporter of Pompey.

- **Quintus Ligarius**, a soldier of *eques* rank and one of Pompey's supporters then pardoned by Caesar after the civil wars. Like his two brothers, he would probably be the victim of proscriptions ordered by Octavian, Antony, and Lepidus.

- **Bucolianus and his brother Caecilius**, two senators close to Brutus.

- **Publius Sextius Naso**, senator or *eques*.

Although we do not know the circumstances of their deaths, we can establish the time frame of their demise. Not one of them was alive by the end of 30 BC. As Velleius Paterculus says, Cassius Parmensis was the last of the conspirators to die. Less than fifteen years after history's most famous crime, all the culprits had been eliminated.

Antony's Escape

Everything we've seen—the stabbings, the screams, the commotion—took place inside the Curia of Pompey. Nobody saw anything from outside. This crucial historical event was witnessed only by senators, their secretaries, and the other personnel in the chamber. But what happened outside? Let's try to discover it through Antony's eyes.

To start with, he didn't give much importance to Trebonius's insistence as he stood in his way, firmly holding him by the arm. The two men had been friends for a long time, ever since the campaign in Gaul, in which they both distinguished themselves for their skill and courage. They spoke for a long time, and Antony initially listened to his friend and replied to his questions. After a while, however, he certainly wondered what he was aiming at but didn't have time to lose patience, because the conversation was interrupted by Julius Caesar's screams inside the Curia. It's easy to imagine Antony's dismay, his frown and the quizzical look he gave Trebonius. At that moment, he notices a movement of the crowd on the right. He sees the mass of gladiators converge toward him, swords drawn. There must be amazement in his eyes, and his instinctive reaction may have been to reach fruitlessly for the sword on his right side. We are no longer in Gaul; Antony is here as a consul and therefore unarmed. For a moment, he feels lost. Then he realizes that the gladiators are walking past him up the stairs to take positions outside the door to the Curia, their weapons unsheathed, stopping anyone from entering. Only then does he feel his friend grip his arm more tightly and shout at him to keep calm. Trebonius has to draw on all his personal determination to explain what's happening, that Julius Caesar is being murdered but that he, Antony, has nothing to fear because Caesar is the sole target of the conspiracy, while his life is being spared on Brutus's instructions.

Perhaps all that is happening is no surprise to Antony. About a year earlier, in the summer of 45 BC, Trebonius had invited him to become part of the conspiracy. Antony had refused . . . but oddly enough had not disclosed anything to Caesar. Cicero would hold this against him in his famous *Philippics*. Did he know that the assassination was being planned? It's reasonable to suppose that, although he certainly had no inkling that it would be carried out today. Another theory is that once he had blocked Mark Antony on the stairs, Trebonius did not beat about the bush but told him right away that Julius Caesar was about to be killed, just as he had intimated a year earlier. The two men's old complicity might explain why it was Trebonius and not someone else who stopped him. He may even have told Antony that if he didn't put up a fight nothing would befall him or his family. This would also explain Antony's lack of reaction. Of course, these are all theories. What's certain is that, faced with the gladiators' drawn swords and the sudden stampede of senators, he would have had little time to decide.

Suddenly, the doors at the top of the stairs were flung open, the gladiators stepped aside, and a true human river burst out in a desperate flight from the Curia. A mass running down the steps toward him.

No one explains what's going on, all the senators are running, screaming and shoving, scaring people outside the Curia, who also start fleeing . . . There are words like "run, close, close!" Rumor instantly spreads that there's a slaughter in process in the Curia. There's general panic. Picture the scene: all over, you can hear the screams of those who have not taken part in the assassination but are afraid that the storm is about to hit everybody, including Caesar's retinue who escorted him in the litter. Those present are certain that the crime has been committed by the Senate with the help of some armed group or other, given the presence of gladiators.

People have rushed into the porticos, knocking everyone down, heading for the nearest exits before scattering down Rome's countless streets, quickly spreading the terrible news.

Faced with this total chaos, Antony does the only thing he can. He runs away, realizing that even he, being so loyal to Caesar, is a potential target. He's not yet sure if they're also looking for him in order to kill him. Anything is possible in this frenzy, which is probably why he blends in with the togas of the senators trying to flee. At some point during his escape he must have hidden in a house or a store in order to remove his consul's toga and put on ordinary clothes, perhaps a slave's. Or else he may have ordered a slave in his retinue to give him his. Then he would have headed home, not running but walking briskly so as not to attract attention.

Who knows? He might have turned during his escape and seen the conspirators calmly coming out of the Curia, still holding their bloodstained daggers.

The Curia of Pompey, 12:45 p.m.:
The Conspirators Leave

Plutarch depicts the scene: "Brutus and his associates, being still warm with blood, left the council chamber together, displaying their drawn swords and heading to the Capitoline. [. . .] They were beaming, bold, urging people to freedom."

Under the portico in the Curia of Pompey, the group has assembled to take stock of the situation. There are many bloodstained togas, and tempers are running high. Someone suggests throwing Caesar's body in the Tiber but Brutus is against this. Others propose eliminating Antony, but once again Brutus refuses. It's essential that people know that they wanted to eliminate only a tyrant and not a whole host of adversaries. The crime is not a political one, but one whose purpose is to restore freedom to Rome (and the Republic). This is the message they want to convey to the people.

As a matter of fact, as soon as they resume their walk down the Roman streets, somebody puts on a spear a felt Phrygian cap, like the one worn by freedmen to symbolize the end of tyranny. A group of conspirators led by Brutus and Cassius heads to the Capitoline. They walk calmly, joined along the way by other senators who support them. Their tranquility is probably based on their political convictions, but also on the solid presence of Decimus's small army of gladiators escorting them down the streets with drawn swords.

The News Spreads Throughout the City and Reaches All the Protagonists

Such an extraordinary event is naturally followed by an equally extraordinary reaction. At first, the commotion and panic are confined to a specific location—the exit of the Curia of Pompey. The doors suddenly flying open and senators rushing out at breakneck speed can be considered as the "patient zero" of an epidemic that spreads across the whole city. The sight of so many armed gladiators triggers much fear. People flee in a disorderly fashion and mingle with frightened senators. What could a shopkeeper or a customer in a *popina* have understood in this panic? Some are saying that an army of gladiators has killed all the senators, others that now Caesar has been eliminated, Rome is being sacked. Many shops close their shutters while people lock themselves in their homes. During these long hours of uncertainty there would be much looting in the stores and warehouses, riots and unmotivated killings (probably settlings of scores).

The news spreads from mouth to mouth, from house to house, and from district to district like the shadow of a black cloud over Rome. And it reaches many of the protagonists we have encountered over the past few hours.

First and foremost, Julius Caesar's wife, Calpurnia. Ancient sources do not tell us how she reacted, but it's easy to imagine her despair and regret at having been unable to persuade Caesar not to go to the Curia. She married him at sixteen or seventeen and is now thirty-one. She feels that her life is irreversibly destroyed and has no future. She will never remarry and will probably spend long stretches of time filled with memories and sadness, watching the sea from her father's, Lucius Calpurnius Piso's, huge villa in Herculaneum. As sometimes happens, history and archaeology go hand in hand: the famous Villa of the Papyri, buried by the Vesuvius eruption in AD 79, belonged to Caesar's father-in-law, Calpurnia's father.

Almost at the same time, the news reaches another wife, Brutus's. Porcia's reaction is entirely different. She has brightened up, and probably sends a messenger to tell him she's feeling better and to congratulate him.

Confirmation of Caesar's death also comes to Lepidus as he is returning to Tiber Island with his soldiers. We don't know what words he uttered. No doubt they expressed sorrow and grief over his lost friend, whom he wishes he could avenge, as well as a myriad of questions about the future, which remain unanswered.

Then there is Artemidorus Knidos. We don't know how he found out. Perhaps he heard the commotion and panic on the streets. Like many Romans, he would have stepped out to see what was happening and somebody would have told him. The light would have gone out of his eyes beneath his bushy eyebrows as he stared into space. He would spend the rest of his days wondering if he could have done anything more or better to save Caesar, and where he had gone wrong. Maybe he should have told him to his face instead of waiting for him to read the papyrus. Wondering serves no purpose now.

1:20 p.m.: Antony's Domus

Walking at a regular pace, that of a long march, the slave slips into the alley that runs along the side of the *domus*, one of the largest and most luxurious on the Palatine. Everybody remembers that it used to be inhabited by the famous tribune Publius Clodius Pulcher, who was murdered some years ago. His widow, with whom he had two children, now lives here. As a matter of fact, she remarried, first to another wealthy, powerful man, the tribune of the plebs Gaius Scribonius Curio, then, when he was killed in Africa by Pompey's supporters while fighting for Caesar, to Mark Antony.

The slave has now stopped outside one of the back doors of the *domus*, a servants' entrance usually used by slaves for kitchen deliveries. Seen from the back as he's knocking, he looks truly humble. His tunic is threadbare and covered in oil stains, while his *paenula* is old, with several holes. It looks like a leather poncho that ends in a kind of cone that covers and protects the head like a medieval helmet. That and the scarf covering his face make him into an unrecognizable slave. No one opens the door although he has knocked hard. He glances around anxiously and starts knocking again. At last, the sound of the bolt instills hope. The door half opens and the face of a house slave appears, bald with a black beard, giving him a suspicious look. Seeing his poor appearance, he asks him what he wants, then notices something odd—well-cared-for hands and, especially, a solid gold ring with very familiar bezel. This man is not a tramp begging for alms.

At that very moment, the stranger pulls down his hood and scarf, revealing his face and identity. It's Antony, the master.

Shortly afterward, the consul is at the heart of the *domus* holding tight in his arms his sons Iullus and Antyllus (diminutive of Antonillus, i.e., "little Antony"), who are just one and two years old. During these dramatic moments his first thought was for them. They don't live in the elegant home where we encountered him this morning. That's a formal residence, where he hosts official banquets, and receives high-profile guests as well as women. His family lives here. And here is where he rushed immediately, fearing the worst. His wife, Fulvia, looks at him quizzically. What is a consul dressed as a slave doing here? In just a few animated words, Antony explains what happened and why he had to wear a disguise. Fulvia immediately grasps the gravity of the situation. She is no ordinary woman but a true protagonist, a tsarina behind the scenes of the Rome "that counts." A determined, ambitious, and calculating woman who is a far cry from the classic matron. She is not attractive: Velleius Paterculus writes about her that "all that was female about her was her body." It's above all her mind and personality that conquer men. In the context of the so-called Perusine War that would be fought in the future against Octavian, the historian Barry Strauss writes that Fulvia was the only woman to have carried a sword and recruited an entire army. Ancient sources report that later she would enjoy sticking a pin into the tongue of the severed head of Cicero, who had been her next-door neighbor. We're not dwelling on Fulvia's personality by chance. The fact that she is a strong woman, a virago, is very important in our story about Cleopatra.

By the time she and Antony married, they had known each other for several years. For Antony, who had been friends with her two previous husbands, his marriage to Fulvia not only redeemed his image—his stormy and much gossiped about affair with Licorys, the actress, banquet entertainer, and high-class prostitute had just ended—but also came as a breath of fresh air for his finances, since

Fulvia was extremely wealthy. At a time of arranged marriages, their relationship is certainly driven by genuine affection—although it's not an equal one. She is the stronger partner, most probably capable of imposing her will on Antony.

For all his being a brave soldier, a skilled commander, and an excellent orator not in the least intimidated by an audience and very charismatic with the people and senators, Antony is weak with women, unable to assert himself with them. A "beta" male, we would say in today's vernacular, quite different from Caesar's "alpha" male.

Even now, men successful in their work—strong and charismatic captains of industry—often prove to be disarmingly naïve, subservient, and indecisive in relation to women who are capable of ensnaring and dominating them.

Was Antony the same way? It's hard to tell after two thousand years. In his case there seems to be more: the search for a strong, protective companion in whom to seek refuge. Something Cleopatra would learn very clearly, because that's what she is like.

We must remember, however, that matches back then were not motivated by physical attraction or feelings as much as the desire to seal unions of politics, power, and wealth. This explains some odd examples of equilibrium within couples that can be understood only in terms of mutual convenience.

Horti Caesaris, 1:30 p.m.: Cleopatra Receives the News

Across the Tiber, in Caesar's sumptuous villa, the news has not arrived yet. Cleopatra is lying elegantly on a bed covered in cushions, her arm resting on a headboard with carved leopard heads at both ends. She's talking with Charmion, her lady-in-waiting, who is confessing a penchant for a charming Roman senator with sky-blue eyes. They're sipping wine enriched with Indian spices. Not far away, a brazier is spreading a sweet scent of frankincense and other essences in the room. This feels not like Rome but somewhere halfway between Egypt and India.

Suddenly, three men appear at the end of the room: Ammonius, the queen's principal adviser; the elderly Serapion, whom Cleopatra trusts blindly; and Olympos, her personal physician. Cleopatra stiffens and stares at them as they approach, followed by a large escort that takes position discreetly so as to defend the room while the Roman guard stops at the threshold. The queen realizes immediately that something has happened, and that there's an emergency—but what? The wise Serapion comes closer. His face is tense despite a gentle smile. He sits next to Cleopatra, looks into her eyes, and gives her the news of Caesar's death, adding that it's no more than a rumor at this stage, that nothing definite is known yet, but that the city is prey to panic, and that a plan of defense has been triggered for the villa in order to guarantee her and Caesarion's safety.

Cleopatra's eyes suddenly lose all their self-assurance. She feels as though she is tumbling into an abyss and is short of breath, about to faint. Her personal physician, Olympos, immediately steps forward, but she clutches at the sides of the bed and pulls herself together. Her fingers sink into the stuffing like claws. She looks Ammonius then Serapion in the eye while hers fill with tears she has trouble holding back. The seconds flow by, endless. Her entire world is crashing down on her: Caesar, the man at the center of her life, their joint projects, maybe another child, and Egypt suddenly vulnerable now that it has lost Caesar's protection . . . Only these few words, and her whole life is crumbling to pieces. She's in shock, staring into space. The evil spell is broken by a door opening and a smiling face appearing: Caesarion, who runs to his mother, followed by the servant who looks after him. Cleopatra's hug may be the warmest he will ever receive. The queen buries her face in her son's embrace, as though to hide. A few seconds later, she looks up again, her eyes now having resumed their strength and vitality, as well as a glint of all the wrath of a wounded lion. Cleopatra looks at Serapion and Ammonius again, and orders them to send messengers out to gather as much news as possible. Accustomed as she is to palace intrigues, over these past months she has worked out who Caesar's enemies are and the traditionalist Roman elite's hostility toward her. Even though she doesn't yet know who exactly the conspirators are, she harbors a strong suspicion about Brutus and Cassius, and is wary of two-faced individuals like Cicero and many other senators.

Here, she will wait for the messengers to return and, depending on the news brought her, will decide what to do.

1:10 p.m.: Caesar's Body Returns Home

Daggers still drawn, the conspirators barricaded themselves at the Capitoline a quarter of an hour ago. Everything is proceeding to plan, so far. Officially, they are here to pray to the gods, but the truth is that the Capitoline is a fortress for them. Parts of it are very steep, therefore easy to defend, not to mention its strategic location, overlooking the Forum.

Caesar's body is still lying in the Curia, lifeless for over an hour, at the foot of the bloodstained statue of Pompey. Many have come to see it, even from the street, but no one has dared touch it. Understandably, none of his supporters are left there, having run away for fear of being killed. As we have said, the conspirators wanted to throw Caesar's body into the Tiber at first but thought better of it, not just because Brutus was against it, but because of the presence of Lepidus's troops on Tiber Island. It would have been too risky.

In the end, three slaves loyal to Caesar lift the body very carefully. How odd it must feel to carry the cold body of this great, powerful man, which is now sliding about as they bear it to the litter. Where are his regality and dignity?

All that's left behind the slaves is a large pool of blood that is beginning to curdle, and red marks on the plinth of Pompey's statue, which would stay there, as Plutarch says, like a "film" of the slow, gradual collapse of Caesar under the merciless blows of his murderers.

In the general silence, a blend of embarrassment and respect, his lifeless body is placed gently on the gold-and-ivory litter that picked him up this morning. Someone puts the laurel crown compassionately next to the body.

Thus begins Caesar's final journey. A slow journey, since there are only three slaves. The litter slowly heads toward the Forum, avoiding the Capitoline for obvious reasons. It's a moving scene, and you can almost see the procession passing down the streets in slow motion, as Romans watch it, paralyzed, from the sidewalks, houses, and shops. Many are weeping. You can hear laments and invocations. Some cover their heads with their cloaks out of respect, a sign to mark the man's sacredness.

It's a chilling sight. The side curtains that shield the litter are raised and they can see the battered body and face, with the stab wounds. Moreover, one detail will be etched in the minds of those who see it for the rest of their lives: Caesar's arm hanging out, dangling in the void with every step of the three slaves.

Nicolaus of Damascus's words describe the scene very vividly: "The curtains on both sides being raised, you could see the dangling hands and the facial injuries. Then, seeing this man who had been honored on a par with a god until just a moment earlier, everybody had tears in their eyes. He was escorted on both sides by the lamentations and moans of people weeping in their houses, on the streets, and in the porches he passed."

His arrival back home is most dramatic. Calpurnia comes out screaming and crying, with her handmaidens and all the servants. We can picture her embracing him, like a mother her child. She probably struggled to recognize in that cold, ashen face carved by death the strong, confident, protective man who only a few hours ago had held her in his arms. The death of a husband, of a man like Julius Caesar, is unbearable. It's not just someone dying, but the certainty on which stand a household full of life (Calpurnia's), a key city in history (like Rome), and a dominion in the process of expanding across the entire Mediterranean.

Shortly after the body is brought into the house, Antistius, Julius Caesar's personal physician, examines it. We can well imagine his devastation, his difficulty in keeping to his role as a doctor apart from that of a long-standing friend. He must have cried a great deal after the autopsy. As we said, he sees that only one of all the wounds was fatal—the second one, in the middle of his chest. Whether it pierced through his heart or a lung, its result was so catastrophic it caused Caesar's swift death—considering the massive hemorrhage that ensued, just a few seconds if it was the heart, a little longer if it was the lung.

About 2–6 p.m.: Brutus Tries to Convince the Crowd

Brutus and Cassius have almost certainly seen the litter with Caesar's body pass at the foot of the Capitoline. We don't know what they thought or said, but it's reasonable to imagine they rejoiced. Subsequently, called by their supporters, they come down into the Forum to speak to the gathered crowd, escorted by a squad of gladiators and slaves. There are high-profile citizens among those congratulating them. Shortly afterward, the two men climb into the Rostra captured from Antium at the battle of 338 BC, to which were eventually added those purloined from Carthage at the Battle of Mylae in 260 BC. The crowd is dumbfounded. Brutus speaks first, followed by Cassius. They congratulate Rome on following the example of her ancestors who chased away the kings, and on gaining her freedom again. Their speech calms the crowd, which now looks at the conspirators with a friendlier eye. Although they mourn Caesar in deep silence, they respect Brutus. The situation alters, however, once Cinna speaks; he's a distant relative of Caesar (the brother of his late first wife), whom

Caesar had only recently appointed praetor. And yet he calls him a tyrant and tears his praetor's toga in contempt. This is a grave error. The crowd becomes enraged, and Brutus and Cassius are once again forced to flee to the Capitoline.

The historian Giovanni Brizzi remarks that although the conspirators "made adequate preparations for the tyrant's killing—even Romulus had been killed in the name of this idea—they have in no way prepared anything to ensure assuming this power, leaving the Senate and magistrates (whose names are Antony, consul, and Lepidus, representative of Caesar as *dictator*) the possibility of seizing it. The idealists at least seem to think that the Republic will rise again as soon as the tyrant is dead, which makes Cicero say that the conspiracy was planned by 'a manly spirit but puerile intelligence.' Caesar's assassination has been described as an error more than a crime. But even if Caesar had died from natural causes, things would probably not have turned out differently. The Republic was drawing to an end, and there would always have been an Octavian capable of realizing that Caesar's greatness had also been his weakness. Like other great men in the past, perhaps even more so, he was a 'memorable man but more in the arts of war than peace,' who had not understood that, in his personal power inevitably about to emerge, justifications were more important than embellishments."

The moment of great confusion is highlighted by Dolabella, the man supposed to be appointed consul much to Antony's anger. Caesar's death has ruined his investiture, and yet he turns up at the Forum in a toga—in practice, a self-proclamation—climbs the Rostra, and delivers a very violent speech against Caesar and in favor of the conspirators. He's not a trustworthy man, blows with the wind, and is now jumping on the bandwagon of the winners, or at least those he erroneously considers to be the winners. Then he goes up to the Capitoline to congratulate them. He's not alone: Cicero is also there, enthusiastic. At this moment, the majority of senators are in favor of the conspirators, who send Antony and Lepidus messengers to make unofficial deals without bloodshed.

In the late afternoon, at around 4:30, a violent storm breaks out over Rome, with terrible thunder and lightning. The wind and heavy rain disperse the last clusters of people talking about Julius Caesar's murder. It's like a curtain falling on one of the hardest days in the history of Rome.

8 p.m.: Antony and Lepidus Evaluate the Next Step

These are difficult hours for those most loyal to Caesar, Antony and Lepidus. What is the next step? The two men no doubt exchanged messages. We also know they met but not where. Lepidus, an impulsive man of action, has a legion in town with him and suggests acting immediately, attacking Caesar's assassins. Antony, on the other hand, is more cautious and prefers to wait. He fears the Senate will support the conspirators, which would spell the end for him and Lepidus. The two men take courage when they realize that even the conspirators are uncertain as to the next step. They don't seem to have a proper plan, and even the support of the crowd in the Forum was rather halfhearted. So they decide to go on the offensive and take the initiative. Tomorrow at dawn, Lepidus's troops will take positions in the Forum, ready to attack the Capitoline if necessary. Meanwhile, Antony sends messengers out of town to summon back Caesar's veterans. He persuades them easily by telling them that now their general is dead they will probably lose all the lands they received as reward for their victorious military campaigns.

Midnight: The First Night Without Caesar

Nobody in Rome can get to sleep. The legionaries on Tiber Island are on alert as though on enemy territory. The streets are deserted, buffeted by a cold wind.

People have returned from the celebration dedicated to Anna Perenna, but have shut themselves at home. In every *domus*, every *insula*, and every apartment, people are gathered, anxious, asking thousands of questions about the future. Caesar was on the side of the people and they had always loved him. Despite the rumors about him and Cleopatra, he was far better than the clique of corrupt senators that have come back into power, strictly bound to aristocratic families. What will happen now? It's not the same in the wealthy *domus* of many senators, where Caesar's death is widely seen as an opportunity to take back control and the Senate's past privileges. More than one drinks a toast or feasts, happy with this change.

Sacrifices are performed in temples to try to work out what will happen now. Antony and Lepidus are holding feverish meetings with their allies. Calpurnia is weeping inconsolably. Porcia is happy. Brutus and Cassius, once the celebrations are over, try to decide what to do next, sensing that Caesar's death has not created an easier world where everyone is in agreement but, on the contrary, has generated an imbalance in the political framework, with problems that are even harder to handle.

Thus concludes one of the most significant days in the history of humanity.

What about Cleopatra? She is shut in her home across the Tiber, surrounded by bodyguards positioned in every corner and every corridor. In her bedroom, lit by the faint glow of many oil lamps, she is curled up in sheets that have folds like a tempestuous sea and tell of her despair. Charmion slowly strokes her hair in silence, trying to comfort her, but Cleopatra doesn't seem even to notice her. Her eyes are wide open, looking into the darkness. This is how her future appears to her. Never has she felt this alone and vulnerable. Like a buoy on the tempestuous sea of life, she holds her only certainty as a woman and a mother: Caesarion, who is sleeping peacefully, unaware of everything, his hair stuck to his forehead with the heat generated by children as they sleep. Cleopatra buries her nose in this hair, smelling its scent. It's the only thing that calms her down.

Caesar's New Die

The days following the Ides of March are frantic. Going into details is not the purpose of this book. We wanted to tell you about Julius Caesar's death minute by minute because, like a die cast on the green cloth of history, it projects the protagonists of the chapters to come: Cleopatra and Antony *in primis*, then Brutus, Cassius, and other new faces, such as Octavian, Agrippa, Maecenas . . . You will see how, as the months and years (as well as pages) go by, these dice roll and flip before they stop and show the winning, then the losing side, then another winning side, and so forth, in a crescendo of tension in which it would never be possible to tell who is about to triumph until they stop altogether, revealing the number destiny has allocated to each and every actor on the scene. It's not easy to tell in a mere book fourteen years' worth of political events, battles on land, epic naval clashes, love affairs, children coming into the world, protagonists who die. Because it's not possible to describe everything, we will try to travel through this important period by focusing on the most relevant events and covering others in less depth.

The day after Caesar's death, at dawn, Lepidus moves his troops from Tiber Island toward the Forum. Like many Romans, Cleopatra will have certainly seen the marching soldiers, and we can easily imagine that everybody must have feared the situation getting out of control. Letting an army into the city, past the *pomerium,* is sacrilege. It breaks one of the most sacred prohibitions of the government of Rome. And yet this violation illustrates the level of tension and how close we are to civil war.

The legionaries commanded by Lepidus take position in the Forum at the foot of the Capitoline, where they are joined by Antony, who is wearing the consul's insignia. An assault seems minutes away.

Brutus and Cassius, barricaded on the Capitoline, are within earshot and can hear very clearly the centurions' orders to the soldiers; at this point they start to fear the worst.

Both Antony and Lepidus are stirring the crowd in the Forum, claiming that Caesar's murder must not go unpunished. The crowd reacts and there's turmoil. We're a step away from a massacre in the city's most sacred places, the Capitoline and the Forum.

Confusing and contradictory news reaches Cleopatra. Naturally, she takes Antony and Lepidus's side, but to whom can she turn at this chaotic time? She probably sent messengers to Caesar's most trusted men, such as Lucius Cornelius Balbus, Caesar's true *éminence grise*, or else Gaius Oppius, described by some modern authors as the great military leader's eyes and ears, the only ones with whom he had an open channel. But how much power do they have now that their great leader is dead? Alternatively, there's Aulus Hirtius, one of Caesar's most loyal lieutenants and a friend: she knows him well because he, too, was in Alexandria when they had to defend themselves for months, holed up in the Royal Palace and the Portus Magnus. This is another emergency, and Cleopatra probably trusts him. There's nothing more she can do, so she anxiously waits, seeing the fires in the military encampments in the Forum and on Tiber Island, as well as those of the conspirators on the Capitoline, glowing in the night.

Many want to attack the Capitoline and put an end to Brutus and Cassius, but, surprisingly, it is Antony who saves the situation. He decides to confer with the conspirators and suggests a Senate meeting for the following day, thereby proving to be a skillful strategist, excellent negotiator, and forward-thinking politician. He discloses his trump card discreetly, going to Caesar's house to see his widow, Calpurnia. She entrusts to him the bulk of her husband's documents and a large portion of his fortune, believing they will be in safer hands this way. Within minutes, Antony has in his care an astronomical sum: 4,000 talents, the equivalent of 100 million sestertii. It's hard to make a comparison with our times, but it's probably around $700 million. He is like a poker player suddenly obtaining a mountain of chips. From the financial point of view, he now has the backing to try to win. But the documents are another card he plays with skill. According to Plutarch, these are notes on everything Caesar had decided and planned to do. And so, over the coming weeks, Antony would add new names—agreeable to him—to Caesar's list. He would appoint these people as magistrates and senators, each time saying he found their names in the notes and it was therefore Caesar's will. Likewise, he would free friends of his from jail and summon back other citizens from exile. Romans are not stupid, and would call these people miraculously saved in a shady manner by someone who is already beyond the grave "charonites," with reference to Charon, the ferryman of the dead.

Antony is bound to have seen Caesar's body when he went to visit Calpurnia. In keeping with tradition, his corpse has been washed and prepared with ointments by the *pollinctores*, who will also then insert a coin into his mouth to pay the toll to Charon in the afterlife. After being dressed in the most luxurious garments, the body was put on display in his home for a few days before the funeral.

Time may have stopped forever for Caesar, but outside his house it's rushing at great speed toward a yet unknown future.

That same evening, Antony orders the soldiers to guard the gates of Rome. The negotiations continue all night. Romans have begun to realize that the conspirators and their supporters are few. Public opinion starts to sway toward Antony and Lepidus and the Caesarians, those loyal to Julius Caesar, as a whole.

The following day, the senators gather at the Temple of Tellus, goddess of the earth, symbol of fertility. The famous Dolabella, who, sensing the strongest side, has changed his allegiance once again, is among the senators, on the Caesarians' side. Outside, the crowd of veterans is shouting "Revenge!" Antony speaks to them and only just manages to pacify them, but Decimus's armed gladiators respond by crying "Peace for the Republic!" There's a tense atmosphere both inside the temple and out. The discussion gets heated. At this point, Antony delivers a splendid speech able to persuade everyone by suggesting a compromise: to grant impunity to Caesar's assassins and at the same time maintain all his government decisions (*acta Caesaris*). Apparently, this saves everything and everybody: the veterans have their lands, those raised by Caesar to the rank of senator or appointed governors, praetors, or other positions keep their posts and benefits, and nobody will kill the conspirators. Obviously, everyone stands to benefit. Swords and daggers are set aside in favor of discussing and building the future with the laws and the Senate. It's an example of democracy. This saves Rome partly because it prevents a civil war. But many people know that it's just a way of postponing the settling of accounts that, as you will see, will, like a river bursting its banks, fuel the coming years with wars, treaties, conquests, betrayals, and encounters—like that between Antony and Cleopatra. This meeting of the Senate represents the victory of the Caesarians and the defeat of the Caesaricides (as the two factions are called by historians). Above all, it's Antony's political masterpiece: he has no troops, so if it came to an armed struggle, Lepidus would win and victory would be attributed to him and not Antony. Moreover, by keeping all Caesar's decisions valid, Antony does himself a favor above all, because he then keeps the powerful post of consul. When he leaves the temple, he is acclaimed by everyone as the country's savior, someone who prevented a civil war.

In order to understand what happens next, we must add that the provinces are distributed according to provisions made by Caesar: Crete is assigned to Brutus, Africa to Cassius, Asia to Trebonius, Bithynia to Cimber, and Cisalpine Gaul to Decimus. This is how a "geography" of future clashes is unwittingly established.

Not all the perpetrators of the assassination, such as Brutus, Cassius, and many others, have taken part in this meeting, for fear of being killed. On the other hand, all the senators who supported them were in the chamber, and subsequently went down into the Forum to shake Antony's and Lepidus's hand. But the degree of mistrust still present is illustrated by their first demanding a hostage exchange. Antony and Lepidus have agreed and sent their own sons to the Capitoline: Antyllus himself, not much more than two years old, has become the pivot of Rome's stability.

In the evening, reciprocal banquets of reconciliation took place. His hand still bandaged, Brutus went to dine in Lepidus's house, and Cassius to Antony's. It's easy to imagine the atmosphere. We know from Cassius Dio that at one point, Antony said to Cassius, "Do you perhaps still have a dagger under your arm?" and Cassius replied, "Of course, and a long one at that, if you, too, aspire to tyranny."

Caesar's Will Ignores Antony and Cleopatra

A crucial moment during these days is the reading of Julius Caesar's will, kept by the Vestals in their temple. What's interesting is that it was not Calpurnia, Caesar's widow and closest relative, who requested it to be read in public and went to pick it up, but her father, Lucius Calpurnius Piso—as we said earlier, the owner of the splendid Villa of the Papyri in Herculaneum. How come? We are still in an essentially patriarchal society despite an undeniable opening toward female emancipation. In many families, it's still the man who makes the decisions, or, in his absence, "the most important" male available. When a man and woman get married, the marriage can be *cum manu* or *sine manu*, *manus* referring to the bride's possessions. In the former case, the "property" of a woman goes from her father to her husband; in the latter, even though she marries a man, she remains the "property" of her father and her husband has no legal rights over her. Hence the well-known modern expression "asking a father for a girl's hand." Contrary to belief, it's not a request to take her symbolically by the hand in order to lead her to a new future, but a request to take possession (*manu*) of her from her father. It's only an elegant figure of speech, with no bearing on present reality.

Caesar's marriage to Calpurnia was therefore *sine manu*, since it's not the wife but her father who picks up the will.

We can picture Caesar's father-in-law, his beard unshaved as a sign of mourning, received by the *Virgo Vestalis maxima*, the eldest Vestal. The Vestals are the six priestesses in charge of the cult of Vesta, the Roman goddess of the hearth. Their temple, as well as the attached "convent," is in the heart of the Forum because the cult as well as the temple effectively represent the heart of Roman culture and, as we know, the fire inside the temple must never go out, on pain of death to the responsible Vestal (who would be shut away in an underground room in the *campus sceleratus* at Porta Collina, on the Quirinal, and die of thirst and starvation). The same fate is reserved for the Vestals who soil themselves by having sexual relations with men: they must remain virgins for the entire thirty years they are in that position (they would be selected at the age of ten and "freed" at forty), but were allowed to marry once that period was over. Caesar's will, which the eldest Vestal hands to Calpurnius Piso, must have been made up of a few carefully bound scrolls with Caesar's seal clearly visible on the wax. It had most probably been kept in a wooden chest, also sealed.

The reading of the will did not take place in Caesar's but in Antony's house, the one for official events.

Picture the scene.

It's a *domus* where servants are accustomed to seeing meetings between high-ranking individuals and official guests. But on the morning of March 19, at about 9 a.m., its rooms transcend all imagination. There are senators from both sides, magistrates, many of Caesar's colleagues and loyal men, including a few of his soldiers, and, finally, relatives. What servants sense in comparison with all the other meetings is the dark, heavy atmosphere, a blend of tension, sadness, solemnity, and spasmodic expectation. Indeed, because everybody knows that after the reading of the will many things will change and the world will be different. There's widespread fear regarding what are about to be, truly and forever, Caesar's final words and, above all, final decisions. We know he has a large estate. In addition to the 4,000 talents Antony has taken from Calpurnia, there are many properties in Rome and other cities. And yet something even more important will emerge from these scrolls, much more important than money or possessions. Something impalpable but worth more than gold: Caesar's political bequest. Being appointed his heir will also mean assuming a dominant position during this phase in the life of the Republic.

The scrolls are opened in general silence. Interminable seconds flow by before Caesar's lines are read out. Antony stares without blinking at the scroll held by a slightly trembling hand. The silence is then broken by the voice reading. Everybody focuses on the meaning of every sentence, afraid of misunderstanding something. Few realize that this is still Caesar speaking, and although he is dead, he is deciding Rome's future.

As a matter of fact, much to everyone's surprise, he appoints as heirs his three nephews on his sisters' side: "Three quarters to Gaius Octavian, and the remaining quarter to Lucius Pinarius and Quintus Pedius." This Gaius Octavian will later become Gaius Julius Caesar Octavian, the future Augustus. . . . He's a slightly distant relative but the connection is clear: he is the son of Atia, the daughter of Caesar's sister Julia Minor. This may sound a roundabout way of doing things but it's logical for a male-dominated society where the purity of lineage is sacred. Moreover, Caesar follows a consistent principle: his sister's daughter and grandson are certainly his blood relatives, whereas his daughter Julia may not be, but, theoretically, the fruit of an adulterous relationship between his wife and another man. This is in no way odd. There is an African tribe where traditionally the father does not bequeath the inheritance to his own children but to those of his sister, because they have his blood for sure.

At the end of the will, to confirm his wish to appoint Octavian as his successor, Caesar adds an important provision. As Suetonius tells us, "he adopted Gaius Octavian into his own family and name," in other words, into the *Gens Iulia*, and by doing this he grants Octavian the right, if he should so desire, to call himself Gaius Julius Caesar Octavian. In just a few seconds he has conferred huge power on an ordinary young man. And a prime position in history.

Some thought this was a provisional will, since Caesar did not think he would be killed so soon. The fact that he did not realize the serious danger he was in on the day of his assassination is evident from the following lines in his will. In case Octavian (and his other nephews) do not wish to accept the inheritance, Caesar appoints other, "second-degree" heirs, as we say. And who are they? Antony—and this is logical since he was one of his most loyal men—and Decimus, one of the chief conspirators. He then added the names of other assassins to his list . . .

What's perhaps most surprising is that Caesar leaves nothing in his will to Cleopatra and especially Caesarion, who might be his son. But there is another devastating blow in store for these two.

In his will, Caesar also bears in mind the people of Rome. He leaves 300 sestertii to every Roman citizen, a huge sum. And that's not all. He donates to the city of Rome his properties across the Tiber, so that they may be turned into a public park. That's the Horti, where Cleopatra is currently living.

In other words, the queen and Caesarion are abandoned to their fate.

After being read in Antony's house, Caesar's will is also read out in public, so that all Romans may hear his final wishes.

It's easy to imagine how moved people must have been by such a generous bequest to all the residents of Rome, and the sadness at having lost such a great man.

Cleopatra's Reaction, and Then Antony's

How does Cleopatra react? She was probably one of the first outside that room to hear of the contents of the will. No doubt one of her advisers was present and immediately informed her. She is an intelligent woman and has no illusions. As a foreign queen, she knows perfectly well that she cannot be included in her lover's will. Caesar is Rome's supreme leader, he cannot leave his fortune to a foreign monarch, let alone appoint her a political heir (neither is Octavian—he would have to earn this inheritance). The same applies to his son, Caesarion. No doubt she also thought of this during her sleepless nights. What the queen perhaps truly didn't expect was that Caesar would have given to his people the place where she lives, the Horti Caesaris.

At this point, Cleopatra immediately understands something: that her exclusion will be seen by Caesar's adversaries and especially by the people as a clear sign of her weakness because of his little consideration toward her. The underlying hostility now risks becoming extremely dangerous. She realizes that Rome is no longer a safe place and, in the afternoon, after consulting her advisers, gives instructions for her departure. She must leave the city as soon as possible. Her destination: Alexandria.

If Cleopatra had envisaged this kind of event, Antony, on the other hand, is bitterly surprised by it. None of the ancient historians mention his state of mind, but it's fair to imagine his deep disappointment. Maybe he was even hoping for an adoption, and so takes the reading of the will as a kind of personal "rejection."

Octavian, the appointed heir, doesn't scare him—he's still a boy. Now Antony is concentrating on Caesar's funeral, which is taking place tomorrow. He has been chosen to deliver the funeral oration in his role as consul, friend, and distant relative (his mother, Julia, was Julius Caesar's cousin). Most probably, immediately after the reading of the will, Antony will have held a restricted gathering with relatives and friends in order to prepare his speech and study the organization of the funeral. It was probably his wife, Fulvia, who suggested a spectacular solution for showing everybody the injuries Caesar received: erecting a wax statue next to his body in the heart of the Forum (it was she who showed everyone the mortal wounds of her previous husband, Clodius, murdered by the men of his political rival Milo).

Caesar's Funeral and Antony's Speech

Julius Caesar's funeral takes place on the morning of March 20, five days after his assassination. The program includes transporting the body to the Forum and Antony's solemn speech. Subsequently, the coffin is to be taken to the Campus Martius, where there is the tomb of Caesar's daughter Julia, who died young in childbirth, and where the funeral pyre will be erected. Things will turn out completely different, and Antony, excluded from the will but determined to exploit Caesar's funeral politically, will play a deciding role.

From the first light of dawn, a huge crowd gathers in the Forum, and not just Romans. Many have come over the past hours and days from neighboring cities, as well as the soldiers about to leave on the expedition against the Parthians, and Caesar's veterans, who, shrewdly incited by Antony, will play a crucial part in the day's events.

The funeral cortege approaches the Forum, preceded by men carrying torches; they're accompanied by many mourners, singing praises to the deceased and weeping histrionically. Everybody sees Caesar's body laid on the ivory litter covered in crimson and gold, carried on the shoulders of magistrates and ex-magistrates. According to Barry Strauss's reconstruction, there are also actors wearing wax masks with the semblance of Caesar and his triumph garments, gesticulating theatrically according to the custom of Roman funerals, recalling the great general's five triumphs. Appian adds that there is also no shortage of his veterans escorting him on this final journey, like bodyguards. At the rear, behind the coffin, come friends and family.

There are noteworthy absences, like those of the conspirators, who realize this is not the time to be seen. Above all, there's no Cleopatra. As a foreign queen, she may not enter the *pomerium*. But, as expected, across the Tiber, in her gilded home, she keeps thinking about her lover while preparations for her departure are under way. Everything is changing for her. Again.

As the cortege enters the Forum, feelings are rising high and the crowd bursts into a single, collective weeping. It's a sad roar heard all over Rome. Tears run down the cheeks of the women but also on the hard, lined faces of his ex-soldiers. Everybody feels they have lost something more than a general: a father who is now leaving them orphaned. This gloomy sound is accompanied by the veterans, who begin to strike their shields, as is customary among the legions, to show the strength of their formations to the enemy, but also to salute their general. Imagine this atmosphere even just for a moment, with all the shouting, crying, and rhythmical beating of shields. Many approach the coffin and reach out with their arms, as though to touch it or protect it.

The funeral litter on which Caesar's body lies is taken to the Rostra and placed in the middle of a small golden construction prepared in advance, very similar to the Temple of Venus Genetrix, so close to Caesar's heart. Symbolically, we could say that Cleopatra is there, because inside the temple that inspired this golden *aedicula* stands her gilt bronze statue.

The toga Caesar was wearing when he was assassinated, soaked in blood, is put on full display over this sort of glowing canopy. Everyone senses that Antony's speech will be full of tension. As a matter of fact, the crowd abruptly falls silent as soon as he climbs the Rostra, next to Caesar for the last time, raises his hand, and stretches his arm, an unmistakable signal that he's about to speak. His head is covered with a veil. Those closest to him notice his five-day beard, a sign of mourning.

An Echo That Reaches as Far As . . . Shakespeare

What exactly does he tell the crowd? We don't have his exact speech. Only two ancient authors, Cassius Dio and Appian, have transmitted his words, almost certainly reconstructed from ideas he expressed during those minutes, and which tradition remembered. These testimonies help us sense, however, the theatricality of his contribution. Relying on various ancient authors, I will try to reconstruct this very important moment in his life and in the history of Rome. It's also interesting to see the form of what was more of a political speech than a funeral oration, two thousand years ago.

In this surreal silence, Antony must have looked at the speechless crowd with a solemn movement of the head, from one side of the Forum to the other. Looking down for a moment, as though to gather his thoughts, he then slowly raised his head again. According to Appian, this is how he began: "Fellow citizens, it is not right that the funeral oration to such a great man should be uttered by me alone, but by the whole country."

Suetonius tells us that at this point, "as a eulogy, consul Antony got the crier to read out the ordinances by which all human and divine honors were once conferred, as well as the oath all the senators took for his safety, and added only a few words of his own." It's clear from the beginning that Antony wants to highlight the cruel betrayal that killed Cesar, in order to show his adversaries in a negative light.

Antony addresses the crowd once again. According to Cassius Dio, he starts speaking about Caesar's ancestors, his lineage, and then his personal virtues, dwelling in particular on his generosity to friends and the clemency he always showed his enemies. He then remembers all Caesar's lifelong feats. It's a long list of military victories and their benefits to the Roman people. "His initiative and boldness conquered for us places we didn't know existed and whose names were completely unfamiliar to us; he made previously unknown places accessible, and previously unexplored regions navigable. And if some men, envious of his luck, your luck, in fact, hadn't stirred unrest and forced him to return to Rome before his time, he would certainly have subjugated the whole of Britain as well as its surrounding islands, and the whole of Celtica as far as the North Sea, so that our future borders would no longer have been lands and peoples, but the sky and the faraway sea."

It is however the final part of the speech that's emotionally the most powerful and violent.

"But, alas, this father, this supreme pontiff, this inviolable man, this hero is dead. He died not defeated by illness or undone by old age, or wounded far from his city in some war, or suddenly carried away by some misfortune. Here, within these walls, the man who led a successful expedition to Britain was ambushed [. . .] The man no enemy could kill was killed by citizens [. . .] The man was killed by his companions, he who had forgiven them so many times. Where, o Caesar, have your goodness, your inviolability, and your laws gone? You were ruthlessly murdered by your friends, you who made so many laws so that nobody could be killed by his adversaries. You lie in the Forum across which you walked so many times, with a crown on your head; you fell, pierced through with injuries, on the tribune from which you so often spoke to the people."

Imagine Antony's theatricality. We know that with every sentence he turns to Caesar's body, motioning to it with his hand. At this point, Appian describes a very specific gesture. We know through some authors that he very much likes to show off his chest and muscles, and often ties his tunic on one side, somewhat like Hercules. "Then, as though inspired, he tucked in his garment, intertwining it like a belt to free his hands."

Perhaps it's at this moment that, taking it off the hook from which it was hanging, he starts waving Julius Caesar's blood-soaked toga about, showing it to everyone with increasing theatricality, as Cassius

Dio tells us. "Alas, bloodstained gray hair, the torn toga you wore, it seems, only to be killed!"

Then, Appian writes, raising his voice and stretching his hand toward the Capitoline, he booms, "O Jupiter, protector of this city, and all the gods, here I am, ready for revenge, as I solemnly swear."

A shudder probably runs up the backs of many senators, who sense that Antony is referring to them. Yet he knows how to measure out the venom in his voice and, in a more peaceful tone, takes back part of what he's said, adding that the decree of amnesty for the assassins is a good thing, and that one should be "concerned with the present and not the past [. . .] to avoid being struck by civil wars." It's clear to everyone that the future will bring the death of many conspirators. Just as Antony has sworn to the gods.

The Rostra are by now a theatrical stage on which the principal actor, Antony, is playing; the only one on the scene next to Caesar's body.

Appian writes that "he stood in front of the coffin, like on a stage, bowing then straightening up, and praised Caesar like a celestial divinity, raising his hands toward the sky to witness the birth of a new god." During this litany (which some historians consider as no more than a highly "emphasized" version of the traditional Roman funeral hymn), the crowd follows Antony, providing a responsory to all the things he lists as good that Caesar did and to his own distress; like at a church mass, when the faithful echo the words of the priest, or a singer on a stage who stops in order to get the audience to sing. Antony's skill lies in emotionally involving the crowd in his speech and not letting it be just a spectator and nothing else. On this front, he has an incredible sense of the stage, a rare histrionic and charismatic talent for carrying the public along.

It's not over. Real actors now climb on the Rostra "stage" to celebrate Caesar's feats. One of them in particular, who impersonates the dictator, provokes a roar of emotion in the crowd when he starts to list the names of some of the men to whom in the past he had granted favors if not actually life, which included some conspirators. "The people found it especially monstrous that, instead of being punished, the assassins [. . .], imprisoned while on Pompey's side [. . .], were instead raised by Caesar to the magistrature of Rome and to the command of provinces and armies."

Antony knows stage timing very well and is perfectly prepared. No wonder this speech of his would be taken up by Shakespeare and performed in theaters around the world for centuries to come. He has even studied twists to set the crowd alight. At this point Caesar's will is read in public again, and we know, again from Appian, that there is almost a surge of rebellion among those present upon hearing Decimus's name among those Caesar has mentioned among his heirs.

Antony's words are like fuel to the fire. Worked up already, the Romans are now alight. And Antony stokes this fire further. Maybe on Fulvia's suggestion and the complicity of many theater friends Antony had while frequenting the much-gossiped-about actress Licorys, he stages—as we've already mentioned—an authentic *coup de théâtre*, by producing the wax statue of the deceased.

The scene is described by Appian and is quite incredible: "In this tense situation, by now on the brink of an explosion of violence, someone lifted above the coffin a semblance of Caesar made of wax. The body was lying in the coffin and could not be seen. Thanks to a mechanism, the wax effigy turned on itself, showing the twenty-three brutal injuries all over the body and face. The people could bear that sight no longer. They gave a lament and, tucking in their clothes, set the place on fire."

By now the situation is out of hand. The soldiers just about manage to contain the crowd but are afraid that the fire might spread to the houses, theaters, and temples. People want to cremate Caesar's body but don't know exactly where—in the heart of the Temple of

Jupiter Optimus Maximus or in the Curia of Pompey, where he was assassinated?

At this point the action of two men, probably following Antony's suggestion, proves decisive. They grab lit candles and try to set the funeral bed on fire.

Everything starts to degenerate. Plutarch describes the chaos leading to the cremation of Caesar's body: "Some were shouting for the assassins to be killed, others [. . .] yanked benches and tables from the shops and, having piled them up, erected a huge pyre; then they placed the body on top of it and burned it there in the midst of many temples and many other sanctuaries and inviolable places."

The location of the pyre is therefore not the Rostra on which Antony delivered his speech or where Caesar was killed. Instead, it's in the Forum, a few yards from the Temple of Vestals, in a spot where even now, more than two thousand years later, tourists throw roses, flowers, and touching notes, thus reiterating Caesar's greatness.

The pyre is fueled with objects the crowd has brought as gifts, and not only that. "Moreover, the musicians and actors, having torn off their garments [. . .] threw them into the flames," Suetonius says. "The veterans of his legions threw in the weapons they were carrying for the ceremony and the matrons even their jewels." The soldiers struggle to prevent the fire from spreading to the surrounding buildings.

But the pyre does not just receive objects but gives out firebrands, which are picked up by the most overexcited individuals. The crowd then turns its anger on the conspirators and wants to use these firebrands to set the houses of Caesar's assassins on fire. A stream of enraged people heads to Brutus's *domus* and Cassius's *domus*, then to that of Publius Servilius Casca, the man who stabbed Caesar first, and is pushed back by the slaves of these houses or, again, by Decimus's gladiators. However, there are many casualties, and the home of at least one conspirator, Lucius Bellienus, is set on fire.

A chilling episode also takes place, featuring a friend of Caesar's, Helvius Cinna, who, ill, was staggering to the Forum to attend the funeral. The crowd mistakes him for his near namesake Lucius Cornelius Cinna, the praetor who previously removed his toga and called Caesar a tyrant, and murders him in the middle of the square. Then, Suetonius adds, "they carried his head around on a spike."

Some suspect that these attacks on houses and this manhunt were devised and organized by Antony, something Cicero declares openly. The lack of protection by the soldiers is another element in favor of this theory. However, it's also true that at some point the situation entirely escapes Antony's control.

Caesar's funeral pyre, fueled by a large number of thrown objects, burns for hours, with an endless procession of people. When the flames finally go out, the dead man's remains and charcoaled bones are collected by his freedman and carried to the family tomb, in the Campus Martius, together with the golden *aedicula* shaped like the Temple of Venus, into which his bloodstained toga is also placed.

An interesting detail: the ashes have fueled various legends, even several centuries after his death. A medieval tradition, found in the *Mirabilia Urbis Romae*, a kind of tourist guide that began circulating in the twelfth century, claimed that they were kept in the gilt bronze orb at the top of the obelisk in Saint Peter's Square. This is untrue.

(This obelisk has a fascinating history. It was transported from Heliopolis to the Forum Julius in Alexandria by Cornelius Gallus, Egypt's first prefect, then to Rome by Caligula in AD 40. And when, in 1586, Pope Sixtus V had the obelisk moved to Saint Peter's Square, he replaced the golden orb with a cross, the one we see today. The metal sphere, now on display in the Capitoline Museums, bears the marks left by the arquebus shots of the *Landsknechte* during the sack of Rome in 1527.)

At the end of the day, Antony is the unchallenged ruler of Rome. He is clearly the principal leader of the Caesarians, overshadowing

Lepidus. With incredible political wisdom, he continues to consolidate his power. Using the violence that broke out at the funeral as an excuse, he gets a law approved that forbids anyone in the city to carry arms (with the exception of legionaries) and this way stops any adversary from using gladiators or bodyguards as a small private army, as done by Decimus, who, meanwhile, has become one of Rome's most hated men.

The conspirators realize that their plan has failed across the board and leave Rome in dribs and drabs, some withdrawing to their villas outside the city, others taking advantage of their positions in the provinces, received from Caesar (and confirmed by the amnesty). Decimus, for example, relocates to Cisalpine Gaul with his gladiators. Cassius and Brutus also leave the city in mid-April. By now Rome is in the hands of Antony and his allies.

4

Cleopatra Returns
to Alexandria

Does Cleopatra Meet Antony?

When the last glow of Caesar's funeral pyre has gone out and his ashes have been placed next to those of his daughter in the tomb in the Campus Martius, history resumes its course. Cleopatra has decided to return to Egypt. Except that she needs some guarantees. And there's now only one person who can give her any certainties or reassure her. Contacting him is the only thing to be done. With Caesar dead, Antony, being a consul, is the highest authority in charge (with Dolabella, who has proclaimed himself consul) and, after the funeral, also the unchallenged leader of the Caesarians.

What guarantees is Cleopatra asking for? And, above all, do the two meet face to face? It's possible, even though we have no evidence of it. Maybe they just exchange messages. It's the opinion of many scholars that Antony prefers not to be seen with this widely unpopular queen. It's not to his political advantage.

Cleopatra has at least three requests. First and foremost, she wants guarantees for her safety and that of Caesarion. Then she seeks reassurance that Rome is not going to change its position toward Egypt now that Caesar has gone. Through the agreements he had subscribed to, he granted Egypt high recognition, allowing it into the narrow circle of "friends and allies of the Roman people." Moreover, he had recognized Egypt's sovereignty over the island of Cyprus, strategic for trade routes and politics in the eastern Mediterranean. Finally, there are at least 16,000 legionaries in Egypt, left there by Caesar to ensure stability in the region. Cleopatra's question to Antony is simple: To whom are these legions loyal? To the Caesarians or the Caesaricides? To Antony or Brutus and Cassius? Before returning to Egypt, she wants a reasonable certainty that they will not depose her or, worse, kill her.

Antony reassures her on all fronts, agreeing that it's better for her to leave the city.

We don't know if the two of them met or only exchanged messages, but at this point a more than logical question arises: Do they already know each other? Have they already seen each other on some occasion?

The answer is: most probably yes. It's probable that they have met on several occasions during Cleopatra's stay in Rome. There must have been many banquets and formal occasions (although, as we've said, in theory the foreign queen could not enter the *pomerium*). Who knows? Antony might well have been to Cleopatra's home across the Tiber.

But there is an even more intriguing theory. They could have already met in Egypt many years earlier, even before the start of Caesar and Cleopatra's relationship, when she was just a teenage princess and Antony a strapping young officer recently introduced to the army. There are a few ancient sources to suggest this first meeting. But what is the truth? Let us try to discover it.

Did the Two Already Meet Many Years Earlier?

Let us go back thirteen years before the Ides of March, specifically to 57 BC, when Antony is a young officer stationed in Athens. He is twenty-six or twenty-seven years old. (Strangely, we don't have his exact birth date, which could be 83 or 82 BC, although we know the day: January 14.) There he meets Gabinius, who has just been appointed governor of the very wealthy and strategic province of Syria, which more or less encompassed the territories between Cilicia, from the Gulf of Alexandretta, and the Euphrates, and in the south then included Lebanon and Palestine. Gabinius asks Antony to follow him, appointing him cavalry commander (*praefectus equitum*). He accepts. He's ambitious and this is an excellent opportunity for beginning his ascent to military, political, and personal success. He does, in fact, immediately distinguish himself for his passion, courage, and military acumen. He successfully suppresses an uprising in Judea single-handedly and, by order of the governor, performs reconnaissance operations with the cavalry in the east, in the territory of the Parthian Empire, Rome's great enemy. But his masterpiece is the Egyptian military campaign, which aims to restore to the throne Cleopatra's father, Ptolemy XII Auletes, deposed in a dynastic war by his daughter Berenice, helped by her husband, Archelaus of Comana. Antony was seeking great feats and this sounded like the right one. Conquering Egypt had never been easy, and the last one who succeeded was Alexander the Great, almost three hundred years earlier. Egypt is defended by deserts in the east, south, and west, while in the north there's the sea, navigated by its powerful fleet. Antony shows remarkable courage and great military skill by conquering the city of Pelusium, a kind of gateway to Egypt from Gaza, and then boldness and strategic nous in the successive stages of the campaign. Moreover, he's very magnanimous toward the defeated as well as the body of the enemy chief, Archelaus of Comana, after he finds him dead. He gives him a royal funeral. All this increases his fame not only among his soldiers but also among the Alexandrian insurgents. Once the rebels have been defeated, Antony, Gabinius, and Ptolemy XII enter Alexandria.

Antony stays there for several weeks, and this is his first contact with the Eastern world, something that marks him deeply—as Professor Giovannella Cresci Marrone remarks—and his intellectual curiosity is rewarded by a basically Hellenistic culture with exotic influences. After reinstating Ptolemy on the throne, he often goes to the royal palace and is entertained by the court on various occasions. And it's on one of these occasions that he meets Cleopatra.

She is a very young princess, barely thirteen years old. A little girl who probably takes little notice of a thirty-year-old. Nothing happens between them except a formal, public introduction. Nothing to herald the affair that would overwhelm them in the future. Appian claims it's true that Antony, according to widespread rumor, was always willing to fall in love, and that he "caught fire" at the sight of Cleopatra. But these are only rumors, unconfirmed by ancient sources.

Antony, a Soldier That Looks the Part

But how would Antony have come across to the very young Cleopatra? Although we have almost no information about her as a girl, we do know about Antony as a young officer through a nice description by Plutarch. "He had a noble air and an attractive beard, a wide forehead and an aquiline nose that gave him a lusty appearance like that of Herakles as represented in paintings and statues. Besides, according to an ancient tradition, the *Antonii* were Heracleidae, descendants of Anton, a son of Herakles. And he decided to confirm this legend with his attitude, as we've said, and his clothes. Whenever he had to appear in public, he always tucked his tunic in at his hip, carried a large sword there, and wore a cloak of coarse cloth." Antony therefore looks athletic, muscular, and strong, which automatically brings him closer to the superman model in vogue in ancient times: Hercules. It's easy to picture how all this translates into a virility obvious to women.

He is also charming, an extrovert who enjoys company and good food. As Plutarch writes, "His bragging, joking, drinking in public, sitting next to someone who was having lunch, and eating standing up in the soldiers' mess inspired an extraordinary affection and attachment on the part of the soldiers."

The ace up his sleeve is his innate gentleness in love: "Even his love life did not lack courtesy but, on the contrary, won him the goodwill of many, because he assisted those in love and took it on the chin when others made fun of his affairs. His generosity and the favors he readily granted to soldiers and friends without cutting corners gave him a wonderful starting point for power."

On this subject, we should add that Antony was chronically in debt all his life.

Cleopatra Leaves Rome

Cleopatra leaves the Horti Caesaris at dawn. This is just the final act of a complex series of preparations that have been keeping its residents busy for days. Cleopatra probably held a small ceremony the day before to thank the guards and retinue that had attended her for months during her stay in Rome (and protected her during the violent days of Caesar's assassination). They will stay here, unlike the court and nearest workers, who will all leave this house en masse with the queen, creating a giant procession worthy of a royal parade. The villa is already crowded with all kinds of wagons, from the ordinary ones customarily used for carrying goods (*plaustra*), pulled by mules or oxen, to the most common ones like the *redae*, strong, four-wheel vehicles with seats for members of the court. Many wagons are heaped with the royal furniture that embellished the villa, from Cleopatra's throne to prized silks, to ornate banquet tables, to statutes of divinities, etc. This isn't a simple move but a royal palace relocating. Documents are also placed in the wagons, as well as courtly items and, last but not least, the queen's luxurious personal effects: countless precious dresses, jewels, and dishes, pitchers, and drinking receptacles made of gold, silver, malachite, and alabaster, delicately wrapped in straw and placed in chests. Not to mention the fact that, in addition to the queen, there is also a "king" (her brother Ptolemy XIV) and Cleopatra's son, Caesarion, each with his own personal effects and servants in attendance.

She comes last, stepping regally, slowly, toward her carriage, and everybody bows as she walks past. Before getting in she turns her head in a very human gesture and looks at the place where she has lived for such a peaceful and happy time. Her eyes take in the windows, the pillars with their curtains undulating in the light spring breeze, and that *pergula* with the elegant wooden trellis where she often watched the dawn over Rome, running her fingers over the timber arabesques while the crisp air caressed her face and hair. This morning's dawn is the same. Cleopatra closes her eyes for a moment and fills her lungs with a deep breath, as she has always done. Except that this is the last one. She opens her eyes again. Her expression suddenly alters and becomes sharp and focused. She turns her head and gets into the carriage. It's a *carpentum*, a solid, splendid vehicle with pillars supporting a timber roof. It looks almost like a golden temple traveling on four wheels, with brightly colored silk curtains between the uprights. Cleopatra glances out one more time then, with an elegant movement, disappears behind the Eastern silks with her ladies-in-waiting.

At a signal, the procession starts. The queen's carriage is in the middle, protected by a large ring of bodyguards. Some are even in the carriage, swords ready.

They decided to leave at dawn for security reasons and while the streets are empty. The huge bronze gates of the estate open majestically, allowing the royal procession to leave by the light of the last torches. There's a huge contingent of Roman soldiers on horseback waiting for them. It's the substantial escort sent by Antony to ensure the queen's safety. The cortege is very long and never seems to end as it exits the Horti Caesaris. It's a flashy, noisy caravan that wakes up many Romans, who open their windows in astonishment. Which road does it take? Given the delicate political situation they have chosen the quickest way to Ostia, from where the queen will set sail. Even though Cleopatra owns a luxurious vessel moored at the private pier of the Horti Caesaris, it's not advisable to use it: Horace says that in the days following Caesar's death, the level of the Tiber is unusually high and overflowing in parts. The procession therefore probably crosses the river across the large Pons Sublicius in the south of the city and reaches Porta Ostiensis, Rome's largest southern entrance. From there, the caravan heads to Ostia.

Today, this trip is just over half an hour's drive, but in Cleopatra's time it took at least half if not a whole day. This is only the beginning of a long and very arduous journey. We tend to forget it, but in antiquity traveling requires time and effort, even if your name is Cleopatra.

In fact, once in Ostia, the queen doesn't embark immediately—the baggage first has to be loaded, and that requires several hours. So Cleopatra probably spent the night there (in some sumptuous villa) and set sail the following morning.

The Long, 1,200-Mile Sea Voyage Begins

The queen and her retinue probably board rather small ships, about 30 to 45 feet long, not suitable for the open sea, but ideal for sailing fast along the coast.

What is she thinking as she feels the sea beneath her once more? It's certainly a moment when she realizes, even physically, that her life will resume only once the rolling stops completely and she touches dry land in Alexandria and smells in the air the scents of African soil she has missed so much. That's where her future awaits her.

Maybe, as she holds Caesarion close to her, her hair fluttering in the wind, she watches the harbor and the lighthouse grow distant, knowing she is turning a page of her life forever. She will, in fact, never return to Rome. Antony's escort also leaves her and goes back to the city. It will take about a day to reach Pozzuoli (*Puteoli*), where large vessels, suitable for the open sea, will finally take her to Alexandria.

We do not have ancient sources to describe this first stage of the journey, but she probably went by ship, since it would have taken at least three or four days by land and carried risks to her safety. Better to sail along the coast—and it will take less time. And so a small Egyptian fleet travels en masse from Ostia, southbound to Pozzuoli.

In the first stretch of the journey, the color of the sea varies according to the depth and the current. It can be emerald green then suddenly take on the hue of the earth because of the Tiber sediments. But at one stage it becomes a clear blue with dolphins blowing as though escorting Cleopatra's ship.

It's just the start of a 1,200-mile journey, an enormous distance in ancient times. It must be very carefully prepared, with planned stages and large supplies of food and water. Let's remember that it's an entire court traveling, with baggage, and all this requires time, which is what Cleopatra does not have at her disposal. Caesar died suddenly, the political equilibrium has changed, and she might even be risking her life. Besides, she has to leave her home. She probably takes advantage of a coincidence: her Egyptian ships were ready to sail on Caesar's expedition against the Parthians, and this had made her sudden departure easier.

But there's another problem—the bad weather. Navigation in Roman times stopped almost entirely during the winter because of the storms. The Mediterranean can become a true killer from one moment to the next. Travel was therefore concentrated between May and October; in other words, during the warm months. In actual fact, maritime traffic did not stop altogether in the winter but was limited to exceptions: transporting troops, foodstuffs to relieve a famine, etc.

Unfortunately, Caesar was killed at a time of year when navigation was still considered dangerous. Not only that, but in order to travel to Egypt you had to wait for favorable winds, summer winds the ancients called Etesian winds, which facilitate southbound journeys. Produced by high pressure over the Balkans and low pressure over Egypt, they can be considered true toboggans for anyone wanting to go from the western to the eastern Mediterranean, for example, from Rome to Alexandria.

This explains why Cleopatra did not leave right away. As well as waiting for Antony to confirm the agreements stipulated by Caesar and organizing a truly complicated voyage, she had to wait for the best moment to depart. In other words, at least a month after the Ides of March, to take advantage of the first Etesian winds, even though these are not constant yet. One could practically say that she jumps on the first train. Many clues, in fact, including letters by Cicero, suggest that she left Rome at dawn sometime between April 11 and 14.

After reaching Pozzuoli, the queen glimpses a familiar sight: that of the large, deep-sea Egyptian ships moored at anchor. She begins to savor the power of her kingdom.

Pozzuoli is actually a real hub of ancient navigation. All the trade from and to Rome goes through it (Ostia will have a large port only starting with Emperor Claudius). Just like in a modern international airport, the crossroads of many routes to many destinations, here, too, we notice many cargo ships of different nationalities, Egyptian included. But there is more.

Cleopatra feels even more at home because in neighboring Naples, as in most of the Roman Empire, Greek is a very widespread language. It's a city of Greek origin, Greek culture, built according to Greek town planning.

She doesn't waste time, however. She must return to Egypt as soon as possible and boards the flagship. She certainly has at her disposal one of the largest and fastest vessels in the Egyptian fleet, one of the best at the time. We don't have details about this ship from ancient sources but it was probably a galley, possibly similar to the imposing *Antoniade*, which she will use in the future Battle of Actium, with a tall hull, a huge surface of sails, and several banks of oars. We're talking of a ship more than 130 feet long, with a crew of two hundred rowers. There are also other, smaller deep-sea ships, which, as we've said, must carry a hundred or more people, from servants to counselors, to the intellectuals and artists she brought with her from Alexandria. In addition, there's her substantial bodyguard and all the personnel of her brother and husband, Ptolemy XIV. As we've said, it's a small fleet that leaves Pozzuoli.

The queen of Egypt's sudden arrival can't have gone unnoticed, any more than her quick departure. The news had spread instantly and must have been at the center of comments for days. We can imagine a small crowd on the pier, watching inquisitively all the procedures until the departure of Cleopatra's fleet.

The Long, Final Leg Home

The trip would not have been comfortable. Ships back then were not devised to carry passengers. There are usually no cabins. People sleep wrapped in blankets on the decks. They wash and eat on the deck. And there's precarious shelter in case of rain. This, of course, isn't the case for Cleopatra (nor, perhaps, for some of the more important members of her entourage), who enjoys all the comforts of a queen.

Moreover, we must consider the superstition of sailors. Roman ones are highly superstitious, so we can imagine that the Egyptians were the same. During a voyage you don't dance and don't cut your nails or your hair. It's bad luck to sneeze when you board, and the perpetrator is sent back to land. Even the dreams you dream that night are significant. For example, depending on which animal you dream of, you can expect storms or fair weather. If before leaving you see a piece of driftwood floating, or else a crow sitting in the yard, it's best to postpone the departure: these are sure omens of a shipwreck. The sacrifices performed just before setting sail also give you the all-clear—or not. Finally, there are inauspicious days for traveling, such as August 24, October 5, or November 8. And, above all, never be in the open sea on the last day of any month.

All these superstitions are typical of a prescientific world unable to understand the reason for storms or explain the cause of lightning. After all, by limiting significantly the presence of ships at sea, this "irrational" behavior statistically lowered the incidence of wrecks, although they did take place and were dramatic. Death in the open sea was a certainty. There were no lifeboats on board, like on modern passenger ships, nor life buoys, let alone immediate rescue, and few could swim. Embarking on a sea voyage was therefore a truly risky business.

But at this moment, perhaps all these considerations are put aside. Cleopatra is a queen and moreover considered to be the incarnation of a goddess, Isis. Consequently, all it takes is an order from her and they set sail.

It's a very long journey. Going from Rome to Alexandria has been estimated to have taken Cleopatra two or three weeks.

We can try reconstructing the route. The fleet heads to the Strait of Messina, which it reaches in one and a half or two days. From there it crosses the Ionian Sea, following a route as far as the island of Zakynthos, then follows the Peloponnese coastline for a day and a half to Tenaro (Cape Matapan). Once the cape is on the left-hand side, Cleopatra's ship sets course for Crete, getting there after just over a day's sailing. From there it heads straight to Alexandria. Most probably it skirts around the coastline of southern Crete, then, once it has reached the uninhabited island of Koufonisi, it takes the leap of a week in the open sea, toward Alexandria.

Does Cleopatra Miscarry?

Although in antiquity it was usual to put up with all kinds of discomfort, especially in comparison with today's standards, many authors—especially Cicero, who writes about it in his letters—claim that the journey was so stressful for Cleopatra that she had a miscarriage.

A private tragedy in addition to the collapse of all the certainties she'd had until then. Besides her status as a queen and everything we might think of her as a historical figure, she is also a woman, a human being who suffers life's ups and downs like the rest of us.

So was the queen expecting a baby?

Ancient sources suggest that Cleopatra was pregnant when she left Rome, and her pregnancy is a theory that has always intrigued scholars. Did the queen and Caesar have the opportunity to make love in the home across the Tiber? Was it possible, among guards, aides, and royal counselors, for them to have enough privacy to indulge their affair? Or were they just brief, passionate encounters, nights of love no longer beneath the stars of Alexandria but those of Rome? It was not advisable to be seen together too often. Everybody's eyes were on Caesar, and Cleopatra was frowned upon. Besides, he already had a wife in Rome. We will never know how things were. While Cleopatra was traveling from Rome to Alexandria, Cicero wrote at least six letters (between April 16 and June 14, 44 BC) to an acquaintance of his, a tycoon of the time, rejoicing at the queen's escape and repeatedly mentioning rumors concerning her alleged miscarriage, although he was not sure. Sentences like "I hope that the rumors circulating about the queen and also that man Caesar are founded" clearly suggest that Cicero rejoiced at the possibility that Cleopatra may have lost a child.

If these rumors were true, we can only sympathize with this woman who, at night, when the sea is calm, goes to sit at the prow, away from everybody (but with bodyguards ready to intervene), and quietly watches the horizon, with that huge weight in her heart and soul.

A Friendly Light in the Night

All you can hear is the waves lapping against the hull, like a lament, as, beneath, the waters are sliced by the sharp prow of the flagship. The sea is black, but Cleopatra feels it as a friend that cradles her with the rocking of the ship. The noise of the rigging, with cables creaking and squeaking, accompanied by the hollow clicking of the sail swelled by the breeze, also provides a background to her thoughts. The queen looks up at the sky. It's lighter than the sea. A thousand luminous dots are mirrored in her eyes, like fireflies on a summer night. It's not possible to describe the feeling you get when beneath the stars on these seas. They are not stars but sparkling diamonds, and you feel as though you could almost touch them with your hand. Thanks to their soft light, everything on board is visible, even faces.

It's not difficult to make out familiar constellations when you travel by sea in April, such as Orion or Cassiopeia (queen of Ethiopia), a constellation mentioned by Ptolemy.

Cleopatra looks for the constellations her tutors taught her to distinguish when she was a little girl. She can almost hear their voices. She has always enjoyed listening to their stories and myths, adores Homer and knows the *Iliad* and *Odyssey*, and Ulysses's extraordinary journey, very well. It's not improbable that she may have learned entire passages by heart, as many Greeks did in her times. In the Hellenistic world, teaching is truly stimulating to a mind as inquisitive and eager to learn as hers. Homer's poems are not just literature but also teach you about history, religion, law, and technology. The same is true of mythology. They're not just sacred stories, with divinities and feats, but a true encyclopedia of knowledge and, even then, a benchmark of cultural reference: they provide lessons in several subjects with just one book. It's a multidisciplinary way of discovering one's world and a typical characteristic of the Hellenistic mentality, the expression of a great broad-mindedness that is at the root of the Western way of thinking.

Her eyes, full of sweet memories from the past but also stark questions about the future, are disturbed by the helmsman at the back of the ship: "The lighthouse!" he shouts, and it's a liberating cry everyone's been awaiting for hours. Before them, at the border between the black sea and the starry sky, a small light seems to be floating on the surface of the Mediterranean. It's the Lighthouse of Alexandria.

At times it vanishes behind a wave, at others it quivers because of a problem in air currents, perhaps. We're actually still a very long way away, but Cleopatra's fleet is now within its range.

It's easy to imagine the queen's relief. There's a joyous roar on board, as everybody looks for it and points at it. After weeks at sea, the end of the journey is now imminent.

As minutes and hours go by, its light becomes increasingly visible and strong. The Lighthouse of Alexandria projects a beam of light that reaches out as far as the limit of the Earth's curvature, in other words thirty miles. How can this be possible? It's the fruit of the ingeniousness of ancient minds, and this extraordinary era in particular. It was designed and built by the architect Sostratus of Cnidus, by order of Ptolemy I, although it was completed during the reign of Ptolemy II, one of Cleopatra's ancestors. That was in 280 BC, twenty or so years before the Carthaginian wars. We can call Sostratus of Cnidus a true superstar of the time. The cost was exorbitant, 800 talents, but the result was one of the seven wonders of the ancient world.

In order to send a beam of light so far, it was first and foremost necessary to build a very tall tower, so he devised a structure more than four hundred feet tall, the equivalent of a forty-story building, made up of three parts. The base is square, the central body is an octagonal "trunk," and the summit an open cylinder, probably with many pillars. Three different geometrical forms, then. On the top, the golden statue of Alexander the Great (or, some say, Zeus or Poseidon) shone. Beneath it, between the pillars, burned the fire that represented the point of reference (and safety) for all the sailors who navigated at night. It was a large, oil-fueled flame, but how could its light go across almost thirty-one miles of open sea and reach out as far as a modern lighthouse? The trick was the presence of a series of mirrors that focused the light into an intense beam able to reach where the coast was no longer visible. But that was not enough. It's possible, even though we have no evidence for this, that what contributed to focusing the beam so effectively may have also been large lenses shaped in a particular way (with a "bulb" and "steps"), like authentic parabolic mirrors, just like the ones you see in premodern lighthouses. In Cleopatra's time, people already had the knowledge to produce lenses like that, even though they couldn't obtain such pure materials.

Charmion approaches Cleopatra, and together they stare at the light, mesmerized, while a few locks of their hair whip against their cheeks. They have a past to forget behind them, and before them a future to build and defend.

Whether the rumors circulating in Rome about her pregnancy and miscarriage are true or false, it all now belongs to the past. Cleopatra is back home.

The sky is quickly paling and a shade of blue slowly extinguishes all the stars, leaving only one glowing, sitting on the black profile of the coast—the Lighthouse of Alexandria. The sun will soon rise, and at its first rays offerings and rituals will be held to thank the rising of Ra or Helios, depending on whether you're Egyptian or Greek. Above all, the travelers will thank the gods for reaching Egypt safe and sound.

The spectacle that opens before the eyes of Cleopatra and all those on board is indescribable.

The beam from the lighthouse suddenly seems to split in two. Another light appears next to its powerful glare, an even more intense one: the first rays of the sun appearing exactly behind the lighthouse. Cleopatra's fleet is following a route that aligns it with the lighthouse and the rising sun. For ten seconds or so, the tower is perfectly framed by the red sun that has appeared on the horizon. A typically flattened, oval sun, the way you see it at dawn in this part of the world. Its red color is caused by the floating desert dust. April is the month when the Khamsin blows, a wind capable of raising terrible sandstorms, one of which, about five centuries ago in the Egyptian desert, swallowed an entire Persian expeditionary force that was never found. As it rises, the sun quickly shakes off the desert dust and a few seconds later turns orange, then pink, then yellow, until it glows with such intensity that you cannot look at it anymore. Cleopatra is still there, her eyes shut, welcoming the warmth as though pure energy for her heart. When she opens her eyes again, she sees the city and many sails on the sea coming toward her. It's the entire Egyptian fleet, leaving the harbor to welcome its queen. There's an entire nation waiting to celebrate her return.

Alexandria Welcomes Its Queen

The large flagship stops at a certain distance and is joined by Cleopatra's beautiful royal ship, much smaller but so refined and precious that it shines like a casket in the bright African morning sunlight. From the shore, everyone can see its gold parts sparkle, the elegant undulating of flags, fabrics, and silk curtains between the pillars that hold up a canopy under which the queen is sitting. The rowers have adopted a slow, perfect rhythm, fueling an almost sacred atmosphere. As soon as they heard the news, the Alexandrians came out of their homes en masse and are now crowding the piers, shores, and even the roofs and terraces of the houses. They want to see the queen and express all their love and support. Partly because she is their only guarantee of independence and wealth. As she draws closer to the royal pier, Cleopatra hears more and more clearly the individual cries of her subjects, the sounds of tambourines, flutes, and *sistra* that turn into a single loud clamor as soon as she's within earshot.

Many start to sing a hymn to Isis, one of those used at the climax of the orations in the temples dedicated to her. Others gradually join in, and at one point, Cleopatra feels that they are singing this hymn together for her. Only now, facing the love of her subjects, does she realize how long she's lived surrounded by the mistrust and hatred of Romans, segregated in the gilded residence of the Horti Caesaris. Standing on the ship, looking proud, she makes an elegant gesture with her right hand to greet her people, who burst into a roar. The ship approaches the pier and the rowers hold their oars up toward the blue sky. In the silence, a gangplank is quickly positioned by a few attendants. Two wings of royal guards have already drawn up, along with the main dignitaries waiting for her at the rear. To one side, but with colored shields and armor in full view, a platoon of legionaries with insignia on display surrounds the commander of the three Roman legions stationed in Alexandria, as well as the commanders of individual legions, the legates. Their presence in full uniform is a form of respect toward the queen and a confirmation of Antony's promise to respect the agreements Julius Caesar drew up with her, and this reassures Cleopatra, partly because it conveys a very clear message to all Alexandrians: nothing has changed. On the contrary, the queen is perhaps even more powerful than before, since she is respected even without Caesar's protection. Then drums start to roll like distant thunder. Their rhythm is heard miles away by peasants scattered in the fields, who raise their heads, as well as from boats in the marshes of the Nile Delta. Now it's wind instruments, harps, and dozens of *sistra* playing an obsessive rhythm. The queen emerges from the forest of oars and slowly walks down from the ship.

Despite the long journey and the difficulty in getting her ready aboard the flagship, Eiras and her assistants have performed a true miracle. Cleopatra surprises everyone with her freshness and naturalness. She advances solemnly between the rows of soldiers until she reaches the dignitaries who have held the reins of the city in her absence. All, except the legionaries, bow and prostrate themselves before her. After the courtesies and a few welcome rituals (about which, sadly, we have no information), Cleopatra gets into a covered litter that raises her above everyone's head and begins the trip to the royal palace. There's a celebrating crowd around her, kept at a distance by the royal guards that act as a shield.

Cleopatra has a regal poise. She holds her head high and gives the crowd slow nods of approval, but even though she cannot show it there's a whirlwind of emotions in her heart. In just a few seconds, she has landed in an explosion of colors, of radiant faces, and the happy smiles of people she has not seen for a long time, but also smells to which Cleopatra is very sensitive: pungent dry land, the acrid plants of the marshes, fruity flowers, and the intense scent of the desert. She is home, yes, welcomed by the strongest and most ancient charm— that of Africa.

A City out of Homer's *Odyssey*

Let's allow Cleopatra to continue on her journey to the royal palace. Let's let the crowd in her wake parade past us and let us try to be alone. For us, too, this is a new experience. A few pages ago we were in Rome, with its crowds, its very tall buildings, countless temples, and cool spring air. We're now feeling a little disoriented. The first thing we notice is the scorching sun. Every ray seems concentrated by a magnifying glass and burns your head. Unlike on the boat, where there was always some wind, here we sweat because it's hot and humid. We're in Africa and, in addition, at the tip of the Nile Delta.

You can't see the great river because it has spread out like the roots of a tree in an infinite series of canals and minor waterways (it's a bird's foot delta, as they say) that, before ending in the sea, fuel a substantial humid and marshy area, so large that it can be seen from space. Another thing that strikes us is the flies—so many of them, apparently with a penchant for our skin and eyes. Swiping them with our hands, let's try to explore the city.

Alexandria is now the second city in the Mediterranean, after Rome. If you look at a map of the Nile Delta, Alexandria is on the coast, slightly to the left, in the west.

It's strange how the capital of Egypt is not in its heart like the famous Thebes, where you can now admire Luxor, Karnak, the Valleys of the Kings and Queens, but practically on the border, with one foot in the sea. How come? The reason is that it was not founded by ancient Egyptians but by Alexander the Great in 332 BC (not many cities have such a specific date of birth). The great Macedonian military leader had a very clear plan: the city had to become one of the main commercial ports of call in the known world. Behind it was the Nile, with its very fertile lands thanks to regular flooding that nourished its highly sought-after farm produce. All kinds of goods came from the east, mainly destined for Greece and then the west. There was no sense in creating a city in the heart of the desert, along the Nile. In that position, perched on the sea, Alexandria constituted a perfect point of contact among these various trade routes, like a Hong Kong of the ancient seas, which was to enrich and strengthen Alexander's dominion over the Mediterranean.

There's another, more symbolic reason this place was chosen for the location of the city, which looks to Greece in many ways. Alexander the Great was a great fan of Homer, and of the *Odyssey* in particular. The island of Pharos, on which the Lighthouse of Alexandria would eventually be built, is mentioned in Book IV. Alexander must therefore have decided to refer to this book and pay tribute to it by founding a city right on the spot described in the poem. A private extravagance that however gave birth to what eventually became the capital of a long dynasty, the Ptolemies, which in turn gave rise to Cleopatra, and to our story.

They say that the shape of the city was not coincidental but the result of another extravagance on the part of the great Macedonian military leader. Alexander wanted his plan to be a faithful reproduction of a chlamys, a short, light cloak fastened with a pin, which he liked to wear. To all the Greeks, the chlamys was a symbol of male power and virility. Commanders used to wear it and boys were given one when they reached puberty to emphasize their approaching manhood.

Unfortunately, Alexander the Great did not get to see his city completed (he actually built at least seven places with the same name all over his Middle Eastern and Asian empire: Alexandria Asiana, Alexandria Bucephalous, the one in Egypt, and in the Caucasus, Eschate, Nicea, and Troas). Alexandria was not built from nothing. There was already an inhabited settlement, called Raqote, a kind of citadel, fortified to defend the coast from pirate attacks. This small center became the starting point and turned into the most ancient and working-class district of Alexandria in Egypt, under the Hellenized name of Rhacotis. It was where most of its Egyptian residents lived, while the rest of the city was populated mainly by Greeks. This already tells us that under Alexander the Great and all the Ptolemaic dynasties, including Cleopatra, it was the Greeks who were in charge in Egypt, in other words invaders who essentially settled in Alexandria. The rest of the country is inhabited by its original people, the Egyptians, who, however, when all's said and done, are viewed as second-class citizens. Greeks were the kings, Greek was the official language, and, as we said, Cleopatra's name is Greek. Even some of the nouns we think are Egyptian are Greek—the word *obelisk*, for instance. It means "skewer" in Greek, and was the word the Greek invaders used disparagingly to describe these magnificent, elegant monuments. Was there was any racism toward Egyptians, the descendants of the pharaohs? Yes, but this did not amount to apartheid or violent discrimination. Were Greeks and Egyptians treated differently regarding the law and taxes? Again, the answer is yes. The world in which Cleopatra was born was therefore that of a conquering people who had taken command of an entire nation and kept its residents under its yoke, just as the Persians had first done, followed by the Romans. However, Cleopatra was the only one in her lineage who opened up to the Egyptians, spoke their language, took a step toward them, and respected them. That is why they loved her.

The Secret of Alexandria

When we look around, we see a city not as large as Rome though densely populated, with squares, temples, and palaces in a mixture of architectural styles. What's especially striking is the swarm of people and the bubbling of commerce in every corner, which make it alive, like all large harbor cities, a crossroads of trade, nationalities, ethnicities, and different cultures that manage to coexist in the same place with their own habits.

It wasn't easy to build Alexandria. Its terrain is sandy. Alexander may have seen its first buildings but nothing more, since he then headed to Asia on his great conquests, only returning from these after his death. After that, his generals split the empire among themselves through a series of struggles, alliances, and clashes. Egypt went to Ptolemy, who gave birth to the Ptolemaic dynasty, of which Cleopatra is the last reigning descendant. That is why she speaks Greek, dresses like a Greek woman, and has Greek culture. A far cry from the history of Ancient Egypt as we think of it, that of the dynasties of pharaohs who have become legendary, like Ramesses II or the skillful military leader Thutmose III.

The great builder of Alexandria was therefore Alexander the Great's successor, Ptolemy. He realized that this would be the new capital city of the Egyptian kingdom, so transferred the court here (it had previously been in Memphis). Subsequently, every one of his successors added new buildings and elegant edifices, transforming what was the early settlement into a beautiful, fascinating, and above all "new" city that had nothing in common with what had sprung up along the Nile for centuries before that. Somewhat like our modern metropolises, complete with skyscrapers, in comparison with medieval cities. Its urban model is Greek and revolutionary. Alexandria was designed by an architect called Dinocrates, who used an idea so simple and effective that it remains at the root of modern cities. It's the so-called Hippodamian Plan, the fruit of the genius of a very sensible Greek architect, Hippodamus of Miletus, who lived four centuries before Cleopatra. For thousands of years, cities grew haphazardly, one house after the next, and the streets were built in the spaces left between the various buildings. This always led to a chaotic agglomeration, made of winding alleys. Hippodamus turned everything upside down. The starting point for building a city became the streets and not the houses. First, streets were planned and afterward, around them, the city would develop. This made every facet of daily life easier, from the transportation of supplies to cleaning the city, etc. His idea was simple. Streets met at right angles, forming a plan similar to a chessboard. The streets that followed the direction of the sun, east to west, were called *plateiai*. Those that went from north to south, *stenopoi*.

As often happens, success comes from simple, concrete ideas. This new layout has been at the root of almost all Greek cities, then Roman ones, and even modern ones like New York. A good example is the "Spaccanapoli": the famous street that, so perfectly straight, cuts right across the historic center of Naples.

Therefore, Alexandria, too, is built according to this plan. Its principal axis is called the Canopic Way, and it crosses the entire city from one end to the other. It's about four and a half miles long (which corresponds to about 40 stadia, as a resident contemporary of Cleopatra would have said, since a stadium was the typical Greek unit of measurement, corresponding to just under 200 yards). You get the same feeling as when standing on Fifth Avenue in New York. You see the street disappearing on the horizon, surrounded by buildings. And so in ancient times, Alexandria is as electrifying as Paris in the late nineteenth century or New York in the modern era. For those who arrive from outside, it's a huge city with all kinds of extremes, but which also offers great opportunities.

At one point, the Canopic Way has a perpendicular intersection with another large street, known as the Soma (the name of Alexander the Great's tomb). The junction of these two roads constitutes the center of Alexandria, and widens into the Agora, the main square.

Wandering Around Cleopatra's City

What do you see and feel in Alexandria? Let's take a stroll around the city. The street we have taken is not one of the main ones and yet it's extremely busy, like an Indian city at rush hour. The buildings are tall and elegant, with light plaster. There are many terraces, since the climate is warm and less rainy than in Europe. There are almost always shops and places of refreshment at the foot of these buildings, and each of them has a curtain to keep the entrance and the sidewalk outside it in the shade. The curtains are of various colors, sometimes with stripes, sometimes with a decorative pattern. Often, the sun has bleached their early beauty. The result is an endless series of multi-colored curtains, similar to Tibetan prayer flags, that stretches all the way to the horizon, past various intersections.

The streets are paved with stone slabs, like in Rome, but the atmosphere you breathe in is definitely more eastern than in the Urbe. You can't walk on the long sidewalks, because they are almost always taken up by the goods on display in the shops. You often have to get off the sidewalk in order to avoid baskets piled up atop one another, or else amphorae and pillars of terra-cotta cups, or else more heaps of brightly colored linen fabrics arranged on stalls. And then there's the sun, much stronger than in Rome, almost unbearable, which gives the streets and districts a blinding glare as well as making them scorching hot. Within seconds, your eyes must get accustomed to the semi-darkness behind the curtains, only to be blinded again as soon as you're back in the sun. There are impressive stalls with bronze and metal objects, an infinite spread of cups and pitchers of every kind, and oil lamps with chains, almost all finely decorated. There's no shortage of shelves with statuettes of divinities of every kind, from those representing Hercules and Aphrodite to the Egyptian ones of Horus, Isis, and Osiris, but also those originating from the Middle East and Persia. They are all dominated by Serapis, a divinity especially loved and worshiped in Alexandria. This expanse of statuettes, which can look cheap and go unnoticed, is in actual fact a clear sign of the whirlwind of cultures and religions across the city.

Then there are shops displaying glass objects. We can see glass ointment bottles with bright stripes, splendid little amphorae with walls so thin you think they'd crumble instantly in your hands, cups, pitchers, and elegantly decorated, long-necked vases. Glass manufacturing in the eastern Mediterranean is far more refined than in the rest of Europe, and Alexandria's shops are full of high-quality goods.

The fragrances you can smell on the city streets are also different. As you walk, you can at times smell burning wood. It's different, sweeter and aromatic because the trees used are African and don't grow in Rome. Everyone who disembarks here after a long journey in Europe notices it. In perfumers' shops there are also essences and fragrances unknown in the Western world, which come from faraway cities in the Middle East, many even from India. They are the same as those that envelop you when an Alexandrian woman walks past you: intense, fresh scents, full of exotic charm. It's impossible not to realize that some of Cleopatra's secrets, like perfume, cosmetics, or her inter-cultural approach, are the natural result of the world in which she was born and grew up, but to a "foreigner" like a Roman, for instance, they can seem new and overpowering.

The sacks of spices around a shop (there are even more inside, making you wonder how the shopkeeper can move around) suggest faraway trade. As we speak, the owner is haggling with a customer in broken but understandable and direct Greek, while carefully placing on small, bronze scales a few precious root stalks of turmeric, the "saffron of the Indies." It arrived here after a very long journey from India, or perhaps even farther.

The exotic origins of these many products on display are also reflected in the faces we pass in the streets. Some passersby are clearly Greek, while others look more Middle Eastern, like that bearded man with olive skin, who comes from the Arabian peninsula and is having a lively discussion with a short Carthaginian seller with a big belly and curly hair. And here comes slowly a tall, slender woman with dark skin and very white teeth. These days, with her elegant poise, she could well be seen on a high-fashion catwalk. We are suddenly cut off by a cart pulled by two oxen, carrying a large block of pink granite from Aswan, which will no doubt be turned into the statue of some divinity by one of the many sculpture workshops in Alexandria. Behind the vehicle, two men are talking while walking in the middle of the street. They're wearing very elaborate clothes, with colorfully embossed embroidery, and we can tell from their hats, which we've never seen before, that they come from a long way away, maybe Syria or Armenia. Three amber-skinned men go past them, slouching. All three are thin and are wearing clothes made from Eastern fabrics that fall in elegant folds. We can't be certain, but they're probably three Indians who have come here with some goods unloaded in one of the Egyptian ports on the Red Sea. Inevitably, you also come across soldiers. Here are three of them crossing the road. They are legionaries on leave, although they're armed. They have a large presence in Alexandria and have been at the origin of many problems, especially in the past: rapes, brawls, and abuse of power. Alexandrians don't like them, but many of them have settled in the city and started families.

Every person you meet has his or her own story, languages, ideas, ways of cooking, culture. On this front, the streets of Alexandria remind us a little of modern London or Paris.

Continuing on our walk, we are struck by some of the details in this city. No doubt it looks like a large capital, with wide streets, tall, elegant buildings with light, shining walls, but it also has its shabby side, signs of neglect. There are tufts of dry grass sprouting on the sidewalk, in the corners we can see garbage through which some goat is rummaging, and we come across donkeys and cows standing in the middle of the street.

Alexandria truly is a collage of goods and people, and a glimpse of all the worlds and kingdoms it binds with the same invisible thread of commerce. Commerce is based on the drachma, the Greek currency, here. But if you pay with a different currency, people will accept it without much of a fuss, unless it's an unfavorable exchange. The same as any modern-day currency exchange would be anywhere in the world.

A valuable piece of advice when visiting Alexandria, like all Greek cities, is to pay serious attention to the front doors of the houses. Unlike the ones in Rome, which always open inward, these sometimes open outward, so there's a real risk of getting hit in the face by one, especially in small alleys. This is why people are used to knocking not only when going in but also when coming out. At one point, the street we are walking down cuts across the main road, the Canopus or Canopic Way. It's flanked by a huge portico, with countless shops. Thanks to its constant shade, the open stores, and the likelihood of bumping into people you know, this is one of the most popular streets for taking a walk, in an atmosphere not unlike the modern souk in

Tunis or Istanbul. Various goods are on display, often piled up, and sometimes you suddenly feel your head caressed by fabrics on sale, hanging in midair. A little farther away, there are men sitting on simple stools, chatting and drinking spiced wine. Every now and then they slap their legs to kill mosquitoes, of which there are many in Alexandria. During our walk down this "tunnel" crowded with people and objects, we sometimes come across a small altar that gives off the scents of exotic essences burning under the painted and slightly flaking image of a divinity. They may not look like much but are actually a very important detail and remind us that we are in a city and a world (a Hellenistic one) where there is maximum religious tolerance. This also derives from syncretism, the fusion of many elements from different religions until a hybrid divinity is created, with which very distinct peoples and cultures identify, like for example Greeks and Egyptians. The great openness and the culture of welcoming differences ensure that no one is discriminated against because of their religious beliefs, as long as these do not constitute political resistance to the Roman government. And if we join this characteristic to freedom of dress, speech, expressing one's opinions, and the respect of others, that's what we can truly call a civilization. Naturally, in Alexandria, too, there's room for improvement in coexistence, laws that don't work, and obvious privileges for the Greek community, which dominates the country. But in comparison with other places, we are very much advanced in many ways. Perhaps only Rome can compete with Alexandria on this front.

Amid all the increasing chatter around us, it doesn't take long before the Canopic Way takes us to Alexandria's main square, the Agora. Emerging from the cool shade, it's not easy to get used to the blinding glare of its marbles. After the narrow portico, the open space feels even larger than it is. There are clusters of people talking, women walking past with "umbrellas" held up by slaves, children running after one another, soldiers walking in step, beggars asking for alms. We also see characters who are very common in everyday life in Alexandria: peddlers displaying all kinds of goods—from fritters to chilled, flavored drinking water, to small lucky amulets—on simple boards hanging from bands around their necks. These characters are invisible in history books and museums, and yet together with so many others they make up the living body of everyday life in all cities throughout the centuries, including Alexandria.

Being at the intersection of two main streets, the Agora gives you a perfect view of all four sides of the city. When you're in the center of the square, facing north toward the sea, the Canopic Way stretches east and ends up in a new district, inhabited mainly by the Greek community, which would eventually be called Nikopolis (*nike* means "victory" in Greek) because it is through the Gate of Canopus (or Gate of the Sun)—which stands at the end of the road—that Octavian will enter a few years from now, having vanquished Mark Antony and Cleopatra . . . In the west, the Canopic Way leads to its counterpart, a very poor area, the Rhacotis, the Egyptian quarter, the original nucleus of the city, as we've said, mainly inhabited by Egyptians. It's a working-class area where poverty reigns.

In the south, just outside the city, there's a very exclusive, elegant quarter. Around a large lake called Mariout, the wealthiest families (almost all Greek) have built their luxurious villas to keep away from the strains of Alexandrian life.

From our vantage point, the exact center of the Agora, we have the north in front of us. Following this direction, you reach the two ports of Alexandria and its extraordinary lighthouse. Let's go and discover it. As we walk, we realize that the heart of Alexandria is dominated by masterpieces. All around us, in the Agora district, immersed in the street grid, there are its most beautiful monuments, such as the Soma—Alexander the Great's monumental tomb—and many gardens. It's impossible to describe them, partly because we don't have any testimonials as to their appearance anymore. But there are also less spectacular places that are more a part of everyday life. Besides the many "cafés" and refreshment spots, there's no shortage of brothels, with young women leaning against the entrance, waiting. The bulk of their clients are those who arrive in the city after a long sea journey. It's no wonder that the closer we get to the port, the more brothels there seem to be.

After a few more minutes' walk westward along the Canopic Way, the sound of the sea starts to grow louder. Then, gradually, its smell penetrates your nostrils. Finally, a sudden breeze ruffles your hair. And, at the bottom of the street, as soon as you walk through another entrance to the city that practically leads to the port, and has the evocative name of Gate of the Moon, suddenly, here is the sea, magnificent and endless, deep blue. You can't possibly stand in the doorway for too long. It's always too windy and your clothes slap anxiously against your skin.

A little farther north, Alexandria's road network continues across the water thanks to a very long breakwater that connects the city to a small island on which the lighthouse was erected. The breakwater is called Heptastadion, "seven stadia," which tells you how long it is: 1,300 yards. It's a masterpiece of Hellenic engineering that takes us to another wonder of this culture—the lighthouse. It stands before us, imposing, the whiteness of its blocks making it visible from a very long way away even in daytime.

The island is called Pharos, and that is where the name of the seventh wonder of the world comes from. From it derives the word for lighthouse in some Latin languages (for example, *faro* in Italian and Spanish).

Once on the island, we try to go up into the lighthouse. After going past the guards and climbing the innumerable steps up to the top, we see a breathtaking spectacle unfold before us. Alexandria spreads out in front of us with its temples, palaces, and houses, surrounded by its thick city walls. You can clearly see the famous Library and, next to it, the Musaeum, a unique center for knowledge in the ancient world. A little farther, you can make out the theater and then, just outside the city, the Hippodrome. Between them, in the tangle of houses, there's the Jewish quarter (in Cleopatra's time, the Alexandria community was one of the largest on the Mediterranean).

According to Diodorus Siculus, more than 300,000 people live here, which means that with an estimated population of 7.5 million in Egypt, almost one in twenty people lives in the capital.

Beyond Alexandria, there's a never-ending expanse of cultivated fields and low vegetation, with palm groves whose bright green gradually disappears on the horizon, through a thin, humid mist that rises from the Delta, mixed with the hovering desert dust. The whiteness of the city, the green of the vegetation, and the blues of the sky and the sea are the four colors of Alexandria. And they linger in everyone's memory.

From up here we can clearly see the breakwater dividing the bay, effectively creating two ports. On our right, there's the commercial port Eunostus (which means "happy return" in Greek), complete with a row of warehouses and a frantic loading and unloading of many moored ships. On the left, though, we see the so-called Portus Magnus, with the royal pier where Cleopatra disembarked this morning. We can clearly see her shining ship, still moored. Next door, we can admire the royal district and the palace to which the queen has now returned. I wonder if she is looking at us from down there.

Cleopatra Is Back Home

Alexandria is a wonderful city with Eastern charm, the heart of a dense network of trade and capital of a very wealthy kingdom. Don't be deceived, however. Egypt's power has been declining for many decades and, lacerated by succession wars, the country is increasingly dominated by and dependent on the new superpower expanding on the Mediterranean: Rome.

And this is precisely what Cleopatra is thinking while she is looking at the port and the lighthouse, her head leaning against the edge of a large window. Her eyes are anxiously searching all the places she's known since she was a child. She sees the pier where she disembarked this morning from her gilded ship that's still moored there. Now the pier is empty and the images of her festive return are gradually replaced with other memories that emerge from her deepest self. Her gaze has turned fixed and dreamy. Once again, as we draw closer to her eyes, the way we did at the beginning of our story, we can see images mirrored in them: the port of Alexandria, of course, although we can sense that she sees more than that in this landscape. It's the harbor of her heart, where, lining up like sailing ships, so many dreams are arriving, along with distant emotions, which the palace and these familiar places are bringing up so overwhelmingly. This journey into the memory of reality is a cry for help, a way of seeking refuge and protection from the past, given that the present is so uncertain. In her eyes, the gilded vessel moored in the port becomes that of her father. How many times did she see him, from this very spot up here, getting on or off his ship with a solemn gait, accompanied by a procession of guards, counselors, and courtiers? She would watch him in secret, her nurse frantically looking for her in the palace. The memory of this childhood atmosphere is like a gentle caress to the heart. But what was Cleopatra like as a child?

5

Cleopatra Remembers Caesar

Cleopatra's Mother and Father

Unfortunately, we don't have any information on Cleopatra's childhood and adolescence, although it's fair to imagine that she would have been born in this same royal palace. It was in 69 or 70 BC, but we don't know the day. Her father was Ptolemy XII, also called Auletes, or "flutist," because he thought of himself as a "new Dionysus." A little like Nero, he enjoyed playing and singing in public, especially during Dionysian celebrations, hence his nickname. He was, however, a terrible ruler. He loved art and music more than governing, which is why Egypt went through frightening political confusion and economic upheaval under him. He would purchase his legitimacy on the throne and the protection of Pompey and other Roman politicians—including Caesar—with promises of colossal amounts of money. We're talking of 6,000 talents on one occasion, and even 10,000 on another, the equivalent of entire yearly taxes received by the Egyptian government. Since Ptolemy did not actually have such sums at his disposal, he turned to a big Roman banker, Gaius Rabirius Postumus, who lent him the money at exorbitant rates. This is how Egypt obtained its status as "friend and ally of the Roman people," as we said earlier. The residents of Alexandria did not like this subordination to Rome. When, despite the agreements,

Romans occupied Cyprus, a very rich island on Egyptian territory, there was a popular uprising that forced the king quickly to flee to Rome. He remained there in gilded exile, still corrupting politicians and powerful men, until he obtained his return to the throne. Later, to make sure they were paid, the Romans even managed to impose the very same Rabirius on him as an administrator of the kingdom's finances, with disastrous consequences. The banker plundered so much wealth that he then had to be sent back to Rome under protection.

Ptolemy Auletes's debts were so substantial that they were still a burden on Cleopatra. That was one of the reasons that led Caesar to Alexandria, when he met the queen for the first time. He was there (in part) to call in his markers, asking to be repaid at least 10 million drachma and "remitting" another 7.5 million.

Even though Ptolemy was a totally inept ruler, Cleopatra remained loyally at his side until his death, hence her nickname "Cleopatra Philipator," or "she who loves her father." If we had to translate her full name into English, we would therefore have before us a true hymn to her father: "father's glory" (Cleopatra) and "she who loves her father" (Philopator), the fruit of a male chauvinist society in which the figure of the father was at the center of everything. This illustrates how skillful Cleopatra was at shattering the patriarchal structure of Greco-Macedonian culture.

We know nothing about her mother, on the other hand. We don't know her name, what she looked like, or where she came from. Some say she was a woman who frequented the court, a concubine of the king, so possibly an illegitimate wife, although she appears to have been highborn, perhaps an Egyptian woman who came from the circles and families of Memphis high priests, and so Cleopatra's blood and features were probably half Egyptian.

Another theory suggests she belonged to the Greek people. It could have been the king's first wife, who, in keeping with Ptolemaic tradition concerning royal marriages, may have been one of his sisters, a namesake called Cleopatra Tryphaena. In that case, Cleopatra's blood and features would have been Greco-Macedonian.

Childhood

Cleopatra is now walking down a wide corridor between two rows of guards who silently bow as she passes them. She is reclaiming these locations, so dear to her, with their smells, sounds, and light.

She remembers running down this same corridor, pursued by her nurse and an escort who never let her out of their sight. She recalls picking up the pace, laughing at the prospect of forcing adults clumsily to run after her, a little girl. She has very fond memories of those years: painted terra-cotta dolls with linen dresses and fake jewels, and her rocking horse. They were the toys of any other child of that time, except that they were luxurious. Later, she discovered parlor games such as senet, with a long, narrow chessboard and pawns, and the Mehen game with its board, the Egyptian-age equivalent of checkers or chess. But who did she play with? With other children, the sons and daughters of Alexandria's most aristocratic and high-ranking families, which formed *in nuce* her very first court. In other words, already as a child, she would get used to a world that would one day be her everyday life.

But in Cleopatra's case, it went further. From a very early age, she has been raised to become a queen. She was the last, truly the last of a very long tradition. From the times of the first pharaohs, princesses had always received an education of the highest, finest standard.

Cleopatra walks into a little room where she is going to change in order to take a bath. Lying on a kind of gilded little couch upholstered in leopard skin, she is sipping a chilled tonic drink. Behind her, a servant is waving a huge ostrich fan.

She no longer notices, but all the drink and food is sampled by a servant, to make sure it isn't poisoned. Being a food taster is a strange, worrying job.

The bath is ready. Cleopatra goes to the bathroom, still wrapped in her elegant white linen dress. Behind her, her silent escort has been joined by two handmaidens carrying ointments, perfumes, and linen cloths to be used as towels. She crosses an entire garden, a real oasis inside the palace, with fragrant plants, often in bloom, and here and there animals emerge from the greenery, including a peacock. She stops to admire this paradise (and so does the small procession behind her). The sound of water gurgling from fountains creates a natural soundtrack with the song of many colorful little birds drinking, perched in an orderly manner on the edge of a marble basin.

Cleopatra remembers perfectly well that in this garden, when she was still a little girl, philosophers, kings, dignitaries, and ambassadors would stroll before her, and sit on the elaborate marble benches to enjoy the atmosphere. In this place, each of them would cease to be a king or a philosopher, and show his more human, almost childlike side, their faces lighting up with surprise and admiration before this peace and these water features.

Her Sign in Stone

Cleopatra keeps walking through the palace rooms, amid marbles and pillars. Her eyes suddenly come to rest on a black stone statue of herself. The queen is represented advancing solemnly, in slinky clothes. She looks straight ahead. The style is undoubtedly Egyptian, but the details are Greek, a sign of the culture that currently dominates Egypt. It has healthy, rounded features, full breasts, soft cheeks, fleshy lips, and you can no longer see the chiseled line of makeup (kohl) stretching to her temples. Moreover, she is portrayed holding a cornucopia in her left arm, a sign of wealth and abundance. On her forehead, there are three standing cobras, the uraei, representing Cleopatra's greatness and the lands she has brought to the kingdom of Egypt. The other queens had two at most, but she has carried Egypt to new heights. What will become of this land now? Will the Romans keep their promise and guarantee the integrity and autonomy of her kingdom? Cleopatra's anxiety swells and a sense of the void envelops her, so she picks up the pace and leaves behind her this statue you can admire, even though it's broken and its face is damaged (we'll never know if it's because of a fall or the hammer blows of the *damnatio memoriae* after her death), at the Museo Egizio in Turin. For decades it belonged to collections and now its rediscovery has aroused amazement and curiosity, even though scholars cannot agree on whether it is truly a statue of Cleopatra. We, however, have imagined that it used to stand here, perhaps even temporarily, in the Alexandria palace, before finding its definitive (unknown) location, where it was eventually found.

The queen continues absentmindedly past a stele with a text in hieroglyphics that includes her name. Like those of all the kings, it's in an oblong frame, the so-called cartouche.

It can be found written in three different ways in Egypt: in Greek (Κλεοπάτρα), in Latin (Cleopatra), and in Egyptian.

Cleopatra Becomes a Capable Queen

There is a bow at every encounter with the queen as she walks across the rooms. But how long has Cleopatra been in power? For at least seven years, even though she had actually been getting ready for the throne for a very long time. Berenice, her elder sister, destined to be queen, died eleven years earlier. From that moment on, although her father was still alive and in power, Cleopatra became the first in line in dynastic succession. That's why she received an appropriate education, as well as making visits and traveling in order to get acquainted with the country she would probably get to rule. Three powerful tutors took care of her and her brother's education: Pothinus, a very clever, shrewd eunuch; Achillas, the supreme commander of the army; and the rector Theodotus. Moreover, her father had also asked the Romans to act as "tutors to his two children," something that, as we are about to see, will have strong implications in history. Given her independent nature, Cleopatra had clashed with her powerful tutors soon enough, so they turned against her and took her brother's side.

When, at her father's death in 51 BC, destiny came knocking at her door, she was ready even though she was only eighteen. She was formally invested in a lavish ceremony, probably in Memphis, before Egypt's supreme priest. Her younger brother, just ten years old, stood next to her. She had married him in keeping with the dynastic tradition the Ptolemies had adopted for the purpose of self-celebration from the ancient Egyptians, who, in turn, referred to Isis and Osiris. It was substantially a marriage more in form than practice. From that moment, Cleopatra had taken a series of intensive state trips along the Nile and the rest of the kingdom so her people would get to know her. From the outset, everybody noticed and liked the fact that she spoke fluent Egyptian without the need for an interpreter, a real exception among Ptolemaic kings.

Even during these encounters, she had begun to weave a web of contacts and support, especially with the powerful caste of priests, in order to consolidate her own power. Hers had been a very sophisticated strategy. Being older than her brother, who was still a child, she had gradually excluded him from power by consigning him to the shadows. There was only one face—hers—on the coins, and, especially in the beginning, portraits of the queen were in Alexandrian style, to highlight the direct link with Alexander the Great and legitimize her power and her actions. Moreover, official documents ended with her signature alone. In everyone's eyes, it was she who commanded, and rightly so, as the only sovereign.

The first two years of her reign (51–50 BC) were not easy, however. Because the Nile did not overflow as abundantly and the harvest was poor, the entire population had been affected by hunger. Cleopatra had had food supplies distributed in every district for as long as possible, then ordered them to be diverted to Alexandria, which was now in a full state of emergency. Because of the shortages, people flooded into the city and surrounding area, fleeing the countryside along the Nile, where food was scarce. There were riots, with plundering and raids in many districts. It was basically a very difficult period, which she managed to overcome, however.

As the months and years went by, the rivalry with her brother got worse. In truth, it wasn't just the two of them but also and above all two contrasting "teams" of counselors behind them, who were plotting to consign the opposing regent to obscurity.

This is where all Cleopatra's intelligence and subtle political skill emerged. We know from a stele that in 51 BC she sailed on the Nile to Hermonthis to take there the new sacred bull, Buchis, after the previous one had died. According to the ancient Egyptians, bulls were the reincarnation of the supreme divinity, the sun god, Amun-Ra. Moreover, Cleopatra had made generous donations to various Egyptian cults across the kingdom. It was a way of strengthening her bond with the country's religion, by pleasing the kingdom's two great protagonists, the priests (as we've already said) and the people, who saw her more and more as a protector. Ptolemy XIII, on the other hand, spoke only Greek, and was therefore confined to the Hellenic circles that permeated the city of Alexandria.

Escape to the Desert

An interesting episode took place in 49 BC, when Egypt had gotten involved in the civil war between Caesar and Gnaeus Pompeius Magnus. The latter had sent one of his sons, Gnaeus Pompeius, to ask Cleopatra for ships and grain, and she had responded by providing sixty ships loaded with grain and five hundred Roman legionaries, chosen among those stationed in Egypt. Rumors subsequently circulated about the meeting between Cleopatra and Gnaeus Pompeius, according to which she gave herself to the young Gneus, the son of the Pompey who seemed to all intents and purposes like the future winner of the civil war. However, this is probably malicious gossip circulated after Cleopatra's death in order to discredit her in the eyes of history and paint her as a sort of "Egyptian Messalina" (and, to be fair, Messalina wasn't at all the lascivious figure we have inherited and was also the victim of a smear campaign). Cleopatra did not have sex with Gneus.

Still, it was the support provided to Pompey that triggered an insurrection among the Alexandrians, who, tested by a bad year for the harvest and the terrible ensuing famine, had accused the young queen of selling out Egypt (and its grain) to the Romans. As you can imagine, the three powerful "tutors" jumped on the bandwagon of the protest and fueled the fire, taking advantage of the difficult period the country was going through.

In 48 BC Cleopatra was forced to flee Alexandria, and the trio used this moment to put her brother, Ptolemy XIII, a boy easy to manipulate, on the throne.

It's a little known but impressive escape. In a long march made up of several stages, Cleopatra had crossed the eastern border of the kingdom, crossed Palestine, and stopped in southern Syria. In the end, she encamped in the middle of the desert, barricaded in a tent with an army of mercenaries that protected her on all sides (we don't know where she'd obtained the money to pay them)—a scene seldom seen in history, which sounds more like something from an episode of *Star Wars*, and, if you think about it, the ingredients of our great story about Cleopatra do bear a strong resemblance: "imperial" fleets, deserts, queens at war, rebels, camp battles with masses of exterminated soldiers and vehicles, heroic actions by individual men, charismatic women, betrayal, sumptuous palaces, sudden attacks, and hasty escapes, except that instead of the universe and planets for hiding or fighting, like Naboo and Hoth, there's the

Mediterranean with its islands and coastlines. The amount of action and drama in history, with its repeated *coups de scène* at every moment, is almost identical.

Don't be annoyed with me for this deliberately provocative comparison, since it's intended to show how history can sometimes go beyond imagination, even that of the most highly paid Hollywood screenwriters. None of them has ever succeeded in matching the story of Cleopatra, albeit having access to the best special effects and the most fervid creativity, because every page of her life is even more astonishing than the previous one, and involves us in the story. If we didn't know that she really existed, a film about her would not be very plausible. The real events truly outshine fiction. So what can possibly happen now to a queen barricaded in the middle of the desert?

Pompey's Severed Head

In chess, if she were the king in a corner, with just a few pawns to protect her, we would all assume that there's an imminent checkmate. Ptolemy XIII had traveled with his powerful army, drawing up in Pelusium, located in Lower Egypt, next to Gaza, in the Sinai area, at the far northeast of the Delta, thereby blocking her way, ready to attack. He was just one step away from killing her.

And yet, almost like a life lesson to us all, it's just a matter of waiting and enduring, because the events themselves alter a desperate situation and open a crack (which you must, however, be capable of glimpsing). This is the case for Cleopatra.

Because there weren't only two players (she and her brother) on her chessboard, but several others, and one of these suddenly burst in and, unwittingly, changed the cards on the table. His name is Pompeus Magnus. He has just been defeated by Julius Caesar at the battle fought on August 9, 48 BC, in Pharsalus in Greece, in the Thessaly area to be exact, and is fleeing by ship. He heads to Egypt, to Cleopatra's brother's encampment, relying on and hoping for his support, because Pompey helped their father, Ptolemy Auletes, when exiled in Rome, and received, as we said, the promise of huge payments. Pompey, sure of his immense credit, is not only hoping for the young king's protection but is planning to rebuild his power by exploiting the wealthy Egyptian kingdom. But things will turn out differently.

It's September 28, 48 BC. As soon as Cleopatra's brother sees Pompey's ships, he sends him a small boat to bring him to shore. On it are Achillas, the supreme commander of the Egyptian troops, and two Roman soldiers: Salvius, a centurion, and Lucius Septimius, whom Pompey recognizes, having fought under his command in previous campaigns. There is silence—a strange silence—when he comes aboard. Pompey doesn't know it but his murder has been planned. The boat approaches the shore. From the galleys at large, Pompey's friends and his wife, Cornelia, who are anxiously watching the events, take heart when they see many of the king's courtiers running onto the beach in sign of greeting and homage. Pompey stands up, but right at that moment, Septimius strikes him in the back with his sword, as do Achillas and the centurion Salvius. Pompey covers his face with his toga and collapses, still showered with blows. What follows is horrifying. As the writer Lucan says, "The merciless Septimius [. . .] tears off the veil, uncovers the venerable face of the dying Pompey, grabs the head, which still has breath in it, and rests the neck, abandoned by now, across one of the rowers' benches. He then severs the nerves and veins, and, with repeated blows, breaks the vertebrae—they didn't yet know how to separate the head from the bust with just one cut of the sword. [. . .] that hair, made even more beautiful by his noble brow, was violently seized with one hand and—while the face still bore marks of life, the mouth was still murmuring a rattle, and the eyes, wide-open, were stiffening—a pole was stuck under the head [. . .]. This is how, with execrable technique, the blood, humors, and brain were removed from the head, the skin was dried, and everything that could have rotted taken away, and, with the help of a poisonous concoction, the face solidified."

Why did Ptolemy XIII order Pompey's assassination? In order to secure the goodwill of Caesar, the new rising star. By now, Pompey was a loser; his severed head was prepared and preserved so as to constitute proof of his royal murder, to be shown to Caesar. And, just four days later, in pursuit of Pompey, Caesar docks at Alexandria on October 2 with ten warships and 4,000 men (about 3,200 infantrymen and 800 cavalrymen). He is welcomed not by the teenage king but by his delegation with the rector Theodotus at its head—perhaps the best man for finding the right words in these delicate circumstances. He shows him Pompey's ring, with a lion holding a sword. Then, from a wooden box, the macabre trophy emerges. Caesar's reaction, however, is not as hoped. On the contrary.

Caesar weeps before Pompey's severed and "restored" head (or pretends to, since Ptolemy has actually done him a favor by physically eliminating his powerful adversary). In any case, this is a very serious event: Pompey, a powerful and acclaimed son of Rome, has been killed by a foreign king without consulting the Senate or even Caesar. This is one of the most odious crimes for a Roman like Caesar, who rages against Ptolemy XIII and his delegation. He insults them, orders them to cover the head with all the required honors, and gives instructions for Pompey's remains to be returned to Cornelia, who, according to Plutarch, "put them into her property in Alba" (now Albano Laziale, near Rome).

The rector Theodotus manages to escape Caesar's wrath. He flees Egypt but then, through a strange twist of history, will be found by one of Caesar's assassins (Brutus or Cassius, it's not very clear) and put to death.

Caesar takes up residence in the royal palace, to prove that Egypt is no longer a powerful kingdom but just a Roman protectorate. He almost certainly has a bath where Cleopatra is now, then summons both siblings to try to decide which to support. In practice, he has become the referee in this dynastic struggle. Ptolemy refuses to go, considering it an affront that a Roman general should command him to appear before him. As for Cleopatra, she is in the middle of the desert and would be willing to meet him but is afraid that during her journey, away from her troops, a mercenary sent by her brother might attack and kill her.

Cleopatra's Beauty and Cunning

Cleopatra is now undressing before her bath. The white linen robe immediately falls to the floor without making a sound. All that remains is the queen's naked body. The white linen on the floor and Cleopatra's curves remind us of a candle, a flame undulating on melted wax. It's a seductive, toned, and beautifully proportioned body. Her breasts are full although not large, her buttocks firm and well-formed, and her small waist emphasizes her wide hips. Her skin is very smooth, and the total absence of hair on her body makes the queen look like a statue. Petite but perfect. But it's not just Cleopatra's appearance that gives her that incredible sensuality. Although her body is pleasant to look at, there's nothing rare or extraordinary about its beauty. Unfortunately, we don't have any specific descriptions of her body, but judging by what the ancients wrote about her (often without having seen her, after her death, clearly reporting other people's descriptions or common assumptions), we can imagine that what makes Cleopatra a woman superior to any other is not so much her body as the way she uses it. In practice, when she activates it with her movements, voice, and intelligence. And this affects everyone. Like a musical instrument, seeing it is one thing but listening to it is another. Similarly, if we believe the ancients, Cleopatra showers whoever is near her with unexpected music, becomes pure grace, and conveys an unusual feminine symphony. What's bewitching is the elegance of her movements, the gentle way she proffers her hand, for instance, or turns her head when called, as well as the pride in her poise. If we add to this her soft way of speaking and her insight, we can immediately see why she makes a breach in the mentality of the manly Roman used to dominating women. Like Paris, Cleopatra aims her arrow at the bare heel of this man as swiftly and dangerously as a scorpion.

She takes just a few steps toward the bathtub, a small pool in a room clad with precious marbles. She makes one final, very natural gesture, as though lost in thought: she reaches out with her foot to try the water temperature. Then she slowly goes down the steps into the tub. The reflection of her naked, swaying body is perfect and very sensual, but only for a moment before shattering into a thousand fluid shards, created by the ripples in the water as she enters it. First, her calves disappear, then her harmonious thighs. Her hips and stomach slide elegantly into the tub, as though slipping on a new garment. She stops for a moment when her breasts brush against the surface, allowing the water to embrace her gently. Then she immerses herself.

A specific memory surfaces in her eyes and mind, a memory that's sweet as well as dramatic. During those terrible days in the desert, facing the dilemma set by Caesar's invitation, it was water that proved her most valuable ally in solving her problem.

Cleopatra thinks back on those anxious hours, spent in the tent with her closest advisers. Her only hope, in the middle of the desert, was to meet Caesar and obtain his support before her brother did. But how? Going to Alexandria was very risky. During the journey, she and her delegation would have been too vulnerable a prey for mercenaries sent by her brother, so she devised a bold but very risky plan. No one would have imagined that the queen could travel incognito, without guards or retinue. No one would therefore have taken notice of an ordinary boat with two passengers on board, a man and woman, arriving in the port of Alexandria at dusk. And that's what she did. She secretly left with her most loyal servant, Apollodorus the Sicilian.

The Famous Meeting with Julius Caesar

Imagine therefore this boat entering Alexandria's eastern port at night and drawing close to the royal palace walls. But the real stroke of genius is yet to come. There's a serious risk that the palace guards may recognize her. Apollodorus brings her inside in a hemp sack, the kind used for storing blankets or rugs (an incorrect translation of the text in ancient Greek made many believe that she had been rolled into a rug). As soon as they reach land, Apollodorus puts a strap around the sack with the queen inside it, puts it over his shoulder, and heads to the palace. This episode tells us two things: that Apollodorus must have been a robust man to be the queen's bodyguard and carry her a long distance, and, at the same time, Cleopatra must have been a slender, short if not tiny woman, like so many in antiquity (in Roman times, the average height of a woman was five feet one).

He somehow gets past the guards (by bribing them handsomely? Showing himself to those who were loyal to them?—we don't know), walks into the palace gardens and then Caesar's apartments with the excuse of having to take him a gift.

Hence the famous scene of the meeting between Caesar and Cleopatra depicted in so many movies. No doubt you will all remember the 1963 feature with Elizabeth Taylor emerging from an unrolled rug in front of an astonished (and timeless) Rex Harrison in the role of Caesar.

It might be the most spectacular meeting in history between two leaders. What happened exactly? Did Cleopatra really come out of a sack after a journey that must have been at least uncomfortable, if not exhausting? According to Cassius Dio, she found a way of making herself presentable, attractive, and, above all, regal. "She adorned herself and dressed her hair in such a way as to appear as a woman worthy of both the utmost admiration and the utmost pity." The scholar Stacy Schiff thinks that after such a journey it's highly improbable that Cleopatra had "decent" hair; it's more likely she would have worn a royal diadem on her head to show her regality. We can try to imagine these moments, Cleopatra suddenly appearing before Caesar and, acting before the general has a chance to get over his surprise, giving her all in terms of sensuality, grace, regality, and words (she certainly must have prepared a perfect speech). Only the ancients can help us here. Plutarch highlights the fact that "Caesar was struck by this initial stratagem of Cleopatra, who appeared nonchalant, and charmed by her conversation and grace." Once again, Cassius Dio provides more detail. "She was a truly beautiful woman, and, being then in the flower of her youth, was in full splendor; she had a very gentle voice and could converse with anyone most amiably. That is why she fascinated whoever saw and listened to her, and she could subjugate any man, even one who might have been disinclined to love and of a somewhat advanced age"—precisely like Caesar.

But what language were they speaking? Greek, naturally, Cleopatra's mother tongue, which Caesar spoke perfectly. And the true "elixir" that ensnared and seduced Caesar was her voice, as Cassius Dio confirms. "No sooner did Caesar see her and hear her speak than he was immediately so fascinated that, without wasting time before dawn, he sent for Ptolemy and tried to get them reconciled: and so while earlier he had declared himself Cleopatra's judge, he was now taking her defense."

The First Night of Love

Cleopatra has come out of the bath and dried her body, toned by the cool water, with snow-white linen cloths that have captured every drop running down her skin. She is now on a marble bed, covered in cloths and cushions. There are oil lamps in the corners of the room and on the ceiling, and braziers scent the air with frankincense mixed with other Eastern essences. Sunbeams struggle to penetrate two windows, shielded by very fine silk curtains that rise with every breath of the sea breeze.

Skillful hands are massaging her. She is lying down, displaying all the sensuality of her back, while amber hands and fingers travel down her body desired by so many, thumbs lingering on the two provocative hollows in the lower back. The experienced, regular movements dissolve the long-stored tension in every muscle, every inch of skin. Cleopatra shuts her eyes. In her memory, the hands touching her now belong to Caesar, strong, determined, capable of giving death but also love. She remembers perfectly the shudder throughout her body whenever his hand caressed her shoulder. A hand full of desire, that firmly drew her to him, to his manly body, holding her in an intense embrace that made her drop all defenses, enveloped as she was in the daze of this smell—so masculine—of his skin.

Did all this also happen *that* night? Cleopatra smiles and reveals nothing . . .

According to many stories, at that very moment there was a spark between them, followed by an entire night of passion and sex. Though we can't be certain of this, according to many scholars, and at the risk of disappointing many lovers of Cleopatra and Caesar . . . there was no consummation that night.

Not so much thanks to Caesar, who was an unrepentant womanizer, but Cleopatra, who was barely twenty-one years old. Caesar was just over fifty and would have appeared somewhat elderly to her ("old enough to be her father," people often say, but perhaps even her grandfather, given antiquity's precocious childbirths). That certainly wasn't what stopped Cleopatra. Let's remember that at the time this kind of age gap was very common, especially in politically motivated arranged marriages. Something much more technical could explain the absence of sex that night. As we said, the Ptolemaic dynasty stipulated marriage between brothers and sisters, and procreation often took place between them (Cleopatra was probably an exception, since her mother had perhaps been one of the king's concubines). Given that Cleopatra's brother and first husband, Ptolemy XIII, was only fifteen, and considering their disagreements from the very beginning, it's unlikely that they ever had intercourse. In other words, on the night when she met Caesar, Cleopatra was almost certainly still a virgin and not inclined to give herself easily. That was the reason for her refusal.

But there were also the fate of her kingdom and her own safety at stake, and perhaps even the male charm of a great conqueror in battle and in bed. A seducer with graying hair (and then some), manly, protective, in the style of Sean Connery or George Clooney. Moreover, a man of power and success, probably more attractive characteristics than his sex appeal, especially for Cleopatra, who, as we said, was twenty-one (quite old at an age when girls had their first pregnancies at fifteen) and had to choose a man worthy of her status as queen and also woman. Between Julius Caesar and her fifteen-year-old brother, the choice is self-evident. Finally, Cleopatra was going for broke. She had risked her life to get to the royal palace and had to persuade Caesar to support and protect her. Knowing her, her impetuousness, and her subtle strategies, it's equally possible and even probable that she might have given herself to him that night, bypassing the obstacle in favor of her heart. It's in character with Cleopatra.

In any case, if it wasn't that night then it would have been one of the following ones, since she probably got pregnant with Caesar's child after a few months.

Being a virgin or at least inexperienced (we'll never know), she might have been a little shy and awkward on her first night of love. Nobody could imagine Cleopatra like that, and yet she was still a woman who had to go through life's various stages like all normal people, with anxieties, fears, and doubts, a side of her we tend to forget, always picturing her in her *femme fatale* role, aggressive and very experienced.

Whatever happened, Caesar may have been the first man to guide her in the discovery of the pleasures of sex. They say that from that night on, the two of them became inseparable lovers, and it truly is a great, beautiful love story. But how much attraction and overwhelming passion was there? And how much was mere convenience? Neither of them was naïve. They knew all too well that there was something more than kisses. To Caesar, Cleopatra was a determined, independent sovereign, therefore much more reliable than her brother. Above all, their strong bond allowed him to control her better. On the other hand, to Cleopatra, Caesar was a powerful ally on whom she could rely in order to ascend the throne and stay there permanently.

Besides passion, it was also pure convenience that kept them together.

Her Brother's Reaction

Cleopatra has been very clever and brave, let's be honest. She risked her life, first by coming to Alexandria without an escort, then by entering the palace concealed in a sack. She had no idea how Caesar would react to her sudden appearance . . . and yet she gambled—and won. The meeting with Caesar clearly illustrates the nature of a woman who would prove capable of scaring the Senate and the Romans. Cleopatra can defy destiny with strength, determination, ambition, and a life force that even over two thousand years are very impressive and make her one of a kind. Partly because, every time, she's alone, and needs to obtain consent by fighting for it tooth and claw, because nobody gives her anything for nothing. Moreover, she's a woman in a man's world, which makes her a truly exceptional human being.

The move to meet Caesar by surprise, that gamble, turns out to be a political success.

When her brother, Ptolemy XIII, arrives at the palace to meet Caesar, he discovers that his sister, whom he believed still to be barricaded in a tent in the desert, has preceded him and ended the game. Worse still, there's love at first sight between her and Caesar. Imagine his astonishment and anger at seeing Cleopatra (who, in theory, is also first and foremost his wife) with the Roman general.

Ptolemy realizes he's lost and has an adolescent outburst, which is described by Dio as follows: "He lost his temper and, running among the people, started to shout that he was betrayed and in the end tore the diadem off his head and threw it aside." The historian continues by saying how this *coup de scène* unleashed a true uprising in Alexandria, to the point that "Caesar's soldiers abducted the young man, while the Egyptians were in revolt and attacked the royal palace both from the land and the sea."

The crowd calms down only after Caesar convenes an assembly and reads in public the will of Ptolemy Auletes, the father of Cleopatra and the young king, which states that the two of them are to rule together in accordance with Ptolemaic tradition, and under the guardianship of the Roman people. Caesar is cornered: he has few men, and there's an entire city against him and a powerful Egyptian army ready to attack him. He is therefore forced to grant a further concession in order to calm everybody down. On his own initiative, he gives the island of Cyprus to Cleopatra's younger siblings, Arsinoe and Ptolemy the younger, who had been excluded from the will. We will hear more about them later . . .

Cyprus is essential on the Mediterranean chessboard, as a true "deposit" of resources for Egypt. Thanks to the copper mines, it allows the monopoly of this metal and, with its forests, enables a mainly desert territory to have an abundance of timber.

To Assassinate Caesar and Cleopatra at the Banquet

In order to seal the reconciliation, they unanimously decide to organize a lavish banquet over the following days. There is still fire smoldering under the ashes, however. Young Ptolemy XIII has officially agreed to the deal, but his counselors, Pothinus and Achillas (Theodotus has run away, meanwhile), are much more astute than the young king, and begin to plot. They discreetly call back the Ptolemaic army, which has been watching Cleopatra's now empty tent for weeks. (Who knows? Maybe her loyal lady-in-waiting has been dressing like her for days, and remained in the tent so as to make potential spies believe that the queen was still there.) More to the point, they organize a plot. The aim is to kill Caesar and Cleopatra during the banquet.

They know very well that Caesar is just stalling, and that he will eventually end up eating his words and giving Cleopatra the throne. This for them means the end of power; they will be excluded from the rule of the kingdom, since not only is Cleopatra an adult and has no need for tutors but she is also hostile toward them.

On the day of the banquet, everything is organized with great lavishness and regal perfection. Sophisticated foods are served on tables sumptuously set with precious dishes, while expensive wine flows into cups. Meanwhile, in the inner rooms of the palace, away from prying eyes, the material executors of the killing are perhaps meeting with Achillas himself to pick the right moment to act. It isn't easy, given the large number of legionaries on guard, but the murderers are playing "at home," so to speak, because they know the palace, how to avoid surveillance and strike the two chosen victims at lightning speed. There's just one problem, and he looks like a harmless character: Caesar's personal barber. He's an anxious man, afraid of everything, and notices anything that doesn't look right. That includes strange conversations. According to Plutarch, it is he who, while the others are eating and celebrating, discovers the imminent conspiracy by chance, perhaps by listening behind a door or perhaps, unseen, glimpsing Achillas talking to armed men hiding in a room. We don't know. In any case, he immediately warns Caesar, who has an explosive reaction.

Imagine the scene. No sooner does he hear the news, probably whispered in his ear by the said barber, than he immediately calls his legionaries and commands them to surround the hall. Then, in the general silence, his eyes flashing with anger, he orders a centurion to kill the unsuspecting Pothinus, and the soldier runs him through with a brusque motion. For a moment, the man remains motionless, as though frozen. Then everybody starts to scream, having witnessed firsthand the death of the shrewd counselor, and rushes out of the room, leaving Pothinus's body on the floor, prey to its final convulsions. Achillas, the chief of the Ptolemaic troops, is immediately sought, but he has managed to disappear and join his army, triggering the so-called Siege of Alexandria.

With this conspiracy, it's impossible not to think of the one of which Caesar would be the victim back home four years later. In this case, he was unaware of the plot, and yet his reaction had been swift. In Rome, on the Ides of March, on the other hand, he knew people were plotting against him, perhaps he even read his philosopher friend's message, and yet, unbelievably, he remained inactive. Why? It's a question to which scholars have been searching for an answer for a long time. But the only one who could provide it is Caesar himself.

The Siege of Alexandria: Cleopatra Barricaded with Caesar

You've noticed how every single corner of this palace reminds Cleopatra of the past and her affair with Caesar.

With a very delicate touch, the loyal Eiras spreads nourishing cream on Cleopatra's face, marked by the long sea journey and anxiety. Eiras is assisted by an entire team of handmaidens who take care of the queen's body and appearance, while she tells them about what happened in Rome and the difficult return to her country.

Only now that she can allow herself some relaxation does Cleopatra start to feel all the tiredness accumulated over the past weeks of tension and distress. While she's lying down and the handmaidens take care of her hands and feet (using henna to paint her nails), her eyes focus on a detail on the paneled ceiling. There's a large chip in the gilded timber. Nobody has noticed it, or else it hasn't been fixed yet. It was there that, four years ago, a stone ball hit it, hurled by a war machine. She's suddenly assaulted by the feelings of those months of fear, when she and Caesar were besieged with little hope of surviving.

The war lasted only six months, but it was one of the most difficult, even according to Caesar. Maybe it was because the enemy was not an army deployed in the open field but a monster created by the intrigues and politics of the Alexandria palace.

When he first landed in Egypt, Caesar had no way of knowing what a snake pit he was getting into.

Achillas had joined his army and the command was straightforward: surround the city and attack it. There were not only Ptolemaic troops but also a band of marauders and pirates from the provinces of Syria and Cilicia, as well as many men sentenced to death or exile, and many slaves who'd escaped from Roman dominions and who were not pursued if they enlisted. A total of 20,000 men (in addition to the city's population, stirred up by the news that Caesar was holding the young Ptolemy XIII prisoner). Caesar, who had only 4,000 legionaries, gave the order to barricade the royal palace by fortifying it, erecting barriers, and turning it into a fortress. Even the two emissaries he sent to negotiate met a dismal end. One of them was killed, the other gravely wounded. Then the attack began with a "rain of arrows falling on the palace," as the writer Lucan says. Then there were waves of frightening, violent but disorganized mass assaults that the experienced legionaries managed to block and push back. Arsinoe, Cleopatra's younger sister, suddenly ran away from the palace to join the rebels and was, by the rule of the mob, elected the new queen of Egypt. This made the situation more complicated. As the historian Michael Grant underlines, "this was a serious blow for Caesar, since it meant that the war could no longer be regarded as a purely private revolt against royal authority." He was caught up in the middle of a struggle for power to secure the throne of Egypt.

In the hours, days, and weeks that followed, many things happened that are now going around Cleopatra's mind. Like when Caesar realized that the death trap was about to close in on them. They were surrounded by land but not yet by sea; the palace was being attacked from the alleys and surrounding districts, while behind him, there was the royal harbor and the open sea. If the Alexandrians had captured Egyptian ships anchored outside the harbor, they would have surrounded the Romans completely and prevented any contact with the rest of the world. Caesar swiftly ordered the Roman ships to row out of the port and attack the Egyptian ones, setting them alight with arrows coated in pitch. However, encouraged by the wind, the fire spread from the ships to the arsenals and then to the houses by the sea. According to popular belief, it was on this occasion that the Library of Alexandria was destroyed. In actual fact, scholars now concur in refuting this historical howler (if that had been the case, many educated men in antiquity, like Strabo and Didymus, would not have been able to consult it just a few years later, under Augustus). What was destroyed, though, were apparently a few storerooms near the harbor that, according to the historian Luciano Canfora, contained books bound for export. Caesar did not stop. Taking advantage of the chaos created by the fire, he occupied the lighthouse with a rapid night action, thereby controlling the entrance to the port and sending calls for help.

Arsinoe, the new queen of the enemy camp, had the commander Achillas killed and put in his stead one of her most loyal men, Ganimede, who devised an evil trick. Using large machines, he introduced a huge amount of seawater into the water supply of the area where the royal palace stood, so that its drinking water would gradually become unfit for purpose. But Caesar had wells dug and handled the problem thanks to his legionaries, who, as well as being skilled soldiers able to defend the city, were also engineers, blacksmiths, and carpenters capable of building roads, aqueducts, and wells.

Another recollection, linked to this one, returns vividly to Cleopatra's mind: an episode in which Caesar risked dying. And it's as though time was turning back to that day . . .

From the top of the royal palace, Cleopatra watches Caesar and his men trying to conquer the long breakwater that connects the lighthouse to dry land (the famous Heptastadion). They cover it all then, very quickly, start building a barricade to prevent access to the city by the Egyptians. Only the fast approaching Egyptian ships behind them threaten to cut off any escape route, so, in a panic, the legionaries backtrack despite Caesar's exhortations, diving into the water, rushing en masse to their ships along the breakwater. Even Caesar ends up boarding his ship but is followed by so many men that the vessel capsizes and sinks straight to the bottom, dragging many men with it. Only at the last minute does he manage to dive into the water with his heavy armor and swim almost 220 yards, beneath enemy arrows, and apparently even managing to keep some of his notes above water. Today, there are many doubts about this particular detail, told by Plutarch. However, considering that he was over fifty, this episode illustrates the fact that he was a man of action as well as a man of physical strength. It isn't an old man Cleopatra has before her but a man at the height of his power. It's also possible that his relationship with the queen may even have invigorated him, leading him to extremely risky but important feats . . . Especially if he knew she was watching him from the palace.

In the end, as Cleopatra well remembers, safety arrived with the much-awaited reinforcements he had asked for. It was not a formation of Roman legions that appeared at the Egyptian border, however, but a king, Mithridates of Pergamon, at the head of a heterogeneous army gathered in Asia Minor, Syria, and Arabia. There was also a large contingent of Judean troops commanded by the supreme priest Antipater, supporters of Caesar because they were hostile to Pompey.

Meanwhile, Caesar had cunningly freed the boy king Ptolemy XIII to create confusion among his adversaries. (Who would rule—the boy king or the new queen, Arsinoe?) A few days later, the two formations had clashed in the Delta, in a location not far from the city, called Land of Onias. Caesar and his soldiers joined the "savior" army. Before them stood the entire Egyptian contingent, commanded by the boy king. The battle raged for hours, but in the end Caesar's formation won, making their adversaries flee. Ptolemy XIII, who had also fought with honor, had quickly fled and boarded a ship which, however, sank from excessive weight. Ptolemy had ended up in the water but, unlike Caesar, had drowned because of the weight of his golden armor.

That evening, Caesar returned to the city, acclaimed by all the residents (the same ones who wanted him dead that very morning). He then had Arsinoe captured and arrested and, as we've seen, she was paraded in chains during his triumph in Rome.

Caesar actually did not want Egypt, a strategically important land for its grain and raw materials, to become a province, thus risking it being assigned to an untrustworthy, greedy, and unscrupulous governor, seeing that these positions were always picked from among senators, with all that involved of friendships, nepotism, business, and personal ambitions.

He therefore decided to leave a large military contingent there, made up of three legions (the XXVII, the XXXVII, and another, unspecified) under the command of a trusted man called Rufio, or Gaius Iulius Rufio. He was the "son of one of his freedmen and his lover," Suetonius wrote, using precisely the jargon word *exoletus*, which refers to passive adult homosexuals.

It's odd that Caesar should have a wife in Rome, Calpurnia, and at least two lovers of different sexes in Alexandria—a woman, Cleopatra, and a man, Rufio. But perhaps this is just an exaggeration.

From that moment on, only Cleopatra was left on the throne of Egypt, and in keeping with tradition, Caesar symbolically brought her together in ruling with the last brother she had left: Ptolemy XIV.

Love with Caesar and the Honeymoon Cruise

With these last images in mind, Cleopatra opens her eyes again. Her makeup is finished, and Eiras and the girls are holding a mirror up to her, anxiously waiting for her judgment of their work. The queen nods approvingly. The makeup is perfect. But she has other things on her mind. For the first time in Alexandria, she sees her face emerging from the shining bronze surface, as though appearing out of the mists. She doesn't recognize it. She realizes that her eyes are dull, lacking the vitality that has always fascinated everybody. Those who know her have probably noticed but didn't tell her, to protect her. She will now have to wear a "mask," appear determined and full of energy, and conceal her feelings, the infinite sadness that almost turns to deep despair, and above all her fear of the future. Only she and her lady-in-waiting Charmion, whose arms have often cradled her tears as an ordinary woman and not a queen, will know the truth of her soul. Nobody else. It would be a disaster for everyone if her vulnerability were to surface, especially Caesarion. The thought of her carefree son playing and smiling at her triggers within her unexpected strength and determination. She takes a deep breath, stands up, and leaves with a resolute step.

But her steadfastness doesn't last long and crumbles at every step; destiny is after her and attacks her like a predator. Every room, staircase, and window reminds her of Caesar, his voice, his embrace, his optimism about the future even in the darkest moments of the siege. It's his very optimism and confidence that she now misses, like air to breathe.

It's not surprising. Caesar and Cleopatra experienced the beginning of their love affair in this palace, perhaps the most beautiful on the Mediterranean, in the worst possible conditions, surrounded by the enemy and afraid of being killed. She clearly remembers running at breakneck speed through the porticos, or else suddenly waking up in the middle of the night, with guards clutching their swords, quickly escorting her to a safer part of the residence. It's more a huge castle than a palace, a true gilded district with squares, pavilions, gardens, galleries, and fountains. Everything is built with lavish, splendid Hellenistic taste. Living their passionate love affair in this extraordinary setting, with the terror of dying that day or the next, fueled their relationship in a very unusual, sublime, intense way. So many times, overwhelmed with fear during an attack, they pledged everlasting love to each other, while soldiers around them were shouting and arrows and stone balls were falling everywhere. Their relationship was based on uninterrupted, intense, deep passion. Fiery nights before an attack. Infinite embraces afterward. Kisses stolen behind a pillar. Cleopatra remembers clearly Caesar's chest pressing against her body, as his mouth and hands conquered her with a heat few men granted her.

So many times, she gently stroked her lover's neck. These moments of great passion, which no author ever wrote about, but which we imagine did happen, fueled by love, the joy of being alive, and the fear of death, all blossomed in this place that no longer exists. Now there are only anonymous buildings, restaurants, and shops. Cleopatra, Caesar, the legionaries, Alexandria, and all its residents (mothers, children, sailors, servants, the Musaeum philosophers) have vanished and not even their bones remain, except in rare cases. But they've left us an extraordinary story. A story we are trying to piece together.

Caesar arrives in Alexandria on October 2, 48 BC, as we've said, so let's continue with our story, assuming that Caesarion is Caesar's son and that he was born the following June (47 BC), which means that Cleopatra would have gotten pregnant in October, so practically very early on in her relationship with Caesar (maybe even on the first day?). According to the historian Michael Grant, she was already certain of it by December. Everything seems to fit together perfectly in the splendid design of an extraordinary love story. We must stress that quite a few scholars these days believe that Caesarion was not Caesar's son, thus bringing out in Cleopatra a sinister skill for political calculation and propaganda.

We can all imagine the couple waking up in the morning in an enormous bed, their bodies wrapped in colored silk blankets, surrounded by countless cushions, Cleopatra's head on Caesar's muscular chest as he slowly caresses her. A beautiful picture of one of history's most famous love affairs.

But that wasn't the way things were.

Caesar and Cleopatra slept separately, which is in no way surprising. In ancient Rome and privileged classes in the past, even not long ago, husband and wife almost always slept in separate bedrooms, possibly partly because marriages were arranged and not love matches. It was a different custom than ours, which Cleopatra and Caesar followed, even though they spent the rest of the day together. But there was also another reason. Grant himself emphasizes the fact that during those months it was particularly important to spend the night in separate wings of the palace, if not in different buildings. During the siege, it was suspected that there might be traitors and assassins inside the palace. Just like when modern royals travel on different planes to avoid any disasters that would wipe out the whole family at once. It was therefore more prudent to sleep in buildings far apart, surrounded by a barrier of bodyguards and trusted men.

It is therefore highly probable that Caesar would have retired to a pavilion protected by his officers, and the young Ptolemy XIII to another home with his large court (made up of members of Alexandria's prominent families, as well as infamous prime minister Pothinus). On the other hand, there were probably not many people with Cleopatra, since all the Alexandrians of consequence were probably thinking that she was a step away from political and physical elimination, so she would have been surrounded by just a few trusted people. Moreover, her court was still in the desert or at least across the border. In this, too, Cleopatra proved that she could always tackle a difficult situation head-on. She could perhaps be called, in the most intimate sense, a queen facing history on her own.

When the war was over, however, on March 27, 47 BC, Cleopatra and Caesar treated themselves to some time just for themselves. Many historians (even Napoleon Bonaparte) have been surprised by this break Caesar granted himself despite the problems in his country. He hadn't been to Rome for a year now, and people were complaining about Antony's actions because, taking advantage of his role as head of Italy in Caesar's absence, he was managing the property confiscated from Pompey to his own exclusive advantage in an attempt at self-promotion. Moreover, although he had beaten his enemies at Pharsalus and Pompey had been defeated, the Republican forces were still active and far from tamed. These months of waiting were a danger, and nobody could explain Caesar's absence, except Caesar himself and Cleopatra.

By now the two of them were Egypt's absolute rulers, and with great reciprocal advantages. Cleopatra financially supported Caesar's political ambitions, and in exchange he supported her in controlling the kingdom. That was when they decided to carve themselves a real dream, a fairy-tale trip together—a cruise down the Nile.

This certainly was a unique event in the history of the Mediterranean. Two of the most famous figures in history taking a romantic trip in one of the most fascinating places on the planet. It's like something out of a novel. And yet it truly happened. Anybody who's been to Egypt knows what a sunset over the pyramids or on the Nile, by Luxor, means, with a red sky and sailboats sliding calmly on a surface like a mirror. Well, imagine this atmosphere with Caesar embracing Cleopatra from the back and kissing her neck. No ancient writer has ever told us this, but we can imagine it must have happened very often.

Caesar's decision to linger in Egypt, however, was only irrational in appearance. The country had only just been pacified and he wanted to make sure there were no more disturbances after he returned to

Rome, and was checking firsthand the mood of the people, that of the priests, and the situation in the countryside. Also partly because as far as Caesar was concerned, Egypt with Cleopatra on the throne was an essential source of income. Also for Rome, with its supply of grain.

However, his decision was influenced by other elements too. Few people realize that Caesar wasn't just a soldier and a man in command but also an extremely inquisitive character very interested in geography (just read his *commentarii*). The opportunity to explore Egypt and the wonders he'd heard of, like all noble Romans, since he was a boy, must have been an irresistible temptation, the territories along the Nile in particular. He'd said so himself at a banquet, as Lucan reports: "There's nothing I want to know more than the causes—still unknown after so many centuries—that trigger the Nile's overflow, and the matter of its unknown source. If you give me a definite hope of seeing the source of the river I will abandon the civil war."

Finally, Caesar had one last reason for staying in Egypt. A reason with a specific name: Cleopatra. We discover for the umpteenth time this woman's extraordinary gifts of persuasion. Lucan puts it most explicitly: "Cleopatra was able to vanquish the resistance of an old man with her magic arts." Instead of calling it "magic arts," it might be more correct to use terms like *oratorical ability*, *talent for persuasion*, *seduction*, and *sex appeal*. A cocktail of talents that for some reason always turns out to be devastating for Roman military leaders, as we will see with Antony.

The couple left at the beginning of April and "disappeared" for at least three months. Caesar sent no news. He vanished entirely from the radar of politics and command. In Rome, people embarked on all sorts of speculations. For instance, as we know from Cicero, a rumor began to circulate that Caesar was in serious trouble in Egypt, even though he was absolutely fine. The mud-slinging machine had been triggered against him.

Don't expect this to have been a romantic cruise for two. There were many ships, as many as four hundred according to Appian. It was therefore also a military expedition with many soldiers. Above all, it was a political mission to show everybody that Cleopatra had powerful support and thereby to strengthen her position in charge.

Even so, for both of them, the main reason for this trip was a honeymoon to be enjoyed to the very end.

Appian is very clear on this point: "Caesar sailed up the Nile with four hundred ships, visiting the country with Cleopatra and entertaining himself with her in many ways." Without going into the details about the "ways," we can imagine the setting of what was in all effects a honeymoon even though they were not officially married.

The ship on which they set sail was colossal. The Ptolemies owned incredibly luxurious vessels for this kind of journey, the magnificent *thalamegos*.

In his book about Alexandria, of which we have large sections thanks to the Egyptian writer Athenaeus, the Greek historian Callixenus of Rhodes tells us that these ships had flat bottoms suitable for the river, but with tall hulls that rose high into the air: "The upper sides, especially in relation to the prow, were very tall and formed a regular arc." This description already leads us to picture something great, but then we have further astonishing details from other authors. We know that the first example of this ship, ordered by Ptolemy IV, was almost 300 feet long, and taller than a modern seven-story house: about 90 feet. In practice, it was a sailing building, something akin to modern cruise ships or perhaps even more. We could call it a small floating palace.

Just like in modern transatlantic ships, there were outside promenades on several decks, as well as sanctuaries, small gardens, salons, dining rooms, colonnades, and imposing gilded statues. Naturally, the furnishings were extremely luxurious, with an abundance of gold and ivory, fine sculpted timber, decorations, and perhaps even slabs of expensive marble. We can also picture elegant locations for ablutions and baths and, to finish, a sumptuous bedroom for the two lovers.

So picture these vessels stretching along the Nile with, in the center, Caesar and Cleopatra's immense *thalamegos*.

The sailing must have been slow, partly the aim of the voyage, which was a kind of triumphant procession. So the couple experienced one of the happiest times of their lives. Everything was looking up.

Is it possible to retrace the stages of Caesar and Cleopatra's romantic voyage along the Nile? Some historians have tried. After leaving Lake Mariout in Alexandria, the convoy went up the Nile Delta as far as Heliopolis. There, Caesar and Cleopatra admired the pyramids and the Sphinx, which had already been there for about 2,600 years. They were still in perfect condition, with their smooth coating, light and shiny. Who knows what Caesar would have thought? And what would Cleopatra have told him about the history of the pharaohs who had preceded her?

They would have undoubtedly gone to the temples at Karnak. Could Caesar have visited a pharaoh's tomb? A few generations later, many Roman emperors, physicians, and officials passing through Egypt would (their graffiti are still visible on the painted walls). According to the archaeologist and ancient history lecturer Duane W. Roller, Cleopatra and Caesar probably stopped off at Syene, the present Aswan, where Eratosthenes had succeeded in calculating the Earth's circumference. It's easy to picture Caesar's interest. Alexandrian scholars and intellectuals also took part, and it's perhaps there that he got the idea of reforming the calendar. Finally, they stopped off at Elephantine, where Caesar was able to see the Nilometer, depicted in the famous Nile mosaic in Palestrina. It was a structure made up of a ramp of fifty-two steps, with notches along the walls for measuring the water level during the floods. Knowing the level also provided information on the progress of farming.

Suetonius evokes the atmosphere: "[Caesar] especially loved Cleopatra, with whom he often banqueted until dawn, and, on a ship equipped with rooms, he went deep into Egypt and almost as far as Ethiopia, which he would have entered had the army not refused to follow him." Was it his soldiers, then—as in the case of Alexander the Great—who refused to go any farther and persuaded him to turn back? We will never know. But this gives us an idea of how extraordinary this journey was. And also its end.

The trip had to be concluded at the end of May. Caesar received dispatches about the threat of Farnace in the east. Quickly returning to Alexandria, he prepared to go to Syria. He left Egypt at the beginning of June. He left a strong garrison in Alexandria formed of three legions, that is, 12,000 legionaries, under the command of the loyal Rufio (to defend Cleopatra, but also to "control" her movements). He was not present at the birth of his alleged son, which may have taken place two or three weeks later. He did, however, expect Cleopatra and Caesarion in Rome over the following months, unaware that his life would brutally end on March 15, 44 BC . . . with Cleopatra nearby.

So one morning he left, after holding his beloved Cleopatra in his arms one last time and saying goodbye to Egypt and Alexandria, which had become a paradise for him.

A few years later, another man would have the same thoughts: Mark Antony.

How Caesarion Was Born

Walking through the wide corridors of the royal palace, Cleopatra sees in the distance the rooms where she gave birth to Caesarion. She approaches, as though wanting to connect the present with that moment that was so important for her—the birth of her first child. How did a Ptolemaic queen give birth? Like practically all Egyptian women of her time—on her knees.

How do we know it was the same for her? Thanks to a temple she had built in Hermonthis, the city she had been linked to ever since she had ascended the throne because it was also the city where she had taken the sacred bull Buchis. Unfortunately, this temple has been destroyed (dismantled by the Mamluks in order to erect new buildings); it was in perfect Egyptian style and was a "temple of birth" (*mammisi*), which Cleopatra had dedicated to Caesarion. Following an ancient tradition of the pharaohs and their wives, the Ptolemies performed complex rituals relating to the birth of their children. Cleopatra is depicted on her knees, helped by female divinities (we will never know if there was also a male physician, an obstetrician, to assist her during the birth, given the very advanced knowledge in surgery and gynecology of Alexandrian scholars, and also the political delicacy of this particular birth). Above her figure there's the hieroglyphic of her new name, "Mother of Ra" (the sun god), and a scarab above the newborn, to symbolize the fact that Caesarion is the god of the rising sun. A little farther, Caesarion is breastfed by two divinities with the heads of a cow. There's another child with him, the god Horus. An association between two newborn babies, one royal, one divine, had never been seen.

The explanation, however, allows us to understand what Cleopatra had in mind: the god Horus had the mission to avenge the violent death of his father, Osiris. According to Michael Grant, during the Ptolemaic period Horus was still called "avenger of the father." So the queen's message was clear to everyone: Caesarion would avenge Caesar's death. Besides the feud it led to, it was a blatant declaration of intent: Cleopatra was still on Caesar's side and hostile to all those who had killed him or who were pushing for the Republic. The message was also a kind of hand proffered to Antony and his faction on the part of the "Mediterranean granary," that is, Egypt.

But at this moment, the temple probably had not been built yet. For now, Cleopatra has presented Caesarion to everyone as the fruit of hierogamy, that is, of a divine union, and has had coins minted representing her holding the child in her arms. In other words, Caesarion is no longer just her son but a political manifesto that signals to everyone the supporters and alliances of the queen, as well as those to whom she proffers a hand. Temples like the one at Hermonthis and Dendera, where she is always portrayed with Caesarion, are also intended to connect Cleopatra to Egypt's past and its pharaonic traditions. And that's not all. Even the decision to be depicted in a 250-year-old style (like on the coins) carries a clear reference to the "winning" Ptolemaic queens that preceded her, like Arsinoe II, who is still much loved. So Cleopatra wants to recover all that energy, including that of the past, in order to have more strength in her march toward the future.

Cleopatra's Needles

Another example of Cleopatra's skillful "message politics" is the Caesareum, a huge, extraordinary building that looked over the port in Alexandria, a true sanctuary in Caesar's honor, but which Caesar would never see completed. Admired for centuries, it was rich with votive offerings, including silver and gold paintings and statues. Magnificently decorated and enriched with porticos, libraries, rooms, gardens, arcades, wide terraces, and large, open gardens, as described approximately a century later by Philo of Alexandria, a philosopher at the head of the city's Jewish community. There were certainly various statues inside, some made of gold, representing Caesar deified after his death, with priests officiating at rites in his honor. Strangely enough, this temple would not be finished by Cleopatra or Antony, but Octavian, in memory of his adopted father. Finally, there is a curiosity that brings us to the present day. Little remains of this magnificent temple in the modern era, except a few sections of the walls, twelve feet thick, found buried, but if you want to admire an example of its majesty, you can do so by taking a walk in London or in New York. Outside the Caesareum, in 12 BC, Octavian had two giant obelisks erected. He had taken them from the neighboring city of Heliopolis, and they were the work of a great pharaoh from the past, Thutmose III, who had lived 1,400 years before Cleopatra. These rose granite twins from Aswan, carved with hieroglyphics, are sixty feet tall and weigh more than 200 tons each. They are nicknamed "Cleopatra's needles." As time went by they fell, perhaps as a result of an earthquake, and remained buried for centuries. Subsequently found, they were "given" by Egyptian monarchs to nineteenth-century superpowers—to Britain in 1819, in order to strengthen diplomatic relations, and to the USA in 1881 as thanks for the funds it had given for the modernization of Egypt. After complicated journeys across seas and oceans, these two obelisks now stand majestically in the two metropolises—in London along the Thames, and in New York in the middle of Central Park. But how many people, among those on double-decker buses or in cars driving past the obelisk by the Thames, or those jogging with earphones in the New York park, truly realize what they have before them? Or the extraordinary events Cleopatra's needles have witnessed? Very few, unfortunately. The majority just go past these monuments, absorbed in their own thoughts. If they only stopped for a moment, they'd have a chance to take an incredible journey in time.

6

The Battle of Philippi

Starting Again with a Heavy Heart

Caesar is dead. Cleopatra is back in Alexandria. Her principal objective now is to protect herself, Caesarion, and Egypt, because she knows she will have to face new challenges and new threats from outside the country. First and foremost, she reorganizes the administration of the kingdom in order to increase its productivity, because an economically strong country can purchase alliances, build ships, and train fearsome armies. And Cleopatra's politics has always aimed at independence as well as at safeguarding Ptolemaic culture and identity, even though she is aware that she is within a Roman protectorate.

There is also a natural giant that helps the queen: the Nile. An exceptional flood tide brings the kingdom great fertility, and the conviction starts to circulate among the people that a new era is beginning, full of luck and prosperity.

These are months of peace during which Cleopatra has the opportunity to recover and consolidate her position. By her side, on the throne, out of pure respect for tradition, sits the co-regent king, the last of her brothers, Ptolemy XIV, who was in Rome with her when Caesar was assassinated.

But the first clouds begin to gather on the horizon. One of these has the face of her sister Arsinoe. She was the young woman involved in the Siege of Alexandria, and was subsequently paraded in chains in Rome at one of Caesar's triumphs. Seeing her had struck and moved Roman public opinion, and in order to please the people Caesar had set her free. Arsinoe had then taken refuge in the Temple of Artemis in Ephesus, one of the seven wonders of the ancient world. Like many sacred places, the temple guaranteed the immunity and safety of whoever was received there. As a matter of fact, Arsinoe is treated with every honor there, and we know that the high priest of the temple, a eunuch, calls her "queen." The young woman therefore continues to be a menace to Cleopatra. She hasn't ended up in a jail, and is only temporarily on the sidelines in a gilded exile, so there is a concrete threat of her returning to her country, summoned back by her supporters in Alexandria and even at Cleopatra's court.

Another problem is the legions left by Caesar in Alexandria, which have gone from three to four because of the imminent campaign against the Parthians, provisionally suspended following Caesar's assassination. We're talking of at least 16,000 legionaries, over whom Cleopatra has no power even though their commander, Rufio, is a friend and is trustworthy. These legions could easily deprive her of the throne in a rebellion if they were led by powerful Romans who were her enemies. But above all, they are very attractive to anyone who, after Caesar, tries to emerge by force and demand these legions from the Egyptian queen. And to whom should she concede them? The first one to step forward is Dolabella, who has renounced his own position as consul in order to go to Syria because he has been given command of the province. He's ambitious for power and glory, especially in hunting down Caesar's assassins. After surrounding one of them, Gaius Trebonius, governor of the province of Asia, he's had him beheaded after a brief trial, carrying his head on a spike and dragging his body through the streets before hurling it into the sea. Trebonius is the first of Caesar's assassins to be killed.

Dolabella is now looking for new support in his fight against the Caesaricides, and asks for Cleopatra's help. Essentially, he tells her: Give me the four legions and naval support and, in exchange, Antony and I will confirm Egypt's status as "friend and ally of the Roman people." At the same time, Cassius, who is now in the Middle East, gathering troops and alliances, also makes a similar request. Who can she trust? On her decision depends the future of Egypt and that of her son, Caesarion. In the end, Cleopatra chooses to help Dolabella, who is anyway seeking revenge for Caesar's death, and embraces his faction. Dolabella therefore sends a legate to take the four legions, but, as soon as he leaves, the legate "donates" them to Cassius. An incredible volte-face and a true betrayal. Maybe there was already a secret agreement between the two.

As a matter of fact, the legate, called Allienus, is an old friend of Cicero, who is on the side of Cassius and Brutus. As you can see, history sometimes also goes through secret, invisible routes. According to other historians, more simply, when the legate found himself before Cassius's troops and saw that the enemy was far superior (four legions against seven), he spontaneously gave them up. Cassius now emerges as the true master of the Middle East. The commander hands over to him the legions without any bloodshed and he insists with Cleopatra once again—he now wants the powerful Egyptian ships. She prevaricates and says she cannot oblige him because there is a severe famine (which is true: Egypt has been affected by low flooding and consequently an epidemic of bubonic plague). But here, too, there is a dramatic turn of events. The governor of Cyprus, which is under Egypt's control, unexpectedly provides Cassius with the ships and betrays the queen. The emerging design is crystal-clear. The Cyprus governor's disobedience toward Cleopatra probably means that he is a supporter of Arsinoe, and that he and Cassius are planning to put *her* on the Egyptian throne. As though this weren't enough, Cleopatra receives the news that Dolabella, by now without his legions and besieged by the infamous Cassius in the city of Laodicea, in Syria, has committed suicide.

These are difficult times for Cleopatra. She has helped a losing faction, has no legions, has been betrayed from inside her kingdom, and has lost the very valuable island of Cyprus. As though this weren't enough, Brutus and Cassius are by now swaggering about the Middle East, extinguishing the last glimmers of pro-Caesar resistance, eyeing Egypt as their next objective—a rich, fertile prey—probably intending to eliminate Cleopatra and place Arsinoe in her stead. As Appian says, toward the end of 43 BC, "Cassius turned his attention to Egypt. [. . .] For some time he had been thinking that Egypt's circumstances were particularly favorable to his plans, since it was devastated by famine and could not rely on a consistent army."

We can imagine Cleopatra's state of anxiety. Caesar is no longer there to defend her, and Antony is too busy in his country, consolidating his power and enduring Cicero's famous *Philippics*, the country is on its knees from the famine and the enemy at the gates . . . What can she do?

Actually, she already has done something. She has a new "husband" beside her on the throne. Ptolemy XIV died at the end of August 44 BC, in never entirely understood circumstances. Many modern historians suspect she had him murdered, to avoid his being put at the head of some conspiracy to get rid of her. If this were the case, it would be an act that reveals the ruthless coldness that distinguished her all her life. By now, almost all Cleopatra's close relatives are dead—her father, mother, older sister, Berenice IV, and her brothers, Ptolemy XIII and XIV. The only one left is Arsinoe, but Cleopatra has a very definite—and murderous—opinion of her.

Sitting on the throne next to her is her new "husband" and new king: Caesarion. This, too, is a crystal-clear message for everyone. His name becomes Ptolemy XV Philopator, or "he who loves his father." And who is his father? Perhaps, as we've seen, Caesar himself. Ptolemy XV Philopator is Cleopatra's way of saying that he is Caesar's true heir, his natural child, much more so than Octavian, who became so only by way of adoption, according to a will.

But these proclamations, royal attributes, and references to Julius Caesar take place at a wrong time in history. An army led by one of Caesar's assassins is marching on Egypt. All seems lost. But, just as has already happened in the past, it is history that will save Cleopatra. Cassius, while marching, receives a dispatch from Brutus, asking him to turn back, because a grave danger has materialized on the horizon. The conquest of Egypt and Cleopatra's elimination can wait.

That Pointing Finger

Cicero's pointing finger is like a spear stretched out toward an enemy to be eliminated. It hangs in the air for a few seconds, with a slight tremor because of tension and age. This is how Cicero has ended a long verbal attack on Antony, in the surreal silence of a room crammed with senators. Then, to underline the conclusion of this oratory masterpiece, as usual holding his chin with his left hand, he looks straight at his fellow senators with venom and a scornful smile. The entire Senate bursts into a roar of applause but also shouts and protestations. It's the end of the first of the famous *Philippics*, a series of fourteen (or perhaps seventeen or eighteen, according to some scholars) orations that Cicero would deliver in the Senate against Mark Antony. Their name is an homage to the speeches with which the orator Demosthenes, centuries earlier, had attacked the father of Alexander the Great, Philip II of Macedonia (hence the commonly used term *Philippic*). In these invectives, some of which were never publicly read out in the Senate but circulated in book form in Roman political circles, Cicero attacks Antony and his allies (his brothers especially), describing and emphasizing often made-up events, actions, and reprehensible episodes. Cicero's smear campaign probably contributed to creating a negative image of Antony over the centuries, painting him as greedy, violent, ambitious, and de-voted to all kinds of pleasures and lustful transgressions. In the *Second Philippic*, never uttered in public, for instance, he says that Antony had drunk so much wine at a wedding that he actually vomited in front of everybody at a state assembly. He continues by attacking him for appropriating Pompey's possessions and having frequented then left a questionable "dancer," the infamous Licorys. Cicero's attack is a clear sign of how events deteriorated in Rome. But what happened?

The *Philippics* were delivered over a year prior to Cassius's imminent attack on Cleopatra. They began on September 2, 44 BC, six months after Caesar's death, and went on until April 21, 43 BC.

What happened during those months was a very violent and sur-prising evolution of the military and political landscape that would lead to the emergence of the two great protagonists of the chapters to come: Antony, naturally, but especially Octavian.

It's during these months, just as Cleopatra was trying to consolidate her power in Egypt, that there are clashes between Antony's and Octavian's legions, and the famous proscription lists are drawn up, with cold-blooded murders of hundreds of people. We won't go into detail, because it was a very complicated series of events, but it is essential to understand what happened, and how, during those months, the world of Ancient Rome wrote one of its darkest pages.

A few days after the reading of Caesar's will, Octavian lands at Brindisi. He had been in Apollonia, the present Albania, with Caesar's legions ready to go to war against the Parthians. He had been waiting for Caesar, who had asked him to accompany him on this new adventure (thereby already confirming in a way his decision to make him his heir in his will).

Octavian is little older than a boy. He is not yet nineteen, but shows impressive caution and political instinct. He was no doubt left speechless in the military encampment at the news of Caesar's death, and even more so on discovering that he was his principal heir. Fearing for his life, his mother, Atia, and stepfather, Philippus, beg him to decline the inheritance so that he does not get involved in the dangerous political conflict triggered by Caesar's death, but he decides instead to go to Rome to accept it. Before arriving in the city, however, he contacts Caesar's former advisers, such as the powerful Marcus Nonius Balbus, and other influential people who can give him sensible advice. Then he stops in Campania to forge relationships with many of Caesar's veterans and secure their support. His arrival almost coincides with Cleopatra and her royal retinue's departure for Egypt. The situation he finds in the city is not an easy one. Antony is the uncontested master who swaggers about, using the fact that he has Caesar's notes (*Acta Caesaris*) and, as we've seen, is applying them according to his own interpretation, placing his own men in key positions.

Moreover, he is administering the huge sum (at least 700 million sestertii) destined for the expedition against the Parthians and deposited in the Aerarium. Over these weeks he has consolidated and increased his power base with concessions to veterans, granting Roman citizenship to all Sicilian residents and also with provisions in favor of the Jewish community previously promised by Caesar.

In the beginning, Antony underestimates Octavian, taking him for an inexperienced boy, but soon changes his mind. Octavian strings together a series of important political feats that endears him to people, like for instance collecting funds independently to pay for what Caesar had bequeathed to the people of Rome, or else financing and organizing games (gladiatoral combats and chariot races) to celebrate the victory of Pharsalus. It's during these games that the Romans are deeply impressed by an unusual event. It's been four months since the death of Caesar. A star appears in the sky and shines for an entire week, its light so bright you can see it even during the day. Usually, a comet is considered an ill omen, but

Octavian manages to turn it into a positive divine message. He says it's a sign that Caesar is now in heaven, before the gods. A god amid the gods. This is why he has a star called *Sidus Iulium* placed on top of statues of Caesar. As the U.S. historian Barry Strauss says, "this made splendid propaganda," so much so that even soothsayers adhere to this interpretation, claiming that, like the sun, the comet heralds a new era.

Soon enough, the contrast between Antony and Octavian escalates into a head-on collision with an exchange of insults. Octavian, with an underhand technique that would always distinguish his modus operandi, persuades entire legions arrived from Macedonia and destined for Antony to defect, paying huge sums to individual legionaries (500 denarii per head, the equivalent of two years' salary). It's only the beginning of a tug-of-war that will involve the two of them over the months to come and give rise to an incredible series of events that we will summarize as follows: field battles, the siege by Antony of cities like Modena, where Decimus has barricaded himself, and even clashes between the legions of Antony—declared "public enemy" thanks to Cicero's intervention—and those of Octavian and two other consuls. Yes, we can call it a civil war. Exactly as Julius Caesar had foreseen. But then there are twists: Octavian reaches an agreement with Antony and stages the famous "march on Rome" at the head of his legions (following the same route as Caesar after crossing the Rubicon) and reaches Rome to force the Senate to make him consul. Such an extraordinary act that, several centuries later, it even inspired Napoleon, who would imitate it to perfection, entering the Senate with his soldiers, all weapons deployed, to take power. During this time, Decimus, who had dined with Caesar the night before the Ides of March and gone to his house to persuade him to attend the Senate meeting, meets a terrible death. Abandoned by his men, who have joined Octavian, he tries to cross the Alps with a handful of Gallic horsemen, going a long way around to join Cassius and Brutus in Macedonia. But, once he enters Sequani Gallic territory, between France and Switzerland, he is recognized and murdered. His head is then sent to Antony.

At this point, the Caesarians' front has reunited. All that's needed is a formal agreement, which is reached just outside Bologna, on a small island on the Reno River. Here, Antony, Octavian, and Lepidus meet and create the so-called Second Triumvirate (to distinguish it from the first, much more famous one, formed by Caesar, Pompey, and Crassus). The atmosphere is very tense. Each arrives with five legions that line up facing one another, ready to fight. Then the three men advance on the bridges across the river, each with three hundred men. The first to arrive, Lepidus, inspects the little island and the temple that stands on it and waves his military cloak to signal to the others that the place is safe. At that point, Antony and Octavian leave their men and join him for a two-day discussion.

Today, the river has moved, so the little island has gone, but there is still a long-forgotten memorial in a locality called Sacerno, on the edge of a field. It's the last in a long series of memorial stones and monuments that have followed one another to commemorate the place where the Second Triumvirate met. We know that Antony, Octavian, and Lepidus chose this location because it was equidistant from their respective areas of power. We also know that the island ensured ideal security conditions, not only because it was surrounded by water but also because the temples were considered neutral zones. According to the archaeologist Nicola Cassone, the name Sacerno almost certainly derives from the Celtic nature divinity Cernunnos, represented with stag antlers. This implies the presence, during antiquity, of a place consecrated to this divinity right there, which would confirm the choice of this "holy" island for the triumvirate's meeting. Instead of the ancient pagan sanctuary, which is no longer around, there now stands a church that replaces (and has erased) the ancient local beliefs with a place of Christian worship, as has happened elsewhere.

Here, Antony, Octavian, and Lepidus reach an agreement, provisionally putting aside differences of opinion so that they can form a united front against Caesar's assassins, Brutus and Cassius in particular, who are by now the masters of the east. They establish a form of threefold power similar to a consulship—in other words a triumvirate—by dividing provinces among themselves and promising their soldiers eighteen thriving, prosperous Italian cities as colonies, including Capua, Rhegium, Beneventum, Venusia, Nuceria, Ariminum, and Vibo. In practice, as though they were cities conquered in war, freely divided up among them.

At that point, having sent away their closest advisers, the three men drew up lists of enemies to be killed, thereby creating the infamous Proscription Lists.

The Proscription Lists

Imagine suddenly being judged as somebody to be killed, without being guilty of anything, or having had a regular trial. As though an "alive or dead" arrest warrant were hanging over your head, like a kind of antiquity *Wanted* poster, and anyone could report or kill you—and even get a reward for it. The proscriptions mark one of the most dramatic points of the civil wars. In a kind of social grinder, the most different kinds of people end up on these lists: Appian says, "Those suspected because of their power, as well as personal enemies; they gave each other the names of their own friends and relatives to be eliminated [. . .] New names would sometimes be added to the list, some through enmity, others through resentment, or else because the victims were friends of their enemies or enemies of their friends, or else because of their wealth, since the triumvirs needed a lot of money in order to finance the war [. . .] The number of senators sentenced to death and whose possessions were all confiscated amounted to almost three hundred, while that of the equites reached almost two thousand. The proscription lists featured the brothers and uncles of the triumvirs, and even a few officers who had served under their command."

It's a massacre. Before returning to Rome, the three men send mercenaries to the city to kill twelve adversaries with big political weight (including Cicero). Four are executed immediately, caught unawares during a meal or in the street.

The arrival of the triumvirs' mercenaries in Rome triggers panic in the city. "People were running everywhere, shouting and moaning," Appian writes. "Everybody realized that people were being captured and killed, but as they didn't know who had been sentenced, they were afraid of also being among the wanted."

A few days later, the triumvirs return to Rome with their soldiers, who occupy strategic spots, guarding the doors. The proscription lists are posted in several parts of the city. The names don't all appear at once but are added sporadically, day by day, fueling the climate of fear and uncertainty. The tariff is also written on them for anyone who kills or provides information on the proscribed. As Appian quotes: "Those who kill the proscribed must bring us their heads and they will receive the following: 25,000 drachmas per head if it's a freedman; if it's a slave, freedom, 10,000 Greek drachmas, and his master's citizenship. Informers will receive the same reward." This is how a climate of fear is created, where everyone is suspicious of everyone, from the next-door neighbor to the relative with whom you've had a row.

Death at a Banquet

The first magistrate to fall under the mercenaries' blows is a tribune called Salvius. In principle, his position should make him untouchable, but he knows that since he's a loyal colleague of Cicero, his fate is sealed, so he organizes one final farewell banquet with family and friends. While they're eating and talking, soldiers break in, telling everybody to keep still. The centurion at their head takes Salvius by the hair, pulls him over the table, and with sharp blows, severs his head and takes it away in front of the horrified dinner guests.

Two-Faced Relations

Even relatives of the triumvirs themselves end up on these lists. Antony adds the name of an uncle of his on his mother's side, Lucius Caesar, and Lepidus his own brother Paullus, who saves himself, however, and manages to escape to Asia and withdraw to Mileto, "with the complicity of centurions, who respected him as the brother of a triumvir," Appian tells us.

Sons Against Fathers

There's no shortage of episodes where sons betray their fathers in order to take possession of their estates. So whom could you trust at home? The ancient historian Velleius Paterculus says that "wives were the most loyal, freedmen were only moderately so, slaves hardly were, and sons weren't loyal at all."

Innocent Victims

The violence of these proscriptions does not even spare young people or children, whose only sin is to belong to families considered enemies, or else to be wealthy orphans. Appian tells us that "one of these was murdered while going to school with his master, who put his arms around him to shield him with his own body and so died with him."

Loyal Wives

In most cases, those who are on the list try to hide or flee but almost never succeed. In some cases it's their wives and a little luck that help them. This happens to a former commander of the XI legion who had fought in Gaul with Caesar. His name is Gaius Antistius Reginus. Appian tells us that his wife "hid him during the night in a sewer where the next day the soldiers did not have the courage to enter because of the stench. That same night she dressed him as a coal burner, gave him a donkey to lead loaded with coal, and left shortly before him in a litter. One of the soldiers guarding the city gates was suspicious and decided to search the litter. Worried, Reginus picked up the pace and, as though an ordinary passerby, asked the soldier not to importune the woman. Taking him for a coal burner, the soldier was about to respond rudely but, recognizing him (having served under his command in Syria), said, 'Go along your way, General, because that's the title I should use when addressing you.'"

Disloyal Wives

Appian also tells us of a chilling case: "Some women betrayed their husbands in a wicked way. Among these was Septimius's wife, who was having an affair with one of Antony's friends. Eager to turn this illicit relationship into a marriage, she asked Antony, through her lover, to help her get rid of her husband. Septimius was immediately put on the proscription list. When he discovered this, he took refuge in his wife's house, unaware that it had been she who had betrayed him. Feigning to be lovingly concerned, the woman shut the doors and stayed with him until the murderers arrived. She remarried on the very day her husband was killed."

The End of Cicero

The most famous victim of the proscription lists was undoubtedly Cicero, Antony's great enemy. Their hatred dated back to before Caesar's assassination. When he was a consul, Cicero had had Antony's mother's second husband killed; Antony had been very close to him, having lost his real father as a boy.

But it was his *Philippics* that sentenced him to death definitively. Antony insisted on including him in the proscription lists, a decision Octavian did not share but was forced to accept. Cicero tried to escape, but in Formia, on the shady avenues leading to the sea, his litter was intercepted by soldiers. When he saw them, the famous orator realized his end was nigh and ordered his slaves to put the litter down on the ground. "He touched his chin with his left hand," Plutarch reports, "the way he always used to, and looked straight at the mercenaries [. . .]. His head, which he'd leaned out of the litter, was cut off." A tribune decapitated him, Marcus Popillius Laenas, whom Cicero had actually defended from the accusation of patricide. He was unable to sever the head neatly. Appian says, ". . . he had to strike it three times, almost sawing it off through inexperience." And the barbarity doesn't end here: Seneca the Elder says that both his hands were cut off because of what he had written against Antony, and that these macabre trophies were displayed on the Rostra, on the exact spot where he had spoken against him a few months earlier. One final, gruesome detail marked Cicero's death. Before his head was put on display, they say that Fulvia, Antony's wife, asked to hold it in her hands and, full of resentment, spat on it. Then she put it on her lap, pulled the tongue out, ran it through with a pin she used for her hair, and insulted Cicero's head. They also say that Antony ate at a banquet with Cicero's head placed opposite him. But these are probably just rumors circulated afterward to discredit Antony.

The proscriptions carried on for many months, and finally concluded definitively only in 39 BC. The first few weeks were the most terrible. As time went by and the proscribed fled, a manhunt spread throughout Italy. Those who were on the list were desperately trying to get to Pompey's son, Sextus, who was in Sicily and taking in all the fugitives, or else Brutus and Cassius, who were dominating the east. And it's precisely to them that the triumvirs turned their attention, and prepared what would, to all intents and purposes, be the final showdown to decide who would be in charge.

This is when a new cult is born, that of Caesar, or rather the divine Caesar, *divus Julius*. The Senate ratifies the decision to include him among the gods of the Roman state and build this new god a temple in the Forum. The person who stands to gain most from this is Octavian. As Strauss writes, "This entitled Octavian to call himself *divi filius*, the Son of a Man Made God. Acclaimed as an Imperator, Octavian became 'IMPERTOR CAESAR DIVI FILIUS.'"

Cleopatra Risks Shipwreck in the Mediterranean

The sky is dark and blinding lightning bolts illuminate the horizon. The helmsman's eyes are on the waves, trying to detect from any slight changes in the sea and sky the progression of the weather. The white-hemmed crests, everywhere by now, the wind growing stronger, the black clouds approaching, menacing, and no birds flying. All signs that make one fear the worst. Many eyes are searching the horizon. Two in particular: Cleopatra's.

The Mediterranean is a dangerous sea, sometimes more than an ocean, because it can alter within just a few hours and turn into a bloodthirsty monster. And that's what everybody on board fears.

Cleopatra is sitting, motionless, her hands clutching at the royal throne, in the middle of the ship, beneath a baldachin with gilded, impalpable silk curtains that are now quivering in the wind, practically hysterical. The wind has been blowing even stronger for the past few minutes. The sky has turned gray over their heads. The waves send up spray that wets everyone's face, and the sea slowly heaves up and down. It feels like being on the chest of a giant breathing deeply, like bellows. A giant about to wake up. The sea has lost its colors. It's no longer dark or bright blue, or green. Now it's just gray, like lead. Between the black of the sky and the gloomy gray of the sea, Cleopatra's fleet advances, undaunted, almost in defiance. The colorful vessels have also lost their bright hues in the pale light that reminds everyone of death. Powerful and imposing, these sailing ships, which belong to one of the most feared naval powers in the entire Mediterranean, now seem extremely fragile. The sea is swelling and their sails

look like small feathers between the fingers of giants. Like in a game
of death, the sea rises, swells, and lifts Cleopatra's enormous flagship
high up, as though, for a moment, it were weightless. At the peak of
the giant wave, the bow emerges from the billows as though about to
take flight, then starts the crazy descent down the slope of this huge
mountain of water. In a fraction of a second, it vanishes from the sight
of the escort ships and the fleet. Cleopatra's eyes and those of everyone
aboard are staring, waiting for it to end this descent, and it does so
with an explosion of creaking. The flagship shudders and shakes. Its
bow dives entirely into the sea before resurfacing after long, interminable seconds, like someone gasping for breath. Meanwhile, on board,
everything, including the sailors, is rolling around. Many items have
flown overboard. But nobody is concerned about them. Everybody is
gripping masts and stays, terrified of an imminent death.

What is Cleopatra doing in this immense, stormy sea?

We don't know when the queen heard about the dreadful slaughter
triggered by the proscription lists. She probably did not receive comprehensive accounts of it until early 42 BC, maybe even during the
spring. She would have been shocked by Cicero's death, delighted
by the decision to deify Caesar, and certainly angered by the news
of Octavian calling himself *divi filius*, thus placing himself in direct
competition with Caesarion. The triumvirs have contacted her because they need allies, in the east especially, given the imminent war
against Brutus and Cassius. And her formidable fleet is essential for
landing in Greece where—it has become evident by now—the final
clash will take place. We do not know the terms of their request to
Cleopatra for help, but just as Dolabella had done the previous year,
they most probably promised her autonomy for Egypt and the ac-
knowledgment of Caesarion as the country's ruler. Given Cassius's
imminent attack on Egypt, Cleopatra had no choice but to respond
positively. And so she armed a powerful fleet in order to join those
of Antony and Octavian, and is leading this mighty attack force in

person. A queen at the command of her own fleet has never been seen in Ptolemaic dynasties, and this illustrates the strength, initiative, and uniqueness of this woman. Cleopatra was a true rarity among the Greek queens and can only be compared with another great queen, Artemisia of Halicarnassus, who lived four hundred years earlier. As Duane W. Roller remarks, it reinforces her identification with the goddess Isis, also given her meaningful connection with the sea. It must have been an amazing sight—a large fleet setting sail into the open sea, leaving the Alexandria lighthouse behind it, like a comet with a trail of sails advancing across the blue sea.

The expedition ends in disaster, however. We're in the summer of 42 BC, and Appian provides an eloquent detail witnessed by an enemy commander, Staius Murcus, sent to intercept Cleopatra with his fleet: "He saw the wreckage of destroyed ships driven by the waves as far as the coast of Laconia and heard subsequently that she had returned home with great difficulty and in poor health."

Regarding this, it's worth specifying a surprising fact, that the Mediterranean is probably the largest, most richly stocked archaeological museum on the planet. If you consider an average of three shipwrecks a day of all kinds of vessels (a reasonable estimate, considering that this sea extends from Gibraltar to the coast of Lebanon), in two thousand years you obtain the exorbitant number of more than two million wrecks at the bottom. Each with its often valuable cargo.

We do not know what kinds of problem the queen might have had; perhaps she was simply exhausted by seasickness because of the terrible conditions in the Mediterranean. Seasickness is one of the most devastating discomforts for a human being. In any case, it was a truly unfortunate baptism of fire at the command of a fleet. After this episode, we have no more information from ancient sources about Cleopatra's participation in the ongoing war. We will have to wait for her to meet Antony and start her love affair with him before we see her once again in command in a battle.

This event highlights an aspect that gives an insight into Cleopatra's skill and foresight. Her identification with the goddess Isis is not a random one but, on the contrary, a constant in her propaganda that justifies her position on the throne.

As the incarnation of Isis, Cleopatra is also automatically the "mother" of the kingdom and all her subjects. Like a mother, she defends them from injustices and outside perils, provides them with food, and protects their future. No other Ptolemaic queen has drawn quite so much from ancient Egyptian culture and religion. Like an accomplished politician, Cleopatra uses her knowledge of the language, her concessions and aid to the powerful clergy, and references to ancient deities, like Isis, so that her closeness to the people and their culture may be felt, and presents herself as the one who guarantees the survival of the kingdom and its residents.

But her design goes beyond this. She exploits even the birth of her firstborn, Caesarion, for propaganda. There are many similarities between Cleopatra and Isis in that they both raise their children alone (since in both cases the father is dead), and not ordinary children but generated by divinities. This is especially obvious in Caesarion's case. We've seen how Cleopatra presented him as the son of Caesar, who has been deified by Octavian, and Cleopatra herself is the reincarnation of a goddess. Consequently, Caesarion is entitled to access the throne and is associated with Horus, the Egyptian divinity with the hawk's head, the son of Osiris.

With this solution, Cleopatra's skill goes beyond the boundaries of Egypt. The cult of Isis actually dates back to the Ancient Kingdom, but it was revived by the Greeks, especially during the Hellenistic period, after they assimilated her to various Greek divinities like Demeter, Io, and Aphrodite, and do you know what that means? Thanks to this "fusion" of beliefs (syncretism), the cult of Isis spreads across almost the entire Mediterranean, especially among women, by attributing to the goddess, among other things, virtues linked to fertility and the protection of sailors. In Rome, this cult has enjoyed great success, and favored the propaganda led by Cleopatra, who, by presenting herself as Isis, conveys a message also immediately understood by the Romans.

Toward the Clash

As time goes by, it becomes increasingly obvious, as the historian Antony Spinosa underlines, that Caesar's murder was in fact a settling of accounts, a bloody act that triggered a civil war, rather than the first step in a great political project. Even Cicero, when writing to his friend Atticus, would comment that Caesar was more alive than ever, and it made no real sense to draw comfort from the memory of the Ides of March. The conspirators had proved manly courage but not shown enough foresight, because the tree had been cut down at the base but not uprooted, so new suckers kept sprouting. And it's true that this tree, Caesar's heritage, is now marching toward Brutus and Cassius with many legions, as many as nineteen, led by Mark Antony and Octavian, to annihilate them in a final showdown.

Both Cassius and Brutus reinforce their positions in Asia Minor and the Middle East, eliminating the last pockets of resistance, such as the one on the island of Rhodes, which had supported Dolabella. The city of Xanthus, in Lycia, in the southern part of present-day Turkey, also falls. These are episodes none of us takes into account, lost as they are in the whirlpool of events in ancient history. But let's stop and think for a moment. For many people, thousands and thousands, all this has meant a violent, painful, and atrocious loss of lives. Xanthus, for instance, is conquered after a long siege, and many of its residents commit mass suicide rather than end up in the hands of Brutus's troops. Plutarch writes that "they would search for any means to kill themselves, and not just men and women, but also small children, with shouts and screams, some would throw themselves into the fire, others headfirst from the walls, while others would proffer their bare necks to the swords of their fathers, asking them to strike. The city being thus destroyed, a woman was seen, who, with a dead child tied to her neck, had hanged herself from a noose . . ."

To prefer that kind of death means the alternative was even more terrible. Legionaries (and the allied foreign troops) don't have that professional soldier's aura of nobility that we tend to attribute to them. They are extremely disciplined in their ranks and in battle, of course, but they are also unscrupulous individuals. They enlist and risk their lives in wars essentially prompted by the desire to accumulate loot, to plunder, to build a career, or to obtain citizenship if they are foreign (like the Auxilia). United by a powerful esprit de corps that engenders acts of pure heroism, they are at the same time capable of absolute, cruel, ruthless violence like that of an ordinary militia. In order to appropriate valuable items, food, or women when assaulting a city, they don't shy away from slaughtering anyone, even defenseless children, in a shocking crescendo of collective ferocity. Roman legions, like all armies throughout history, terrorize civilians with their brutality. What makes them different from others is their training. They are a modern army insofar as organization and professionalism go, but their ferocity is ancient. And now two armies with these same characteristics are about to confront each other.

On one side, Brutus and Cassius's formation, made up of nineteen legions, out of which only two have complete ranks, amounting to 100,000 men: 80,000 foot soldiers and 20,000 on horseback. An international force insofar as it is constituted of troops from the various Roman provinces, from Gallic, Lusitanian, Iberian, Thracian, Illyrian, Parthian, and Thessalian cavalrymen to Arab archers on horseback.

As we've already said, nineteen legions are advancing against nineteen legions, a total of 108,000 men: 95,000 infantrymen and 13,000 cavalrymen. Some modern historians tend to halve the effective number of the soldiers in both armies, thinking the sources are exaggerating, but even if you reduce the numbers you still have a clash of titanic proportions.

Brutus and Cassius choose the battlefield. It's going to be the plain of Philippi, in Greece. It is crossed by an important road, Via Egnatia. Brutus deploys his troops on one side of the road, and Cassius on the other. There's barely a mile between the two armies. They unite their two encampments with a long defensive palisade that blocks Via Egnatia. It's a strategic position, since their sides are protected—they have the mountains on one side, and a marsh on the other. Moreover, Via Egnatia continues behind them as far as the port of Thessaloniki, which ensures a constant supply of food, weapons, and men. No doubt they could not have picked a better spot, in view of a battle that promises to last a long time.

Their adversaries' situation is quite different, however. Antony and Octavian cross the Adriatic with their formidable attack force (Lepidus remains in Italy with nine legions, to protect the peninsula from any possible Republican coup). No sooner do they reach Dyracchium and the march begins, however, than the enemy naval forces gain the upper hand on the Adriatic. Do you know what that means? That, unlike their enemies, they will not be able to receive help and new soldiers from Italy. They're on their own, and cannot rely on provisions from the zones behind the front. Moreover, Octavian falls ill (with a never fully disclosed illness) and his health will be precarious throughout the entire conflict. For starters, he is obliged to be confined to his tent for ten days.

Antony is the first to arrive on the plain of Philippi. Alone before the enemy, he immediately realizes that he is at a disadvantage. As well as being unable to rely on supplies from the zones behind the front, the enemy army is blocking his way, and is in a favorable position. So what does he do? He plays the psychology card. He builds his encampment, complete with fortifications, palisades, etc., a very short distance from the enemy, just a mile away. His courage impresses

Brutus and Cassius's soldiers, and gives him an undeniable advantage. After all, he had no choice. The plain where he positions himself is the only place (far from the marsh) where wells of drinkable water can be dug.

Ten days later, carried in a litter, the famous sick man, Octavian, arrives on the battlefield. The two generals understand the situation will soon become critical. Fall is at the gates, and there will soon be rain, cold, and no help from Italy in terms of food and men. The enemy must absolutely be forced into a conflict. On the opposite side, for the selfsame reason, Cassius is stalling. He is a highly experienced general and knows perfectly well that time is on his side; very soon, the enemy will run out of resources and defections will begin.

Brutus, on the other hand, who has no war experience, wants to fight right away in order to impose freedom on the last representation of Caesar's tyranny, and also to intervene before the triumvirs complete the construction of a dam that would impair the Republicans' supplies and make an escape by sea impossible. We can imagine their conversations in the Praetorian tent in the center of one of the encampments, with Brutus pacing up and down in front of Cassius, making grand speeches about politics and their country's freedom, quoting the ancients . . . While Cassius sits, his eyes constantly upon him, turning the gold ring on his finger, his mind on quite different problems.

The First Battle of Philippi

A mile away, in the enemy camp, in another command tent, we can picture a mirror image of the scene, with Antony talking around a table with (a still feverish) Octavian and the main legion commanders.

Meanwhile, they may have drawn up maps of the area based on observations by scouts who approached the enemy lines unseen, and information extracted from captured prisoners. If that was the case, we can picture Antony, leaning on the table with both hands, seeking his adversary's weakness, his eyes reflecting the glow of an oil lamp and searching the maps for a long time.

You cannot trigger a frontal attack. The enemy has the same number of soldiers and is safely entrenched inside his fortifications. You cannot even try to go around him, because of the marsh on one side and the mountain on the other. What is to be done? At one point, Antony smiles, lifts his head, and looks at the others, standing around the table. Perhaps he's found a solution.

Brutus and Cassius aren't engaging because they're constantly receiving new supplies. What if Antony tried placing the enemy in that same condition by blocking their provisions route from the sea? With no more supplies, they'd be forced to come out in the open and agree to the battle.

It's a daring notion, but how to bring it about? With the experience of so many years of battle in the legions, Antony resorts to the military genius of the army. Because the legionaries are not just soldiers but, when needed, as we've already seen, can become engineers, plumbers, carpenters, and blacksmiths. Every legion can rely on a multitude of specialists, which makes it into a perfect war machine capable of destroying the enemy and also building roads, bridges, aqueducts, and cities.

The plan is simple—to build a "road" across the marshes by piling soil and stones, and laying timber bridges where the water is too deep. They will do this in the utmost secrecy. Antony decides that every morning, the army will go out and line up facing the enemy camps with all their insignia in full view, as though all the regulars were present. In actual fact, a large number of soldiers, hidden by the bed of reeds, will undertake the work in total silence. After a final glance at his commanders, Antony orders work to start immediately while, silent in his corner, Octavian nods.

For ten long days, without respite, the legionaries build an embankment in the marsh. When everything is ready, Antony orders a contingent to cross the marshland along this "road" by night and occupy the high ground between Cassius's encampment and the sea, to cut them off from their supply route.

The following morning, Cassius realizes that he has been surprised, but instead of attacking the large enemy contingent on the high ground, he orders a similar "road" to be built in the marsh, shielded by a palisade, which would intercept Antony's so that his troops are cut off. It's a true stroke of genius.

Cassius is undoubtedly an old fox of the battlefields, but so is Antony, who, realizing the enemy's strategy, orders the assault. His troops attack those of his rival. It's a fierce clash and, like a wildfire, gradually spreads to Cassius's encampment, which is conquered and sacked. While all this is taking place, the battle also flares up on the other wing of the formations. Brutus lets his troops out of the encampment and attacks Octavian. Cassius Dio tells us that the legionaries of the two formations "gave the cry of war, struck their shields with their spears, and threw javelins at one another, while slingers and archers were shooting stones and arrows. Finally, they confronted one another [. . .] with the cavalry and armored troops coming from behind." Octavian's formation is overwhelmed and flees. Brutus and his army don't stop, but fight until they occupy Octavian's encampment (although he is no longer there, having just gotten himself transported somewhere else). "And so he was presumed dead," Plutarch writes, "and his litter, now empty, was pierced with enemy arrows and javelins." Everybody in the encampment is put to death. The captured soldiers are slaughtered, including the two hundred Spartans recently arrived as reinforcements.

Toward the end of the day, the situation is as follows. On one side, Antony has occupied Cassius's camp, and on the other, Brutus has occupied Octavian's. At this point something incredible happens. Cassius commits suicide because of a dreadful misunderstanding, possibly caused by problems with his eyesight!

But let's take it one step at a time. Overwhelmed by Antony's troops occupying his camp, Cassius withdraws to higher ground with a few men, "but he could see nothing except, barely, the sacking (he had poor eyesight)," Plutarch tells us; "the cavalrymen with him saw many other cavalrymen moving in their direction: they had been sent by Brutus, but to Cassius they looked like enemies in pursuit of him."

The general sends one of his high-ranking officers toward them to see who they are. The cavalrymen surround the officer to welcome him, happy to see him still alive, and get off their horses to hug him and shake his hand, but Cassius can't see very well from a distance and thinks that, on the contrary, the officer has been surrounded by enemies who are about to kill him. So he goes into his tent with one of his freedmen, Pindarus. "Pulling the mantle over his head," Plutarch concludes, "he bared his neck and proffered it to the freedman so the latter would cut it. As a matter of fact, his head was found severed from his body." He adds that Cassius died on his birthday.

His death is a severe blow to Brutus's formation, so Brutus does not organize a lavish funeral, in order not to demoralize the troops. But he's in despair and, again according to Plutarch, calls his friend "the last of the Romans." Thinking about it, this is a death that goes beyond the loss of an able general; it's the exit from the stage of one of the most important authors of Caesar's assassination, perhaps even the principal one. It's the culmination of a destiny that was unleashed on the day of the Ides of March, and which would kill all the main conspirators one by one. Now only Brutus remains.

Cassius's death, so inconceivable, will play a decisive role in the outcome of the conflict. The Republican formation has suddenly lost its most able, most skillful general.

The Second Battle of Philippi

After the clash, the two much-tested armies withdraw to regroup and nothing happens for several days. There have been heavy losses on both sides: 8,000 dead in Brutus and Cassius's formations, 13,000 dead and wounded in Antony and Octavian's.

Now Brutus must think about the future. He is alone and certainly does not have Cassius's military experience, quite the contrary. He's a politician and a lover of philosophy, but knows very well some of the deep motivations of the legionaries. He's aware of the fact that his soldiers do not like having an inexperienced commander. And so in order to secure their support and avoid defections, he promises that in case of victory they will be free to sack the cities of Thessaloniki and Sparta. In a way, he donates cities and thousands of residents to the devastating fury of the soldiers, who will have license to kill, rape, ravage, and set on fire.

Brutus is equally cynical about the prisoners captured in Octavian's encampment. The scholar François Chamoux highlights the fact that, although on the one hand he sets all those with Roman citizenship free in order to gain their goodwill and support, on the other he has all the slaves killed in cold blood, since there are too many to feed and monitor.

A mile away from him, in the triumvirs' encampment, the situation is no better. A large naval detachment with two of Caesar's best legions on board was crossing the Adriatic to come to their aid when it was intercepted by the enemy fleet and completely destroyed.

Moreover, the weather is deteriorating. It's raining, it's very cold, and the camp built on the plain is partially flooded (partly the making of Brutus's forces, who have deviated a stream). Then there's a shortage of supplies, and it even becomes necessary to send an entire legion to the rear, to Greece, in search of food.

Morale is high, however, thanks to Cassius's death. It's clear to everyone that Brutus is not adequate to this conflict. As highlighted by the historian Ronald Syme, "Brutus could win a battle but not a campaign."

Aware of his lack of experience, Brutus adopts Cassius's strategy, that of wearing out the adversary without waging battle on him.

But this time it's his men who ask him for a clash with the enemy. Every day, Antony lets out his troops and deploys them facing Brutus's camp, hurling insults at their enemies and urging them to desert. A psychological war Antony is very good at implementing, given his experience. Finally, what puts pressure on Brutus are the defections of the units of eastern allies, who abandon the battlefield and return to their countries.

In the end, Brutus has to give in and agree to the engagement. It's October 23, 42 BC, twenty days exactly after the first battle. Imagine the scene: to the sound of war bugles, facing Antony's formations, Brutus's units, joined by Cassius's, come out in order and prepare to stand before the enemy. We have Rome's two currently most powerful armies facing each other now: two endless lines of shields standing on the ground, on several rows, with a forest of *pila*, the legionaries' typical javelins, made up of a wooden pole that ends with a long, narrow metal part with a solid point. The chessboard of the legions' formations is clearly visible from above, with the squares of the centuries, crowds of cavalrymen at the sides, and the standards and heraldic flags in the wind.

Looking at these legionaries, you realize that they are not at all the way you imagine them. These are soldiers of Rome's Republican era, and not of the Empire (perhaps more often pictured in movies) that will come later. They are not wearing the armor formed of the typical metal strips (*lorica segmentata*), but a kind of chainmail sur-coat (*lorica hamata*). Their shields are not rectangular like tiles, but oval. Even so, they are very colorful, painted with the symbols of their units and with visible marks of the most recent clash. More-over, the helmets are those classical ones you generally see in books and documentaries, with a large protective "fan" on the back of the neck and a kind of thick visor on the forehead to ward off blows. They are still the "Montefortino" kind, spherical with a point on top, from which an unusual tuft of horsehair springs, forming a "fountain" that undulates when fighting or marching. There are often also elegant bird of prey feathers attached to both sides of the helmet, erected like antennae. (The custom of wearing bird feathers belongs to an ancient tradition of Italic warriors, and we still find a trace of it, for instance, in the hats of *bersaglieri* and *alpini*).

It looks like a very simple and primitive army, when compared with the imperial ones that would come later. But, in fact, it's this kind of legion Caesar used to conquer Gaul, land on the British Isles, and cross the Rhine, inflicting a resounding defeat on Germanic peoples. With this kind of armor, the soldiers of Pompey, Cassius, and Antony have fought in Spain, Asia Minor, Egypt, and North Africa. These legions are driven by a thirst for victory that would forge the boundaries of Rome and shape the future Roman Empire that would last centuries.

The two formations remain facing each other for hours without anything happening. Every so often, a psychological war starts. A soldier insults the enemy commander or else emits a war cry, followed by thousands of fellow soldiers who produce a deafening roar. The other formation responds by beating their spears or swords rhythmically on their shields. Allied barbarian warrior units sing their own battle songs and often produce a lengthy sound by pressing their lips against the hollow of their shields, producing a dismal collective howl the Romans call *barritus* (the same root as the word *baritone*, which suggests the depth of its tone). The shields diffuse this sound at low frequencies, and in the long run it stimulates the sympathetic nervous system of the enemy soldiers, triggering anxiety.

It's hard to describe in modern times just how these battles must have looked, but they relied especially on the large number of the people involved. Now, the only places where you can witness a similar phenomenon are stadiums, with crowds singing in chorus or shouting en masse when someone scores.

At a glance, it's an impressive sight—tens of thousands of legionaries ready to spring forth, helmets gleaming in the sun, banners waving in the wind, hands on the pommels of swords ready to draw, or, sweaty, clutching at *pila* ready to hurl. They know that there's going to be a battle, they know that it's going to be the definitive one, they know they will become a part of history . . . and they know that many of them will die. What's most shocking is that these are two "twin" Roman armies in a fratricidal clash. Never has this term been so accurate. The soldiers in the opposite formations often know one another and are sometimes friends and even relatives. A tragedy within a tragedy.

Mark Antony is wearing his commander's armor, which gives him a chiseled, athletic chest. Beneath the helmet pulled down over his head, his eyes have become cold and don't lose sight of the enemy even for a second, darting left and right like those of a tiger in a cage, seeking potential weak spots in the enemy formation but also in the best units, against which he can put up a solid resistance. Experience is relentlessly projecting possible strategies and scenarios in his mind, like a chess player before moving his pawns.

Antony is on the field, among his troops, and keeps moving around to get a better view and encourage the men. His horse bears the wait in silence, shaking its head nervously every now and then. Octavian, on the other hand, is far in the rear, staring into space and looking vacant since they left the camp, which shows he does not enjoy fighting and action, preferring strategies and intrigues. He's caught the odd glimpse of Brutus, far away, at the rear of his formations, in his scarlet cloak. This morning, before leaving the encampment, Caesar's assassin has given the soldiers a patriotic speech, using dignified words, like a philosopher, some of which many legionaries probably did not understand. He has no way of knowing this but his *adlocutio*, the pep talk commanders give their soldiers before every battle, would be the last of any general from the Roman Republic. This chapter from ancient history would close in a few hours. In a few hours' time, the sun will have set and the Republic of Rome would cease to exist, and with it any hope of bringing it back to life.

Compared to Antony and Octavian, Brutus has a disadvantage: he's not sure he can trust his soldiers one hundred percent. According to Plutarch, some internal reports have indicated possible desertions. The legionaries are worried by his lack of military charisma and scarce battle experience, and they are afraid of dying because of their commander's naïveté in war. As a matter of fact, after a few hours' wait comes the first dramatic defection. A brilliant Gallic cavalryman called Camulatus approaches the enemy formation and literally changes sides.

Brutus watches him, as do thousands of soldiers in both armies. His face turns red with anger and, before others can follow and trigger a devastating chain effect, he orders the attack. Like an echo, his command generates an endless series of shouted orders that spread down every row of the army. The war *tubae* sound the signal to attack. The banners and flags with the symbols of the legions and centuries are pointed at the enemy. Thousands of shields are raised and forests of spears are now undulating in the air. The shouts, screams, and war chants become deafening. This is history snarling, knowing this day will be remembered for thousands of years.

In the Fray

It's three o'clock in the afternoon. The sun begins to set. Its light suddenly seems to dim slightly, the way it does when flocks of birds fly by. But what's really darkening its luminous disk is a rain of arrows, darts, and projectiles hurled by both armies at the same time. The hiss of thousands of arrows fills the air for a few seconds, muffling all other noise. It's like the buzzing of a colossal swarm of huge wasps equipped with deadly stings. In those few seconds, everybody realizes that life is about to end for many. But there's no time to think. Tens of thousands of shields are raised above the soldiers' heads, forming a kind of roof. The legions cover themselves with scales, like the body of a fish. But many arrows find a gap between shields and pierce through many men, who fall to the ground. Even more devastating is the impact of the huge "arrows" from the *scorpiones*, which are like enormous crossbows on trestles, to all intents and purposes the equivalent of our small-caliber cannons. Their blows are dreadful, like thunderbolts that fall on the crowd of soldiers with a surgical precision still surprising to experts.

This rain of death resounds with thunder-like shots from the various war machines. The *onagri* (literally "a kind of wild donkey"), similar to catapults, are positioned behind the soldiers on the attack, and with canting hurl on the enemy stone balls, their sizes ranging from coconuts to watermelons. Every blow crushes skulls, bounces wildly, and mutilates more bodies before it stops. It's chilling to hear the hollow sound of imploding shields; the metallic ones of cracking helmets; the deep ones of heads splitting; the raw ones of flesh tearing; the sharp ones of bones shattering . . . and even worse is hearing them all at once. That's how death seizes so many soldiers in just a few seconds.

It's a nauseating sight for those nearby. The companion at arms with whom you were speaking just a few seconds ago is now on the ground, a shapeless mass of blood and armor. Those who have never seen this horror start retching with vomit and terror. But they cannot flee. There are new waves of projectiles, called "sling bullets." They're the shape and size of a date and are launched with incredible precision, the same way that David slew Goliath. The whirling of the slings in the air has a choral sound, like that of sirens, which reaches the enemy and generates enthusiasm in the friendly lines, but dismay in enemy ones, preparing them for a rain of death. Whenever they are thrown en masse, the projectiles act like modern ones, since they are made of lead and have an elongated shape, which enables them to arrive with a frightening power of impact and penetration, and go through helmets and bodies.

The first ranks of dead are already being counted and yet it's only the beginning of the battle.

Now the legionaries are advancing with the auxiliary troops in the front row. A wall of shields is coming toward you. Each is a bright blue, green, yellow, or red, depending on the centuries, units, and soldiers. They're decorated with painted figures of animals (symbols of the legion or century), thunder, lightning, large stars, or ornamental "frets." There are many variations, although they all respect the unit's symbol, and there are many differences between shields; especially in comparison with the *albae* plates (the white or undecorated shields of the recruits), the decorated shields of the veterans are particularly recognizable—and frightening.

On the left wing, Brutus himself commands the troops, and perhaps this is why they are so decisive and forceful in their attack.

Once the enemy lines are within their shooting range, the legionaries stop and throw broadsides of *pila* to perforate the enemy's shields with their solid points and follow it with the pole, which, being thinner, penetrates the hole easily and goes "in search" of the enemy's body. If it cannot find it, then the whole metal pole bends and crumples on the shield, making it unusable. And, in the imminent hand-to-hand fight, the fate of a man without a shield is sealed.

The equivalent of a volley from a machine gun, the broadsides of *pila* kill many other enemy legionaries, who in turn have hurled the same weapons at Brutus's men. It's a fratricidal war, with identical weapons and techniques.

A few seconds later the two lines engage. The last few yards are covered running, the men screaming at the top of their voices, sword in the right hand and shield in the left. The general clamor is broken by the thud of colliding shields, which sounds like many poles dropped on the ground. Then there's the metallic sound of the weapons. Confused cries, heart-wrenching yells. Ever heard the sound of a blade penetrating flesh? The fray produces a deafening chorus of eerie sounds that are like a powerful slap to all that makes man different from animals.

By now, all you can see is a huge, confused crowd of human beings struggling, with swords rising for a moment before plunging into the fray and taking lives. The expanse of fighting soldiers looks like an ocean of bodies seething as far as the horizon. The standards and symbols of the units are undulating in the sea like ships' masts in a tempest. You truly wonder where every man finds the strength to fight unless it's in a desperate urge to live, or survive.

At a signal, Brutus's cavalry appears on one side. Hordes of Gallic cavalrymen and allies lunge at Antony and Octavian's army, in support of the troops of Caesar's assassin. The horses knock the legionaries over, the riders' blades coming down like cleavers on the bodies of those who don't move out of the way. Like a huge ram, the mass of cavalrymen breaks through the enemy formation, which is now swaying, coming apart, and giving ground. Brutus's move is successful: his formation is breaking through the enemy front that is now beginning to scatter. Brutus is winning, and it's a clear victory.

But what's happening on the other side of the battlefield?

On the left-hand side, things aren't going well for Brutus. On the contrary. Octavian and Mark Antony's soldiers are hanging on and slowly pushing away Brutus's, who give ground "as though they were pushing back a very heavy machine," Appian says.

It's a crucial time in the battle, and Cassius Dio gives us a vivid report of this moment, like a special envoy in the middle of the fray. His words are terrible: "The collision was powerful and so was the clash of swords. In the beginning, everybody was trying to strike his adversary without being struck back, fully intent on killing anybody in front of him, saving himself; then, as the impetus and ardor for war grew, the fight became widespread and disorderly, and heedless of their own safety, everyone felt the urge to slaughter the enemies, defying danger. Some were throwing down their shields and, attacking the enemies in front of them, were strangling them with their own helmets and striking them in the back, or else tearing off their armor and wounding them in the chest; others were holding their enemies' swords still, making them practically defenseless and running them through with their own [. . .]. Some clung together so they couldn't strike at each other and so died in this tangle of swords and bodies. Some fell after a single blow, others after several; they didn't even notice their wounds because death preceded pain, nor did they give death moans because they did not get to feel pain. There were those who, having killed an enemy, did not, in the joy of their action, even consider that they could be killed; and those who fell lost any ability to feel and did not realize what had happened to them."

Cassius Dio's story is that of a furious, savage battle where any order or strategy is lost. Where you just try to kill in order to survive.

The fray ends up exhausting Brutus's formation. His left wing grows increasingly weak in the center, then yields and breaks up. At this point, the soldiers flee. In just a few seconds, the goddess of victory has chosen which formation to support (this is why she is represented with wings: she flies over the battlefield for a long time then lands suddenly and unexpectedly on one of the contenders): that of the triumvirs Antony and Octavian.

It's a bloodbath. Mark Antony knows he mustn't stop now and gives the order to attack the gates of the enemy camps to prevent them from taking shelter inside. Despite a rain of arrows from towers and palisades, his soldiers storm the encampments, forcing their adversaries to flee to the hills, forests, or toward the sea. Antony does not stop and orders his soldiers to pursue them, and goes after the fugitives himself with just one goal—to capture Brutus.

Many die trying to defend Brutus, and many sacrifice themselves to allow him to flee.

Regarding this, there's a peculiar episode told by Plutarch, who describes the courage of one of Brutus's companions, called Lucilius, who pretends to be Brutus and hands himself over to enemy soldiers, asking to see Antony. Antony, of course, knows Brutus very well, and when he sees Lucilius brought in by his triumphant soldiers, he real-izes there's been a case of mistaken identity. He does, however, show magnanimity (a characteristic he would always have and one that many great Roman military chiefs—Caesar above all—always liked displaying in order to increase their worth), apparently uttering these words: "You were searching for an enemy and you came bringing a friend; by the gods, if I had Brutus here alive, I would not know what treatment to afford him; may I be granted men like these as friends rather than enemies." Having said this, he hugs Lucilius, who from then on would remain at his side and always serve him with loyalty.

The End of Brutus

Mark Antony and Octavian look at the battlefield strewn with motion-less bodies lying in unnatural positions, wounded men dragging themselves, broken spears, shields bashed in, abandoned swords, and poles stuck in the ground with standards fluttering sadly. In this land-scape of death and desolation, the birds have started singing again and the sun is setting, restoring a surreal kind of peace. In their eyes, we see the reflection of what is more than the end of a day on the battlefield: Caesar has been avenged.

Meanwhile, Brutus has vanished and cannot be found. He's not actually very far, but with a few companions in a secluded valley, where he meditates all night. They would eventually say what happened during those hours. As a highly educated man, he finds comfort, in-spiration, and strength to face the final hours of his life in philosophers rather than his soldiers. He recalls the verses of Greek poets. And, according to Cassius Dio, it seems that at some point during the night, he recites those of a tragedy in which Hercules, exhausted after many successful trials and full of bitterness (just like him), says: "Oh, miserable virtue, you were but a word and yet I worshiped you like a real thing. But you were the slave of chance."

In the middle of the night, after giving his final instructions to his servants, who burst into tears, he asks his friends to help him commit suicide, but they all refuse. He then takes advantage of a moment of confusion, when someone cries that everyone should flee this place, which has now become dangerous, and leaves with two companions, one of these Strato, his great friend from the time he was studying rhetoric. They are all armed, clutching swords, since they could be discovered and captured at any moment. At a certain point, Brutus draws close to Strato, takes his sword in both hands, and stabs himself, dying in his arms. According to other accounts, it is Strato who, in tears and persuaded by his begging, pierces him with his sword while turning away. Showing great courage, Brutus allegedly pressed his chest hard against the blade, pushing without hesitation in order to be run through.

This is how the last great conspirator of the Ides of March allegedly died, he too killed by the sword, he too with pain and bleeding. Of course, at this point we all wonder what would have happened if Julius Caesar had not been killed. At this time of night, Brutus would have been in Rome, sleeping in his wife's arms after a banquet. Cassius would have been able to give advice to his son, now of age. Cicero would have been busy writing by the light of an oil lamp his umpteenth oration, which later thousands of schoolchildren would have had to translate. Caesar would have been in a tent somewhere in the Middle East, Syria perhaps, enjoying his success in the company of Octavian. The legionaries lying in the plain of Philippi, injured, dead, or dying, would have been with him, many of them still alive.

But things turned out differently in this kind of sliding door of history. And now we're here, in a valley not far from the battlefield, with Mark Antony before Brutus's lifeless body.

He is looking at the most complete vision of his victory. He has fiery words for the body—a few months earlier, Brutus had been responsible for the death of his brother Gaius, executed to avenge Cicero's death. But then he has the body wrapped in a scarlet cloak and orders the remains to be sent to Brutus's mother, Servilia.

This would not actually happen because of two unforeseen events. The scarlet cloak would be stolen and, on hearing this, Antony would have the thief killed. Things would be disrupted by that weak, sickly young man unsuited to war, that is, Octavian. A young man who, however, is already showing the overwhelming cynicism that will mark him all his life. He is the one who orders that Brutus's head be severed and sent to Rome to be laid at the feet of Caesar's statue, but, as Cassius Dio writes, "a wave came crashing on the ship that was transporting it, and carried Brutus's head away in the billows." No ancient writer, in fact, ever described Brutus's head in Rome, at the feet of Caesar's statue. Thus concludes the long account of Caesar's assassination. By now, as night envelops the plain of Philippi, history literally turns a page. Dawn marks the beginning of a new chapter that will feature three protagonists who survived the events we have just related, driven by two kinds of passion—love and hatred. They are Mark Antony, Cleopatra, and Octavian.

7

Cleopatra and Antony Meet

Destiny Elects to Go Toward Cleopatra

As often happens after a large battle, the following days are spent collecting the weapons of the fallen, stacking up all those belonging to the vanquished in large heaps, and counting the dead, who are stripped of valuable items. It's impossible to cremate 30,000 to 40,000 or more bodies, so this was done only with the most illustrious ones (and belonging to the victorious side). In the tents, military physicians, almost all originally Greek, are working relentlessly, cauterizing wounds and amputating limbs with a skill and speed that would leave modern surgeons speechless. Bacteria have not been discovered yet, but physicians know that nature grants them a window of only twenty-four hours to intervene before the wounds get irremediably infected. Modern anesthetics do not exist, and all they have are a few mild painkiller compounds derived from opium, not enough for the thousands of wounded and dying streaming into the camp infirmaries. Many die in dreadful torment. The air is filled with the screams and moans of the wounded, which gradually grow weaker before dying out altogether.

The fate of the prisoners is no less cruel. Valuable as professional soldiers, legionaries are generally spared, partly because they are ready to be reassigned under the banner of the winner. Those who do fall are usually men in command or high up in the hierarchy. In Philippi, however, there are dramatic exceptions. During these hours, Octavian is shockingly cruel and cynical. He almost seems to take sadistic pleasure in ordering the deaths of enemy soldiers, like the father and son who are brought to him and forced to kneel before him. They both ask to be spared, but Octavian orders them to draw lots for their lives. The father offers to die instead of his son and is killed by Octavian himself, and the boy, overwhelmed with grief, takes his own life.

To a modern reader, Octavian's cruelty may seem surprising, and can only be explained as the immaturity of a twenty-year-old who has a sense of omnipotence because of the unlimited power obtained thanks to the civil war. It's a dangerous mix that turns his insecurity—he is sickly and without military skills, among tough, experienced soldiers— into arrogance. An arrogance that, on the battlefield, becomes the power of life and death over everyone. He already harbors the steeliness and calculating nature that he will always have, and that will allow him to build his future empire.

At present, the unrivaled master of the scene is Mark Antony. He is the true author of this victory, and everybody agrees that he is the most powerful man in Rome. According to Appian, in time he built himself "the reputation he earned in Philippi of being invincible, which continued to inspire terror."

Over the following days, Antony and Octavian decide to change the terms of the pact that led to the triumvirate. They effectively curtail the authority of Lepidus, accused of having struck secret pacts with the enemy faction (particularly Sextus Pompey and his powerful fleet), and divide up the dominions of Rome. Octavian gets Spain as well as the thankless task, since he's still the least influential of the three, of seizing lands for the victorious legionaries of the Battle of Philippi; Antony gets Gaul and the eastern provinces, and Lepidus, Africa. From this moment on, Cisalpine Gaul, which includes a large section of the Po Valley and the Veneto, ceases to be a province and is included in Italy, for the first time politically uniting the entire peninsula and anticipating by at least nineteen centuries a large portion of Italy's geography.

On the basis of this agreement, Antony would have to bring some order to the eastern provinces from where Brutus and Cassius attacked, and neutralize potential pockets of resistance. The real aim of this geographical "cleansing" is something else: to raise a lot of money for the soldiers, as promised when the triumvirate was formed.

In fact, it's the army that determines history at this time. Power still revolves around the legions, and you must have a large number of them on your side if you want to rule, but even so they need to be paid, and raising money (if you're not extremely wealthy) involves getting it from cities and people by force.

Mark Antony therefore goes to the east with two legions supplied by Octavian, to whom he pledges in exchange the same number of men to fight Sextus Pompey in Italy.

It is a crucial decision that will lead him to meet Cleopatra.

But how come he chose to leave Rome, the heart of power? There are two reasons for this. The first is to leave Octavian, who returns to Italy, with a hard nut to crack—to honor the promises made to the veterans by giving them money and land. A difficult, complicated task that will engender many problems. The situation in the east, on the other hand, is different. There are many minor vassal rulers over whom to extend his dominion, thereby increasing his own financial power in view of new projects. The second reason for Mark Antony's decision is that he has the great expedition against the Parthians in mind, the expedition never carried out by Caesar, but which all Romans have been awaiting since the humiliating defeat at Carrhae (which occurred eleven years earlier and in which thousands of soldiers died, including Crassus, who, alongside Caesar and Pompey, had built the famous First Triumvirate). He intends to avenge the shame, and thereby be included in the Pantheon of the greatest Roman military leaders of all times, next to Caesar and other famous names in the history of Rome.

There may be something else driving him to the east and into Cleopatra's arms. Antony has already fought there as an anonymous cavalry officer. He has certainly experienced the charm of the local atmosphere and its people. He wants to experience them again, return to Greece to admire what all the Romans consider as their cultural homeland, and lose himself in parties, rituals, traditions, and the lifestyle. Moreover, he wants to go farther into eastern lands, to Egypt, a country he already knows and that casts a particular spell over him. "The same felt by all its conquerors," the historian Hermann Bengtson says, "from Alexander the Great to Caesar, and Napoleon," adding, "How could Antony give up all this? [. . .] Everyone warmed to him. It was the first time that a Roman had understood the east and its inhabitants; his arrival would have signaled the beginning of a new era for these lands and left an indelible mark on all his contemporaries."

A New Dionysus

Antony leaves the battlefield after setting up a colony with the veterans of the XXVIII legion, who have fought their final battle here, and goes to Athens, where he spends the winter.

It is his entrance into history's great eastern fresco, and he immediately volunteers as protagonist. He orders the restoration of temples, lavishes donations on the city, etc. He knows that as far back as 44 BC, Brutus was welcomed in Athens like a philosopher-leader, so he too shrewdly takes part in literary conversations, mystery initiations, and competitive spectacles. He then visits Megara and the Delphi sanctuary, which he decides to restore substantially. Moreover, he presides as an arbiter over a few controversial judicial matters, proving to be very levelheaded. In other words, he shakes off the label Greeks often pin on Roman generals, as being uncouth and stupid fighters. As Giusto Traina says, it was a diplomatic success: "This policy earned him important titles like 'philo-Hellenic' and 'philo-Athenian'; celebrations were held in his honor, called 'Antony's Panathenaic Games.'"

Just a few months later, after the Athenian triumphs, Antony moves to Asia Minor. Here, too, he reaps an impressive series of successes. Plutarch's words are emblematic: "Kings would come to pay him homage and the kings' wives would let themselves be seduced by him, competing in giving him presents and looking beautiful." But there is also a darker side to this journey, one that overshadows his fun. He does not give up his taste for luxury, idleness, and entertainment, and surrounds himself with characters of a dubious reputation and low extraction in addition to the ones who joined him from Italy after the victory of Philippi. It's a kind of "court of lust," excesses, vulgarity, and especially ignorance, which Plutarch describes in a terse and interesting manner, with words that immediately bring to mind the similar "courts" of many powerful people over subsequent centuries and even more recently. "Cythara players like Anaxenores, flutists like Xuthi, a certain dancer Metrodorus, and some other congregation of Asiatic artists, that outshone by their impudence and silliness the gloomy company from Italy, flowed into his court and became its rulers. There was no more measure, since everyone would get carried away with this entertainment. The whole of Asia, in fact, was full of incense smoke and paeans and moans."

Strong words in which, centuries later, we should however read Plutarch's veiled propaganda in favor of Octavian.

Even more triumphant is Antony's arrival in Ephesus, where a coin is minted in his honor, bearing the faces of the triumvirs. His entrance through the city gates is memorable. He is preceded by women dressed as Bacchae and men and women dressed as satyrs and Pan, with buildings and roads covered in ivy, while zithers, bagpipes, and flutes accompany his progress. People are looking out their windows and forming rows on each side of the procession. Everybody is celebrating him like benevolent, gentle Dionysus. Antony probably hears the acclamations in Greek (which he speaks fluently) that compare him to this god, one of the most important in the Hellenic pantheon. The same thing occurs in so many other cities.

Dionysus is associated with wine, ecstasy, the setting free of instincts but also with the theater, so appears to describe and sum up perfectly Antony's pleasures during this tour of eastern lands.

In fact, being nicknamed the "New Dionysus"—one of the main Greek gods—illustrates the great hopes that these cities and people are putting in him. According to the historian Joachim Brambach, "this wasn't an act of mere adulation. Greeks and Eastern people in general pinned important hopes on their new lord, a much friendlier Roman than characters like Silla, Caesar, Brutus, and Cassius. Both in Greece and the Middle East, Antony received marks of enthusiasm like no other Roman before or after him." Moreover, "media-friendly" acts, as we'd call them now, come easily to him. Remember the city of Xanthus, destroyed by Brutus after a long siege? Well, Antony provides help for its reconstruction and exempts the residents of the entire region from taxes. He does the same thing in Laodicea (where Dolabella died) and Tarsus, the very city where he will meet Cleopatra a few months later. Even though he cannot imagine this, his life is going to change in just a few seconds in this city, after he sees the woman of his life arrive.

For the time being, Mark Antony enjoys his success without forgetting his reason for being here: restoring order and preparing an important war against the Parthians. He therefore meets many rulers from client kingdoms located along the eastern borders, and whips back in line those who had sided with Caesar's assassins.

Although they were delicate formal occasions, these encounters at times led to other "sectors" of life, drawing out the Latin lover (quite literally!) in Antony. This happens in Cappadocia, for instance, in the large settlement of Comana, where a beautiful woman called Glaphyra lives. She is the wife of the high priest of Bellona, who rules the city. No sooner does Antony see her than he takes a fancy to her and the two have an incandescent, intense, and long-lasting love affair. Apparently, she was famous everywhere for her sunny, feisty beauty. But she's not merely beautiful. She is also an intelligent, talented, and shrewd woman, like Cleopatra. Thanks to her intimate relationship with Mark Antony, she succeeds in getting the throne of Cappadocia assigned to her eldest son, Sisines. We do not know how her husband reacted, but there's not much you can do when dealing with the most powerful general of the time and his two legions. Glaphyra acted very much like Cleopatra, ensnaring Antony so that she could place her son on the throne. Moreover, this is no fleeting romance. We know from the ancients that it took five years of dynastic contention, since the throne of Cappadocia was already occupied by a legitimate ruler, Ariarathes X. This would therefore be a gradual usurpation, which Mark Antony would eventually close with his "seal," since he would remove him and appoint Glaphyra's son as the new king under the name of Archelaus of Cappadocia. All this happens in 36 BC, and do you know what it means? That despite already "going steady" with Cleopatra, Antony was almost certainly still in an open relationship with Glaphyra.

During the months he spends in Asia Minor, Antony summons the kings and heads of religious communities of various cities to obtain consent and form numerous alliances he will then use as a base for the war against the Parthians and also to strengthen his own power in the east.

Among the sovereigns he contacts and convenes there is also Cleopatra. As the queen of Egypt, she has a large fleet and huge wealth, which make her support essential to military operations.

The Invitation to Cleopatra

It's the beginning of summer 41 BC. On a warm morning, surrounded by the white marble of a building beneath a bright blue sky, Mark Antony hands a trusted man a letter in which he asks the queen to come to Tarsus, a city in southern Turkey. This man is Quintus Dellius, a seasoned diplomat, an expert on the east, and a lover of wine and the good life, whom Antony will use for ten years as a negotiator in all the most important and delicate matters concerning the Middle East. He is so clever that he manages to ride, unscathed, all the changes in power that rock this era. After Caesar's assassination, he went from being a Caesarian like Dolabella to a Caesaricide like Cassius; following the latter's death in the Battle of Philippi, he joins Antony's ranks and remains there for ten years. Then, shortly before the Battle of Actium, which will involve the defeat of Antony and Cleopatra, he will join Octavian, and live the rest of his life peacefully under the Augustan regime. A first-class "turncoat" or, as they say, "a man good at rushing to the rescue of the winners."

Dellius's trip has been preceded by various letters Antony sent Cleopatra, inviting her to Tarsus, without receiving a reply, however. The reason is obvious and connected to etiquette. A queen does not stoop to reply to a Roman magistrate and, besides, there is still a definite anti-Roman feeling among the people of Alexandria. But what do these letters say? According to Plutarch, the queen is summoned so that she might "respond to the accusations against her of having provided many means to Cassius and his legates, and of having helped their war effort." This is a reference to the legions stationed in Alexandria, which, led by Allienus, had switched to Cassius's side without fighting.

We now know that Cleopatra was in no way responsible for this, but Antony possibly wanted to have a clear view of these events, as well as an explanation about the failure on the part of the Egyptian fleet to come to his aid before the Battle of Philippi. Here, too, we know that the queen was forced to turn back by a tempest, but Antony wanted a clarification. Given Cleopatra's silence, he was forced to send a trusted man to Egypt.

When the queen and Dellius meet at Alexandria, he immediately realizes he has before him an extraordinary woman who could be of great help to Antony. Plutarch says, "He then began to flatter and exalt the Egyptian to 'go to Cilicia well adorned' [. . .] and not to fear Antony, who was the most amiable and benevolent of commanders."

Cleopatra consents to meet him in Tarsus. According to Plutarch's account, the queen seems to have been somewhat afraid of Antony initially, and of what could potentially happen to her once she reachs the appointed place. In the end, she makes up her mind. She knows what kind of man Antony is, and besides, she has learned how to deal with Romans and is aware of her great importance in view of their campaign against the Parthians.

After obtaining from Dellius the reassurances she needed, Cleopatra prepares to meet Antony.

From Plutarch's description—one of the most famous of Cleopatra—we perceive all the strength of this woman who does not rely so much on her status as a queen as on her beauty, charm, and ability to conquer men with her intelligence. "Persuaded by Dellius and, judging by the kind of relationships she had had with Caesar and with Gnaeus, Pompey's son, she was hoping to ensnare Antony very easily. After all, the others had known her when she was still a girl and inexperienced, but now she was about to meet Antony at the moment when a woman's beauty is at the peak of its splendor and her intelligence is developed in all its maturity. She therefore prepared many gifts, money, and ornaments, as befitting an important state and a prosperous kingdom, but went pinning her main hopes on herself, the spells, charms, and attractions she possessed."

At the end of summer 41 BC, having ordered her personal fleet to be armed, Cleopatra leaves Alexandria and heads to Tarsus, in

Cilicia. The love meeting that will capsize history is about to take place.

The Location of Love at First Sight

Cilicia is a mountainous region in southern Anatolia, which has been part of the Roman dominion for only a few years. Very rich in timber used for building ships, it had long been infested with pirates, definitively swept away by Pompey Magnus in a famous battle (Korakesion, 67 BC). Historically, it's a land associated with the Ptolemaic dynasty, and the island of Cyprus, the junction of commerce in the eastern Mediterranean and famous for its copper mines, is not far from its coast. Tarsus is Cilicia's most important city and the setting for the grandiose—to say the least—meeting between Antony and Cleopatra. They are surrounded by marbles, colonnades, fountains, statues, libraries, as well as schools of philosophy and oratory. There's an expanse of forests and mountains all around. A river, the Cydnus, runs across this natural paradise, and it's up this river that Cleopatra arrives.

In truth, this river has an odd precedent in history. While bathing in it before the famous Battle of Issus, Alexander the Great nearly lost his life. It was the middle of summer, and to cool down in the summer heat, the great military leader removed his armor and clothes in front of his soldiers and immersed himself in the cold water. Perhaps it was the contrast in temperature that caused him suddenly to feel unwell. He blanched, his limbs stiffened, and, had it not been for the prompt intervention of his nearest companions, he would have drowned. He was carried unconscious into his tent and recovered later. We can imagine this story being passed on by Tarsus residents for centuries, and someone would have most probably pointed out the spot of the near tragedy to Antony.

Cleopatra Prepares for the Encounter with Her Future Lover

The queen of Egypt is very clear about the fact that her meeting with Mark Antony will be crucial to her future, her son's reign, and the kingdom overall. Following years of instability and dynastic struggles, Antony appears to be the absolute master, and by all considerations will be so for a long time. It's therefore essential that she brings him over to her side and persuades him that it's also in his best interest to stand by her both on the personal and the governmental fronts, just as Caesar did. In other words, she will need convincing arguments to get him on her side. And what are these arguments? Two thousand years later, we can see through Cleopatra's strategy pending this encounter as though we were standing right next to her. She decides to attack on two fronts—public (official) and private (personal). She most probably followed Antony's triumphant journey to Greece attentively thanks to letters and informers, and has taken note of the fact that people like to call him the "New Dionysus." This expression may make us smile now but in antiquity, in a prescientific and pretechnological society, beliefs were deeply rooted and daily life was permeated by the presence of the gods. Speaking of somebody like a god was not simple flattery but implied a personal faith and hope in a better future. Although not quite in the same way, of course, it's somewhat like when present-day popes, men of faith, or ordinary people undergo the beatification process and are proclaimed saints. Two thousand years ago, people truly thought that some human beings, especially great military leaders and benefactors, could be deified (this had just happened to Caesar, by now considered a god, complete with temples, rituals, and priests). It's no wonder that even Cleopatra spread the notion of herself as the reincarnation of Isis. This small parenthesis was necessary in order to understand how the queen of Egypt was able to exploit to her advantage these popular as well as honorific religious beliefs to strengthen her union with Antony.

If he is considered the New Dionysus by everybody, then she will go to the meeting as Aphrodite (the Roman Venus). More especially as "Venus emerging from the waters" (*Venus Anadyomene*), since she will travel to Tarsus by sailing up the river Cydnus. Cleopatra therefore decides to change the meaning of the encounter from a simple diplomatic meeting to a marriage between two gods—him, Dionysus, with the power to grant her immortality, and her, Aphrodite, goddess of love, beauty, and fertility.

It's a very astute move that only Cleopatra could have devised, further confirmation of her fine mind and her strategic way of thinking about power, far superior to almost all the sovereigns of her era and those to come.

The encounter about to take place must impress not just Antony but the whole of Asia Minor, like a modern royal wedding broadcast worldwide. As Michael Grant points out, this would after all be the union of two gods that all the people of the Mediterranean knew, albeit in different ways. In Egypt, Dionysus (Antony) corresponds to the Egyptian god Osiris, while Aphrodite (Cleopatra) corresponds to Isis, of whom she is the actual earthly incarnation.

For the Egyptian people, there is a further intrinsic meaning that the queen considers in order to seal the consensus back home. Isis (Cleopatra) is both the sister and wife of Osiris (Dionysus-Antony) and this automatically legitimizes their bond because in Ptolemaic dynasties, as we know, it's always a brother and sister, united in marriage, who sit on the throne.

Naturally, Antony is totally unaware of all this. While waiting for Cleopatra in Tarsus, indulging in parties, banquets, and meetings, she is spinning a web all around him, in which he stands no chance. Apart from the official and religious aspect of the encounter, there's also the personal one. And on this front, Cleopatra is preparing an unprecedented surprise with which she will truly surpass herself.

The Incredible Encounter of Cleopatra and Mark Antony

No sooner does she arrive in Cilicia than the queen of Egypt equips a large ship on board which she plans to sail up the river Cydnus to Tarsus and meet Antony. We don't know if it's the gigantic *thalamegos* she used for her honeymoon with Caesar on the Nile.

Antony and his officers are bombarding her with letters, asking her to hurry, but she pays no heed and, on the contrary, like a film star, makes them wait and leaves only once the ship is ready. The look of the vessel has been altered so much that it will be memorable for centuries to come.

Picture therefore this large ship that casts off its moorings and starts gliding majestically through the water with triumphant slowness, entering the Cydnus from the sea and sailing upstream. The local people follow it from both shores. Children run while the elderly stand still, mouths agape. To them it might as well be a spaceship. Nobody has ever seen anything as elegant or lavish. The news spreads like wildfire throughout the region, and even Tarsus residents drop everything and run to admire this floating wonder.

And Antony? He is sitting in the middle of the main square of Tarsus with his officers, waiting for the queen's arrival. They are surrounded by a huge crowd of onlookers but also illustrious guests, waiting for this historical encounter. Antony is probably annoyed by Cleopatra's attitude and her constant stalling, but knows that the long wait is over.

At one point, something happens. Antony and his officers turn to look right and left. The crowd grows restless and sways. The entire square is invaded by an increasingly intense perfume. The light breeze diffuses an unfamiliar fragrance that is both refreshing and pungent and that seems to fill people's lungs with a thousand olfactory colors. People look around, trying to work out where this exotic aroma is coming from. It's not just the perfume that fills the air. There's now also a distant and equally gentle sound growing louder. People look around, trying to understand, then somebody shouts, pointing at the river, and everybody runs to the bank, as though drawn by a powerful magnet.

Antony and his entourage are left alone, astounded, amid the marbles and colonnades of a suddenly deserted square. The huge magnet that has attracted the residents is Cleopatra. Her ship appears on the river.

The queen has planned her arrival very well, stimulating one sense at a time—smell first, with the scents, then hearing, with music, and now it's the turn of sight. It's a memorable spectacle and even Antony is speechless.

Cleopatra's large ship appears on the calm waters of the river in all its splendor. The stern, completely decked in gold, is gleaming in the sunlight. Orders of oars with a silver glow rise and drop into the water in solemn rhythm to the sound of flutes, zithers, and bagpipes. To all eyes, the ship looks like a gigantic pink cloud hovering over the water because of the large sails dyed crimson. And we know what this pigment costs. It can be obtained only in tiny amounts from a kind of sea snail. An ordinary tunic dyed in crimson is worth a fortune, let alone a sail!

It is these sails that are steeped in the essences and fragrances from faraway lands that the wind has blown into the city, enveloping the crowd in the square. Large braziers are scattered on the deck, in which incense and other Eastern substances are burned, and which give off sweet, penetrating aromas. It's a "special effect" ordained by Cleopatra, who seeks every way to surprise and bewitch. But the best is yet to come . . .

As the ship approaches, surrounded by small escort boats, just like a queen bee encircled by her workers, Antony gets a clearer view of the semi-naked women amid the deployed crimson sails. They are the most beautiful among Cleopatra's handmaidens. They look like Nereids and Graces, and have been symbolically placed at the helm or the cables of the ship (which is actually being maneuvered by the queen's best mariners, hidden from sight).

And here she is, Cleopatra. Antony stands up, wide-eyed, mouth agape. The queen of Egypt is lying beneath a gilded pavilion, and children, like cupids in frescoes, are fanning her with fans made of ostrich feathers. She is at the center of an incredible mythological vision, an authentic *tableau vivant* with a calculated erotic impact, but the true *coup de théâtre* is that she presents herself like Venus "adorned like Aphrodite in paintings," Plutarch confesses. This means Cleopatra may be partly naked or even completely naked. A queen arriving without veils, or almost, for a formal encounter is an unprecedented event. There is no memory now of a meeting like this one. In modern terms, her arrival is in the style of Lady Gaga, it's so eccentric and provocative, but it does obtain the hoped-for result. Because Mark Antony's expression is not far removed from that of Jim Carrey in *The Mask*, with his jaw dropping to the ground.

He keeps looking at her, at times astonished, at times excited like a little boy, turning to his officers and friends, who are as in awe as he is. However, everybody immediately realizes that the queen is literally offering herself to the great Roman military leader.

This atmosphere of an imminent mythological union is accentuated by the crowd, which by now openly considers the event the arrival of Aphrodite with her procession, come to meet and, above all, unite with Dionysus for the good of Asia.

Cleopatra proves to be extremely skillful at this. She understands the people's weaknesses and satisfies their desires by exploiting their beliefs and religion. And she does the same with Antony, aware that he has a soft spot for women, theatrical events, and parties that turn to lust. Her eccentric arrival on board the "mythological" vessel is proof of her reasoning.

But if Antony's objective is now to conquer not only a woman but also a woman who is a queen (politically very convenient), Cleopatra aims much higher. She intends to seduce Antony and, through him, obtain the protection of Rome for Egypt, herself, and her son, Caesarion.

The Invitation to Antony

When the ship docks at the river pier of the city of Tarsus, Antony and his entourage are overwhelmed by a wave of even more intense fragrances. After their initial awe at Cleopatra's *coup de théâtre*, they have resumed a more rigid, severe attitude. At least outwardly. They are sitting on a podium, waiting for the queen to disembark and appear before them, thereby underlining their superiority.

There's an empty stretch of square between them and the ship, with two wings of legionaries struggling to restrain a cheering crowd. A gangplank has been lowered to the ground to allow the queen to disembark. Except that Cleopatra is not coming down.

Growing impatient with her games, Antony sends an officer to ask her to disembark. He follows the soldier with his eyes as he approaches the ship, speaks to one of Cleopatra's emissaries who has come ashore, and returns, obviously embarrassed. He approaches Antony and tells him that the queen will not come ashore but is inviting him and all his most important officers aboard. Perplexed, Antony looks around. Cleopatra has surprised him once again. Only then does he realize that she has been leading the game from the very start. He looks up and sees his officers and colleagues staring at him with an intrigued, amused expression. The crowd is clamoring for their meeting. So he makes up his mind. He will go aboard. Officially, he does it out of "affability and courtesy," as Plutarch would eventually say. In reality, he's about to take his first step into Cleopatra's web.

The queen is down there, waiting for him, watching him from behind a grating. Her eyes are those of a tiger staring at her prey in the half-light. It is a crucial moment for her. Everything depends on what the Roman military leader will do over the next few moments. Will he accept or, on the contrary, force her to come ashore, as a test of strength?

Cleopatra notices a sudden movement on the podium. The Romans have stood up. Are they offended? These are interminable seconds. Then, from the back of the marble esplanade, she sees Antony and his generals and trusted men, almost certainly including Quintus Dellius, walking toward her. Cleopatra half closes her eyes and smiles. Her plan is working. She turns and orders her people to give the last touches to the great inner hall—that's where the meeting will take place.

Antony suspects nothing. He imagines it's a simple banquet on the river and is curious to sample the exotic dishes they will serve him, but above all he wants to meet Aphrodite up close. He heads for it with a light heart, calmly, like someone who feels like the master of the world.

Picture a group of Romans going aboard, the sounds made by these men as they walk up the gangplank, and the creaking of the wood in the large ship. They're welcomed with Eastern music, royal dignitaries who bow before them, and handmaidens with bare breasts and wearing few, very sheer veils, with sinuous gestures, watching them with languid eyes. The ship is enveloped by the inebriating fragrance of substances in the braziers, so intense it practically knocks you out. Everywhere, veils and colorful, impalpable fabrics are fluttering in the wind. The Roman soldiers, Antony at their head, feel as though they've walked into a dream. But Cleopatra is not to be seen. Where is she?

The master of ceremonies invites them into the belly of the ship, following a double row of lit torches, their smoke snaking through the air like fragrant tentacles. After a few steps, an incredible set unfolds before them—one of the most spectacular banquets passed on to us by ancient history. Let's allow a writer like Plutarch and his astonishment (on a par with Antony's) the task of describing the impact:

"Finding himself before a setting superior to any description, Antony was especially struck by the number of lights. They say that so many were shining everywhere at the same time, standing on the floor and hanging from above, and they were arranged so artistically together, at such clever angles, that they formed squares and circles, creating so much light that no human eye had ever seen anything like it."

It must be said that Plutarch describes this day and the banquet more than a hundred years later. Understandably, there are a few inaccuracies, especially in terms of exaggeration, bearing in mind the dark *femme fatale* aura that surrounded Cleopatra for the Romans of the generations that followed. There is however an interesting fact. The Greek author says that only one banquet was held on board the ship. Another ancient writer, on the other hand, mentions a string of parties, each more splendid that the previous one. It's the Greek historian Socrates of Rhodes. Although full of gaps, his descriptions, which have reached us thanks to the erudite Egyptian Athenaeus of Naucratis, allow us to continue with our story and to discover what we could have found on the tables and walls. His words illustrate all Cleopatra's seductive art and the finesse of the trap into which Antony falls. Let's try to understand what the Roman military leader's eyes saw.

Even though we're on board a ship, the room is very large. The Romans walk through a galaxy of torches and oil lamps arranged everywhere and at various levels, like stars forming complex constellations. There are carpets and curtains interwoven with gold and silver thread on the walls. And in the middle stand triclinia for Antony, his friends, and his closest officers, with fine covers and perhaps expensive silks. The inlaid tables in front of the beds are covered with gold dishes and cups studded with gemstones. In other words, real, high-quality jewels are used for tableware. Antony is overwhelmed by the wealth on display. Cleopatra smiles at him sweetly and tells him that everything he sees is his, a gift from the queen, which he can take away with him.

According to Socrates of Rhodes, Cleopatra invites Antony to dine with her again the following day, with his friends and officers, and the day after that, for several days.

The following day, she organizes an even richer, more lavish banquet. The gold cups and very fine glasses are so precious that they make the ones in the previous encounter seem coarse. Once again, she gives everything to Antony. And not just to him. Each of his officers may take away the valuable triclinium on which he lay, along with the drapes that cover it and the gold cups from which he has drunk. And every time they leave, late at night, she provides for the high-ranking guests litters and porters, and for the others horses with silver harnesses, as well as Ethiopian slaves with torches to light their way home.

But it's on the fourth day that Cleopatra surpasses herself. She even spends a talent (now roughly the equivalent of 10,000 euros, since an Athenian/Attican talent corresponds to approximately 26 kilograms of silver) to buy a huge quantity of roses so as to make a "carpet," about a foot thick, in the dining room. There are other roses arranged all over the place as garlands and festoons, adorning every wall in the room.

Although potentially something of an exaggeration, this description gives us an idea of how Cleopatra wagers everything on this meeting. It's been seven years since, as a girl, she emerged from a sack before Caesar. Now she is a woman aware of her charm and very skillful at managing the instincts of the men before her in order to ensnare them.

We can try to imagine the first meeting between the two, when Antony walks into that room for the first time. Where is Cleopatra? Certainly not on her feet, playing the host. Most probably she is lying on a bed, amid a large number of cushions, with a multitude of cupid-like children gently fanning her. We assume she is less naked than when she first arrived on the ship, and that she is in a tunic, maybe even one of the white, delicate, pleated ones she likes to wear in public, which emphasize her figure. And we're not wrong in thinking that the sheerness of this tunic is complicit with Cleopatra's cunning, able to set Antony and his men's eyes alight. She's likely to be showing off the richest jewels of her time: a triumph of gold with sapphires, emeralds, lapis lazuli, and malachites in the form of rings, earrings, pectorals, and bracelets (these perhaps shaped like snakes, dear to Isis). She probably wears on her head the symbols of her status as queen of Egypt, with the uraeus, or head of an erect cobra, over her forehead.

In fact, we don't know how many of these jewels are at this banquet. After all, Cleopatra has presented herself as Aphrodite, a barely clad goddess adorned almost exclusively with Egyptian symbols. We will never know but we can picture the queen on her bed, her curves rising with every breath, as she gazes at Antony confidently, intensely, invitingly, her full lips half open.

No doubt she slowly got up to approach the triumvir with a regal step, moving her body with elegant sensuality. And when, once the formalities were over, she came closer to Antony, she would have enveloped him with an invisible embrace of intense perfumes but also desire, as her eyes captured those of the military leader and her lips protruded almost imperceptibly, turning into a mirage of lustful, sensual kisses.

Antony would have felt her breath, as well as a strong desire to kiss her and hold those provocative curves under the tunic—so close within his reach—in his arms. A moment later, Cleopatra would have probably skillfully walked away, just far enough to make all this impossible and light a growing desire in her future man.

Cleopatra's Beauty

In Antony's eyes, Cleopatra is no longer the little girl he met in Alexandria so many years earlier, or Caesar's young, determined lover. She is now an alluring woman of seductive beauty and with an intense gaze.

Over the following few days, Antony will make efforts in vain to return the invitation. Challenging Cleopatra is a venture bound to fail. Even Plutarch says it: "Antony tried to surpass her in splendor and refinement, but was defeated on both fronts and was the first to joke about the poverty and coarseness of his hospitality. Noticing that Antony's humor was truly that of a vulgar soldier, Cleopatra also adopted a straight, fearless tone with him. As they say, her beauty on its own was not unique or stunning to those who saw her, but her company had an irresistible hold. Altogether, it was the charm of her conversation and her way of dealing with others that made a mark." Plutarch's famous words describe Cleopatra's beauty and charm. But what did she look like? Can we see her face?

Unfortunately, we do not have Cleopatra's mummy, so it's impossible to reconstruct her appearance or obtain her DNA to get an idea of her ethnic or geographic background. Very little is left of her. There is scarce information and description of Egypt's last queen, because after her death Octavian, the winner, would order the destruction of all the images representing her: statues, frescoes, mosaics, paintings, bas-reliefs.

So what did she look like? Is it true that she had a large nose? There's a widespread belief that Cleopatra had a prominent nose. We've all heard this. But it was positively stated by the seventeenth-century French mathematician, philosopher, and theologian Blaise Pascal, who said, "If Cleopatra's nose had been shorter, the entire face of the earth would have changed." Except that, just like us, he didn't know what Cleopatra looked like, so is not reliable. The fact that no ancient writer mentioned her large nose (which would have been excellent ammunition for her critics) means it can't have been all that prominent.

Even two thousand years ago, people didn't know exactly what her features looked like. Ancient writers describe only two representations

of Cleopatra in the whole of Ancient Rome: the statue of gilt bronze
in the Temple of Venus Genetrix, ordered by Julius Caesar, and the
painting of the dying Cleopatra, carried as a symbol of victory at
Octavian's triumphal procession.

All reconstructions must therefore consider the almost total lack
of information. How can we remedy this? We can still try to picture
her face with the little we have. Now we have a few busts and statues
that cannot be attributed with any kind of certainty. It's a different
story, however, when it comes to coins that represent her but which,
strangely, bear no resemblance to the statues (except perhaps in one
case). This adds even more mystery to the beauty of the Egyptian
queen. How can this be possible? Let's proceed in an orderly manner.

There are various bas-reliefs, busts, and statues of Cleopatra in the
Egyptian style. One of these has been in the Museo Egizio in Turin
for generations and only recently become the focus of a possible at-
tribution. Unfortunately, the style of Egyptian art, so unrealistic and
tied to very strict canons, doesn't show what Cleopatra's true features
were like.

Among the few other busts that represent her, two are particularly
striking. One was found in the Villa dei Quintili in Rome, and is in
the Musei Vaticani (in the Museo Gregoriano Profano), and the other
is in the Altes Museum in Berlin. They look similar and are both
of a very young woman with hair in a bun held up by a band that
goes over her forehead. On the Berlin bust, the nose is not large but
just slightly pronounced. According to experts, these are two marble
copies made in Roman workshops, representing a Ptolemaic queen
with a Greek hairstyle, like Cleopatra. Theoretically, they could be
of other queens that preceded her, like Berenice IV or Arsinoe IV.
But why would a Roman aristocrat have had an expensive copy of
an unknown queen made to display in his home, unless it were the
famous Cleopatra who had endangered Rome? This argument leads
many other experts, including Matteo Cadario of Udine University,

to believe that this is "our" Cleopatra (since unfortunately there are no inscriptions engraved on either bust to support that). What's interesting is that the sculptors depicted a twenty-year-old, because that's how old Cleopatra was when she arrived in Rome as Caesar's lover. Moreover, they softened her features slightly, to make her look like Venus. We therefore have before us two idealized, youthful portraits of Cleopatra.

On the coins, on the other hand, the queen looks more mature and her features are more defined, with a very evident aquiline nose. Which shall we therefore trust—the busts or the coins? Well, the coins are of a different time: Cleopatra is no longer Caesar's twenty-year-old lover but an established monarch, at the height of her power, and at the head of a nation and army. For that reason she may have decided (although this is just a theory, however plausible) not to care and to highlight her royal traits, even going as far as to make them more masculine, in order to give her authority more strength and credibility, and to resemble her father even more, so as to legitimize her power (in antiquity, coins were always a propaganda tool).

The truth therefore lies somewhere between these two faces, one made softer, the other more pronounced, one made more feminine, the other more masculine. Based on all these characteristics, is it possible to outline an "average" face that's closer to the truth or is at least plausible?

An attempt was made by the scientific department of the Rome Carabinieri, by Captain Chantal Milani, an anthropologist and forensic odontologist, for an Italian TV program. It was an anomalous study, full of challenges. In the absence of a skeleton or a mummy, they gathered anthropometric characteristics of Cleopatra's face from the statues and coins. More than an actual facial reconstruction, it was a facial composite of the queen, as though the witnesses were the artists who portrayed her in the past. The busts taken into consideration were the ones at the Musei Vaticani and the Berlin museum, as well as four coins in circulation during Cleopatra's lifetime, therefore manufactured by artists who knew what she looked like (although, as we said earlier, making alterations for reasons of propaganda among other things). Without going into technical details, let's say that they then calculated relationships and distances between anatomical points, corners, and proportions, since some areas of the skin suggest the underlying bone structure. This way, they quantified statistically how much Cleopatra's face deviated from the reference standards of an "ideal face," by using dentistry, cosmetic medicine, and plastic surgery parameters. Just to clarify: an "ideal" face can be divided into three equal horizontal strips. This wasn't the case with Cleopatra, the upper part of whose face—that is, the forehead—is rather low, while the central strip is broader than in an "ideal" face, with a nose that is higher and more pronounced than the norm. The bottom part of the face, on the other hand, is within the norm (and, we can add, with a small mouth and defined lips). We must reiterate that, although this is a theory based on correct scientific principles, it's not an analysis performed on a real body but on its artistic representation (the marble busts and the coins), and therefore has objective limitations. It does, however, confirm what the ancients always said: Cleopatra was not beautiful but alluring. And that important nose was not ugly or out of place (otherwise, the ancients, especially those who were hostile to her, would have pointed that out), but it clearly matched the rest of her face and was in harmony with her character and her eyes. Today, we'd say her nose gave her face personality.

On the other hand, if you think of all the beautiful, famous actresses, you'll often come across one with a nose that's not very small, but which emphasizes the charm and strength of her face. There's even Maria Callas, who, like Cleopatra, was of Greek origin, had charisma, a pronounced nose, and . . . a very sweet voice.

Unfortunately, there's nothing else we can say about Cleopatra's appearance, nor the color of her skin. Being Greco-Macedonian, with ancestors who married within the community if not within the family, it's not impossible that she may have had fair skin and perhaps brown, blond, or red hair, and even pale-colored eyes. If, however, her mother, as some theories claim, came from the entourage of Theban high priests, then it could have been the opposite, and she could have had darker skin, frizzy hair, and dark eyes. In support of this second theory we should say that in Roman times, the model of the ideal woman was eastern Mediterranean. Both Caesar and Antony would have attracted more envy and approval with this type of woman.

In the reconstruction by the scientific department of the Carabinieri, despite the difficulty presented by this kind of study, another interesting aspect emerges. The facial parameters suggest that Cleopatra's face may have had mainly Caucasian and not African, let alone Asian, characteristics. Significant details also emerge about her famous nose. The tip looks slightly down, giving it an aquiline form but, above all, the collection of data suggests it was larger than average. How much larger? An "ideal" nose, used as reference, protrudes from the face by 67 percent of its diagonal length. In Cleopatra's case it's by 73 percent, in other words, a rather pronounced nose that, in the final depiction, has been slightly adapted in order to make it more plausible. These are the suggestions resulting from the Carabinieri analysis.

Observing the coins and busts, we'll add another characteristic to the previous ones, one that is not really considered when speaking of Cleopatra's beauty—her large eyes. Perhaps they rather than her nose or height (Cleopatra was probably short) were the Egyptian queen's true weapon of seduction. Maybe she captured the hearts of the Roman military leaders thanks to those deep, expressive eyes. Besides her mind, of course, which was capable of uncommon intelligence.

Slave of Love and Sex

Despite his extensive experience with women, including able and shrewd ones, Antony capitulated immediately. On that, all the ancients concur. Cassius Dio writes tersely, "Antony met Cleopatra in Cilicia. He fell in love with her and, with no regard for decorum, became her slave and devoted all his time to love." Appiano echoes him: ". . . he yielded to her charm no sooner than he saw her. And this passion ended up attracting ruin on them and the whole of Egypt." He adds that Antony allegedly let himself be seduced by Cleopatra "like a boy, even though he was forty years old." Josephus, always hostile to Cleopatra, reinforces the message, stating that Antony was so much under the Egyptian queen's thumb that he granted her every wish, not like an ordinary man in love but actually as though he were under the influence of a drug.

And did she, Cleopatra, make Antony drop into her arms only through calculation or because she fell in love with him? Maybe she fell in love with him from the beginning, tripping into the very trap she had laid out. And for good reason, because he truly is an attractive man. Tall, with a wide, muscular chest, broad shoulders, a solid, powerful body like Hercules, a square, manly jaw, and a mass of curly hair (unlike Caesar, who was almost bald). He's forty-two years old and oozes virility. Today, we would say that he has the charm of a silver fox. And that's not all. He also has the allure of power. Being the most influential man in the Western world, all men bow before his authority, while women compete to give themselves to him, since he is by now famous for being a skirt chaser. Someone said that power (with its consequential success and wealth) is the most irresistible aphrodisiac for a woman. This also applies to Cleopatra, who is drawn to this charismatic character everybody views as a leader.

There's almost certainly a spark of sexual attraction between them from the first few evenings. Both are in the prime of life, on a dream-like ship, amid banquets, music, carefree laughter, and in the middle of summer. In a steamy affair of passion and sex, they are drawn to each other, their bodies cling together, their mouths come together, and their senses blend. Only to seek each other out and get together again the following night.

But it's not just a sexual affair. Cleopatra and Antony like each other, are strongly drawn to each other, and soon develop an unexpected understanding and complicity. That something has blossomed between them is confirmed by the fact that they meet again in Alexandria not long afterward.

Cleopatra stays in Tarsus for only a few days, just long enough to obtain the essential reassurance for herself and her country. From the diplomatic point of view, the mission is an incredible success. She had come to provide an explanation and instead leaves with important concessions snatched from Antony. Admittedly, not many men would have been able to hold diplomatic discussions in these conditions. It's their emissaries who do that while the two of them enjoy the banquets. This way, Cleopatra obtains important results. Once her behavior during the war against the Caesaricides is cleared up, Antony once again acknowledges Caesarion as Egypt's legitimate sovereign. In exchange for the queen's support for the imminent expedition against the Parthians, he reiterates that the important island of Cyprus belongs to her.

Cleopatra's requests are increasingly pressing. She asks for the physical elimination of all her most dangerous enemies, so Antony orders the cold-blooded murder of all potential contenders to the throne of Egypt who could oust her and her son. The most dangerous is her sister Arsinoe IV, author of the great popular and military uprising in Alexandria against Caesar and Cleopatra. As we saw, after being dragged in chains at Julius Caesar's triumph in Rome, she was freed and took refuge in the Temple of Artemis at Ephesus, one of the seven wonders of the ancient world. Cleopatra asks Antony to eliminate her. He agrees and sends mercenaries to Ephesus. However, since the Temple of Artemis is a sacred, inviolable area, she cannot be executed inside it. So the assassins drag her out of the temple by force and kill her quickly. On Cleopatra's suggestion, Antony also orders the killing of Serapion, the master of Cyprus, who had supplied ships to Cassius, betraying Cleopatra, Antony, and Octavian.

At a stroke, she eliminates almost every external and internal threat to her power, reinforces her place on the throne and that of her son, and strengthens her relationship with Rome, now a powerful ally that protects Egypt. It's victory across the board.

8

True Love

The Two Seek Each Other Out

Once the banquets and the days of unadulterated passion are over, Cleopatra's ship casts off and returns to Egypt, while Mark Antony, at the head of his troops, resumes his journey to bring order and stability to the Middle East. Apart from their expectations and objectives for this meeting, they have both been more deeply struck by each other than they had anticipated. Antony has been conquered by the sunny disposition of a woman who's different than any other he's met so far. Cleopatra, on the other hand, certain she could outsmart this man stirred by basic instincts, falls under the charm of his protective manliness and the male energy he oozes, in spite of herself. Don't forget that Cleopatra is, first and foremost, a woman, and because of her royal status cannot, unlike Antony, allow herself love affairs or sexual relations, whether transient or long-lasting. So, for all her being an ambitious woman of power, she most probably misses having a companion at her side. Given how the situation will then turn out, as you will see, we can suppose that she feels especially involved in this relationship. Something she certainly had not taken into account when engineering the encounter with the clear intention of making Antony fall at her feet, going as far as leaving her son back home so she could devote herself to him fully. She, too, has also been affected by the "side effects." We can therefore imagine that as the days go by, they both feel an increasing need to see each other, even though they don't confess this to a soul.

In the Middle East, Mark Antony must first and foremost tackle the threat of the Parthians across the border. What's surprising is that this enemy empire, strange as it might sound, now has a valiant Roman officer in its ranks, and Antony must confront a fellow countryman who has gone over to the enemy.

It is Quintus Labienus, the son of one of Caesar's most loyal supporters (read *The Gallic Wars* and you'll find his father, the legate Titus Labienus, always at the general's side), but who had switched to the side of Caesar's assassins. Brutus and Cassius had sent him as an ambassador to Rome's fierce enemies to forge an alliance with them and beat Mark Antony and Octavian. Reaching an agreement with someone who wants the end of Rome is absurd enough, but fighting on their side is even more so. Orodes, the king of the Parthians, has in fact entrusted Labienus with a large army, which he uses to stage raids in Syria and Asia Minor (Turkey). Antony therefore reorganizes the Middle Eastern region, strengthening bonds with the Jews in Judea and turning his attention to those who rule the area, like the priest Hyrcanus and the powerful governor Herod.

Then, in November, he decides to go to Egypt, to see Cleopatra again. It's only been eight weeks since their great encounter. His decision is probably partly motivated by diplomacy, but one thing is certain. In order to get to her, he crosses the entire arid desert expanses of the Middle East, which makes you realize how much he is in love with her. Naturally, the queen doesn't discourage him, because she desires him most ardently.

That this is a chiefly personal visit is proved by the fact that Mark Antony comes into Alexandria not as a military leader at the head of a military procession (he remembers well Caesar's problems when he disembarked with insignia as a Roman consul), but as a private citizen, without an escort of soldiers. He probably has with him only a few bodyguards in civilian clothes.

In the future, he would be much criticized for this decision. "While the threat of a Parthian army [. . .] was hanging over Mesopotamia and about to invade Syria," Plutarch writes, "Antony let Cleopatra take him to Alexandria. And there he indulged in amusements appropriate for an idle boy, eating and squandering [. . .] the most valuable thing one can squander, that is, time"—implying that it was Cleopatra who invited him. Who knows, perhaps Antony thinks of winter as the time for a break and a holiday, since not only must one not sail in the Mediterranean then, but the weather also discourages big military campaigns.

And so the two of them embark on a relationship that is to become no less legendary than their encounter in Tarsus. It's a very long "honeymoon" in the extraordinary setting of Alexandria.

A Honeymoon That Lasts Six Months

We can imagine their encounter. Since Antony arrives incognito, there are no formalities or ceremonies to abide by. It's nice to picture Antony walking into the palace and being left alone in a large hall, a door at the far end of it suddenly opening, and Cleopatra running to him, breathless, into that intense, much-awaited embrace. His hands sink into the queen's colorful garments as his muscular arms envelop her slender body like the branches of an old oak tree. We can imagine her perfume wrapping around them both, her golden crown falling to the floor while their minds melt into a lingering, intense kiss as smoldering as the flames of the desire setting their bodies alight. There's no need for words; it's the silence that speaks, as do their hands and eyes. But it's the kisses that speak above all, first to the lips, then to the neck, then to the chest, stripped, offering a panting breath, while the mouth of one who has waited so long lands on the skin and kisses slide gently, writing the invisible words of a love poem only the heart understands.

They are no longer a general and a queen, Dionysus and Aphrodite, but just a man and a woman longing for each other, who love and like each other. They are Antony and Cleopatra.

From this moment on they're inseparable. They spend every minute together, every hour, every dawn, and every dusk. Perhaps they realize that they have, after all, always been alone, and that the person in their arms completes them to perfection. They're happy, want to make each other happy, and sense that their happiness exists only if they are united.

This is what we sense, two thousand years later, even though we are not in the palace with them. Putting aside mutual political convenience, they both need love and protection: Cleopatra because of her loneliness, so unfair on a young woman (Caesar's "widow"), and Antony because of his need to have at his side a strong, independent, protective woman in whom to seek refuge despite his physical prowess and numerous female conquests.

He feels so comfortable with Cleopatra that he seems to forget about everything else, as though suffering from amnesia or under a spell. He takes off his Roman clothes and puts on traditional Greek garments and footwear.

She, for her part, does everything to make her new lover happy. She panders to Antony's every whim. She does so out of calculation, of course, but we think also from instinct, desire, and just for the sake of it, simply because she's falling in love with her man. She's always devising some new form of pleasure. Above all, they're like two teenagers in love. They're never apart. They play dice together, drink and go hunting together, and if he trains in military exercises then she is beside him. Even though some ancient writers see all this as a sign of the progressive dominion of the Egyptian queen over Mark Antony, we see two people desperately in love. They love to indulge in nighttime outings, incognito, down the streets of Alexandria, mixing with people, roaming around dressed as ordinary people if not actually slaves.

In the working-class areas, Antony often pauses outside a door or a window to make fun of whoever is inside, and, according to Appian, occasionally even gets hit. Does nobody really recognize him? Plutarch replies, "Most people suspected his identity. Even so, Alexandrians enjoyed his pranks and joked with him politely and without overstepping the limits."

In this three-dimensional dream, Cleopatra and Mark Antony live their love for months. A love made up of parties, intimate strolls, fiery sunsets admired in silence in each other's arms, and smoldering nights, united by a passion that never ends.

Love and Banquets in a Gilded Nest

Even though she's a very active woman capable of traveling far by sea and land, only one setting provides the background to the most significant moments in Cleopatra's life, and that's the royal palace of the Ptolemaic kings in Alexandria.

For centuries, the "pharaohs" of the dynasty to which she belongs have lived here. Every one of them, starting with Alexander the Great, the founder of the city that also began Hellenism, has enriched it with new buildings and structures. Cleopatra has therefore inherited an architectural jewel that's unique in the world, which she knows like the back of her hand because this is where she was born and grew up with her family. Every corner reminds her of her father, her mother, her nurses, her brothers, and her sisters, now all dead. But there's also the place where she met Julius Caesar, the location of the siege she experienced with him, and the rooms where Caesarion took his first steps. Now life is writing a new chapter of her existence, this time beside Antony, but still on the same "pages" as the palace.

It must be said that in no way does it look like a classic royal palace and is much larger. Rather, it looks like the Forbidden City in Beijing or the Topkapi in Istanbul. And it has a name: Brucheion.

We can call it a kind of royal district, a city within a city. It extends along the coast, taking up almost a quarter (if not a third) of the city of Alexandria. Inside, there are temples, porticos, gardens, and numerous buildings and pavilions. Statues, mosaics, and fountains can be admired everywhere. The tomb of Alexander the Great is also located here, as well as the necropolises of Ptolemaic sovereigns, the great Library of Alexandria, and the famous Musaeum, a kind of university of that era.

At the heart of this royal district, there is also the residence of the monarchs, the Ptolemies' "presidential residence," which contains streets, gardens, porticos, buildings, and even a theater. In every building, the visitor is impressed with the furnishings, which bring together the best of the three continents: Africa, Asia, and Europe.

Let's try and picture this place. In a single room, you can most probably see surfaces in ivory from African elephants, coatings made from the shells of turtles from the Red Sea, ceilings covered in layers of mother-of-pearl from oysters from the Indian Ocean, Persian rugs, drapes dyed in crimson, statues and pillars of marble from quarries on the Aegean Sea, African malachite cups, Baltic amber statuettes, couches covered in African leopard skins, and Chinese silk sheets. The furniture is made of wood from cedars of Lebanon and decorated with ivory and mother-of-pearl inlays, while the doors are coated in gilt bronze, and the paneled ceilings are painted with bright colors. The timber gives off an intense exotic aroma everywhere, at times covered by that of braziers burning incense and other Eastern essences. Moreover, there is a large quantity of gold, plating the details on the beds, drinking cups, and many elements of indoor decor.

Lucan's story confirms this vision of ours, as he describes Cleopatra's palace by adding further details that make our jaws drop. It no doubt has a level of luxury the Roman world has never seen. "That place looked like a temple that a more corrupt age would struggle to erect. The paneled ceilings were full of riches and the beams were covered in solid gold. The palace glowed, clad not with marble slabs applied to the walls, but blocks of agate and porphyry, while all the floors of the entire royal palace were made of onyx. Mareotic ebony did not cover the large doors but constituted, as rough oak usually does, the support and not the ornament of the palace. The lobbies were clad with ivory, and the doors decorated with Indian turtle shells, hand painted and studded with a considerable amount of emeralds. The beds glittered with gemstones and the furnishings with tawny jasper; the rugs shone and most of them, boiled for a long time in Tyrus crimson, had absorbed the tint through various immersions, some embroidered in gold and others a fiery red, following the Egyptian technique of embroidering and warping fabrics."

There's an anecdote that illustrates the unlimited dimension (especially from the financial point of view) of the love between Antony and Cleopatra, and it remains relevant. We know from the ancients that every meal for them is a lavish feast. Plutarch himself states that his grandfather told him a surprising "backstage" story that surfaced thanks to the confessions of a friend of his, the physician Philotas of Amphissa, who had sneaked into Cleopatra's kitchens thanks to his good relationship with one of her personal cooks.

Since it's impossible to tell when Antony will ask to eat, being always busy and unpredictable, the kitchens work nonstop, roasting at least eight boars at the same time (Plutarch specifies) with appropriate side dishes and many other dishes. Although it could appear like the preparations for a crowded banquet, according to the cook, there are never many guests, a dozen or so, but every dish has to be cooked to perfection, no matter at what time. Hence the large amount of meat on the spit: "Not just one but several meals are prepared," he admits, in a kind of 24/7 restaurant.

We can picture Antony and Cleopatra's feats thanks to a story by Lucan, which actually concerns an event four years earlier but certainly still applies to their "honeymoon" in Alexandria.

"And again here comes a crowd of handmaidens and entire mass of servants. Some could be told apart by the color of their skin, others by their age. One group wore their hair in Libyan style, another was very blond [. . .] and another, from a race scorched by the sun, had such curly hair that it never fell over their foreheads. There were also hapless youths, castrated and deprived of their manly attributes; there were other young men ahead of them, more mature but with just a light down covering their cheeks."

The description of the banquet continues by saying that every food yielded by the earth, sea, air, and the Nile is served in the gold dishes—often animals and birds Egyptians venerate as divinities. The diners' hands are washed in Nile water poured from glass chalices. They sip wine from goblets carved from gemstones (probably sardonyx agates, like the splendid Farnese Cup in the National Archaeological Museum in Naples, which is from the Hellenic era and of Alexandrian style). All the diners wear crowns interwoven with spikenard flowers and roses that will not wilt soon—their oiled foliage is sprinkled with exotic cinnamon and cardamom freshly picked from a neighboring field. In other words, everybody is decked out and fragrant. And sometimes, before the other (bewildered) guests, as many ancient authors would write, Mark Antony gets up lovingly to massage Cleopatra's feet.

Cleopatra's Pearls

The queen is sitting next to Antony. She is wearing heavy makeup and is covered in jewels. Lucan describes an interesting detail: "Covered in Red Sea pearls, she flaunted her jewels on her neck and hair even though all that adornment was heavy." Cleopatra looked on pearls very much as ornaments, so much so that they also appear on some of the coins representing her. And on that subject, it's worth telling an anecdote by Pliny the Elder.

The two lovers compete at surprising each other with gifts and stunning delights. During a banquet, to astound Mark Antony, Cleopatra uses an extremely rare oriental pearl.

According to Pliny, Cleopatra owns both the largest pearls of all time, gifted to her by kings from the Orient. They now hang from her ears.

While Antony is stuffing himself with splendid, refined dishes, Cleopatra complains and says they can do better. On cue, before the splendor and extreme luxury of the banquet, he asks what more one could hope for, and she replies with defiance that she could eat at least 10 million sestertii in a single sitting. Antony doesn't believe her and so they have a bet. The following day, Cleopatra has an extraordinary dinner prepared, although not that different from the usual. Antony points that out to her, laughing, and she assures him that this dinner will cost the wagered price, and that she will single-handedly eat ten million sestertii by the end of the banquet, then orders the second course. Before Antony's incredulous eyes, the servants bring her a single goblet of vinegar. The queen then removes one of her earrings, with one of the wonderful, rare pearls, and drops it into the vinegar, "so acidic as to dissolve the pearl completely," Pliny the Elder remarks.

From the chemical point of view, a pearl is basically formed of calcium carbonate and dissolves in a concentration of acetic acid higher than that of table vinegar, equivalent to 5–7 percent. Cleopatra's pearl is therefore turned into calcium acetate, producing water and carbon dioxide in the form of a fizzy veil. This way, the acidity is partly neutralized, making the vinegar drinkable.

Once the pearl is liquefied, Cleopatra swallows it. But that's not all. The queen reaches for her other earring to do the same thing with it, but before the second pearl can go into the vinegar one of the guests, Lucius Pnacus, the arbiter of the bet, puts a hand over it and proclaims Cleopatra the winner, thus saving this second natural masterpiece from disappearing forever.

After Antony and Cleopatra's death, this pearl would end up in Rome, where it would be cut in half to make earrings for a famous statue of Venus in the Pantheon. As Pliny the Elder would remark with humor, "When the queen was captured, [. . .] the pearl was cut in half so that both ears of the statue of Venus, placed in the Pantheon in Rome, should bear half that dinner of theirs."

This episode was re-created by numerous famous painters and artists, like Giambattista Tiepolo, who, in the mid-eighteenth century, turned it into an immortal work on one of the walls of Palazzo Labia in Venice.

Antony's Prank

Mark Antony and Cleopatra spent most of their time together. They enjoy joking and entertaining themselves with games, which we might consider childish. For instance, we know from Plutarch that they went fishing.

So here they are on board an elegant boat, going into the network of canals in the Delta, not far from Alexandria. The vessel seems to glide on the flat water. It has a peculiar shape. The bow is straight and very tall, with the head of a mythological animal on the top. From here it looks like Anubis but we could be wrong. It's covered in gold surfaces, ivory sculptures, and chiseled slabs of silver. It has three oars on each side, operated by as many rowers, who rise and fall in unison with mesmerizing perfection and slowness. The stern rises to the sky even higher than the bow, curving forward over the boat to then go up vertically like the dorsal fin of a shark. On this "fin" a silk ribbon dyed in crimson flutters majestically. The helmsman sits in the hollow of the stern and directs the two lateral rudders with few but determined movements. In the middle stands a kind of small gilded house with carved wooden gratings. Inside, in the semidarkness, two bodies are clinging to each other in love. In a corner of light, you can only see Antony's hand sliding down Cleopatra's thigh, pushing away her tunic then traveling up her hip. She moves one of her thighs to welcome her man, but suddenly the shade, like a curtain, hides everything from our sight, following the change of direction chosen by the helmsman. He's noticed the head of a hippopotamus at the bow. There are also crocodiles, but there's nothing to fear, they are a regular presence in the Nile and its Delta, and besides, the personal bodyguards who escort Antony and Cleopatra on other boats watch over every movement. It's not easy, because the vegetation is luscious. They sail among reeds, tufts of papyri, and elegant water lilies with petals open on the water, like fans. Their surface is studded with small drops of water that sparkle like stars.

The royal boat advances into a cone of shade produced by tall trees. A group of wild ducks swims away. It's the perfect spot. The ship stops and everybody waits, but it takes a few more minutes for the curtains of the gilded little house to part. Antony emerges first, rearranging his tunic embroidered in gold. Cleopatra follows him a few seconds later and everybody bows. It's not the first time they have come here, one of their favorite spots for fishing . . . and in truth just an excuse for being together, away from the palace. Meanwhile, the rowers and helmsman have moved to another boat to leave the royal couple alone in this small paradise. Only two servants have stayed on board, apart, ready to serve the two lovers food, wine, and small sweetmeats.

Antony and Cleopatra slide down on cushions in the shade of a drape dyed in crimson. The queen rests her head on his chest and he gently strokes her hair. He takes her smooth, amber-colored hand, on which she wears two rings, one with the royal seal. It's so small compared with his hand, rough and marked with scars from many battles. Cleopatra's fingers feel the softness of Antony's lips as he kisses them one by one.

Between a goblet of wine and a snack, two hours have gone by already, but Antony hasn't caught anything. His fishing rod has remained motionless. Cleopatra tries to conceal a mocking smile. Although she says nothing, the Roman general has understood perfectly and feels an increasing sense of embarrassment that stings his pride. So he finds an excuse to go see one of the servants. We know his plan: he orders him to go fetch some fish from a few local fishermen and, secretly swimming under the water, attach it to his fishhook. Then he returns to the queen and resumes frolicking with her. A few minutes later, the rod suddenly bends. He leaps to his feet, feigning excitement, and engages in a brief but intense struggle with the prey . . . until he pulls up a large fish he quickly gives to the servant, so Cleopatra doesn't notice it's already dead. Antony throws the fishing line in again and, a few seconds later, there's another miraculous catch . . . then another again. Cleopatra congratulates him on his courage and good fortune, expresses surprise and excitement, her eyes are open wide, but in actual fact she has worked everything out. And already she is thinking of an appropriate response.

The following day, she tells a few friends about Antony's miraculous catch and invites them to take part in a new fishing trip. Naturally, he agrees, thinking he'll resort to the same trick. Once everyone's in the boats and Antony throws in the line, Cleopatra orders her servants to go underwater before Antony's and to attach to the hook a salt fish from Pontus. She then waits, smiling. When Mark Antony hears the rod bend, he enacts the usual show of a difficult catch and finally pulls aboard the ready-salted fish. Naturally, everybody bursts out laughing. Then, Plutarch writes, Cleopatra says to him, "Leave the fishing rod to us who rule over Pharos and Canopus, oh great commander. Cities, kingdoms, and continents are your prey." This brief episode, told by Plutarch and which we have fictionalized a little, shows what kind of woman Cleopatra is. Even in games she likes to dominate and doesn't like losing.

The Temple of Knowledge: the Musaeum and the Library of Alexandria

The two lovers don't spend their days only on these simple pastimes. They also enjoy culture, and in Alexandria there is a true temple of knowledge. It's the Musaeum, a cross between a university and a monastery, and they often go to this magnificent place.

Alexandria is not just a trading city but also the most important cultural hub in the entire Mediterranean. And it's not the only beacon of knowledge. There are other centers like Athens, Pergamon, Rhodes, and Ephesus that are no less important, depending on the era and field of knowledge (Ephesus, for instance, is one of the capitals of ancient medicine and surgery, the way Atlanta, Baltimore, and other cities in the United States or other parts of the world, where there are research centers and cutting-edge medical schools, might be now).

It was the first ruler of Alexandria, Ptomely I, who lived about three hundred years before Cleopatra, who, thanks to huge investments, built the two beating hearts of ancient culture: the Musaeum and the very famous Library, which constitute an extraordinary temple of knowledge and the best that man can express in this part of the world. We are truly witnessing the first organized steps that would lead to scientific thought and modern scientific research.

Let's go into the Musaeum. Don't be deceived by its name. It bears no relation to our museums. It has no display of ancient artifacts or art masterpieces. In Cleopatra's time, it's the equivalent of a university or research institute. Once past the entrance pillars, you immediately get a sense of being inside a hive of knowledge, amid a multitude of people walking past you, whose sole activity is to produce the honey of knowledge. As you cross halls and courtyards, you realize right away that here people are completely different from those you left just seconds ago, in the streets. They are not merchants, soldiers, or navigators, but scholars from every corner of the known world. Many are Greek, others from Asia Minor and the Middle East. And there is certainly no shortage of Eastern faces, from as far as Persia and India. You recognize them the moment they emerge from a colonnade, talking to other scholars, because they dress in exotic fashions.

Exploring the Musaeum's various rooms, you notice many long beards, always a characteristic of Greek philosophers and thinkers. All these scholars, who represent the most enlightened minds of the countries and cities from where they come, have come here to join their knowledge to that of others, challenge one another and learn from those who know more than they do, thus allowing knowledge—a collective game—to grow and find new boundaries.

Here, they have total freedom to consult any book in the library, but also to further their knowledge by debating with others and studying alone. And many give away their knowledge by giving lessons. In other words, it's exactly what we can see in modern universities, with lecture theaters, free-access libraries, and research laboratories. We take it for granted, but in 40 BC it's a glimmer in the darkness, an incredible exception and a hope for the future.

Many of the people you come across often stay here, because the Musaeum, just like a monastery, has a wing for the scholars' accommodation and a kind of refectory for shared meals. There is also a promenade with an exedra, for anyone who wants some fresh air.

Here, about two and a half centuries before Cleopatra, ever-eternal figures lived, studied, and made fundamental discoveries in the history of knowledge; people like Eratosthenes, philosopher, mathematician, poet, astronomer, and the Library's third librarian, famous for his works on geography and history. It was he who calculated the circumference of the earth, with an error—we now know—of only 1.5 percent, an impressive result with one very important implication: the notion that the earth was round was already taken as read 2,300 years ago.

Here, knowledge also took fundamental steps in mathematics, with Euclid, the father of geometry; in medicine with Herophilos, considered the first anatomist in history; in physics with Strato of Lampsacus, author of the theory of void that allowed another scholar, Ctesibius, to design pumps and plumbing systems. As you'll gather, modern knowledge has its roots in this specific place.

But great names in literature and lyric and elegiac poetry are also studied here, like Callimachus and Theocritus. Callimachus was the greatest writer of his time, and even devised a practical system for navigating the endless series of books kept in the Library of Alexandria.

Continuing on our tour, we notice that some men are discreetly keeping an eye on a passage leading to the inner courtyard of the Musaeum. Taking advantage of a worker carrying a chest with papyri, we go through a checkpoint and, a few seconds later, reach the end of the corridor. We are struck by the light in the courtyard and the silence. There's only one voice speaking, uttering words in Greek. We keep walking into the most private area of the complex. After passing the umpteenth checkpoint of armed men (there are some all over the place, monitoring the location and the comings and goings of people here), we sit on a projection at the base of a pillar. Before us, a man is explaining the movements of heavenly bodies. We discover that the discussion here probably isn't about whether it's the earth or sun that's at the center of the solar system—the scholars of Alexandria have known for some time that the sun is in the center and that the earth revolves around it. Aristarchus of Samos, a giant of astronomy, was apparently the first to see the sun as the center of the universe and try to measure the dimension of the Earth and its distance from the sun. These are conversations we would expect to hear at a NASA conference and yet this is—I wish to reiterate—more than 2,200 years ago. Aristarchus taught here, and now the man everybody is listening to in silence is putting forward his ideas. Among those present, we see Antony and Cleopatra. They have no thrones, or dignitaries, or servants at their side. They are dressed simply, in elegant but not luxurious clothes; they are not here as a king and queen, but only to learn new ideas. And they are listening, enthralled.

To Preserve Knowledge or Destroy It

We walk away. A few yards farther stands antiquity's largest library, which probably contains 800,000 books.

We don't know what the building looked like per se, but we can imagine marble everywhere, and rooms and wooden tables where you can consult the works. Light is an essential element for reading papyri (do lenses for those with eyesight problems already exist? We cannot rule it out), and naturally, sunlight is preferable to oil lamps, which constitute a huge danger to the papyri because of their bare flames. It's logical to think that there would have been large windows or small courtyards in the reading rooms, in order to have enough light to consult the works comfortably. Common sense also suggests that these rooms would have been separate from the actual Library. Given the hot, humid climate and the proximity to the sea, as well as the geographical position of Alexandria, the delicate papyri must be kept in dry rooms with the correct ventilation to avoid mold forming. We find an example of similar caution in Rome, 150 years later, in the large grain warehouses in Portus, the harbor of Ostia, another seaside city. To stop the huge quantities of cereals being damaged, the storerooms were lifted and "detached" from the ground (and were not in contact with the surrounding walls) and there were gaps in the floor, still visible today.

Direct sunlight also damages valuable documents, so the rolls of papyrus are probably kept in sheltered places, in the shade, often enclosed in containers that also protect them from insect attack. This is a system predominantly used for the most important works and treatises, which can be consulted only with immense care.

It's unthinkable that anyone can circulate through the rooms freely and pick whatever they like. There is probably staff to assist the scholars in finding the manuscripts, navigate a true labyrinth of shelves and cupboards, and note down which book is borrowed by whom, so that it may be returned safely. It's very likely that they are the only people allowed to get their hands on the shelves, in order to keep the papyri safe. Naturally, these are suppositions dictated by common sense, since we have no descriptions on the subject. Furthermore, the Library also produced hand copies of the treatises it acquired, and perhaps these were the copies handled by the scholars.

The production and acquisition of manuscripts was such that at one stage, the shelf space ran out and another, smaller library was opened in the Temple of Serapis. It is the so-called Serapeum library.

For a moment, picture yourself roaming along the corridors of the Library. You are at the heart of knowledge in antiquity. All the knowledge of the time is concentrated here, the fruit of generations of thinkers. In the semidarkness, you pass young staff members leading the way for some white-bearded, wrinkled scholar. Even if your eyes meet for a moment, you see in his face the wisdom of an old man mixed with the curiosity of a youth, both animated by the same, infinite thirst for discovering the world.

All around you, there's a series of wooden bookcases all the way up to the ceiling. They are not horizontal but diagonal, thus forming many lozenges where papyri can be stored atop one another without rolling on the shelves. At regular intervals, there are the famous *pinakes* invented by Callimachus. These are hanging tablets with many little paintings that indicate the genre to which the papyri in this section belong. Callimachus wanted all the books in the Library to be subdivided into six literary genres (rhetoric, law, epics, tragedy, comedy, and lyric) and five "prose" sections (history, medicine, mathematics, natural sciences, and miscellaneous works). Reading the tablets, we discover that these books are organized in alphabetical order by author. Glancing at the names, we see many very famous ones, and pick one out of curiosity. We memorize the number and section of the bookcase and move away. A few steps away, we reach the correct panel, where many papyri are stored atop one another. Where is ours? Easy—every scroll has a bibliography file hanging from the shelf, stating the title of the book, the author's name and birthplace, the names of his father, his pupils, and a few cultural experiences, in other words a kind of résumé that lists his other works, with brief summaries of their contents. Sliding out one of the scrolls is indescribably thrilling. With the utmost care, we open it and see dense lines, written in Greek in impeccable handwriting (the printing press is fifteen centuries away). We are holding in our hands the peak of human knowledge at the time of Cleopatra. We get the feeling we're at the cultural frontiers of the world as we know it. Beyond it there's nothing but darkness. It's a moving feeling, because everything is so delicate, light, and subtle. This thin page of papyrus contains, in a veil of ink, the mind of the man who has begun to inquire about himself and the world.

All this would be swept away and destroyed . . . When and how, though, is a much-debated question.

Some say it could have been in AD 270, during Aurelian's devastating war against the dissident queen Zenobia, when the entire district would be destroyed, including Cleopatra's palace and the Library with the Musaeum possibly even razed to the ground.

According to others, seeing that the Musaeum is mentioned by some sources a few years later, it all happened in 391, with Theodisius's edict and the proscription of all pagan religions. The temples would be destroyed or turned into churches, the priests murdered, and anyone practicing cults different from Catholic Christianity would be persecuted with a religious fanaticism that reminds us very much of current episodes. It's in this climate that Hypathia, Alexandria's famous female scholar, would be savagely killed in the city streets by Christian fanatics. In truth, this is not just an attack on Greek religion, but also and above all on the Hellenistic way of thinking. It will mark the end of that extraordinary moment in human history, which began in Classical Greece and continued with Alexander the Great, that sparked Hellenism, so fertile in free thought and investigators of the world around but also inside man, and which would evolve further with the Roman Empire. Admittedly, the ancient world is rich in gods, but when all's said and done, it has a secular way of thinking.

The Serapeum, the Temple of Serapis, would be destroyed, and, with it, Alexandria's second library, the main one's "subsidiary," and so tens of thousands of papyri of Greek works (some say even 200,000 or 300,000) would go up in smoke. However, according to many scholars, the Library of Alexandria survived this nuclear winter unleashed by monotheism on people's culture and religion, but finally came to a definitive end, according to other authors, like Franco Cardini and Luciano Canfora, with the Arab conquest of Egypt.

In 642, by order of Caliph Omar, all the manuscripts would be burned. According to a medieval author (Bar Hebraeus, who lived around the mid-1200s), when asked what was to be done with the books of the royal library, the Caliph replied, "These texts contain either things already addressed in the Koran, or things alien to the Koran. If they are already written in the Koran, then they are useless, and if they are not, then they are harmful and must be destroyed." The same author informs us that the scrolls were used as fuel to heat the soldiers' Turkish baths. It would take six months to burn them all.

If this was truly how they ended up (no one can tell for certain), then what was dissolved in that smoke that rose up those chimneys from the furnaces were the discoveries and thoughts of generations of men and women who gave birth to this extraordinary blossoming of the human mind in the ancient world. Professor Cardini adds: "It's hard to dispute the fact that the Greek collection in the Library of Alexandria disappeared in the mid-seventh century. This is moreover confirmed by another datum. It's from precisely that time that the entire Mediterranean experienced a drastic interruption in the arrival of Greek texts from Egypt. There was therefore a hiatus that was excellently remedied starting from the ninth century, when the Muslim-Arab world (by then also Syrian-Muslim and Iranian-Muslim) fully recovered the Hellenistic tradition, studied it, and managed to also convey it to the West during the twelfth century."

Cleopatra's Culture

Every corner of the Library is familiar to Cleopatra. She sits on the benches as casually as a final-year university student. Scholars and librarians probably know her well, and perhaps at times forget that they have before them the queen. She does in fact seem like a woman with her feet on the ground and a sharp intelligence that allows her to converse with them and always provides food for thought.

All this doesn't just derive from her DNA. Cleopatra has a first-class education under her belt, one that perhaps no other Mediterranean woman has been fortunate enough to receive. Her instruction was of a Hellenistic imprint, with training in the humanities. Like all children, she began by learning to read and write Greek, reciting the alphabet out loud and copying letters engraved on wooden panels. But that was just her first step. What made a difference was the royal environment in which she was brought up. Her masters must have been first-class philosophers and scholars who lived in Alexandria. Through them, she learned to recite verses about the myths and legends of her time. Given her status, as soon as she grew up she was probably able to hold a copy of the *Odyssey* or the *Iliad*, both kept in the Library.

Cleopatra adores Homer and can recite by heart large sections of his works, the equivalent of Dante's *Divine Comedy* for Italians. Her ability is no surprise. She is an inquisitive woman with an infinite desire for knowledge. Hearing a queen, Egypt's last official pharaoh, reciting Homer and the feats of Ulysses or Achilles may sound surprising, but we mustn't forget that she is Greco-Macedonian and not Egyptian. She probably knows well the tragedies of Aeschylus, Sophocles, and Euripides; she knows Aesop's fables by heart and regularly rereads Menander's comedies with a smile.

A fundamental role in her career as a queen was the study of rhetoric, with which one learns to speak in public. She has received lessons on how to debate a point and make it persuasive, using not only words but the body. Gestures, voice tone, breath, the position of the head, and the expression of the eye are crucial when you wish to communicate. Pauses, too, are an effective tool. It's what present and past lawyers and politicians can do very well. You need to be able to "act" and persuade.

Cleopatra, too, had to learn a few rhetorical techniques, practice pretending to be a prosecutor or a defense lawyer, and put forward convincing arguments, also to become good at tackling unforeseen events and surprises.

All that was an extraordinary school for her. Almost all the sovereigns, kings, dignitaries, or Roman soldiers she meets have achieved their position through power or influential friends. They certainly do not possess her psychological preparation, and this perhaps partly explains her ability to negotiate with and win over her counterparts.

If we add to this ability in dialectics and oratorical strategy the sensuality of a young body guided by a calculating mind, we no longer have a timid queen but a woman capable of going anywhere. As history has shown.

Did Cleopatra Write Books?

Among the Library's bookcases, are there books, papyri, and treatises bearing Cleopatra's signature? It's a legitimate question, since she is an intelligent, educated woman and an expert in various fields, not least that of poisons, which will play a significant role at the end of this book.

According to Arabic sources, Cleopatra is a scholar and certainly not a *femme fatale*. Strangely enough, they make no reference to her sensuality or physical appearance, mention only her culture and knowledge, and describe her as an expert in philosophy, mathematics, and sciences. We must, however, stress that these authors wrote several centuries after Cleopatra's era. The nearest to her was a Coptic bishop who lived during the seventh century AD, in other words, about seven hundred years after her death.

According to their testimonies, Cleopatra allegedly wrote books on medicine, cosmetics, pharmaceuticals, and toxicology. Unfortunately, we don't know their titles or subjects, or if they were indeed written, or if attributing them to her was just a way of emphasizing her extensive knowledge.

We do, however, have something that might show us Cleopatra's handwriting. Two fragments from a royal decree dated February 23, 33 BC. Discovered at the beginning of the twentieth century by a German expedition to Abusir El-Melek, south of Cairo, these papyri are now kept in Berlin. They were reused to envelop a mummy in a *papier-mâché* mask, the so-called cartonnage.

The papyrus is interesting, in that it states that one of Antony's generals, called Publius Canidius, is granted perpetual tax exemption in exporting grain and importing wine and other produce. And we're not talking small quantities here. The general has clearly set up a small import-export business. We read in the papyrus that the man is authorized to take out of Egypt at least 300 tons of grain and bring in

5,000 amphorae of wine every year without paying a single drachma in taxes. It makes you wonder if this special authorization is the result of Antony putting in a good word for him, because there is no other explanation as to how he would have managed to obtain this kind of fiscal exemption.

Publius Canidius also owns arable land, and the papyri state that these are forever exempt from all taxes or payments, as are the animals used for sowing and tilling, and the ships for transporting the grain. No contribution need be made to anyone who comes to carry out checks, and no payment for the upkeep of their soldiers. (All this casts a worrying light on the fiscal oppression Egyptian peasants usually experienced.)

There is a sentence in Greek at the end: "To be done." The Belgian papyrologist Peter van Minnen from the University of Leuven claims that this is Cleopatra's formal authorization. According to Ptolemaic tradition, she, the queen, is the only one with the authority required to validate this kind of document. So is this her handwriting and signature? It's very tempting to believe so, even though we cannot exclude the possibility that it was a royal scribe who actually wrote it down, under the queen's dictation. In this case we would be hearing the echo of her words, trapped in ink.

Cleopatra Is Expecting Again

It's a late December day. The sun is setting, and the sky has turned into a huge red curtain, the kind you can see only in Egypt. In the natural harbor of Alexandria, a few sails, black because of the growing darkness, are gliding on the flat sea, returning to the protective embrace of the docks and the long Heptastadion. A quiet day is drawing to a close. The gigantic outline of the lighthouse watches over the port and the city, dominating the entire panorama, like a colossal stone guardian. Its powerful light, fueled by reflecting mirrors, grows stronger as the minutes pass. A flock of seagulls flies over the harbor, searching for a place to sleep.

Two luminous eyes admire this slice of heaven that no modern-era person would ever be able to experience. They seem to be looking far beyond the thirty-one or so miles of the beam from the lighthouse. They are staring at the horizon, engrossed, stuck on a thought that occupies their entire mind. They don't move even when a strand of hair suddenly whips her cheek, blown by a gust of sea breeze. They are Cleopatra's eyes.

She is huddled inside a pavilion, with cushions, fluttering silks, and blankets, sitting with her knees under her chin, seeking refuge in Antony's protective embrace as he warms her with his strong body. The couple is wrapped in a thick blanket embroidered in gold. Cleopatra had the same expression in another moment of her life. And she was right here, although not with Antony but with her first man, Julius Caesar. She seems uncertain, lingering on thoughts, silent.

Mark Antony notices this odd atmosphere but says nothing. He's waiting for her to speak first because he knows Cleopatra can't keep quiet for very long . . . He reaches out to a silver platter and takes a date. They are very sweet and large, and melt in his mouth. And just as he's about to bite into another, she turns and looks at him. Her eyes are shining with excitement, and are unusually sparkling. "I am pregnant," she says and, not waiting for a reaction, buries her face in Antony's arms. He freezes, holding the date in midair. Now it's his turn to stare into the distance. A few seconds later, he smiles and enfolds Cleopatra in his strong arms. A son will be a wonderful way to seal their love and especially their political agreement.

It's not the first time for either of them. Antony already has several children, including two with Fulvia—we've already seen that at the start of our story—to whom he is very attached. Although he hasn't seen them for months . . . Cleopatra, too, has a son, Caesarion. But this new pregnancy will be very special. For both of them.

First and foremost because it's the fruit of the love of their lives. Moreover, because not one child would be born, but fraternal twins, a boy and a girl, whom they would give marvelous names: Moon and Sun. Or rather, Cleopatra Selene and Alexander Helios.

This is the imagined reconstruction of a scene that must really have occurred on a cold winter's day between the end of 41 and the beginning of 40 BC. We don't know the exact month of conception, but it was probably shortly after their whirlwind encounter in Alexandria. The twins would be born on an unspecified date, between late spring 40 BC and December of the same year.

Cleopatra had a strange destiny as a mother: Caesar was not present when Caesarion was born, and Antony would not be there either for the birth of his twins. He would already have left, summoned back to his country by serious events.

According to many historians, Cleopatra did not fall pregnant by chance but by a considered choice. Besides the love between them, Antony is currently the most powerful man in Rome. For Cleopatra, having children with him means strengthening her own power in Egypt and on the Mediterranean chessboard. Perhaps she also needs a girl to be the bride of Caesarion, according to Ptolemaic tradition.

No doubt Cleopatra has always been very careful with pregnancy throughout her life. As the archaeologist Duane W. Roller says, she cannot afford the discomfort and risk of motherhood and labor. Her presence on the throne is a daily necessity. Imagine the nausea, the thousand health precautions, and then the birth, with a concrete danger of death for her and the children, not to mention her responsibilities as a mother even though she can rely on hosts of wet nurses. Antony has come along at an ideal moment—no danger within the kingdom, no wars or enemies at Egypt's borders, and the most powerful man at her feet. Cleopatra's decision, calculating even from a mother's perspective, is perfect.

But how does Cleopatra plan the births? What are the contraception methods at the time? Although she is a queen, Cleopatra uses traditional folk methods familiar to many Egyptian women. First, there are physical methods. Since the time of the pharaohs, there is a kind of condom, made from animal gut (although there is no tangible proof); as well as preventing pregnancy, it also wards off venereal diseases. We get a lot of other information from a papyrus that dates back to the New Kingdom (1567–1075 BC), known as the Ebers Papyrus. To avoid getting pregnant, the text recommends using a tampon made of bread, acacia, honey, and dates. According to experts, the fermenting acacia could create sperm-adverse conditions, acting as a spermicide. Another document, the Kahun Gynecological Papyrus, describes frankly worrying concoctions based on crocodile or elephant excrement, mixed with honey or a kind of liquid similar to curd, inserted in female genitalia. This would also act as a chemical and physical contraceptive, but a gentler one.

Later, during the Roman era, various sources (including Pliny the Elder) mention silphium, a wild plant that grew in Cyrenaica, which was used as a panacea for many ailments, as a powerful aphrodisiac, and also as a contraceptive to take once a month. Unfortunately, we don't know it, because it became extinct in ancient times through overharvesting, but laboratory tests on similar plants have proved a temporary cessation of fertility in female mice.

We don't know if Cleopatra uses these strange concoctions, but unlike other Egyptian women she has an ace up her sleeve. She is an expert in toxic and poisonous substances. It's not improbable that she knows compounds or recipes able to temporarily stop female fertility or make the male seed ineffective. Whatever substance or technique she might use—remember that this is still hypothetical—she is certainly able to choose the exact moment to get pregnant.

9

The Start of a Nightmare

Waking Up from a Dream

After spending the entire winter in Cleopatra's sensual, loving company, Mark Antony leaves Alexandria and Egypt in spring 40 BC, when navigation resumes in the Mediterranean. There are serious reasons for his departure. In the space of just a few months, dark new clouds have gathered on the horizon, all the way to Rome and the borders with the Middle East. Plutarch says, "While Antony was wasting time on futile speeches and childish games, two pieces of news reached him. One, from Rome, informed him that, after first being in conflict with, then waging war against, Octavian, his brother Lucius and wife, Fulvia, had lost everything and fled from Italy; the other piece of news, no better, was that Labienus, at the head of the Parthians, was subjugating Asia, from the Euphrates and Syria to Lydia and Ionia." For Antony, who certainly hadn't been in the dark about what was happening in Italy, this is still like a rude awakening from a dream and finding himself in a nightmare. But what happened in the space of just a few months, to go from the triumphs of Philippi to civil war in the country?

The first leg of his journey is to Athens, and when he lands he is in a dark mood, which becomes even darker when he hears that his brother Lucius has been defeated and made a prisoner by Octavian, now the master of the peninsula.

It's a complex period that takes up entire chapters in history books. We will now try to summarize the principal points, especially since, apart from the historical events, a whole new personality emerges for Mark Antony, whom we haven't really known until now—from his ambition to the ability to be an extraordinary man of action, to his charisma, his (many) love affairs, and the (many) children he had with different women.

After parting following their great victory at Philippi, Antony and Octavian had divided their tasks. Mark Antony was to pacify and stabilize the Middle East in view of an important campaign against the Parthians, the enemy empire that extended roughly from present eastern Turkey to Iran. Octavian, on the other hand, was to return to Italy and please the 100,000 veterans by giving them land on which they could live with their families. A thankless, risky task because it involved gifting them land and property that belonged to others. Imagine if today, in order to pay thousands of soldiers, a government decided to allow them to take over the houses, apartments, and land of ordinary people, effectively occupying entire cities and evicting many normal families (though Italic as opposed to Roman). To satisfy the veterans, at least eighteen Italic cities had been chosen and sacrificed, and, understandably, these rebelled and asked for this "tax" to be fairly and equally extended to other cities, many of which were alarmed and joined in the protest. Rome was invaded by masses of protesters. As Cassius Dio writes, "Some wanted to resort to violence, while others did not want to endure it, some wanted to take over other people's property, while others demanded to keep theirs."

Albeit trying to mediate between the parties, Octavian didn't have Antony's charisma or his experience in managing this situation, which degenerated into clashes and casualties. He was even nearly killed at the theater by a crowd of soldiers because of a banal incident.

Antony had taken all this into account and was probably hoping that the chaos would allow him to become the only one in power. Antony's relatives, his wife, Fulvia, and brother Lucius—then consul in charge—had the same idea. Ronald Syme emphasizes this: "They played a double game. Before the veterans they laid the blame upon Octavian, insisting that a final decision be reserved for Antony—for the prestige of the victor of Philippi was overwhelming. On the other side, they championed liberty and the rights of the dispossessed—again not without reference to the popular name of M. Antony and professions of *pietas*." To make things worse, there was a shortage of grain and victuals in Rome. Although they had lost at Philippi, the Republicans still ruled over the seas, with Sextus Pompey's fleet still intact, hindering all supplies to the capital.

The straw that broke the camel's back, in 41 BC, was Octavian's decision to repudiate Clodia, Fulvia's sixteen-year-old daughter from her first marriage to the tribune Clodius, whom he'd married in 43 BC in order to seal his agreement with Antony (Octavian swore in a letter that she was still a virgin).

And so war broke out. Lucius assembled the legions loyal to him in the city of Praeneste and marched on Rome. Easily defeating the enemy troops, he entered Rome, warmly welcomed by the people and the Senate, but a few weeks later, he lost other clashes and was forced to seek refuge in Perugia, where he was besieged by Octavian. It was the end of 41 BC, just when Mark Antony was getting Cleopatra pregnant in the gilded paradise of Alexandria.

The siege lasted for months, and Lucius and the city ended up capitulating because of hunger. Octavian's reprisals made history. The city was pillaged, many residents murdered, and finally Perugia was set alight and razed. In this case, as in Philippi, Octavian suddenly showed his sadistic, cruel, and inhuman side. As the historian Suetonius writes, "To the residents who begged for mercy, he replied, 'You have to die.'" Moreover, he picked three hundred senators and cavalrymen among those who had not yielded and had them taken to Rome. There he had them mass-killed in the Forum, before Julius Caesar's altar. It was March 15, the Ides of March . . . Finally, he updated the proscription lists, giving rise to a new bloodbath. This way, he regained control of the whole peninsula.

After the victory (or massacre) of Perugia, Antony's generals dispersed, abandoning Italy. His brother Lucius was captured but then, oddly, pardoned by Octavian, who reconciled himself with Lucius and sent him to Spain as a governor (where he died a year later in mysterious circumstances). Fulvia, on the other hand, could leave Italy unharmed. By granting pardon to the two of them, perhaps Octavian was hoping to leave room for negotiations with Antony.

The Stormy Meeting between Antony and Fulvia

This is the situation when Antony lands in Athens and sees Fulvia again. What was their encounter like? While the one with Cleopatra months earlier in Alexandria was an explosion of passion, this one, on the other hand, is an explosion of hatred.

Fulvia is a very strong-minded woman, a true virago. As we've already seen, ancient sources relate that she pierced Cicero's tongue with a pin while holding his severed head in her hands. She was certainly the one who organized an army, with her brother-in-law, Lucius, in order to oppose Octavian, so much so that Cassius Dio remarks: "Why be surprised by this, since she even wore a sword, gave commands to the soldiers, and often harangued the troops?" Once they are facing each other, they are both enraged, and harsh words probably fly during the encounter, with both raising their voices and shouting. It's more than a quarrel between husband and wife. Much more.

Antony accuses her of having ruined everything, of managing the situation in Italy very badly and triggering the war with Octavian.

According to many historians, Fulvia resents his many extra-conjugal political affairs while she was in Italy (Cleopatra, of course, but also Glaphyra in Cappadocia), which—we must add—led to his prolonged absence from Rome, leaving Octavian free rein.

It can't have been easy for Antony to stem the anger of a woman as intelligent, active, and full of energy as Fulvia, whose force was known to everyone in the country, including the enemy soldiers besieging her in Perugia. As also claimed by the scholar Giusto Traina, during an archaeological dig there emerged tapered lead projectiles, which the legion's slingers would launch en masse, and on which the soldiers of both factions, while the lead was being melted, had inscribed hostile, at times obscene messages against the enemy. One found in Perugia and kept at the National Archaeological Museum says *Pete culum Octaviani*, literally "aimed at Octavian's ass." Another makes fun of Lucius's sparse hair. And a third, finally, is addressed to Fulvia, whom the soldiers clearly considered on a par with an enemy general: "I'm aiming at Fulvia's clitoris."

Fulvia's jealousy is one of the strongest notes in this stormy encounter, described by many modern historians. The fact that she was a very energetic woman and full of pride makes her in a way comparable to Cleopatra (at this point it's worth giving a sympathetic, human rather than historical thought to Antony, under the thumb of not one but two women like that . . .). It would be wrong, however, to believe that all women acted like this back then. It's true that there was a degree of female emancipation at the time, thanks to a historic decision on the part of the Senate, a few decades earlier, which allowed women, on their husband's or father's death, to inherit the family estate even though it did not permit them to manage it independently. Before that, this had been reserved only for male relatives, such as brothers or husbands, consigning generations of Roman women to the shadows and powerlessness. From that moment on, powerful female figures began to emerge, who were also independent in their daily habits, even sexual ones. Fulvia is, after all, a perfect example of this.

The emancipation enjoyed by women during this period of Roman society is perhaps the only period in Western history when the female condition comes "closer" to the modern one. The quotation marks are mandatory because these same women are excluded from political rights and enjoy very few civil rights, and there are still many other limitations, especially in the lower strands of the population. We are still, after all, dealing with a male-dominated society in which the man, as already mentioned, may have extramarital affairs (something absolutely forbidden to women) without consequence. He has a wife and, if he wishes, he can also have one or more concubines of, naturally, a lower status than that of his wife. And we're not talking only of the wealthy classes. Even a cobbler can have several women. The law does not forbid it.

And there's another element to keep in mind when talking about jealousy like Fulvia's. In Rome, as far as the upper classes are concerned, there are few love matches; there are almost always marriages of convenience between families. The spouses are therefore forced to live together without desiring each other. Once they have produced children, a necessity for the continuation of the lineage, each of them finds passion with others—the men openly so, given the sexual freedom they enjoyed in Roman society (extramarital relationships and visits to brothels are examples of that), while everything is much more complicated for a woman. Marriages of family convenience are almost always between a mature man and a very young girl. After they've given birth to their children, these women, still young, are left alone, with husbands old enough to be their fathers, who are never around and whom they don't desire, probably a reason they are happy to put up with their extramarital affairs, although the women, still in their prime, must act in secret in order to love and have affairs, with all the risks of a secret love. These are things to bear in mind when speaking about Antony, Cleopatra, Fulvia, Octavian, and figures of the past in general, to avoid applying modern stereotypes to the ancient world. It would also be an error to interpret their feelings and actions according to our modern rules and values. It was a similar society, yes, but a different one.

According to the scholar Romolo Augusto Staccioli, a great expert on the Roman era, in Octavian's Rome, that is, the epoch we are describing, we can even talk of a "love quadrille," a reference to how couples change partners with truly surprising speed and ease. Naturally, we're talking about the high classes of the population, the aristocracy, to which all the protagonists of our story belong. Another striking thing is the nonexistence in Latin of a word for "spinster." The closest term is *vetula virgo*, or "old virgin," which, however, puts the emphasis rather on the physical—and not too charming—appearance of a woman than on the fact that she doesn't have a husband.

The explanation for this lies in this constant (and very modern) dynamic of high-society couples, which seldom leaves a woman on her own: physical appearance is not an issue. As we've already seen, Velleius Paterculus (hostile to Fulvia, let's remember that) said that the only thing feminine about her was her body. In other words, it is social status, wealth, and the power of her family of origin that set the tune to this love quadrille.

Moreover, it's not improbable that, because of the high rate of female mortality during childbirth (many women died, given the high infant mortality rate and the duty to have a son to continue the hereditary line), there weren't all that many available women in high society.

Naturally, none of this detracts from the fact that a woman could throw a jealous tantrum at her husband, although it does seem like more of an exception. This may have been the case for Fulvia. With regard to this, Francesca Cenerini, lecturer in Roman history at the University of Bologna, underlines the fact that, as in the case of

Brutus and Porcia, what she demands is more intelligence and a joint political vision, and not the sexual life her husband shares with his concubines, about which she has no reason to complain.

If there was any jealousy (and, we repeat, *if*), it would have been because there wasn't just convenience in Fulvia and Antony's marriage, but also feeling, a constant factor in his relationships with women, as we'll subsequently see. Despite being an impenitent womanizer and a "friendly rogue," we think he is especially attractive to the fair sex because he's a strong, successful, powerful, and protective man, of course, but also lively, a lover of jokes and laughter, and therefore so childlike that, as well as love and passion, he triggers something more, perhaps a kind of motherly love that binds women to him deeply. In addition, obviously, his political position and great power increase his social charm considerably.

Antony's Women

Just how many women did Antony have in his life? It's impossible to say, especially since ancient sources claim he also had homosexual relationships. On that subject, it's important to point out that culturally, the Roman man would grow up with a bisexual approach in regard to sex. It was acceptable to make love with men as well as women, as long as he took on an active and not passive role, because the Roman male's supremacy over others had to be total and across the genders. He would sexually dominate not only women but also other men. That's why it was usually a case of "punitive" homosexuality, undergone by individuals of lower rank, from slaves to prisoners. This does not preclude the existence of great love affairs between men and between women. Homosexuality among women was frowned upon, however, because in a male-dominated society, it took away the man's power over the woman's pleasure.

Antony had six documented relationships in his life. And each of them helps us discover a different snippet of his psychology. His first was with Fadia, in 60 BC. Mark Antony was twenty-three and formed with her a relationship that was not altogether disinterested. At the time, he was desperately searching for money and she was the daughter of a very wealthy freedman, Quintus Fadio, who helped Antony straighten his finances. Later, in his *Philippics*, Cicero would allude to the fact that they were married with children, a groundless accusation, since Roman law forbade a nobleman to marry a freedwoman. It was more probably a concubinage, and Antony may well have had children with her, although we know neither their number nor their names, because they would not have been considered legitimate by law.

When he was around thirty (53–52 BC), Antony married a first cousin, the twenty-year-old Antonia Hybrida. In this case, too, the young woman was given to Antony in marriage for financial reasons because he was riddled with debt and in financial dire straits. What did the young woman's family gain from this? Her father, Gaius Antonius Hybrida, former governor of Macedonia, consul and military commander, had been exiled to Cefalonia and was perhaps hoping for rehabilitation, since Mark Antony was a rising figure on the political scene. It was not a happy marriage. Antony constantly betrayed her, one of his lovers being the famous actress Licorys. Maybe she cheated on him too, because he repudiated her, accusing her of having had an affair with Dolabella, something that cannot be verified. They had a daughter, Antonia, who ended up marrying Pythodorus, an elderly, wealthy, and influential figure in the city of Tralles, in the south of present-day Turkey, in the context of the alliance politics weaved by Antony.

The actress Licorys was Antony's third great love. Their relationship began in 49 BC, when she was thirty-four years old. Licorys was one of the most alluring women in the whole of the Roman era. The slave of a rich, prominent Roman, her real name was Volumnia Licorys, but she was known by her stage name, Cytheris. Her master owned a whole array of actors and actresses for stage performances, which he also "supplied" to high-society banquets, where they prostituted themselves. Licorys was his star: beautiful and much valued, she was soon freed so she would be more presentable at the banquets of the Rome that counted. This way, her master increased his network and so his power. But Licorys also benefited from this: while still very young, she first had a relationship with Brutus and then with Mark Antony, who lost his head over her. Their liaison caused a sensation in Rome because they were both famous and because, although he was married, Antony didn't care and, on the contrary, according to Cicero, would travel along the streets of Rome with her on a litter preceded by lictors. It was the modern equivalent of driving around with your lover in an official car. The worst thing, according to Cicero, was that he treated her as a *matrona honesta* and as though she were his wife. This kind of accusation and insinuation could have been devastating to Antony's career, because Licorys was still a prostitute and an actress, considered the lowest echelon of Roman society. Perhaps partly through pressure from Caesar, he reluctantly decided to break off the relationship. She subsequently began a liaison with another prominent Roman figure, the poet Cornelius Gallus, who belonged to Virgil and Horace's circle. He looked upon her as his muse, the way Catullus had done with Lesbia, and when she left him for an obscure commander of the Rhine border, he fell into deep depression. In vain did his fellow poets try to cheer him up (there is a passage in Virgil about his devastated friend). In order to understand Licorys's importance and skill in Roman society, you just need to compare her to Marilyn Monroe: both had an affair with a politician (Brutus/JFK), a man of action (Antony/ Joe DiMaggio), and a writer (Gallus/Arthur Miller). History always repeats itself.

Then came Fulvia's turn. The two got married in 47 BC, when Antony was almost thirty-six, and had two children, Marcus Antonius Antyllus and Iullus Antonius.

Plutarch says about her that "she neither weaved nor ran the household [. . .] but wanted to dominate dominators and command an army commander." He then adds, "Cleopatra was indebted to Fulvia for having gotten Antony used to female rule; so much so that he accepted it in a docile way, already being inclined to serve." In other words, Cleopatra found herself a man easy to boss around, compliant, amply dominated by Fulvia.

Antony, too, is supposed to be a man who is weak with women, subjugated by dominant ones, by whom he perhaps feels protected. The three most important women in his life, in fact—Licorys, Fulvia, and Cleopatra—are just so.

And then came Octavia. He married her at the age of forty-three, in 40 BC. A personality totally different from Fulvia, she would prove to be a faithful, honest companion. A decent person, we'd declare her now, and so much so that, as well as having two daughters with him (Antonia Major and Antonia Minor), she would welcome into her *domus* all the children Antony had had with other women.

The last one was Cleopatra, who gave him three children: Cleopatra Selene, Alexander Helios, and Ptolemy Philadelphus. With her, Antony had his longest ever relationship, which lasted at least eleven years, even though meanwhile he indulged in a long liaison with Queen Glaphyra, and even a wedding with Octavia.

Did Antony and Cleopatra marry? We've never entirely ascertained this, and it is a point still debated today. However, even if they were husband and wife, their marriage would have not been valid in Rome.

Essentially, each of these figures reveals a part of Antony's personality. Capable of falling passionately and explosively in love with deeply sexual women (Licorys, Glaphyra, and Cleopatra), but also of marrying from cold calculation, staying with a wife for a long time and having children (Fadia, Antonia Hybrida, and Fulvia), to then finding a homemaker like Octavia, perhaps the only one with whom he had a "normal" and honest conjugal rapport. Naturally these theories are based on what we know about him thanks to the texts of ancient writers, who often paint a contrasting portrait of him, as a dissolute man devoted to excess. The aim was to discredit him, these being texts in favor of Octavian, his great adversary. Even taking into account this historical distortion, as we said, personal interest involving either political or financial advantage is always a part of Antony's relationships, even his deeply passionate affairs. And yet there is another recurring element. Quite apart from pro-Octavian propaganda, which describes him as dominated by women, Mark Antony often falls at the feet of strong women. The high number of his official relationships (six) and children (eight) shows a psychological profile suggesting clear inconstancy in his relationships, a trait typical of a voracious mind amplified, we should add, by a historical period of great upheavals that require a strong ability to weave affairs and political alliances at the same time. Antony crossed one of history's most tempestuous seas, enjoying life without ever holding back, before dying at just fifty-three.

Antony and Octavia's Marriage

But let's go back to our story. Antony and Fulvia spend the summer of 40 BC together in Athens and their children are also with them. They don't know it yet, but it's the last time the family is reunited.

Toward the end of the summer, Antony goes to Italy with his legions to resolve his issues with Octavian, leaving his wife in Sicyon, near Corinth. He will never see her again: Fulvia is already ill and her condition deteriorates over the following few weeks, causing her premature death. The writers of the subsequent era would say that she died from grief and heartbreak because of Antony's relationship with

Cleopatra. The reason might be an exaggeration but it is likely that at that moment the world came crashing down on Fulvia: she'd lost everything in Italy and was now in exile abroad with a husband who was having a relationship and even children with a foreign queen. But besides her grief, no doubt severe but nevertheless surmountable for her, always a combative woman, she probably had a health problem that weakened and eventually killed her.

Antony must certainly have been heartbroken when, shortly after arriving in Italy, he received the news. The two were genuinely fond of each other, despite everything.

Incredible as it may sound, it is Fulvia's death that unblocks the situation in Italy. Once the one who had fueled the enmity between Antony and Octavian has passed away, the two men immediately grab the opportunity and reach an agreement, averting war. Once again, they divide the territories: the west as far as the ocean to Octavian, the east as far as the Euphrates to Antony, with the dividing line between the two men going through Scutari in Albania (Shkodër, then in Illyria). This is followed by triumphant entrances into Rome, amnesties, banquets with Antony dressed in Eastern and Octavian in Western fashion (in military dress) . . . and to seal their rekindled agreement, a wedding is celebrated: that of Antony and Octavia, Octavian's sister.

During all this time (about three years), Cleopatra seems totally forgotten. Of course, Mark Antony has some very serious situations to deal with, but there is no sign of his overwhelming passion or his attachment to her. It all seems to have dissolved like a bubble of soap, so much so that he marries another woman. Out of official duty, of course, but Octavia is a special woman and, above all, no longer a naïve little girl.

She is about thirty years old—the brink of middle age in a Roman woman. She already has children from a previous husband who died a few months earlier. It is therefore two widows marrying: Antony with, at the time, five children, and Octavia, who has two. But there's a surprise. When she gets married, Octavia is already expecting her third child. Before dying, her husband got her pregnant.

This creates a legal problem. By Roman law, a widow cannot re-marry before ten months have passed after the death of her first husband, to make sure she isn't carrying a child who doesn't belong to the household and bloodline of her new husband (*turbatio sanguinis* and *incertitudo seminis*). A special dispensation from the Senate is therefore required so that Antony and Octavia may marry.

We have no testimonies or descriptions of this wedding but it must have been somewhat bizarre: Octavia, heavily pregnant and still in mourning, Antony not denying his relationship with Cleopatra, though not admitting to having married her.

The union between Octavia and Antony certainly pacified public opinion, at least that of Roman traditionalism, but also Caesar's veterans, for whom the danger of a civil war was averted. Because, as Professor Cenerini underlines, "Augustan propaganda would present Octavia as the perfect representation of the traditional female model, naturally adapted to the circumstances of the time. Plutarch would actually describe her as 'a treasure of a woman' who corresponds entirely to the models praised as the matronly ideal, based on *mos maiorum*." Octavia is even more than that: she is petite and sweet-natured, with a graceful face, and always close to Antony, a genuine wife, faithful, and ready to solve any problem.

This marriage seals a moment of peace and hope in the whole pen-insula, devastated by so many years of war. The minted coins often carry the image of Concordia and even Antony and Octavia: it's one of the earliest times that a Roman woman is represented on a coin, and as many scholars have pointed out, the purpose was to highlight the role of Octavia, one never before played by other women.

As the historian Michael Grant remarked, even Virgil confirms the great hope in a period of peace and wealth and, in his *Bucolics*, writes the fourth eclogue in honor of a hypothetical youth who would bring a golden age to the world: Is it Antony and Octavia's forthcoming son?

"Protect, therefore, o chaste Lucina, the youth about to be born, for whom for the first time the iron age shall end and the golden age begin throughout the world; now your Apollo rules."

As a matter of fact, everything seems to be going well. An agreement is even reached with Sextus Pompey, whose ships were blocking the seas, starving Rome. In this case, too, there are banquets, division of territories, amnesties, and compensations for all those who had fled with him to Sicily during the proscription lists following Caesar's death. And, of course, the engagement between Sextus Pompey's daughter and Octavia's daughter couldn't go amiss.

We know that cutting remarks were made at the banquet that took place on Sextus Pompey's flagship to ratify the peace. The figure of Cleopatra hovered heavily in the air and, although she wasn't present, was the butt of jokes. Her relationship with Antony was still on the lips of the Roman world, fueling all kinds of gossip.

Octavian Also Gets Married . . . Like a God

This is the only time Antony and Octavian truly get along. Their rapport relaxes over the months. This period, happy for everyone, is highlighted by a new marriage: that of Octavian.

As soon as he saw Livia, he fell in love with her. Never mind that she is married (her husband had fought against him at Philippi) and that she is expecting a child. Octavian forces the husband to divorce her at the beginning of 38 BC and marries her without waiting for her to give birth. Here, too, we have a bride getting married while expecting another man's child.

In truth, apart from his feelings, this marriage is a very shrewd move on the part of Octavian on his ascent to the summit of the Roman world, because it cements an alliance with an important section of the aristocracy. There's a lot of gossip among the people, including "The lucky ones give birth to children after three months, and that became a proverb," Cassius Dio writes sarcastically.

On the subject of gossip, it seems (because politically convenient for everyone) that the ex-husband also attended the wedding, and that at this very select banquet, nicknamed "of the twelve gods," all the guests were dressed as gods. Octavian apparently came as Apollo, probably as a response to Antony and Cleopatra being acclaimed in the east as Dionysus and Aphrodite. No royal wedding held today would be like that, but, as we said, when exploring the Roman world, we must always consider that customs and mores were different. This lavish banquet takes place while the people are starving because of Sextus Pompey's naval embargo. The propaganda of his adversaries describes Octavian as a tyrant, a detail that has reached us intact, slipping through the mesh of censorship that operated in favor of Octavian.

Let us conclude this very complex period by adding that after this wedding, Antony goes back to coordinating war operations in Greece, where his generals—Publius Ventidius Bassus in particular—carry off important victories, sweeping the Parthians away from the Middle East, killing the Roman "traitor" Labienus after a fantastical escape, and restoring Rome's honor with a definitive victory on Mount Gindarus, avenging the terrible defeat at Carrhae fifteen years earlier, which apparently took place on the same date, June 9. Because of this victory, never really emphasized by historians but of great significance for the epoch, Ventidius was granted a triumph in Rome on November 27, 38 BC.

Unfortunately, the situation in Italy deteriorates. Despite all the agreements, understandings, and promises of future marriages, a naval war breaks out between Sextus Pompey and Octavian, bringing the latter a series of defeats. Antony rushes back to Italy, meets with Octavian, and they renew their agreement, extending the triumvirate by five years. As well as an umpteenth promise of a marriage (between Antony's son Antyllus and Octavian's daughter, Julia, who's not even two), the agreement includes an exchange of military aid: Antony promises a hundred ships with rostra to the war against Pompey, and Octavian pledges to send him 20,000 soldiers for his wars in the east, in particular for the great expedition against the Parthians. We mention this agreement because it would be one of the sparks that would ignite a war between them in the future: the terms of the pact will not, in fact, be honored by Octavian.

It's the last time they meet outside a battlefield. The next time they do, it will be to annihilate each other with armies and ships.

Antony Reaches Out to Cleopatra Again

After the meeting with Octavian, Antony returns to Greece with his wife and children, but as soon as they arrive in Corfu, he asks Octavia to return to Italy. Why? This decision has been much debated. Some believe it was a reasonable option: Octavia is five months pregnant and it is normal practice among Roman generals that wives, especially if pregnant, do not follow their husbands on military campaigns.

According to other scholars and even a few ancient writers, on the other hand, Antony proves by this act that he is clearly tired of Octavia and of their institutional marriage. His heart still beats for Cleopatra . . .

Plutarch skillfully emphasizes this: "That terrible disease, his love for Cleopatra, which had been lying dormant for a long time and tamed thanks to the best reason, flared up again and grew stronger as Antony approached Syria. And, finally, as Plato says, the insubordinate, indomitable beast in his soul having kicked away every good and healthy thought, Antony sent Fonteius Capito to fetch Cleopatra and bring her to Syria."

In any case, it is the last time Antony sees his wife and children (except for the two eldest). Ahead of him now is Cleopatra.

He has a clear objective in mind. An important campaign against the Parthian Empire requires firm zones behind the front lines in order to ensure supplies, weapons, men, and above all money. Antony therefore reorganizes the entire Middle East, establishing, as emphasized by Grant, strong bonds with some of the sovereigns, who, to all effects, become client kings. It's a change made during Rome's policy of dominion in this region. No predatory governors that plunder entire provinces, but states that administer independently a population they know well (including when collecting precious taxes, a true gold mine for the campaign against the Parthians). The most important among all these client kingdoms, of course, is Egypt. After meeting various sovereigns, it's the turn of Cleopatra, who, invited by Antony through the trusted Gaius Fonteius Capito, arrives in Antioch.

Located practically on the current border between Turkey and Syria, Antioch was the third-largest city on the Mediterranean, after Rome and Alexandria. It's strange and heartbreaking that almost nothing remains of this wonderful city. It's upsetting how time can wipe out entire chapters of history, replacing them with emptiness and silence. It's a phenomenon that should make us value every aspect of our present, most of which is probably destined to vanish.

We have no information on how the meeting between Antony and Cleopatra turned out during the final months of 37 BC, but we can imagine it. Forget their first meeting in Alexandria, with Cleopatra running breathlessly to embrace Antony. We have no evidence of this, but the queen is most probably furious, wounded, and jealous. She's had ample time to get ready for this moment and has picked the most effective words, not leaving out any detail. Perhaps her only obstacle is emotion, which clouds the rationale of her speech. Cleopatra must have been on the offensive at that meeting, equipped with vehemence and all her most effective oratorical techniques transformed, thanks to her female instinct, into weapons of mass destruction.

She must have rubbed Antony's face in the fact that he had been absent for a few years. She must have accused him of never seeing his children, the twins, of having effectively abandoned them, of being an absent father. But, above all, motivated by jealousy and profound grief, she must have attacked him about his marriage to another woman . . . with whom he's had two daughters. It's one of the most intense outbursts of her life and, we're tempted to say, perhaps of the whole of ancient history. It's important to emphasize that, feelings aside, there is also a "geopolitical" kind of anger and resentment: Cleopatra feels she has been discarded in favor of an agreement between Antony and Octavian. Unfortunately, although her jealousy of Octavia is well documented by ancient historians, we don't have even the slightest detail of what happened during those long minutes. Even so, none of us would want to face a Cleopatra blinded by anger and hatred for another woman and by the fact that she has been cast aside in the great power games on the Mediterranean.

Let's remember one thing, though: Cleopatra is not naïve, and knows perfectly well that Antony wants to see her because he needs her help in the campaign against the Parthians, and so this is the best time for her to dictate her conditions. Because as well as being a woman, she's also a great strategist. She uses powerful men just as they use her, and knows that she now can exploit this moment to her advantage. Cleopatra probably presents herself with a colossal blend of anger, jealousy, political calculation, and great oratorical ability. A kind of perfect storm Mark Antony has to tackle.

We can imagine that he let the queen give vent to her anger (what else could he do?) then tried to argue, explaining that his marriage to Octavia was just an institutional façade. But this must have stoked her anger even more, turning Antony into an accommodating man, ready to satisfy the whim of Cleopatra, who—we repeat—is his principal ally and backer in the war against the Parthians. We sense that that's how things went from . . . the consequences of this encounter.

First and foremost, at that moment the names Alexander Helios and Cleopatra Selene are formally given to the twins, partly because, as modern authors like Michael Grant point out, according to Greek tradition, the sun and moon are twins and bringers of victory.

Moreover, Antony makes huge concessions to Cleopatra, gifting her a large number of territories, some of which produce very refined and much-sought-after raw materials at the time:

- Phoenicia;

- a large part of Cilicia, in the south of present Turkey;

- part of Decapolis (a group of ten cities in the present-day Syria, Jordan, and Israel);

- confirmation of her control over Cyprus and its lucrative commerce and mining production;

- a few regions along the Red Sea, in Nabatea, and a monopoly over the exploitation of the bitumen deposits in the Black Sea;

- Iturea, in the north of Galilee;

- the plantations of date palms and balsam shrubs in Judea (the famous "balm of Gilead" or "balm of Judea"), which command astronomical prices as a healing substance and as a perfume.

Mark Antony manages to placate the wrath of the ambitious Cleopatra with these "expensive gifts"—or perhaps, putting it more simply, the territorial concessions are included in a true negotiation to reestablish alliance with the queen. The result is amazing, and Cleopatra suddenly becomes one of the most important Ptolemaic queens, easily surpassing her father. Her dominions almost equal the maximum extent of the kingdom as reached centuries earlier by

Ptolemy II Philopator. Cleopatra's happiness and ambition are so great that she decides to alter the official calendar: from now on, we will be in Year I of her reign.

In Rome, many, even some of Antony's supporters, turn up their noses at these concessions. But he goes ahead and prepares a large army to invade the powerful Parthian Empire.

The Long-Awaited War Against the Parthians

Antony is not alone when, in spring 36 BC, he concentrates all his troops in Zeugma (in present-day southern Turkey). Cleopatra is also with him: the two have made peace over the winter. And very much so. As a matter of fact, the queen of Egypt is pregnant again. Many have wondered if their children are more a political tool than a sign of love between them. We won't go into this detailed analysis because we don't have enough details. One thing is certain, however: that everything seems to go back to how it was before between them, and from now on they will live together until death.

Cleopatra is certainly very impressed. There's a spectacular military deployment before them: it's one of the largest armies ever put together by the Romans. Thanks to the reinforcements obtained from the allies, according to Plutarch about 100,000 men (60,000 Roman legionaries, 10,000 Iberian and Celtic cavalrymen included with Romans, as well as 30,000 men, between foot soldiers and cavalrymen, contributed by other kingdoms). Even admitting that these figures may be exaggerated, it's still an impressive force. As Caesar, who died a few days before his own campaign against the Parthians, had planned (and very probably Antony wishes to pick up his military heritage to prove himself worthier than Octavian in the glory of Rome), the invasion is planned from the north instead of the west, which would be more logical. It's a stroke of genius: the Parthians are taken by surprise, as Caesar had foreseen.

Because of a tactical error, however, the campaign ends in disaster. In order to reach the capital of Media, Fraaspa, quickly and to lay siege to it, Antony divides the army in two near present-day Lake Urmia, leaving only two legions in the rearguard with all the siege machines. The enemy realizes their vulnerability and attacks with thousands of archers on horseback. It's a slaughter, and the siege machines, essential for taking the capital, are destroyed. At that point, considering the campaign compromised, Antony's most valuable ally, the king of Armenia, Artavasdes, abandons him, pulling out his 7,000 foot soldiers and in particular his 6,000 archers on horseback, whose presence was essential to defend the Romans from enemy incursions. Many believe that Octavian was behind this defection, as he was in constant contact with the king by letter.

Mark Antony's troops surround the city in vain: he's attacked from every direction and in the end decides to return to the Roman territories. The march becomes a tragic retreat under continuous assault from the enemy, with legionaries dying from starvation, the cold, or pierced by a host of arrows. Something reminiscent of the retreat from Russia of the Italian army during World War II. In this regard, apparently Antony had one of his bodyguards, Rhamnus (perhaps a gladiator), swear that at a sign from him he would run him through with a sword and cut his head off, so he wouldn't be captured alive by the enemy or recognized after his death. Fortunately for him, an unnecessary measure, but one that illustrates the dramatic nature of this march.

Admittedly, the legions perform heroically, using all their military skills. It's on this occasion that the famous "testudo formation" is described by Plutarch and Cassius Dio—made with shields arranged to cover the heads and sides of the sections, making them into living fortresses. It's such a solid formation that men, horses, and carts can go over the "roof" of shields arranged like tiles, and, although this is not widely known, it was sometimes used for crossing moats and narrow dips, and especially during assaults on enemy fortifications: other legionaries would climb on top of the testudo, forming a kind of human pyramid, to conquer the enemy walls.

When Antony finally reaches the Mediterranean shores with what's left of his powerful army, according to modern historians he has lost between 25 and 40 percent of his soldiers (in other words, between 25,000 and 40,000). He's a destroyed man and calls for Cleopatra's help.

It takes the queen some time to find the means and the money to equip soldiers, but in the end she arrives with her fleet, much to everybody's relief. And it's on this occasion that she shows Antony their new child, a boy called Ptolemy Philadelphus (the same name as the Ptolemaic king who had taken Egypt's dominions to their maximum extent). Cleopatra's fate is strange: none of her children's fathers has ever been present at their births.

There's bitter irony in Antony's new son's name: he wanted to expand the dominion of Rome like never before, with a victory that would have raised him to the level of Caesar or Alexander the Great, and he ends up suffering one of the most bruising defeats for the Romans. Cleopatra must devote all her love and energy to rebuilding her man's destroyed morale. Partly because another bad piece of news arrives from Italy.

Octavian has defeated Sextus Pompey's fleet in an epic naval battle outside the city of Naulochus: he lost only 3 ships, sank 28 enemy ones, and captured another 125. How did he manage to beat the uncontested master of the seas? Thanks to his very able commander, Agrippa. Yes, the same man who would build the Pantheon in Rome. He's a true military genius: he has literally turned the tables and transformed a clash on the sea, where the skill of sailors is important, into hand-to-hand combat, in which the skill of soldiers is essential. And his winning card was the *harpago*, an ancient Carthaginian invention. It's a four-hook harpoon, similar to a small anchor, equipped with a very long rope, which his ships would shoot from long distances with special "crossbows" onto enemy vessels, harpooning them and dragging them toward them: once in contact, they were assaulted by onboard troops, the "marines" of the time. And there was no escape for the enemy sailors.

And that's not all. Octavian has taken possession of Sicily, removing from the triumvirate Lepidus—who has retired into private life in his villa on the promontory of Circeo—making himself effectively the uncontested master of the peninsula and of the Roman dominions in the West.

A steady stream of bad news hits Mark Antony. He also learns that his adversary has been welcomed to Rome like a victor, with honors being dedicated to him, as well as an arch of triumph and even a gold statue. And he has solemnly declared that the civil wars are over. Octavian has undoubtedly taken possession of the scene. While all Antony has in his hand is defeat.

Cleopatra Goes on a Hunger Strike

We have reached 35 BC, a crucial year for Cleopatra, Antony, and Octavian. Because the time has come for all three remaining protagonists to make choices that will direct the future of history on three continents.

And so the first split happens.

At the beginning of the year, Mark Antony is in Syria, where he's trying to reorganize his army. He's discovered that the enemy front is divided: the Medes are on bad terms with the Parthians and are even willing to consider an alliance. And so an opportunity for revenge, designed to succeed against the long-term enemy of Rome, presents itself. But there aren't enough soldiers. Many veterans are dead and Antony can recruit equally able troops only in Italy. So he asks Octavian to send him the 20,000 men he'd promised him in the agreement they'd sealed in Taranto.

But Octavian is ambitious, understands Antony's difficulties, and, instead of helping him, tries to put him under even more strain. He sends him only 2,000 legionaries (Praetorians) as well as seventy ships of more than a hundred that Antony had lent him and that had survived the battle of Naulochus . . . And to make his aid even more venomous, he entrusts Octavia, Antony's wife, with the task of taking these military reinforcements to her husband.

Octavian has realized that Mark Antony's weak spot is his connection with Cleopatra, and provokes him by sending him his wife with a ridiculous military contribution. It's a brazen provocation, to oblige him to refuse and make him lose support in Rome.

The time has come for important choices, the ones that would lead to the epilogue of our story.

Antony is at a crossroads. He can decide to go to Rome with Octavia, to try to reestablish in his country his authority and his image, partly compromised by the defeat against the Parthians. But this obviously means abandoning Cleopatra and all his dreams of glory and power in the east, at least for the moment—but there's no knowing if there may be a future.

Or he could focus everything on the east. Start again with new conquests, new victories, and, consequently, prestige, power, and riches that would allow him to oppose Octavian in a powerful way and to beat him. In other words, to find resources and strength in the east and then rise to power in Rome. Cleopatra's support is fundamental to obtaining all this, but that necessarily means abandoning Octavia, which would inevitably lead to a split with Octavian. There would be no turning back.

It's easy to imagine Mark Antony's torment during those days, so decisive for his future.

And Cleopatra? What is her attitude? The queen is very clear about the situation. And she goes . . . on a hunger strike.

Let's proceed in order and try to understand why. Cleopatra is genuinely worried at the prospect that Antony could return to Italy with Octavia, and not only because she has feelings for him. As an experienced politician, she knows that her position and that of her children will be at risk if Antony reaches an agreement with Octavian. There can never be an agreement or peace between her and Octavian. The main reason for this is Caesarion, whose very existence challenges the political image of Octavian, who presents himself as Caesar's only heir, while the boy claims to be his direct descendant (or at least so Cleopatra asserts). Until the previous year, Octavian was not really seen as a threat to Egypt, given his scarce military skill, but now, after the great naval victory against Sextus Pompey and Antony's defeat against the Parthians, things have changed. If Cleopatra wants to keep her power in the Mediterranean and safeguard her son's future, she has just one option: to hold on tight to Antony and hope he wins the next—now inevitable—battle with Octavian. But how can he succeed?

The first step is to remove Antony from Octavia. Cleopatra hates that woman first and foremost because she is a political threat. Moreover, she is jealous of her, seeing in her a dangerous rival in love, who has taken her man away from her once already. And so, to persuade Antony, she blackmails him with a kind of hunger strike, letting herself waste away by the minute, to make him understand that if he were to abandon her, she would die.

As Plutarch puts it, "She put herself on a slimming diet; whenever he approached her, she would look lost and when he walked away she'd look afflicted and despondent. She made sure she was often seen crying, but would immediately wipe away her tears and try to hide them, as though to stop Antony noticing. [. . .] Playing along with Cleopatra, the flatterers would chide Antony for being hard and letting a woman who lived only for him die. They would say that Octavia had married him only for reasons of state, because of her brother, and exploited her status as a wife; while Cleopatra, a queen with so many subjects, was called Antony's lover, and yet she did not evade or disdain this title as long as she could see him and live with him; she would not survive far away from him. In the end, they softened and moved Antony so much that, afraid that Cleopatra would give up on life, he returned to Alexandria."

We don't know if it was for love, or more probably out of political calculation, that Antony chose Cleopatra and the east. He writes a letter to Octavia, who by now has arrived in Athens, asking her to send ahead troops, supplies, and the eldest children, and to return home.

Naturally, this news creates a stir in Rome, and Octavian, pretending to be offended, asks Octavia to leave Antony's house, where she was living as his wife. But, proving herself to be a great lady, she defuses the situation and tells him to leave alone the personal matters that would lead Romans to a new civil war: she will stay at home as though Antony were present, and raise their children as well as those he had with Fulvia. Clearly, Octavia was a woman of great intelligence and virtue.

Meanwhile, Antony commits another political error that once again makes him lose credibility: Sextus Pompey, defeated at the naval battle of Naulochus, takes refuge in Asia Minor. Hearing of Antony's defeats, he tries to reach an agreement with the Parthians in order to create his own zone of influence, supported by Rome's old enemies, and so get back into Rome's political power struggle. Mark Antony discovers him and sends against him a powerful army commanded by the legate Marcus Titius, who captures, and, incredibly, kills Sextus Pompey without a regular trial, as Roman citizens were entitled to, either on Antony's orders or on his own initiative, we don't know.

The news crosses the Mediterranean at lightning speed. Octavian takes advantage of it and, finally shaken, marks Sextus Pompey's death with all due honors, showing he would have been more magnanimous than his rival, and thereby gaining new approval among the senators and the people.

Finally, a Victory for Antony and Cleopatra

Antony knows that his future now depends on a victory in the east and spends the summer and fall months of 35 BC between Syria and Judea, preparing a great attack and strengthening his bonds with vassal kingdoms. It's on this occasion that he organizes the wedding between his daughter and a high-ranking citizen of Tralles, as we've already mentioned. An unfortunate daughter, who would die shortly afterward, but only after giving birth to a girl who would marry Polemon I, king of Pontus, and become a queen. Strange to think that Antony's DNA would rule again, even after death, through his granddaughter, albeit in a small territory. Her name? Pythodorida of Pontus . . .

Antony and Cleopatra spend the winter of 35–34 BC together in Alexandria, preparing for the big moment: the invasion. But, at the last minute, Antony changes objective: he will attack the kingdom of Armenia. Why? First, because the Romans have not lived down the betrayal of that king (Artavasdes) who pulled out from the war two years earlier, causing the failure of the expedition against the Parthians. Moreover, Antony is informed of the contact between the Armenian king and Octavian: by attacking him he would eliminate a potential and dangerous ally of his rival in the east. Antony's army enters the kingdom, captures the traitor king, conquers all Armenia, stations a few legions there, and turns it into a province of Rome before returning to Egypt as a victor.

Of course, he has not defeated the Parthians, but it's still the conquest of new territories for Rome, in a region close to the enemy kingdom, and of significant strategic importance.

The news, however, does not convince public opinion: besides this successful (albeit precarious) extension of Rome's dominion, everyone feels uncomfortable about this victory, since the enemy is still standing—and perhaps Caesar would have done better. And so Antony's image as a great military leader fades a little more, partly because Octavian is try-ing to minimize his success. In Egypt, on the other hand, the situation proceeds quite differently. When, in the fall of 34 BC, Antony returns to Alexandria, he is welcomed as a hero. A coin is minted for the occasion, on one side of which he features with an Armenian tiara on his head (in memory of Alexander the Great's feat, since he, too, conquered Armenia), and with Cleopatra on the other side.

Moreover, a lavish triumph is organized, although different from the ones seen in Rome, because this one is stage-managed by Cleopatra.

Picture the Canopic Way, the main street, decorated. All the people are out on the street in order not to miss the spectacle, many are at their windows, and many others on the roofs. The triumphal pro-cession finally arrives. Roman symbols pass by along with Egyptian ones, followed by the prisoners, including the Armenian king, Ar-tavasdes, and his family members. It's a public humiliation. People rail against him and insult him. Given his status, the sovereign's chains are made of silver (some ancient authors say gold). Then the crowd suddenly bursts into a roar. Mark Antony has appeared be-hind him on a chariot. He is not dressed as a Roman general but as a god: Dionysus. He wears a crown of ivy on his head, and a luxurious saffron-colored garment, boots on his feet, and holds a sacred stick in his hand. It's clear to everyone that his chariot symbolizes that of Dionysus (for Romans that of Bacchus, which you often see engraved on sarcophagi in museums). Of course, now this kind of proces-sion reminds us more of a carnival parade than the display of an army's power. But, as we've already seen, the symbolic importance of this procession in antiquity is very high. It's no wonder Antony is wearing these clothes, which represent the god of happiness and freedom, but also of liberation, one of the most important gods in the Hellenic pantheon.

Many have never seen a parade like this before, and everybody em-phasizes the greatness of the new era of Cleopatra's reign.

The parade doesn't stop, and soldiers also go by. What about Cleopatra? She is at a crucial spot in the itinerary, where the Temple of
Serapis stands. Here, amid the pillars and precious marbles of the
building, a large silver stage has been erected. We can picture the
guards standing all around, with standards fluttering. The queen is
on the stage, sitting on a golden throne that's gleaming in the sun's
rays. She looks like a goddess emerging from a gold fire. When the
Armenian royal family comes before her, the prisoners neither beg
her nor pay her homage with words of deference (even though, as
Cassius Dio says, they had been made promises if they did so). With
great courage, they address her only by name, without emphasizing
her status as queen. It's an affront for which they would pay dearly.
Cleopatra would, in fact, have the king of Armenia killed after the
defeat at Actium.

After the procession, Antony throws a lavish banquet for the people
of Alexandria, complete with shows and gifts, and perhaps—as many
authors, including Stacy Schiff, claim—Cleopatra herself distributes
food and money to the Alexandrians, claiming with political skill
credit for the victory.

But the most important moment of the celebrations is yet to
come.

A few days later, the couple invites all the citizens into the Gymnasium, where a large silvery tribune has been erected, with two
golden thrones.

There isn't room for everybody, and the place is bursting with
people, eyes glistening in anticipation of the imminent surprise.
Then, amid a tremendous roar from the people, Antony, Cleopatra, and their children enter, dressed oddly. It's not hard to guess
the meaning of their clothes. Antony is wearing the costume of
Dionysus/Osiris, and Cleopatra that of the new Isis. The sacred
significance of their union is thereby repeated. The queen is undoubtedly the protagonist of the ceremony. According to Stacy

Schiff, she appears in a pleated gown with shiny stripes and a fringed hem down to her ankles. We can also imagine that she is wearing the crown with the three uraei.

Antony stands up and, his arm outstretched, asks the crowd to be silent. Everybody becomes quiet. The only sound is that of a child crying in his mother's arms. Then he gives his speech in Greek in a loud voice. Words that would become part of history.

He first proclaims Cleopatra "queen of kings" and Caesarion "king of kings." And that's not all: he states publicly that Caesarion was born from the union between Caesar and Cleopatra. These claims, related by Cassius Dio, constitute a true attack on Octavian, who at this moment seems like merely an adopted son of Caesar and not his natural heir, like Caesarion.

Then comes the moment that made history. Dressed as Dionysus, Antony announces the distribution of Roman territories and provinces to the queen and her children. First, Cleopatra, together with Caesarion, is once again confirmed ruler of Egypt, Cyprus, Africa, and Coele-Syria. Then comes the turn of the other children, who are wearing the traditional clothes of the new kingdoms they are to govern. The youngest, Ptolemy Philadelphus, dressed in the guise of Alexander the Great, is assigned all the territories west of the Euphrates as far as the Dardanelles, including Syria, Phoenicia, and Cilicia. Alexander Helios, dressed like the Medes and the Armenians, is given Armenia, Media, and the Parthian Empire (once it has been subjugated). Cleopatra Selene, his twin sister, is entrusted with Cyrenaica and Crete.

At the end of the ceremony, the hall, which has fallen silent during Antony's speech, explodes into joyful clamor. There's a touching moment of family harmony, with the children hugging and kissing their parents, then leaving surrounded by their respective bodyguards: some with Armenian armed guards, others with Macedonians, etc.

This surprising move by Antony, which has gone down in history as the Donations of Alexandria, represents an extraordinary success for Cleopatra. With these new territorial concessions, the queen is not only able to reestablish the borders reached by the Ptolemaic kingdom during its maximum expansion, with the exception of Judea (which still belongs to Herod), but goes beyond, at least on paper, a large part of enemy Asia. The Donations of Alexandria truly represent Cleopatra's apotheosis.

The reaction in Rome is quite different.

10

The Battle of Actium

The Remote Propaganda War Begins

People in Rome are disappointed, mainly because they feel unfairly deprived of the triumph over Armenia, which Antony celebrated in Alexandria. It's no small disappointment, since traditionally money and food were distributed to people at triumphs. Besides, Antony has been away from Rome for a few years, and rumors about his subservience to Cleopatra are fully confirmed by these donations.

Octavian is also negatively affected by this, since he considers it an affront that Caesarion should have been presented as Caesar's only legitimate descendant.

And so a true remote propaganda war begins, in which Octavian and Antony deal each other every possible blow below the belt.

At the Senate, Octavian accuses Antony of having become totally dominated by Cleopatra and the Eastern lifestyle in general. Antony throws in his face the unfair deposition of Lepidus, the occupation of Sicily without an agreed division, and the failure to send legionaries and ships.

To refute the theory that Caesarion is Caesar's only true heir, Octavian commissions a fake: he asks Gaius Oppius, one of Caesar's closest associates (or perhaps we should say that he forces him), to draft a letter in which he claims that Caesarion is not the great military leader's son.

Then he counterattacks and starts building himself an image as a defender of fundamental Roman values (the *mos maiorum*), and does everything to delegitimize his rival.

But how do the residents of Rome react to this conflict? In reality, Roman society is divided down the middle: as Professor Cresci Marrone has pointed out, the most conservative side with tradition and therefore with Octavian; the young aristocrats and intellectuals, on the other hand, support Antony—unscrupulous and hedonistic, of course, but with a love of life they see as a breath of fresh air, and someone whose openness to the Hellenistic world they value.

In some of the accusations flying around, Antony is depicted as a drunkard, while it's the humble origins of Octavian that are emphasized, with some going as far as describing him as the grandson of a miller and the descendant of a petty money changer ("the flour sold by your mother came from the worst mill in Ariccia, and the Nerulum money changer would knead it with hands soiled from handling money"; so say the insinuations, according to Suetonius).

Cleopatra is also attacked. It's during this period that her image as a wanton woman forms, the one poet Horace defines as *fatale monstrum,* an epithet that would last for centuries.

Naturally, the most venomous accusations concern their sex lives. It's easy for Octavian to attack Antony over his relationship with Cleopatra and his dissolute sex life in general. But Antony also gives as good as he gets: he claims that Octavian was adopted by Caesar because the former was his prostitute as a young man. Moreover, he accuses him of habitually giving himself ambiguous "waxing," burning his legs with the shells of scalding walnuts. He even blames him for taking the hand of a consul's wife in front of her husband at a dinner, taking her to the bedroom, then bringing her back into the dining hall, her ears red and her hair tousled.

The two men also exchange fiery letters filled with insults and accusations. Suetonius reports one written by Antony, which illustrates the tone (and sexual appetites) of the two men: "What has changed you? The fact that I sleep with a queen? She's my wife! It's not as though I've only just started—it's already been nine years. And what about you? Do you content yourself with Drusilla alone? I wish you good health, so much so that by the time you receive this letter, you will already have fucked Tertulla, or Terentilla, or Rufilla, or Salvia Titisenia, or all of them. What do I care where or against whom you erect it?"

Octavian's *Coup d'État* and Declaration of War

By the end of 33 BC, it's obvious that the relationship between Antony and Octavian has been irreversibly compromised and that war between them is not only inevitable, but imminent.

Antony is in Armenia to assess the conditions for a new expedition against the Parthians, the bee in his bonnet. When he realizes that war with Octavian is imminent, he decides to go to Asia Minor and orders most of his legions (sixteen of them) to converge on Ephesus, where he has chosen to establish the army's winter quarters.

He gives the same order to Cleopatra, who joins her beloved with her fleet.

Antony attempts a clever political move. With the start of the new year, 32 BC, two of his loyal supporters (Gnaeus Domitius Ahenobarbus and Gaius Sosius) have been appointed consuls, and he sends them a request to validate all the actions he decides on, including the famous Donations of Alexandria.

It's now up to the new consuls and the Senate to make a decision pertaining to this. The session takes place on February 11, and Octavian does not attend it. We know from ancient sources that Ahenobarbus does not take a position, while Sosius gives a speech in favor of Antony and harshly attacking Octavian. Sosius also proposes a censure motion, which is, however, rejected.

Octavian responds with a blitz that made history, a true *coup d'état*. Summoned by the Senate, he walks into the chamber at the Curia with a handful of soldiers and a few armed supporters, stands between the two consuls, and gives a speech in which he defends his actions. Then he dissolves the Senate and schedules another meeting, at which he promises shocking new revelations about Antony's behavior. In a modern democracy, Octavian's behavior would be considered dictatorial and intimidating. Of course, Rome is not a democracy, but these events throw yet another shadow on the ambiguous, despotic, and often cruel figure of the one who would be called Augustus, the father of the Roman Empire.

The two consuls leave Rome in protest and join Antony with three or four hundred other senators, which illustrates the great support he still enjoys.

Meanwhile, we're in April of 23 BC, and Mark Antony and Cleopatra carve out a little holiday on the island of Samos. It's their last happy time together, and they spend it in a carefree way. Then they move to Athens, where more ceremonies and shows take place in their honor, and Cleopatra tries to regain the favor of the people with many donations. This is when Antony takes a harsh step. He repudiates Octavia. By now he has chosen the east and Cleopatra: it's the queen's first victory over Rome, and it will also be her only one.

And how does Octavia react? It's a deeply sad moment for her, as Plutarch writes: "They say that she left, taking with her all Antony's children except for the eldest, who was with his father. She wept and was devastated by the prospect that she, too, might have been one of the causes of the war. But the Romans felt sorry for her, and even more for Antony, especially those who had seen Cleopatra, who did not surpass Octavia in beauty or youth."

Apparently, Antony's divorce is another heavy blow to Octavian (although in reality he probably wasn't expecting anything else), but this way he has another card up his sleeve, and one he will play very shrewdly. Before the final clash with Octavian, Mark Antony decides to draw up a will, and, as is the tradition in Rome, entrusts it to two of his closest associates, Marcus Titius (who killed Sextus Pompey) and Lucius Munatius Plancus, so they will take it to the vestals, where it will be kept and opened after his death.

After handing the documents to the vestals, however, the two men cross over to Octavian's ranks and reveal to him the contents of the will, which they know well, since Antony drew it up in their presence. Octavian learns that Antony, besides confirming that Caesarion truly is Caesar's son and confirming the inheritance (and territories) left to the children he had with Cleopatra, asks to be buried in Alexandria.

Octavian rewards the traitors with important positions: Marcus Titius will be appointed *suffecto* consul, while Munatius Plancus will become censor. It's Munatius Plancus who will subsequently suggest the name "Augustus," with which Octavian will become part of history.

At this point, Octavian commits a sacrilegious act: he takes possession of the will kept by the vestals and reads it out in the Senate. We don't know if he manipulates it and reads only one part of it, the most compromising part, or if, as many scholars claim, he falsifies a few sections in order to ignite the contempt of public opinion. Some even think that the entire will was a fake created by Octavian.

In any case, the reaction is as planned. The senators and part of the population are outraged, interpreting everything as a betrayal, especially his wish to be buried in Alexandria and not Rome. By now, public opinion is on the side of Octavian, and many leave Antony's ranks and move over to him.

Among those taking a stand with him are also what we could call financial lobbies. Antony's decision to delegate the collection of taxes to various allied vassal kingdoms in the east, leaving them their full autonomy, ended up, as Ronald Syme remarks, "Antony's system of reducing the burdens of empire by delegating rule in the East to dependent princes diminished the profits of empire and narrowed the fields of exploitation open to Roman financiers and tax-farmers. Interest unconsciously transformed itself into righteous and patriotic indignation." Businessmen, senators, and cavalrymen support Octavian in preparing for war, viewing eastern territories as prey to be attacked and fleeced after victory.

It's now all plain sailing for Octavian. He has the people and economic powers on his side.

At this point, he persuades the Senate to strip Antony of his position as triumvir, as well as of all his other powers, thereby reducing him to the status of an ordinary citizen, without duties or official roles.

He then asks the Senate to declare war. But against whom? Not Antony, as one would expect, but against Cleopatra. A cunning move, as it's not against a Roman but at the expense of a foreign queen, which fuels Roman patriotism. Moreover, as Michael Grant underlines, "But what Octavian really meant was that Antony's Roman followers still had an opportunity to change their minds [about Cleopatra]."

The official declaration of war against Cleopatra takes place at a solemn ceremony, in keeping with an ancient Roman formula. Octavian travels in a procession to the Temple of Bellona, the goddess of war, opposite the Theatre of Marcellus, which is still being built. There, he gives a very harsh speech against Cleopatra. As dictated by tradition, he is then handed a spear dipped in fresh blood, which he throws at the *columna bellica* that stands outside the temple.

And it's war!

The Battle of Actium Draws Near

It's the fall of 32 BC. Antony and Cleopatra are inspecting a colossal army, made up of thirty legions with 25,000 light infantrymen and 12,000 cavalrymen.

Eleven legions are sent to Egypt and Cyrenaica, while the remaining nineteen will form the main attack force against Octavian.

Coins are minted for the occasion, and they will remain in history: each represents on one side the eagle and insignia with the name and number of a legion and, on the other, one of Cleopatra's warships.

The royal couple moves from Athens to Patras, which they choose as their winter residence. Antony's troops are not composed only of Roman and Egyptian soldiers. They also have at their side the allied troops of vassal kings, among which familiar names stand out, seeming out of a saga: Mithridates of Commagene, Sadalas of Thrace, Philadelphus of Paphlagonia, Tarcondemus of Upper Cilicia, Bocchus of Libya . . . There is even a section sent by the king of the Medes. There is also Archelaus of Cappadocia, placed on the throne by Mark Antony and the son of Glaphyra, his everlasting passion. Who knows if Cleopatra is aware of this . . .

In addition to this huge land power, there are the naval forces. Antony has gathered at least 8,000 ships at Ephesus, and will use 500 of them in the war against Octavian.

And what about Octavian? He has mobilized sixteen legions with 80,000 legionaries (many of whom are skilled veterans) and 12,000 cavalrymen. Including naval infantrymen and auxiliaries, he can deploy 100,000 men and 400 ships.

Over the weeks, Antony posts various garrisons along the coast and the Greek islands, thereby forming a chain of military stations (Corfu, Ithaca, Zakynthos, Methoni, Cape Matapan, Crete, and Cyrenaica) to monitor the supplies for the army from faraway Egypt. In our opinion, this is its true Achilles' heel and perhaps the main cause of what will happen in the war against Octavian. Antony is a very long way from "home" and his line of supplies is vulnerable, while Octavian is fighting in the proximity of Italy and can rely on constant, fast reinforcements of men, food, and weapons.

But where will this war be fought? Why have Antony and Cleopatra taken shelter along the Greek coast and not disembarked in Italy to face the enemy in a big land battle?

What do they have in mind? They are too far south to invade Italy.

Antony knows perfectly well that, following Octavian's smear campaign, to set foot on his native land with an army and, in addition, with Cleopatra would mean unleashing the hostility of the Italian population and finding himself up against everyone. He therefore opts for a different strategy. His is not an offensive deployment, but an "expectant" one: he wants to force Octavian to move from the peninsula, wait for him in Greece so that he can defeat him, and only then land in Italy. Antony knows that time is on his side because Octavian has few financial resources. He needs a quick victory, so will come out into the open.

Antony and Cleopatra's strategy is actually a clever one, partly because everybody knows that, in a land conflict, Octavian risks heavy defeat. So they shelter with the fleet in the Ambracian Gulf, and wait for the adversary.

Everything will take place against the spectacular backdrop of a deep blue sea, an azure sky, with coves, pale blue seabeds, and wind in their hair—places where you can instinctively feel life and in particular enthusiasm for life, but which will actually be a scene of hatred and death.

Octavian knows he is running a great risk if he faces Antony on a battlefield. But what can he do? He decides to change the game. He will not fight Antony on dry land, where his rival is too strong . . . but on the sea. He wagers everything on his fleet and, especially, on his great commander, the same man who defeated Sextus Pompey in a grandiose naval battle: Agrippa.

Agrippa, the Ace Up Octavian's Sleeve

The same age as Octavian, Agrippa comes from a modest background, but played with him as a child. They grew up together and were together at the Apollonia military encampment when news of Caesar's death arrived. Agrippa has been at his side ever since.

An excellent strategist, he's one of the greatest generals in Roman history and certainly the best admiral of the time. After Caesar, he was the second Roman commander to lead troops beyond the Rhine. A man of incredible physical stamina, he is described by the author Velleius Paterculus as "Unable to be defeated by fatigue, wakefulness, dangers [. . .] in any circumstance unaccepting of delays, usually going from decision to action."

And now he's here, with his innate ability to surprise the enemy with unpredictable moves. It was he who had the stroke of genius to reintroduce the *harpago* in the battle against Sextus Pompey. What will he think up now?

Not long afterward, Agrippa does surprise everybody with an attack that marks the start of the war.

We are at the beginning of March 31 BC, and navigation in the Mediterranean hasn't resumed yet after the winter pause, but Agrippa defies fate and launches a daring action: he sails from Brindisi and Taranto with half the fleet and attacks one of Antony's military bases, at Methoni, defended by the troops of an ally, Bogud of Mauretania, who is killed during the assault. By conquering this important base, Agrippa has effectively broken the line of supply from Egypt. Moreover, he uses this base to launch subsequent incursions.

Some modern historians believe that Antony's entire campaign was compromised by this action alone. And this illustrates the shrewdness of Agrippa's genius and its key role in the Battle of Actium.

The ranks of Antony and Cleopatra suffer their first defections with the city of Sparta, not far away, which crosses to Octavian's side.

But it's not over yet. In an orchestrated action, Octavian moves almost at the same time as Agrippa, crossing the sea, disembarking his men in Epirus, and going south without encountering resistance.

Meanwhile, Agrippa takes off with his fleet again and occupies another of Antony and Cleopatra's military stations, Corfu.

And so Octavian's strategy is revealed: action by both land and sea. While Antony and Cleopatra's deployment anticipated a land clash, he has traveled rapidly over the sea, severing the supply route and effectively besieging the adversary from the sea. On land, too, Octavian marches rapidly toward Antony, who is forced quickly to move his legions. While the two armies are lining up before each other, a further threat arrives from the sea: Agrippa conquers another of Antony's stations, Lefkada, thus surrounding him by sea. Antony's fleet is now imprisoned "at home," shut in the Ambracian Gulf. The inertia of the military giant positioned by Antony is surprising, as are the speed, the strategic ability, and the tactics of Agrippa.

Looking at this closely, as Professor Giovani Brizzi, historian and expert in wars of antiquity, says, although Antony is one of the greatest Roman generals, he is certainly no military genius: a barely competent tactician, he commits extremely serious mistakes on the strategic front, which prove to be disastrous against the Parthians—when he splits his forces and allows the annihilation of the column with artillery and siege machines—and actual suicide at Actium. Professor Brizzi's judgment on Actium is categorical: "This fantastic chess game with the enemy was, to all intents and purposes, already won: the majority of Antony's fleet was exhausted by his continuous action and was now distinctly inferior in numbers and trapped in the Ambracian Gulf, powerless to receive supplies and reinforcements."

But it's not just Agrippa's shrewdness and strategy that deal Antony and Cleopatra's deployment a severe blow. The recent winter was very harsh for the fleet. Its strength has been decimated by malnutrition and disease, and many have deserted.

And so the stalemate phase begins, with the two formations standing still for months, waiting.

The situation doesn't change with the arrival of the spring, then the summer. What affects Antony's crews is the humid, close air, which spreads dysentery, and especially the mosquitoes, which carry malaria. The tents are erected in a marshy area and it's difficult to dispose of sewage in an encampment of tens of thousands of people.

Although he is positioned on the plateau of Mikalitzi (in the north of the gulf), which is better ventilated and more salubrious, even Octavian suffers from the lack of water.

The two factions provoke each other. Antony establishes another encampment on the south shore of the strait and proposes battle. But, sensing the enemy's difficulties, Octavian refuses. Suddenly, his cavalry (led by the betrayer of the will, Marcus Titius) overwhelms Antony's in the Louros Valley. This has a devastating effect on the morale of Antony's troops. Allied kings like Philadelphus of Paphlagonia, Rhoemetalces of Thrace, and even one of the most loyal, Domitius Ahenobarbus, cross over to the enemy. Although very upset, Antony still delivers to him all his baggage, complete with servants and friends, in the enemy encampment.

Despite this, Antony tries to break through the blockade with a dual maneuver, letting his ships out while distracting the enemy with a land action. This move proves to be a failure . . . and more allies leave, like King Amyntas of Galatia and his 2,000 cavalrymen, and then the governor of Greece, and even Quintus Dellius, the skillful diplomat who had persuaded Cleopatra to go to meet Antony in Tarsus.

You can sense the outcome of things in the air . . .

At the end of August, after at least four months of naval blockade, the last war council is held in the encampment of Antony and Cleopatra.

The Last War Council

By now it seems obvious to everyone that they can't win at Actium and that the only thing that remains to be done is to find a way out of this situation. There are two possible solutions.

The first is put forward by Publius Canidius Crassus, one of Antony's most loyal men and commander of the land troops. His plan is clear: send Cleopatra and her fleet back to Egypt, fall back on Thrace or Macedonia with a strategic retreat, and there find an ideal location for the decisive clash with Octavian. Especially since the king of the Getae, Dromichaetes, has promised to help them with a powerful army. Canidius vehemently insists that it would be folly if Antony, a commander with absolute experience of land fighting, were to waste his powerful army pointlessly on ships, trying to break through the blockade.

The other important plan is proposed by Cleopatra: to break through the naval blockade with her numerous ships while Canidius's troops withdraw from the coast and head toward an agreed location where, in the meantime, the fleet and new reinforcements will converge. With this suggestion, the queen is also bearing the climate in mind: the risk of remaining trapped in the Balkans in the winter is a concrete one. Finally, she repeats that by choosing Canidius's land solution, total control of the seas would be left to Octavian: How could they then return to Egypt?

Of all these strategies, Antony seeks the one with the best solution and, in the end, opts for Cleopatra's: he will try to break through the naval blockade while moving way with the greatest possible number of ships.

Today's historians still wonder about the real motives behind this decision, and how important the figure of Cleopatra may have been in it.

One thing is clear, though: the clash at Actium will not be a proper battle, as such, but rather an attempt to break through the naval blockade. If there is fighting, Professor Brizzi reiterates, it will be only for the purpose of opening a route to the open sea, with a weakened and no longer formidable fleet, while the duty of Canidius's land forces is to disengage from the battlefield. To use a euphemism, we could call it a solution of two "strategic" retreats.

"How will it turn out?" everyone wonders. In antiquity, this being a prescientific and pretechnological society, the answer is sought not only in sacrifices on temple altars, but also in the omens perceived all around. Here are a few, rather fanciful to a modern outlook, described by Plutarch and Cassius Dio.

- On board the *Antoniade*, Cleopatra's flagship, a terrible omen appears: swallows have built a nest beneath the stern and others fly in, chase them away, and kill the hatchlings.

- One of the statues of Antony, in Alba, has been sweating and oozing blood for several days despite attempts to wipe it away (the phenomenon of sweating statues or statues weeping blood has ancient origins).

- Jupiter's Chariot, in the circus, breaks down. And a light that has been shining over the Greek sea for several days suddenly rises to the sky.

- A flow of lava from Mount Etna brings destruction to many cities and locations.

The Final Day

In the days that precede the battle, Antony gives the order to burn unnecessary vessels—basically the small transport ships. Octavian and his men watch from their positions, and see dozens of plumes of smoke rise toward the sky, warped by the sea breeze. Some 230 ships—less than half of the initial 500—remain, 60 of which are Cleopatra's, while 400 belonging to Agrippa and Octavian await them at sea. This is a desperate attempt.

Now 22,000 legionaries and 2,000 archers board Antony's ships and are officially told that these are preparations for a real battle. Antony then orders the sails to be loaded—an apparently absurd order, since they weigh down the ships, making them slower and less agile, something highly undesirable in a naval clash where everything depends on the propelling power of the oars. Pilots who ask for explanations are told that they are being stowed on board to stop the enemy from fleeing to safety.

During the troop embarkation procedure, Mark Antony walks past a centurion standing next to some sacks. They look at each other. They have fought many a battle together. The centurion's body is covered in scars. The prospect of fighting at sea is far from appealing to him. Plutarch writes that he says to Antony, "Oh, commander [. . .] why do you distrust these wounds and this sword and, instead, put your hopes in this bad timber? Let Egyptians and Phoenicians fight on the sea, but grant us the land to which we are accustomed, without fear, to die or else vanquish our enemies?" Antony stares at him without a word, then carries on walking, just making a gesture and giving him a look as though to say "Courage!" This exchange is reported by Plutarch (whose great-grandfather remembered clearly how at one stage Antony forcibly recruited Greek peasants) and summarizes perfectly the perplexity of so many soldiers, forced to fight in an alien environment.

Meanwhile, seeing the enemy's movements, Octavian gets eight legions and five Praetorian cohorts aboard his ships, a total of 40,000 soldiers. Both Antony and Octavian have picked men with maximum experience, veterans of many battles.

Bad weather keeps both fleets stuck to the shore for three days, with a strong westerly wind preventing Antony's from taking to the open sea. The two fleets form an endless row of hulls, prows with painted rostra and eyes, a true forest of oars. These are the best ships of the time.

This wait allows us to see how the ships about to clash are made.

Looking at the two fleets from above, we notice a subtle difference. Antony's ships are markedly larger: they usually have three banks of oars one above the other, with two oarsmen on the top and middle tiers and a single oarsman at the bottom. Octavian's ships, on the other hand, more commonly have two banks of oars, each of which is operated by two men sitting on the same bench. There's a striking number of oarsmen: according to the U.S. lecturer Si Sheppard, there were 286 in the former case and 232 in the latter, with a maximum respective speed of 7.7 knots versus 9.65. In other words, Octavian's ships are smaller but faster.

We all remember the famous scene in William Wyler's movie *Ben-Hur* in which a stocky man beats a drum to set the rhythm for the oarsmen. But it wasn't really like that: the pace was given by a man, the *hortator*, sitting at the stern, keeping the rhythm with his voice or else a pipe.

Another surprising feature is the large fighting towers on the decks, like those on fortresses. They are the *propugnacula*. The larger the ship, the more of them there are. During the Carthaginian wars, for instance, some ships had as many as eight: two at the stern, two at the bow, and four in the middle of the ship. Just as in castles, there are soldiers on these towers, equipped with stones, arrows, and all kinds of objects for hurling at the enemy. Naturally, these ships are armed: on the surface of the water there are the terrible bronze rostra, and on the deck and towers you can see war machines like the ballista, a kind of large crossbow able to launch arrows and stones with deadly precision.

It's September 2 and the day of the battle has finally arrived. Antony and Octavian have made their speeches to the troops (*adlocutio*): the former describes Octavian as a loser, and the latter appeals to Roman pride, denouncing the extent to which the rights of Romans have been trampled on by Cleopatra, and how sad it is to see Antony dominated by the Egyptian queen. Octavian labors this point: after reminding his soldiers that Antony now calls himself Osiris or Dionysus, he invites them to no longer consider him a Roman, and not call him Antony anymore but Serapis.

Octavian then boards a *liburna*, a ship with two banks of oars, from where he will watch, since the true strategist is Agrippa.

The ships take their positions for battle.

Octavian's deployment has Marcus Lurius, prefect of Sardinia, on its right wing, Arruntius in the center, and Agrippa on the left. Octavian's *liburna* is on the right, the usual position for the person in charge, but the one who really determines this battle is, as we've said, Agrippa; as ever, the future Augustus disappears during the clashes.

Antony, on the other hand, positions three large, sixty-ship teams and joins the group on the right, entrusting the left-hand one to Gaius Sosius, while there is an obviously weaker deployment in the center. His strategy is simple: to lure the enemy to two large blocks of ships on the right and left while the central one will fall apart and allow Cleopatra, who is waiting in the zone behind the front, to pass unharmed and continue toward the open sea.

Antony gives the signal and leads his fleet to the entrance of the gulf, then leaves it in a north-south position. The enemy is there before them, barely a mile away, and spreads out, forming a semicircle in two rows. It's like a sack ready to trap Antony and Cleopatra's hopes.

Antony is on a rowboat and goes from ship to ship, encouraging the crews. Octavian does the same, on his *liburna*.

On dry land, both armies have stopped checking on each other. They have deployed on the shores at an appropriate distance and on their respective "territories" to watch the naval battle.

It's a stalemate for hours, beneath the scorching sun of September 2. The fleets look like formations of giant dinosaurs ready to pounce. And yet nobody moves . . . until noon.

When the sun is at its zenith, a breeze starts to blow. The battle can begin. Thousands of men are living the final hours of their lives.

The Battle of Actium Rages

Antony orders his ships to advance. A roar rises from the shore where his legionaries have seen their companions go on the offensive. Sosius's team, on the left, moves for the first time. It takes them just a few minutes to cover a mile, before a rain of arrows, stones, and darts of every kind darkens the sky and falls on the decks of both sides' ships. Prior to contact between the hulls and the fearsome rostra, Agrippa gives the order to backtrack and retreat to the open sea. His stratagem is cunning: he wants to lead Antony's heavy ships out there, where his own, smaller and faster, have plenty of room to maneuver and can exploit their greater ability and overwhelming number. He also orders them to spread out on the sides, so as to surround and trap the enemy. But Antony's ships sense the maneuver and also stretch out. The proper clash then takes place. The two formations blend and blur in a furious scrum. Watching these sea giants maneuver with so much dexterity and speed, you realize how extraordinary these ships are, the result of the ancient knowledge of carpenters and shipwrights, able to build by hand perfect hulls that glide on the water with good balance. There's also the skill of the commanders and the crews, capable of turning the ships within a few seconds and sending them back against the enemy at lightning speed. All this is the fruit of coordination and understanding, such as only good training and iron discipline can provide.

You can hear the dull thud of hulls colliding in the fray, as well as the screeching of the planking subjected to tight maneuvers. And the screams. The sound of an entire wooden flank splitting open. We notice, however, that the two formations aren't fighting in the same way. One of Octavian's ships is coming at full speed. The two levels of oars on each side are rising and dropping in the water in perfect coordination, like the gills of a strange creature breathing. It's aiming at a larger, slower enemy ship. We have glimpses of its rostrum emerging from the foaming waves, like the muzzle of a sea monster. It's clearly trying to ram it, but it isn't going about it as we expect. It doesn't approach perpendicularly to the enemy's hull, the way a torpedo might. On the contrary, it aims at it diagonally, from a carefully calculated angle. Seeing the enemy vessel coming at them at full speed, the soldiers on board Antony's ship panic and start running in every direction. They prepare a ballista equipped with an "iron hand," a kind of anchor-harpoon that looks like a grapnel, to strike the approaching ship, anchor it, then slow it down, bringing it alongside, so that the soldiers can then stage a massacre, launching arrows and spears from the fighting towers. Unfortunately for them, their launches miss their aim, Octavian's vessel draws close like a torpedo, and there are only a few seconds to go. At the last minute, it draws the oars in to avoid their breaking in the impact, a maneuver the larger ship doesn't manage. There's a violent collision. The first thing you hear is the crack of the oars gradually snapping, then the dull thud as the hull is pierced by the rostrum, followed by the sharp sound of the two hulls rubbing against each other. Octavian's ship doesn't stop but exploits the headway of its long run-up. This way, its rostrum tears through the enemy hull like a blade, opening a gash into which seawater starts pouring. The two vessels are now standing still, swaying for a few seconds. A metallic object can be seen in the gash. It's the rostrum, torn off the bow of the attacking ship. This is not an error but was planned that way. Rostra are like the bee's sting: once the enemy hull has been ripped open, they often remain embedded in the body of the victim, sinking with it.

Just about everything is being hurled from the towers of the ship that's been struck: arrows, stones, javelins, which kill many of Octavian's men. The soldiers on the towers are the first to notice that something is askew, that there is an alarming tilt. The ship is quickly filling with water because of the huge gash. The rowers from the lower decks come up en masse and mix with the legionaries on board, increasing the confusion. Some, however, don't relent in striking the enemy ship, which is now moving away to avoid as many projectiles as possible. Two well-aimed incendiary shots start a fire on Octavian's ship, which spreads rapidly, generating a lot of smoke that can also be seen from the shore. Meanwhile, the situation on the rammed ship is growing serious. It's now tilting irreversibly and is sinking. There's not much to be done, and those on board must jump into the water. For many, however, this spells the end. Few can swim in these times, and the armor drags to the bottom those legionaries who haven't had time to remove it. Within minutes, the ship disappears, leaving behind just a few survivors clinging to floating timber. Among them, we see the centurion who spoke to Antony. This time, too, he will make it: he'll be rescued a few hours later by Octavian's ships, along with his companions. They may be adversaries, but they're still Romans.

The ramming we have witnessed is not an isolated incident. It's happening all around us. And the rostra don't always remain embedded in the belly of the ship and go down with it. This is how Cassius Dio describes the battle: "Being smaller and faster, Octavian's ships attacked with great impetus, trying to sink an enemy ship, then immediately pulled back. Then they would either suddenly attack it again or else leave it and assault another one and, after inflicting as much damage as possible, go after another, then another, attacking the enemy in the most unexpected ways. Fearing both shots coming from a distance and hand-to-hand combat, they would not linger for long while approaching or during the collision. [. . .] Antony's soldiers, on the other hand, would strike their assailants with a steady and dense hurling of stones and javelins, and throw things against whoever approached with iron hands. If they managed to strike them, they would gain the upper hand; if, on the other hand, they missed their target, their ships would be rammed and sunk. Octavian's soldiers looked like cavalrymen, because one minute they attacked, the next they withdrew, choosing both the attack and the retreat. Antony's, on the other hand, were more like Hoplites, who would wait for the enemies to approach and try to resist them as long as possible."

But attacks with rostra aren't always successful. Antony's ships are large and have strong flanks against which the rostra of Octavian's ships are often powerless or buckle and snap during the collision. The solution is therefore for several of Octavian's ships to attack one of Antony's ships at once. The battle is very much like the siege of a fortress, with soldiers shooting arrows, javelins, and all kinds of projectiles. From the tops of the towers on Antony's ships, precise shots from the catapults cause a massacre on enemy decks.

Cleopatra's Escape

It's been two hours that the battle has been raging on the open sea. It is now that the wind gets stronger. When, between 2 and 3 p.m., the wind is at its strongest, Cleopatra has the sails heaved and orders her entire fleet to advance. Until this moment, the clash has still been even. Agrippa and Octavian's ships have not managed to circumvent the enemy front, and as the wings have spread north and south, widening the conflict, the center has grown thinner, just as Antony and Cleopatra expected. At one point, a breach forms, and that's precisely when the queen's sixty ships slip into the gap. Her move takes pretty much everyone by surprise. The first impression, for Antony's men as well as Octavian's, is that they are witnessing a truly sudden flight on the part of Cleopatra, not a long-planned maneuver. Antony follows her, as foreseen during the last war council. But few realize that. Even Cassius Dio, about two hundred years after the battle, would write, "Thinking they were fleeing out of fright, assuming they had already been defeated—and not by order of Cleopatra—he followed them."

The theory about Cleopatra suddenly fleeing, terrified by the violence of the battle, followed by Antony, would last for centuries. Modern scholars have acquitted them of this infamy. On the contrary, Cleopatra shows a cool nerve when she gives the order at the right moment, despite the risk of being captured or killed. The fact that the entire royal treasure is on board Cleopatra's ships stands as proof that it's a highly risky, delicate action, but one that was minutely planned. Nobody would have loaded it had this been just an ordinary naval battle. As we said, it was a maneuver intended to evade the blockade, to break through the circle and get away. Clearly, no military intervention is intended on the part of Cleopatra's fleet.

As soon as he sees her pass by, Antony joins her with one of his ships then boards Cleopatra's royal vessel and leaves the battle with her.

Antony's plan probably foresees that the other ships in the fleet will get away from the battle and follow Cleopatra. Some do. Cassius Dio does say, "A few ships also raised their sails while others threw their towers and accompanying equipment into the sea so as to be lighter in their escape." It is, in any case, a very small number of ships. We don't know if this is due to the practical impossibility of getting away from the fight in the chaos of the battle, or to the fact that Antony deliberately decided to inform only a small number of commanders. In any case, the plan works: Antony manages to save part of the fleet, particularly Cleopatra's treasure. Only a few enemy ships try to pursue them. They are commanded by a prince of Sparta, Eurycles, who, a few months earlier, had betrayed Antony by going over to Octavian. Even so, he succeeds in capturing only one more flagship escort, ramming it and making it lean on its side, obtaining as loot only the precious tableware. Cleopatra and her treasure are safe and sound.

Flames on the Sea

The battle rages behind them. Antony's fleet continues to fight determinedly, even though its commander has fled. In the hours that follow, the clash grows more dramatic, with boardings and fights to the death. According to descriptions by ancient authors, like Cassius Dio, Octavian's legionaries, on board smaller ships, break the oars and snap the helms of Antony's ships, then climb up on the decks and engage in fierce hand-to-hand combats with the enemy. Antony's legionaries, equally expert in combat, push back the assailants with spears, stone projectiles, and, as soon as the others arrive on deck, break their heads with axes. We're therefore witnessing the kind of struggle we can imagine when soldiers assault the walls of a fortress, while other soldiers defend it.

The fight continues and there seem to be no winners, only a huge slaughter of Romans in a fratricidal struggle. In the end, Octavian must resort to fire. He initially aimed to capture the ships and their contents, but then realizes that there's no other way of winning the battle. Cassius Dio describes this dramatic moment like a reporter: "And so the battle took on a different aspect. Attacking their enemies from several directions at the same time, the Caesarians would strike them with enflamed projectiles. From nearby they would hurl torches and from far they used machines to hurl pots filled with burning coals and tar. Antony's men tried to push back these objects. When one of them, passing between them, clung to the wooden structure and immediately started a large flame, as so easily happens on a ship, they first resorted to the drinking water they had on board and succeeded in extinguishing a few small fires; but as this gradually grew scarce, they started drawing seawater [. . .] Since in this procedure, too, they were losers, they would throw their heavy cloaks and dead bodies into the flames: beneath these, the fire would slowly weaken and seem to go out; but then, partly because of the wind, which blew strongly, it increased even more, fed by these very objects . . . And so some, sailors in particular, died from the smoke before being enveloped by the fire, others roasted in the midst of the flame like in ovens, others perished beneath the burning structures, others, before suffering such a death or else already half burned, threw down their weapons and were injured by shots hurled from a distance, while others threw themselves into the sea and drowned, or sank because struck by the enemy, or else were devoured by the fish."

Thousands of legionaries, men and boys, die terribly. The words of the centurion to Mark Antony now ring like an accusation. An entire army has been sacrificed to allow the royal couple to flee, by embarking it on ships, then onto a battlefield that was far from ideal.

The battle concludes around four in the afternoon, when most of Antony's ships raise their oars in sign of surrender. Around them, there's a chilling scene: the sea is studded with ships on fire, from which thick plumes of smoke rise. There are other, semi-submerged ships floating. Everywhere, there are bodies and fragments of wood, with which the waves toy. And survivors clutching to floating timber, waving their arms for help.

According to Plutarch, 5,000 of Mark Antony's men die on this day, but other ancient authors, like Orosius, mention as many as 12,000 dead and 6,000 wounded, of whom 1,000 died in the days that followed.

In a four-hour battle, Antony loses at least 140 ships (destroyed or captured), which is the equivalent of 60 percent of his fleet. We do not, however, have figures for Octavian's losses.

In *Epitome of Roman History*, Lucius Annaeus Florus says that for days, the waves kept depositing on the beach items decorated in gold and crimson belonging to the fighters. An exaggerated vision, but essentially true.

One of the bloodiest chapters of antiquity has just drawn to a close. The Battle of Actium would become part of history, known to generations of scholars, archaeologists, historians, and students, even though only recently, by cross-referencing data and studies, have we truly understood what really happened.

Antony and Cleopatra's alleged flight is part of a very carefully laid plan that also anticipates joining with Canidius's land forces. But none of that will be possible. First and foremost, it's rather worrying that Ceopatra's fleet should be heading straight to Alexandria without joining the army or at least activating part two of the plan. But there's something else that puts a final stop to Cleopatra and Antony's

Greek adventure. After seeing the Egyptian ships sailing away with the queen, shortly followed by Antony's, and powerlessly witnessing from the shore the naval defeat and subsequent death of so many of their fellow soldiers, the former triumvir's legionaries switch en masse to Octavian's side. Canidius, their commander, is unable to stop them and is also forced to flee by night.

Professor Giovanni Brizzi's assessment thereof is very clear and succinct, summarizing the Actium defeat in just a few points. "It's a total failure because in order to save a handful of ships (not even his own but Egypt's), Antony sacrifices the army (most of which was not embarked) and still loses a large portion of his fleet. This move is suicidal on the part of Antony (where can he possibly recruit another similar army when most of this one, made up of professionals and furious at their commander's betrayal, moves over to Octavian?) but equally peculiar on the part of the queen. What is she hoping to achieve by fleeing? Her fate and that of her kingdom are to all intents and purposes linked to that of Antony. Alone, Egypt cannot resist the power of Rome even for a month. Some explain this crazy act by quoting Cassius Dio, according to whom Antony allegedly expressed his intention, in the case of victory, of restoring the Republic, something that would have induced the queen to abandon him. Antony wanted to unblock the fleet in order to lure enemy ships to the open sea then stop them; but was he aware of Cleopatra's intention to head out into the open sea and return to Egypt? Probably not. Not to mention the fact that there were strong doubts in the beginning about the possibility that their ships, heavier than those of the enemy, could get away successfully."

Regarding Actium, the French historian François Chamoux has written that those hours marked the definitive end of the Hellenistic era. Thinking about it, that incredible moment of grace in culture and antiquity which began three hundred years earlier with Alexander the Great suddenly ends between 12 and 4 p.m. on September 2, 31 BC.

From that moment on, the history of the Mediterranean has one face only: that of Rome.

For Antony and Cleopatra, who until that morning had woken up as the undisputed sovereigns of a great kingdom, the dream of a lifetime is over.

II

The End of Antony
and Cleopatra

What Now?

Antony keeps staring at the horizon, but his eyes are blank, lifeless, and even seem a different color. He searches that flat line as though searching for shelter, for a way of turning back and altering his decisions—so that this time he can win. But that's not possible. It's over, and all that's left is the bitterness of the defeat. His face is pale, his expression vacant. In vain, his hair is swept in the wind, like a standard ready for battle. He's been sitting in the bow of the ship for three days now, motionless, as though turned to stone. Three days. Defeat is hard to take. It's his second since the one against the Parthians, but is even more painful since he's lost the decisive conflict with Octavian—a boy compared to him. Two dreams have been buried in these two defeats: that of becoming the great new Roman military leader after Caesar, and that of routing the enemy. He has nothing left now; no longer a future or even a past: he thinks of all his lost friends, of the veterans with whom he shared so many battles. How many are at the bottom of the sea? There's a dark atmosphere on board the *Antoniade*. Antony is sheltering here, in silence. According to Plutarch, he is prey to a mixture of anger and shame toward Cleopatra. Perhaps he realizes her complicity, but also her responsibility for the abyss into which he is falling. The unmistakable form of Cape Matapan appears before him. He feels a small hand touch his shoulder. A woman's hand. Eiras and Charmion, the queen's hand-maidens, have come to persuade him to come out of his isolation. According to Plutarch, the two women convince Antony and Cleopatra first to start speaking to each other again, then to have lunch together, and finally to sleep in the same bed. Other troopships have joined the fleet around them; those among Antony's friends and supporters who have escaped the defeat.

In this general despondency, Cleopatra shows lucidity and presence of mind. She orders the return to Alexandria, as quickly as possible, because she fears that news of the disaster may have preceded them and that her subjects might rebel and dethrone her and Caesarion. Just in case, on arrival she has the bow decorated with garlands, as though they've won, while songs of victory are sung on board, accompanied by flutes.

Once they've disembarked, the news spreads, but by then they have taken the reins of power again. That's until a message informs them that Antony's large army has also gone over to Octavian's side, and Canidius has had to flee during the night. All hope is gone.

Antony sinks into depression. Once again, Plutarch describes a devastated man: "Antony shut himself in a great solitude. He would roam around, anxious, with two friends, the Greek rhetorician Aristocrates and the Roman Lucilius. He had a house built in Alexandria, near the island of Pharos, complete with a jetty. There he would spend his days, fleeing from human company, saying he enjoyed and wished to imitate the life of Timon, feeling he had suffered the same kind of tribulations. He, too, had been vexed and treated ungratefully by his friends, and consequently mistrusted and hated all men."

While Antony remains in exile in what he calls his Timonium, his incomplete palace on the harbor of Alexandria, Cleopatra carries out the most ruthless revenge. She has the Armenian king Artavasdes killed, as we mentioned earlier, as well as many persons of rank in Alexandria who had rejoiced in her defeat, and then ponders the future. It's only a matter of time before Octavian arrives with his army, so she considers possible escape routes.

Finding a Solution

Cleopatra's most "pharaonic" escape plan is to build a new kingdom with Antony in Africa or the east. Perhaps she thinks of the way in which new colonies have been founded in Greece and Magna Grecia, many young people led by a charismatic leader (in this case it would be she and Antony), abandoning their native city with a group of ships.

But the first thing they need is ships, so, as part of a crazy plan, Cleopatra has part of her fleet immediately transported to the Red Sea, into a bay in the Gulf of Suez. This involves crossing an expanse of desert in a perfectly organized manner. Michael Grant says: "We don't have details of this remarkable undertaking, which probably required arranging the ships on large wooden frames, themselves placed on rollers or wheels, and which were then pushed for more than twenty miles by human strength." But once the ships have reached their destination and been put into the water, they are set alight by the Nabataean king, Malichus. As you see (and will see again), fate is being merciless toward Cleopatra and Mark Antony.

The queen doesn't lose heart and tries to lift the morale of her lover, shut away in his refuge at the foot of the giant lighthouse. She persuades him to return to the royal palace and on his birthday, January 14, throws an extraordinary party "that went beyond any splendor and lavishness, so much so that many guests went to the banquet as paupers and returned home wealthy," as Plutarch tells us.

This moment marks the military leader's return to life. Antony and Cleopatra form a kind of "confraternity": the old partnership they had created years earlier, that of the "inimitable living," animated by parties, dissoluteness, splendor, and astronomical expense, is dissolved and, instead, that of "companions in death" is created. All their friends belong to it and, when they join, pledge to die along with them. They spend their time having fun, carousing, running up expenses, and inviting one another to parties and banquets.

One can't help sensing the anguish of an imminent ending. It's not hard to work out the feelings driving Cleopatra and Antony. After the initial bewilderment, they react with intensity, now they've realized how things are going to turn out. They know very well that they're going to die here in Alexandria when the enemy arrives. So they try to exorcise fate, make light of it with a smile, the good life, the desire to have fun . . . and to live. It's the fall, Octavian's troops will arrive after the winter months, and this gives everyone one final carefree period. Before the end. Before death. Or some extraordinary twist of fate.

As confirmation of what's in their hearts and minds, Cleopatra starts to build a large mausoleum for herself and Antony, not far from the Temple of Isis.

She also prepares the dynastic succession with a great citywide celebration that strengthens the people's loyalty and celebrates Caesarion, who comes of age at the same time as Antyllus, Antony's eldest son.

Naturally, that's not enough. She knows perfectly well that Caesarion will be in grave danger when Octavian arrives. And so, after the New Year in 31 BC, Cleopatra organizes her son's escape to India, with ships, riches, and an escort of loyal people.

Some weeks later, in the spring, Mark Antony and Cleopatra decide to get in contact with Octavian and send him letters. Moreover, Cleopatra sends him the royal insignia and assures him that she will abdicate provided her children can succeed her on the throne. Octavian keeps the insignia and does not give a straight answer.

Antony also sends him a gift. He dispatches a letter in which he reminds him of their bond of friendship and family, the boyish pranks they played when they were young, and the romantic adventures they shared. Then he tells him where he can find one of Caesar's last living assassins, Decimus Turullius. In this case, too, Octavian keeps the gift (and immediately dispatches mercenaries to kill Turullius on the island of Kos, where he has been hiding), but doesn't respond.

Antony then sends his eldest son, Antyllus, to Octavian in Rome with a large sum of money, saying that if he accepts it he will retire to private life. Octavian takes the money and sends Antyllus back empty-handed, without an answer.

At this point, Cleopatra writes another letter, sends it to him with a large quantity of jewels and money, and asks him to preserve her children's succession to the throne. This time, Octavian replies and presents the queen with a dilemma: he will agree to her more reasonable requests if she kills Antony or sends him away. As Professor Brizzi points out, "Octavian is clear, direct, and ruthless. What can the two of them possibly give him that he can't get for himself?"

Many ancient writers hostile to Cleopatra would use these very letters and these requests from Octavian to see every future action on the part of the queen as proof of her betrayal of Antony.

In conclusion, despite all the offerings, Octavian remains impassive. First of all because he's not inclined to be bribed, secondly because he's in the stronger position so has no need to bargain, but above all because he has a desperate need for Egypt and its riches. His strength lies in his huge army—to which the legions that have left Antony's formations have been added—but which must be paid. That's not counting all the veterans waiting for promised lands in Italy. And so to placate ill feeling and potential revolt among the legionaries, Octavian promises them Cleopatra's immense treasure, proving himself to be as cynical and brutal as Brutus and Cassius, who would promise their soldiers entire cities to pillage.

In the summer of 30 BC, Octavian is ready to unleash a massive attack against the residual forces of Antony and Cleopatra.

His plan is simple: to invade Egypt at the same time from the east and the west, with a pincer maneuver. Naturally he will just need to concentrate on the Delta and on Alexandria: once the capital has fallen, the whole kingdom will be his.

Summer 30 BC: The Attack on the West and the East Is Triggered

Prior to the Battle of Actium, Antony had sent four legions to the west of Alexandria, to Cyrenaica and Libya, to defend the western front against potential attack. These troops were commanded by one of Caesar's nephews, the legate Lucius Pinarius, listed in his will as one of his heirs. Pinarius has always been loyal to Antony, and even commanded a legion in Philippi, but after the battle at Actium, sensing which way the wind was blowing, he handed his troops over to a man from Octavian's entourage who had come especially by ship from Rome: Cornelius Gallus. Remember him? He's the poet who had fallen desperately in love with the showgirl-escort Licorys and, after being abandoned by her, fell into a deep depression. Well, he's back again and leading Antony's former legions to Alexandria.

The first step is the conquest of an essential bastion for the defense of the west of the city, Paraetonium (now its ruins stand near the famous tourist location of Mersa Matruh), just 186 miles from the capital. Gallus launches his attack from the sea, swooping down on the city with his fleet and occupying it.

Hearing the news, Antony rushes with his army, determined to play the card of the charismatic commander so that he can reconquer his former troops. He goes to the foot of the walls to speak directly to the men with whom he shared so much, but Cornelius Gallus understands his intentions, and, as Cassius Dio says, "ordered the trumpeters to play all together, and so prevented anyone from hearing anything."

Antony then attempts a naval attack. He sees that the harbor is not watched intently so he lets in the ships with his troops on board. But it's a trap: Gallus has had large chains stretched under the water during the night and placed very few sentinels so as to give Antony an alluring bait. When the ships enter the harbor and approach the pier, he orders the long chains to be heaved, thereby closing the harbor behind them and blocking his opponent's avenue of escape. At this point, a rain of flaming arrows and darts starts falling on the ships, setting them on fire, like at Actium, and the remaining ones are sunk. It's another disaster for Antony, who must accept defeat once again. He realizes that Paraetonium is lost, and that he can only return to Alexandria. And so he does, pursued by Gallus's troops.

On his way back another terrible piece of news reaches him: Pelusium, the other bastion defending Alexandria, on the eastern side, has been conquered. Octavian himself occupied it while Antony was attempting his unfortunate naval action.

Octavian has taken up position outside the city with a colossal army, which includes many allied contingents from the Middle Eastern kingdoms that were once Antony's vassals, among them Herod of Judea. That's right, him.

There was no need even for one javelin to be hurled to conquer the city. Despite being the commander of Egyptian troops quartered in Pelusium, Seleucus, the governor, simply handed it to Octavian. A few ancient writers have hypothesized that there was a secret agreement between Cleopatra and Octavian unbeknownst to Antony: the queen would have kept her status as queen of Egypt in exchange. We don't know if that really happened although it does seem unlikely, partly because Cleopatra's reprisals occur without delay: as soon as she is told that the city has fallen without a fight, she puts Seleucus's wife and children to death.

The conquest of Pelusium took place in midsummer; we don't know when exactly, but all signs point to the end of July. Octavian doesn't want to waste any more time and commands his legions to head to Alexandria on a forced march. The 186 or so miles are covered in just a few days, and on the morning of July 31, 30 BC, Octavian arrives within sight of the city.

A Wait Full of Anxiety

What's the atmosphere in the streets of Alexandria like during these days? It's easy to imagine. It's been less than twenty years since the Siege of Alexandria, but the memory of it is still alive, especially among adults and the elderly. If the fall of Paraetonium has already spread a degree of anxiety, then the news that Pelusium has also been conquered triggers panic. Ancient sources do not describe dramatic episodes but fear must be palpable in the houses and streets. Many shops are closed and locked up. For days, entire families, especially from middle-class Alexandria, have been leaving the city on carts filled with valuables, elegant furniture, and personal effects. But there are also ordinary people abandoning their homes in working-class areas, with household items on their heads, and holding children by the hand. They go to seek shelter in the countryside, hiding far away. In the streets, there's a constant to-ing and fro-ing of soldiers and a few clusters of people making comments, seeking new information, learning and spreading absurd news, as often happens in these cases. Supplies of grain and other foodstuffs have been accumulated in warehouses. The city gates are heavily guarded, as is activity in the harbor. There are many cargo ships lifting their moorings and heading into the open sea toward faraway islands or coasts: on board, as well as goods that mustn't fall into the hands of soldiers looking for loot, there are sometimes entire families.

Then there are the temples, where people gather to ask the gods for all kinds of miracles. Cleopatra is much loved, and many are certainly praying for her and for the safety of the dynasty and the kingdom.

Finally, in some of the rooms in elegant houses and in the dark backrooms of some of the shops, secret meetings are held between officers or legionaries to decide what to do: remain with Antony or move over to Octavian's side and follow the example of other cities and legions?

As the hours and days go by, these behaviors grow increasingly more pronounced, fueled by sheer anguish.

Cleopatra Hides the Royal Treasure

Naturally, the anxiety knows no boundaries and seeps through the walls of the houses, crossing the thresholds of family homes, entering inns, sliding over tavern tables, going deep into harbor warehouses, and penetrating the royal quarter. According to Plutarch, Cleopatra isn't twiddling her thumbs but conducting an intense correspondence with Octavian to negotiate a surrender behind Antony's back. This secret bargaining, exploited by so many ancient authors hostile to her, has fueled over time the image of a treacherous woman, a true viper who "gifted" the bastion city of Pelusium in exchange for her own safety and that of the throne. We cannot rule out the possibility that there may have been contact between them with view to an alliance. However, the atmosphere is probably quite different: if she did receive letters from Octavian, they would have been to reassure her, although they, too, are treacherous. Because he fears Cleopatra will destroy the royal treasure in her possession.

As a matter of fact, there are rumors to this effect, and Plutarch is an example of that: "Since Cleopatra owned funeral cells and monuments of extraordinary beauty and height next to the Temple of Isis, she collected there the most precious items of the royal treasure, gold, silver, emeralds, pearls, ebony, ivory, and cinnamon; but she also added to them a large quantity of torches and tow. And so Octavian, fearing for these treasures, at the thought that, driven to despair, the woman could destroy and burn these riches, kept sending her promises of clemency while his army advanced toward the city."

Octavian's principal objective, more than the royal treasure, is Egypt, which has much more extensive and boundless wealth. At this moment, Cleopatra is cornered and perhaps realizes that her adversary is thinking on a much higher geopolitical scale: the queen stands in the way of his designs since she represents a power that could rival Rome in the dominance and control of the Middle East and North Africa. It's no longer a matter of pacts: there simply isn't any more room in history for the Egyptian kingdom. The future is knocking at the door, on its way to a Mediterranean world that is uniquely Roman.

July 30, the Penultimate Night

It's difficult to describe the silence and sense of icy void in the rooms of the royal palace. Only a few servants quickly walk by. And yet everywhere there's a pleasant fragrance of essences burning in small braziers, blending with the scent of ornamental plants in the inner gardens. It's this very night smell, so intriguing and intense, the accomplice that embraced the love of Cleopatra and Antony, that has now changed face and become the symptom of an imminent end. There are no banquets, no celebrations. Only a stillness that weighs heavily in the air. The faces of the few courtiers you come across are tense, worried, anxious about the uncertain future. A future that will come crashing down on them tomorrow. Will they live? Will they be killed? Who will be here in the palace?

Mark Antony returned to Alexandria a few days ago. He's unapproachable, sad, and in a foul mood. The news from the front is also terrible: Octavian has set up camp in the city of Canopus, a few hours' march from Alexandria and the palace.

Antony has spent the day with his most loyal men, organizing the defenses and weighing up all the options—too few, to be honest—for getting out of this situation. His troops are inferior to those of the enemy, in both numbers and preparation. Besides, they are demoralized and cannot be entirely relied upon, because there's an inclination toward desertion slithering through the ranks. There's also the fleet in the harbor, another weapon Mark Antony is considering using one way or another. Even Caesarion and Antyllus, now grown up, are sitting at the officers' table, caught up in the situation despite themselves. Looking at them, their father has almost certainly thought about an escape to save them at least. And his heart must have filled with anger.

And Cleopatra? We don't know if she attended the meetings, even though she most probably contributed significantly to the strategies, given that her city, her kingdom, her children, and her own life are at stake, and that she is certainly not a woman who lets others decide on her behalf.

According to a few modern historians, there's tension between the two, perhaps partly because of the rumors concerning a pact between her and Octavian after the strange surrender of Pelusium (in actual fact perfectly easy to explain, given Seleucus's choice of side when facing such an unstoppable, and above all already victorious, enemy).

Could Antony and Cleopatra possibly have spent their last night apart? Probably. No general, just before the imminent arrival of a powerful friend, leaves everything and goes to sleep with his beloved. He would have spent all his available hours feverishly counting the remaining forces, anticipating the enemy's possible strategies, and planning surprise moves.

For her part, at one stage Cleopatra will have retired to be with her children, whose fate is no doubt her greatest worry. Especially Caesarion, who would be the first victim to fall after herself and Antony. The queen would have tried to instill calm in everyone but must have been concerned for him. It's not easy to give him peace of mind: at seventeen he understands very well the situation they, and moreover, he, are in. We now feel a lot of sympathy with this boy, given life by an incredible historical couple, but who could be killed at any moment through no fault of his own apart from perhaps being Caesar's son. How can one kill a boy in cold blood? An innocent with life in his eyes? Of course, they will tell you that it's all a matter of power in Rome: Octavian would have another potential rival around whom opposition to his command could form. But we are inclined to see in all this another example of the cruelty of Octavian. A man glorified for centuries, but who conceals a sinister wickedness. Our error, in fact, is to see the ancient world through modern eyes. It's true that Octavian is a cold, calculating, cruel man, but he acts no differently from the others, including Cleopatra. The shocking ruthlessness we see belongs to the era we are describing. It was a world different from ours, with a different moral code. And all we can do is watch without judging.

However, feelings don't change over the centuries. We would like to think that in the end, Cleopatra would have curled up next to little Ptolemy Philadelphus as he slept, hugging him from behind to smell the scent of his hair, the way she did in Rome with Caesarion at the news of Caesar's death. And then, more than ever, she would have missed the great military leader. Why isn't he there anymore? They fought together in this palace. Perhaps he would have found a better solution than Mark Antony. For sure, they wouldn't have been in this situation, starting with Actium.

Dawn, July 31: The Enemy Is at the Gates

The sun hasn't risen yet. The sea is calm, the sky clear. It's going to be a beautiful day. The kind that makes you love life. And yet these will be some of the bitterest days in Alexandria's history. Strangely, there's no activity in the harbor, and the streets are semi-deserted. A few of Antony's high-ranking Roman officers are watching the horizon from the Lighthouse. We can imagine among them the commander in chief, the very loyal Publius Canidius Crassus, a great and brave general. You can enjoy a breathtaking view from up there. Strategically, at the time it was the equivalent of being on a spy satellite. We have no evidence, but the general has probably climbed up there to assess who he's dealing with. The light has been put out so as not to give the enemy a point of reference. All eyes are turned east, to the road that leads from Alexandria to Pelusium. That's where Octavian will be coming from.

At this time, at dawn, the dirt road is a pale strip that disappears amid the dark coastal vegetation. All the legionaries are wrapped in the heavy, red regulation cloak. Although it's summer, the wind and humidity from the sea are sharp before dawn when you're standing so high up. Moreover, the steel armor chills their bodies, like ice.

For the past few minutes, the sky seems to be turning orange and red. Suddenly there comes the piercing first ray of light. In the city, everybody usually sees the top of the Lighthouse turn a fiery red before the sun lights up Alexandria. For generations, that first glow on the top of the Lighthouse has marked the start of the day, like the chimes of a luminous Big Ben. This time, however, it's like a death knell. The faces of all the officers are drawn, marked by a sleepless night spent reading dispatches brought by breathless messengers, spreading open maps of the city to try to work out how to plan the defense, and perhaps write wills while everybody else is running around.

Publius Canidius is offered a cup of hot wine to warm up. His face is now lit up by the red of the rising sun and disappears behind a silver cup embossed with Dionysus and many cupids. As he swallows the last drop, many notice that his cheeks are unshaven and covered in an expanse of short white hairs. They've never seen him like this, and this accentuates the sense of insecurity and fear in many of them, even though they will never say so.

Suddenly, there's a cry: "Over there! Here they are!" (*"Illic! Aspicite!"*)

Publius Canidius drops the cup, wipes his mouth with the back of his hand, squints to see better, grimaces, and murmurs, "So many of them . . ."

The sunlight has reached the ground, flooding the cultivated fields, still covered with a light morning mist. But, in the distance, something frightening is rising on the road. It's the dust raised by marching legions, a huge cloud, lit sideways by the rays of a magnificent red circle on the horizon. By now, through experience, Publius Canidius and his men are able to assess the size of a marching unit or army from the dust it raises. And this looks like an impending sandstorm.

The general goes down to command his men from the land. An officer and a few soldiers have remained on the top of the Lighthouse, ordered to report on the enemy's movements. Now everybody has fallen silent.

The sun precedes Octavian's troops and enters by the east door of Alexandria, not by chance called the Gate of the Sun. Once past the city gates, its long rays continue advancing, instantly lighting the whole main street of Alexandria, the Canopic Way, which is perfectly aligned with the sunrise on the dawn of July 20, the day Alexander the Great was born, as recently discovered by a study by Professors Luisa Ferro and Julius Magli. It's now only eleven days later, and this effect full of significance is still clearly visible, especially today, when the street is completely deserted. There's just a mule, standing still in the middle of the road, having emerged from some bakery where grain is being ground.

The Gate of the Sun, 6 a.m.: Preparing the Defense

On the road leading to Alexandria, a horse is galloping at breakneck speed.

There's no one about and all you can hear is the echo of its hooves. Usually, this street is already filled with people heading into the city:

peasants with their cone-shaped headwear, merchants with carts brimming with goods and country produce, civil servants in litters . . . But today it's deserted and plunged in silence. The few houses the horseman rides past are empty, their doors open, including a few peasant huts, in the distance, made of woven plants, with their typical barrel shape, according to the tradition in the Delta. Everybody has escaped before the arrival of Octavian's legions. And this horseman is also the last one sent to see where the enemy is located, and judging by the speed of his gallop the enemy is very near. They can see him coming from the walls of Alexandria, riding past the tombs and funeral monuments of the city's most eminent families, which line the road. He's now by the large Hippodrome outside the walls, about 1,200 feet long. The young man must be truly frightened, because he doesn't appear to be about to stop and all the soldiers on watch duty are instinctively worried. Like a bolt of lightning, he rides through the Gate of the Sun, and is immediately surrounded by his fellow soldiers and officers, who give him a drink, seeing him exhausted and covered in dust. They watch him gulp the water, which trickles down his cheeks, neck, and armor. Like a marathon runner at the end of a race, he struggles to catch his breath, but everybody wants news. Just as he's about to speak, the circle of legionaries suddenly opens. Mark Antony approaches, with Publius Canidius and other officers. The horseman tenses up. He clumsily tries to wipe off the water and dust, but doesn't have time. Antony's group, now very close, looms over him. He can even feel his breath and smell his ointments. He tells him everything he knows: the enemy is immense, ready for combat, and will be here within the hour. Antony looks at the soldier, thinking that the moment so awaited and feared for months has finally arrived, and that destiny is about to be played out. He pats the horseman on the shoulder and quickly disappears with his generals.

Instructions are given. The few people still outside the walls are brought in. And the order is given to close the gates. The Gate of the

Sun is formed of two separate passages, each with an arch over it: one for incoming traffic, the other for outgoing. There are two large cylindrical towers on either side. It's not easy to close: it hasn't been necessary for years; the salt air and sand have oxidized and encrusted the bronze hinges. Grinding their teeth from the effort, a group of legionaries pushes the gates, which, after initially refusing to budge, start to move as the hinges give way, moaning with small bursts of dust. The heavy gates finally shut with a thud followed by the sound of the large metal bolts; the gates are also propped up with heavy timber planks, effectively isolating Alexandria from the world. Meanwhile, the news of the imminent arrival of Octavian's troops spreads across the city. Few managed to sleep last night: there's fear and stress in everybody's eyes.

Not far from the Gate of the Sun, on one of the city's defensive towers, Antony can clearly be seen standing in his beautiful combat armor, with pectorals and other muscles embossed in the metal, and his hair with thousands of curls. He has Canidius and a few officers next to him, and is speaking to them. The little group might well include Caesarion and Antyllus.

7 a.m.: Octavian's First Units on Reconnaissance

Almost another hour goes by. On the top of the Lighthouse, the officer left on watch is suddenly called by one of his legionaries, who points out a few distant dots on the road. They are the first enemy cavalry units on reconnaissance. Canidius and Antony are immediately informed (they almost certainly use mirrors and luminous signals, or else colored flags).

It's not long before they, too, from the walls, see those dots materialize. It's a small group of very fast and agile horsemen. They have stopped at the entrance to the road, a few hundred yards from the walls, at a safe distance from the deadly *scorpiones*, large crossbows able to hurl long arrows with remarkable power and precision.

The horses' heads are swaying nervously. Before Octavian's cavalry-men, Alexandria appears in all her splendor, with its walls, houses, and other buildings. To their right, on the sea, the Lighthouse towers over the whole landscape. From here, they can make out a few figures moving. It's Canidius's officer and legionaries watching them.

The appearance of the first horsemen has triggered distinct move-ment on the walls, and you can hear alarm signals being sounded on horns. A wave of fear spreads across the city. Anyone who wanted to escape should have done so sooner. It's too late now. The city gates are shut and the enemy has arrived.

7:30 a.m.: Octavian's Legions Arrive

It's the Lighthouse that has been the point of reference for the march of Octavian's legions. Even though it had been extinguished that night so as not to help the enemy, its imposing size and luminous color stood out in the dawn and guided their steps. It hasn't been an easy march, even though it was "only" 12.5 miles: the legionaries' legs bear the weight of more than 155 miles of forced marches.

The sound of the sea stops you from hearing clearly marching le-gions. Usually, their arrival is heralded by a sinister, terrible racket, with the jangling of tens of thousands of suits of armor with their swaying metal fringes, weapons banging, as well as pots and pans— the steps of thousands of legionaries. This grim commotion instills fear even before the actual army is visible.

About ten minutes later, the enemy legions appear at the end of the road, and you can even make out the front rows with their insignia. The rest are shrouded in dust. But somewhere down there is Octavian.

7:30 a.m.: Octavian Sees Alexandria

Octavian is on horseback, surrounded by his generals, wearing a hel-met. When he arrives, he can't help but admire the city, so beautiful, exotic, immersed in an alluring Eastern atmosphere. He's seeing it for the first time in his life and is moved by it: he's heard so many stories about this city. Above all from Caesar, when he would tell him about the Siege of Alexandria.

Once he has recovered from his awe, Octavian returns to reality and immediately notices that the gates are shut. Antony and Cleopatra are not going to surrender like Pelusium.

So he orders his troops to quarter on a small hill near the Hippodrome. He doesn't trust the situation. Even though a sortie on the part of Antony is rather unlikely, he chooses a raised position, easier to defend, and places the cavalry in front of him while his legionaries set up a large encampment with palisades and moats.

8 a.m.: Mark Antony's Last Victory

Mark Antony has not lost sight of the movements of the enemy troops, and as an experienced commander realizes that Octavian's legionaries are very tired after days of marching. So he decides to attempt an action. His cavalry is hiding outside the walls, not far from the Hippodrome. Antony joins his units by exiting through a secondary door. He's wearing his helmet. He looks at his soldiers on horseback, utters a few specific words—there's no time for long speeches—and goes on the attack.

Octavian's cavalry, responsible for defending his troops, is caught by surprise. It is overwhelmed by the assault led by Antony and forced to flee, perhaps leaving casualties on the ground. The charge doesn't relent and heads straight to Octavian's encampment, where the enemy cavalry has taken refuge. Who knows? Perhaps in the momentum Antony tries to break through the enemy lines in an encampment that's not yet complete, to sow confusion and, if he can, kill his rival. After all, isn't this how Alexander the Great staged his attacks? It would be an extraordinary *coup de théâtre*. If you think about it, with

Octavian dead, only he would be left, ready to claim back his power in Rome, with, in addition, Caesarion to justify the victory of the Caesar-supporting faction.

But it's not easy for cavalry to attack a Roman encampment. You need foot soldiers. Seeing Antony's breach, his general Canidius, as no doubt previously arranged, opens the city gates and lets out the necessary troops to aid him. Joined by these troops, Antony goes on the offensive. Meanwhile, Octavian's soldiers have managed to entrench themselves and fortify the camp, albeit provisionally, given the lack of time. And they defend themselves fiercely. The assault comes to an end and Antony desists. He returns to the city, but not before having arrows with messages shot into the enemy camp, promising 1,500 drachmas to every soldier who switches sides. Obviously, Egypt and Alexandria are reputedly so rich that all it takes is a promise to "buy" a soldier. However, this also shows the only true motivating force of the troops: money and loot. Like pirates.

The clash did not involve the two armies, but only a few hundred cavalrymen and legionaries. Even so, it was enough to lift Antony's spirits after all the bad news over the past few months.

10 a.m.: Octavian Regroups His Men

Octavian and his generals are surprised and very struck by Antony's bold action. They expected only weak resistance, and yet the former triumvir attacked them, making the cavalry flee. After the clash, Octavian personally restores order among his ranks and ably—and cunningly—responds to Antony's provocation. This is what Cassius Dio writes: "He decides of his own accord to read the messages to the soldiers, accusing Antony and trying to kindle in their spirits a sense of shame for the betrayal they were being urged toward, and of affection for his cause: this way, they would fight with commitment, contemptuous of Antony's attempt and eager to show that they were not traitors."

11 a.m.: Antony Joins Cleopatra

Mark Antony doesn't know that this was his last victory. Still, for the time being he seems to have regained his former enthusiasm. Back in Alexandria, he's warmly welcomed by his soldiers and General Canidius, then goes to see Cleopatra at the royal palace with a few of the cavalrymen who've taken part in the attack alongside him. According to Plutarch, Antony walks into the palace and embraces Cleopatra even though he's still wearing his armor and has his sword at his side. He presents one cavalryman in particular, the one who fought most bravely today. As a prize, Cleopatra gives him a suit of armor and a helmet made of gold. Unfortunately, Plutarch adds, the soldier accepts the gifts but, that night, will cross over to Octavian's ranks.

2 p.m.: Octavian's Encampment

There's a strange episode that occurs perhaps in the early afternoon. In the sweep of enthusiasm, but also motivated by the problem of the huge difference between the forces in the field, Antony makes Octavian a very arrogant suggestion: he challenges him to a duel.

Octavian almost certainly smiles when he reads the message an emissary has brought to his tent. He replies to Antony, declining the offer with his usual cynicism: he sends word that . . . he has many ways to die available to him.

Nothing happens for the rest of the day. Octavian strengthens his positions and, above all, grants his exhausted troops some rest. The legions draw breath before the final dash. And this is equally evident to those within the city walls, which increases their dismay and fear.

Evening Falls Over Alexandria

All afternoon, the two enemy encampments can be clearly seen from the taller buildings and the Lighthouse: that of Octavian in the east, and Gallus in the west. On the sea, you can make out the ships of the enemy formation controlling all the surrounding waters. The city is completely encircled. Cleopatra and Mark Antony are now in a trap.

What happens at this point? Incredible as it might sound, even though their story (and end) is very famous, we possess few sources describing the final days of their lives. We essentially have two: Plutarch and Cassius Dio. It's necessary to specify that following the succession of events and the denouement of our story by the hour can only be done based on their writings, and that everything else is entirely hypothetical. Even so, even though there are gaps, we can still plausibly reconstruct what happened, albeit conscious of the fact that nobody will ever know how things really went. This clarification is necessary for the sake of cultural honesty.

Royal Palace, Evening: The Last Banquet

Antony realizes his fate is sealed. He will not see the winter to come, he will not see his children grow up, nor will he ever know what his face looks like as an old man. His future now consists of only a few hours. His life has come to an end: by this time tomorrow, he will probably be dead. How would you have reacted? You can't help but think about his state of mind, his anger, and the deep, dark despair he must have felt as he looked with envy at others with their lives ahead of them. And—who knows?—maybe he also thought up other plans to try to turn the tide.

It has to be said that a frequent error is to look at other eras from our point of view as modern men and women: we are used to living a long time and thinking that it's normal to reach old age. We can rely on many remedies to our health problems, and on far fewer difficulties in comparison with Romans or Greeks. But in Cleopatra's time, people didn't live long; on average, forty-one years for a man and twenty-nine for a woman (above all because of complications relating to giving birth). It was a society made up of many children and few old people, where death was waiting around every corner and was a daily presence. Younger siblings died in every family and widowhood was common. A couple rarely remained together as they got old. Over the years, infection, famine, and accidents took away many friends and acquaintances, if not whole communities. Not to mention wars. Although they were no different from us in their fear of death, men and women of that time probably had a higher awareness of the precariousness of human existence. Were they more fatalistic? Hard to say; these days, we have certainly erased death from our minds in daily life (one dies in what are considered "exceptional, unexpected" events, ones like disease, accidents, etc.) and turned our lives into a sort of comic strip from which death has been removed, while in antiquity it was considered a sad reality rather than a tragic exception. After all, that's how our grandparents lived, and that's the reality experienced in many developing countries. Where life is hard, people are stronger.

While we now tend to feel entitled to have a future, it was once not something quite so important. Given how extremely easy it was to die in antiquity, ordinary people tended to live more "by the day," valuing every minute, enjoying every party, banquet, friendship, and family relationship, punctuating life with very close landmarks. Aware that everything could end at any moment, they had more (forced) wisdom than we do, or so it seems.

If we then look at the lives of Cleopatra, Mark Antony, Caesar, Brutus, Cassius, and Octavian, in other words, the leading classes, we notice that they have an even more extreme lifestyle: they throw themselves into great battles, risking everything, to then live on the outcome for a year or two, enjoying huge power in the most unbridled luxury, during which they try to maintain their dominion by constantly engaging in politics, forming new alliances and keeping the old ones; but then, inevitably, they come up against new, crucial conflicts, and wager everything again . . . and so the merry-go-round starts again. Compared with our modern planning, this is an existence focused on all or nothing, where people are conscious of the fact that you live on a large scale, but if you die, then you lose everything, even life.

And that's precisely what Antony has in mind on the evening of July 30, 30 BC.

He orders that a banquet be organized to treat himself to one final pleasure. As Plutarch says, "At dinner, by all accounts, he ordered the servants to pour him drink and treat him with even more zeal and care than usual: because he didn't know whether they would do it again the following day, or serve other masters while he would be lying on the ground, a skeleton reduced to nothing."

His last friends attend the banquet, those who have been loyal to him till the very end. We don't know their names. There's certainly Lucilius, Brutus's friend whom Antony spared after the Battle of Philippi; it's reasonable to expect that the very loyal general Publius Canidius, the Greek rhetorician Aristocrates, and, among his personal staff, his trusted servant Eros are there. It's very likely Antyllus and Caesarion are there too. And, above all, Cleopatra. This is a farewell banquet to everybody and to life.

A mixture of solemnity and affection, the atmosphere of this final dinner is no doubt moving. According to Plutarch, those present are deeply affected by Antony's words: "Seeing that his friends wept at his words, he reassured them, saying he would never have led them into a battle where he sought glory instead of safety and victory."

The ancient biographer then adds an anecdote, more poetical than realistic, to dramatize the inevitable fate awaiting Antony: "At around midnight, while the city was plunged in silence and sadness in fearful expectation of the future, people suddenly heard the harmonious sounds of various instruments and the clamor of a crowd with shouts and satyrs dancing, almost like a Dionysian procession unraveling in a riot. It sounded as though it was moving from the city center toward the outer gate, facing the enemy, and that there, the riot peaked and ceased. Those who took this as an omen said that Antony was being abandoned by the very god he had always identified himself with, trying to imitate his lifestyle."

Antony and Cleopatra's Final Night

The room is enveloped in darkness. At the far end, there's just a balcony, lit up by the moon. Cleopatra is leaning against a pillar. The cool sea breeze is making the sheer curtains on the other side gently sway. She is staring at a distant dot on the Mediterranean, lost in frightening thoughts, while a thousand questions without answers riot in her mind.

The door behind her opens and Mark Antony walks into the room. The queen cannot see him but she hears his footsteps and their recognizable rhythm. He doesn't come near her, however. He has stopped in the dark, in the middle of the room. Cleopatra understands that, after the last words uttered at the banquet, in his heart Antony has given up on life: he's motionless, alone, having lost all hope. Tomorrow, for sure, he will die. And perhaps she will too. She is instinctively overwhelmed by a strong desire for protection. She turns to him with that same thirst for warmth, life, and hope. As though drawn by an invisible force, she moves away from the pillar and, almost without realizing it, goes to him. Antony sees her silhouette approach him against the light, feminine and sensual. The moonlight bounces off the floor and caresses the queen's hips. Cleopatra's final steps are quick, almost a run. The embrace between them is powerful, enveloping, perfect as ever. She lays her cheek on Antony's chest. She can hear his heart beating fast, and senses his anxiety in his quick breathing.

He realizes that it's not the queen of Egypt he's holding in his arms but a very frail, vulnerable person trying to hide in his embrace, like an injured little bird. He strokes her, trying to soothe her. Warm tears are falling on his arms and the body of his woman is shaken with tremors and suffering. Words are unnecessary, and they hold each other even closer. There's warmth and protection in this embrace, and even more: the desperate need to be near each other.

Perhaps now more than ever.

And that's how we leave them.

We don't know from ancient sources how they spend their last night. It's plausible to imagine that their relationship has altered since the previous night and that now, facing an inevitably cruel future, they are seeking each other's support and finding again the person who has given them so much life during all these years. We'd like to think that this was how it went. Because, when all is said and done, they were a man and a woman.

Meanwhile, in Octavian's Encampment . . .

There's another protagonist in the vicinity, Octavian. In this case, too, we don't know from the ancients what's happening in his encampment, but it's not hard to imagine. After exploring and discussing all the options with his generals, he is with his friends in his large tent. They're laughing and joking. They are certain that Rome's history will change tomorrow. So they make future plans while drinking wine and teasing one another. As ever, Octavian is the silent one, drinking little, almost apart from the others. In his head, he has the satisfaction of being one step away from ultimate success. He's also thinking about what comes afterward: Antony is no longer a problem, and that leaves only Cleopatra. Like in a game of chess, when the adversary's king is cornered, all you have to decide is your last moves before the checkmate. But the game is already won.

Laughter and good humor reign in the rest of the encampment. Many legionaries are thinking about all they'll be able to take away from the rich city of Alexandria, about raping women (they certainly have no scruples about the violence they will inflict), and about the fine foods they'll get into their bellies after so many days of rationing. Victory is certain, partly because an impressive stream of deserters from the enemy's ranks keeps flowing in, sometimes en masse. Even Antony's best cavalryman, the one who, as we said, impressed everyone with his courage that day, has come over to their side.

Octavian's generals receive valuable information about the enemy from the deserters. For example, they know that Antony wants to attempt one last surprise attack, this time using Cleopatra's fleet anchored in the harbor. It's Plutarch, once again, who emphasizes Mark Antony's indomitable personality searching for a glorious ending: "Therefore, thinking there was no better death for him than in battle, he decided to fight at once on land and sea." The action is planned for the following morning. Does Antony intend to break through Octavian's naval blockade with his remaining ships, and then escape to Spain, as some have written in the past? It's not very likely. In actual fact, he has a dual maneuver in mind: the fleet will fight on sea while his troops will face the enemy on dry land. It's one last gesture, one last charge. It's a shame he doesn't know that Octavian is aware of everything.

Morning, August 1

At dawn, Antony is already at the head of his troops. He has deployed his legionaries on the hills outside the city, and now he lets the ships out. It's an imposing scene: with strokes of the oar, the galleys, equipped with powerful rostra, slice through the waves and approach the enemy at great speed, while on land both formations watch events unfold. There's a lot of tension, then comes the *coup de théâtre*. Antony and

Cleopatra's first combat ship approaches, is almost in contact with an enemy ship . . . but instead of continuing on its course to ram it, it raises its oars as a sign of salutation. The other responds. Shortly afterward, another ship does the same thing, then another . . . Before Antony's and his generals' horrified eyes, the entire fleet hands itself over to the enemy. So now, of the two fleets about to clash, there's just one, huge and compact, with bows heading to the city.

Much was written in antiquity about this betrayal, behind which Cleopatra's far-reaching grasp was suspected of having arrived at a compromise with Octavian and sold out Antony. Modern scholars believe these rumors were rather the result of pro-Octavian propaganda, and that they were circulated once he was already Augustus. Judging by how things are in Alexandria, it's not necessarily Cleopatra's secret action that prompts his ships to desert.

We can imagine the astonishment and anger of Antony and his loyal general Publius Canidius. They immediately order their troops to attack. But their amazement doubles at the news that the cavalry, the same cavalry that staged that victorious charge only yesterday, has also surrendered without a fight and gone over to the enemy.

Meanwhile, the troops clash with Octavian's, but without the cavalry. Smaller in number and demoralized, they are easily defeated.

Antony disappears and withdraws to the city, "shouting that Cleopatra had handed him over to those against whom he had had to fight precisely for the love of her," as Plutarch puts it.

Morning, August 1:
Cleopatra Takes Refuge in the Mausoleum

News that the fleet and cavalry have surrendered and, later, that Antony's troops have been defeated reaches Cleopatra at the royal palace. The queen realizes that the situation is compromised, that the end is nigh, and that it is better for her not to be in the palace.

Accompanied by her most-trusted handmaidens, Eiras and Char-mion, she therefore heads to the mausoleum she had built for herself and Mark Antony. The plan is to shut herself in this last fortress (which will then become her tomb). According to Plutarch, "fearing Antony's wrath and despair, the queen took refuge in the mauso-leum and had the blinds, which were reinforced with bars and bolts, brought down." And here she takes a decision that still leaves many questions unanswered. She sends a servant to Mark Antony with dreadful news: "The queen is dead." Why?

According to Cassius Dio's interpretation, this would drive Antony to suicide, since he's lost everything and even her, while she would stand a better chance of being spared. However, the Roman historian is hostile to Cleopatra, so his explanation could be biased.

Modern scholars do not supply a unanimous answer. Some inter-pret Cleopatra's gesture as a clear decision to abandon Antony in order to negotiate a deal with Octavian and try to save her life and those of her children.

Others instead view her decision as one final act of love: to prompt her beloved Antony to commit suicide so that he may die in an honorable way and not be killed by Octavian or his soldiers.

This theory does not, however, explain why she did not take her own life immediately afterward and, instead, decided to face Octavian.

Perhaps both theories are actually correct: apart from what Cleo-patra may feel for Antony (who is, after all, the father of almost all her children), she is already thinking about the future and, in cold blood and in a practical sense, chooses the most obvious solution to get an ally, Mark Antony, out of the way in the most honorable manner for all concerned, so that she can begin negotiations with a new ally, Octavian, more for Caesarion's and Egypt's sake than her own. It's not that she has many other alternatives. And if this is her motive, then it illustrates once again her foresight as a politician, her enterpris-ing spirit as a woman, and her courage as a human being: it's not easy to end a relationship this way after eleven years.

We will never know what really happened. It is a shame, though, that at the end of the story, this ambiguity of Cleopatra should still hang between them.

Antony's Death

News that Cleopatra has killed herself has a devastating effect on Antony. After months, weeks, days, and hours of defeats, betrayals, and desertions, the sky seems to be closing in on him in a cold darkness. And now the news of Cleopatra's death brings down everlasting night. Imagine his state of mind: he's lost everything, his troops have abandoned him, the Roman world has turned its back on him (*Tota Italia* has sworn in favor of Octavian), his adversary is at the gates, and the woman he loves is gone, which also means he's lost Egypt as an ally. How would you feel?

Antony believes the news of Cleopatra's death. As Plutarch writes, "He said to himself, 'What more are you waiting for, Antony? Fate has snatched away the only and final reason to love life.'" The act he is about to commit illustrates so many things, including the depth of his feelings for the queen of Egypt. He goes into his room, unfastens his armor, removes it, and lets it drop to the floor. Again according to Plutarch, he exclaims, "Oh, Cleopatra, I do not lament being deprived of you, because I will soon be in the same place as you, but because, although I am a great general, I proved to be inferior to a woman in my moral courage."

Plutarch dramatized this moment but, whether Antony's words are true or false, what happens next illustrates his despair as he faces the fact that he can do nothing to reverse the situation, but above all the strong bond between the two lovers. He draws a dagger and asks his loyal servant Eros to run him through . . .

The latter raises the blade to strike him but no sooner does his master throw his head back than Eros stabs himself violently and collapses at his feet. Antony looks at him, devastated, and, gathering his final laments, exclaims, again according to Plutarch, "Brave Eros! Since you were unable to do it, you have taught me what to do."

In this drama within a drama, Antony is even more alone. All his nearest and dearest have gone (it's not clear where his son Antyllus is during these distressing minutes). Increasingly desperate, he picks up the weapon and, after turning it toward himself, gives a deep sigh, closes his eyes, and, with an abrupt gesture, stabs himself in the stomach. He falls facedown on a small bed, in agonizing pain. It's not a blow that kills him instantly, but a deep wound that leads to a slow death from blood loss amid a thousand throes and torments. Antony writhes with spasms and pain, then faints.

Everybody thinks he is dead. So probably do the bodyguards, who have stayed nearby outside the room. News of his death begins to spread. Shut in her mausoleum and hearing the growing confusion and Antony's name being shouted by everybody walking by, Cleopatra looks out of the sepulcher. The building isn't completed yet, and although the doors can no longer be opened because of a specific contraption, there's still an opening in the upper part.

Gathering what has happened and beginning to feel very guilty, she asks Diomedes, her private secretary, to bring her Antony's body. She obviously wants it beside her before an enemy soldier destroys it by severing the head and taking it to Octavian.

When Diomedes arrives in the room where Mark Antony stabbed himself, he discovers, much to his surprise, that he's not dead. On the contrary, according to Plutarch, the bleeding has stopped because he lay on the bed on his front. Antony comes to but he is prey to a thousand torments and begs those present to finish him off. They run away, frightened. He continues to writhe on the bed in despair. That's when Diomedes arrives. There's blood everywhere. In the middle of the room lies Eros's lifeless body. Antony's face is probably as white as a sheet. Diomedes approaches him and tells him it's not true that Cleopatra killed herself: she is still alive and wants him beside her.

At this news, Antony plucks up courage and tries to get up to go to his beloved, but staggers and can't stand up, probably feeling his legs trembling and giving way. He's lost too much blood and knows the end is nigh. So he asks those present who, in the meantime, have gathered around in disbelief to help him go to the queen and hoist him with ropes to the opening where she leans out.

If these details from Plutarch's story are true, it means the location where Antony stabbed himself is not too far from the mausoleum. This raises more than one question about the couple. When he heard news of Cleopatra's death, why didn't Antony run to see the body, so he could embrace it and protect it, as she is doing for him now? Why did she shut herself in the mausoleum knowing he was in the vicinity and, on hearing of her death, would immediately have come to check and discover it wasn't true? Questions that will never have an answer.

At this point, Plutarch's story becomes dramatic. Antony is pitifully carried to the mausoleum. Unable to open the door anymore, Cleopatra leans out and drops ropes with which she then pulls him up with the help of Eiras and Charmion. It's a tragic, moving image. "Those present claim never was there a more sorrowful scene. Antony, covered in blood, agonizing while being heaved up, stretched his arms toward her. It was not an easy operation for a woman but, with a great effort, Cleopatra pulled on the rope, holding it tight with both hands, her face tense from the effort, while those below encouraged her and shared in her anguish." Mark Antony, however, is a powerfully built man, so how can a small woman pull someone that heavy just with ropes, even though she is helped by two other women? We don't know what Eiras and Charmion looked like, but as ladies-in-waiting they were hardly likely to have large biceps. More probably, since the mausoleum was still being built, there may have been hanging ropes "used for carrying stones," as Cassius Dio says, and Cleopatra may have taken advantage of a device used by the builders, like a hoist or a pulley already in position for lifting heavy blocks with little effort. This way, even three slender women like them are able to heave such a heavy man. Moreover, the seriously wounded Antony may well have been lifted by a rope tied around his waist. He was probably first laid on a plank or something similar, then gradually taken up.

But the most heartbreaking scene is still to come.

Cleopatra takes Antony and, with Eiras and Charmion, drags him into the mausoleum, makes him comfortable, and as Plutarch says, "bending over him she tore off her clothes." Many have seen in this act all the queen's despair, but there could be another explanation. What other purpose would this gesture have had if not to stop the bleeding by pressing on the wound with some kind of bandage? After all, Cleopatra did have a grasp of medicine. Seeing her man covered in blood, his face white, his eyes blank, by now more dead than alive, moaning, screaming, and suffering a great deal from the agonizing pain a wound to the stomach causes, must have been too much for her. All the stress that has accumulated for days, in addition to Antony's "unfair" end, which also represents the conclusion to an incredible adventure in love and carefreeness they experienced together, trigger a total breakdown in her, as well as an emotional outburst. "Beating her chest, scratching it with her fingernails, and wiping the blood with her face, she called him lord, husband, and emperor; she had almost forgotten her woes out of compassion for his." We have here all the suffering of a woman, no longer a queen, who is venting her grief . . . and her love.

Antony has reached the end now, no longer feeling pain but very thirsty, as often happens to someone who has suffered a severe hemorrhage: the body instinctively demands fluids. Plutarch says, ". . . ceasing his lamentations, he asked for wine, either because he was thirsty or because he was hoping to die quicker. Once he'd drunk, he urged her to make sure she was safe if she could be so without dishonor, trusting in particular, among Octavian's friends, Proculeius, and not to weep over his final ordeals but to consider him lucky to have the good things that fate had granted him: he had been the most illustrious of men, had exercised great power, and had now been defeated not in a dishonorable way, but as a Roman, by the hand of a Roman."

His eyes then cloud over and become inexpressive, while his body suddenly flops, as though he's fallen asleep. The hemorrhage has been too abundant, and his brain has severed all contact with the outside world, since with the loss of blood and consequent low blood pressure he is getting less and less oxygen. He's now gradually slipping into death.

And so Mark Antony passes away, in Cleopatra's arms.

Death is less frightening if you're near someone who loves you. No human being should die alone. After the incredible succession of negativity Antony has had to face lately, the gods have granted him the opportunity to go in peace, feeling the warmth and the embrace of the only woman who has ever made him feel truly alive. He is fifty-three years old.

Cleopatra Is Taken Prisoner

After Antony drifts away before the eyes of everybody in the mausoleum, one of the bodyguards, Dercetes, returns to the room where his master has attempted suicide and, on the floor, next to Eros's lifeless body, notices the dagger. Plutarch says that he picks it up, hides it in his clothes, and immediately runs to Octavian's encampment to be the first to announce Antony's death to him, showing the blood-stained weapon as proof.

Cassius Dio, on the other hand, claims that the queen herself sends the news to her great enemy, hoping to be spared.

Plutarch describes Octavian reacting with tears and great sadness (something highly implausible), and adds that afterward he reads to his entourage the letters received from Antony to prove how vulgar and insolent the dead man had been. The historian Giusto Traina emphasizes the fact that he continued to denigrate his opponent even after he died, whereas Caesar, for example, granted the honors of war to Pompey, as a Roman to a Roman. Octavian then orders his friend Proculeius to take Cleopatra alive. His aim is clear: he wants to take possession of the queen's wealth and capture her to parade her during his triumph in Rome.

As we've seen, going in and out of the city is very easy by now, a sign that surrender is close, even though neither the victorious troops nor Octavian have entered it yet. It's that halfway moment when things aren't entirely defined: the last deserters move over to the enemy, the generals hand themselves over, the troops surrender.

Proculeius arrives at the mausoleum shortly after Antony has given up the ghost in Cleopatra's arms. He speaks to her through the closed doors of the building, but the queen won't hear of coming out. According to Plutarch, she asks for assurances that her children will reign after her. He replies that she must place her trust in Octavian. They haggle for a long time, but she doesn't give in. The negotiations must have gone on for ages, hours perhaps, because at one point Octavian sends Cornelius Gallus, the poet-*cum*-commander of the troops encamped to the west of the city, and a freedman called Epaphroditus. His strategy is clear: to capture Cleopatra with a trick. And so, while Gallus, a skilled dialectician and educated man, distracts the queen with an exhausting dialogue, the other man as well as a third man lean a ladder against the wall and enter secretly through the opening used for Antony. They certainly see Mark Antony's lifeless body; now he can no longer defend his woman. They silently go downstairs and reach the door where Cleopatra is speaking with Gallus. They approach. Seeing them, Eiras (or Charmion) screams. Cleopatra turns and swiftly draws the dagger tucked into her belt to kill herself, but Proculeius quickly squeezes her with both hands and makes her drop the weapon. He then shakes her dress to let possible hidden "poisons" fall out. Plutarch's reference to poison and its connection with the queen are truly interesting, because they unwittingly give a formidable clue as to how Cleopatra would die a few days later.

The capture of the queen is the signal for Octavian to enter Alexandria. His legionaries take possession of the Gate of the Sun, open the Gate of the Moon, and occupy all the strategic spots in the city, taking control of them. That's when he also enters. But, remembering the Alexandrians' reaction to Caesar, he makes his entrance engaged in amiable conversation with Arius Didymus, his philosophy master, also well known and esteemed in Alexandria, even keeping him on his right-hand side to emphasize his importance to the residents.

First, he gathers the people in the Gymnasium to speak to everyone. This location has not been chosen at random: it's here that Antony gave his reading on the Donations of Alexandria. They're all terrified and many prostrate themselves. But he climbs on the podium, gets them up on their feet again, and reassures them: he says he acquits them of any accusations, first in honor of the founder, Alexander the Great, second because he admires the beauty and size of the city, and third to please his philosopher friend Arius. He speaks Greek so that everyone can understand him.

The presence of the legions and his assurances obtain the desired result, and there are no riots or revolts. This allows Octavian to visit the most important locations in the city, first and foremost the tomb of Alexander the Great. It's a famous episode that has been passed on to us by Suetonius: "Octavian had Alexander the Great's mausoleum opened: after looking at the body and removing it from the sacrarium, he placed a gold crown on the head and, having had it covered in flowers, worshiped it." Cassius Dio adds an almost humorous detail: Octavian feels the delicate three-hundred-year-old remains so impetuously that, or so they say, "he broke a small part of its nose."

He is then asked if he also wishes to visit the sacrarium of the Ptolemies, the dynasty to which Cleopatra belongs. Sensing a potentially embarrassing consequence to this (worshiping the whole dynasty then putting its last representative in chains), as Suetonius relates, he gives a very enigmatic answer: "I wanted to see a king, and not of the dead." The fate he has in store for Cleopatra is clear.

If those connected to the royal house of the Ptolemies understand that their power is over, the same happens to the Egyptians: when Octavian is repeatedly asked if he wishes to visit the Temple of Apis (the sacred bull), another place dear to Cleopatra, he replies that he is accustomed to worshiping gods, not bulls.

Antony's Funeral

Octavian realizes he is now the absolute master of the Mediterranean and the entire ancient world. Nobody before him, except maybe Caesar, has had power over such a vast territory. Maybe that's partly why he acts with respect toward Cleopatra and Antony, even though the latter is dead. He allows the queen to spend a few days at the mausoleum embalming the body of her beloved. All that time she is watched and given whatever she requires, except anything a woman could use to take her own life. In the end, Octavian allows her to hold Antony's funeral. Cleopatra buries him lavishly, as expected in a royal ceremony, having all she requires at her disposal. In a city occupied by an army and with the change of power at the top, not many people attend the ceremony, probably only the couple's closest friends. The funeral has probably rekindled all Cleopatra's pain. Plutarch adds, "Tormented by so much grief—she beat her breast so much during the funeral that it was inflamed and the wound became infected—she developed a fever. She welcomed the excuse to forgo food and free herself from life." These medical details were probably given to the writer by Cleopatra's personal physician, Olympos. It's likely that the queen is letting herself go and wants to starve herself to death. But Octavian is informed of her attempted suicide and orders her to eat and treat her wounds, threatening, if she does not comply, to retaliate against her children.

The Meeting Between Cleopatra and Octavian

The most surprising fact is that Cleopatra and Octavian met only once. And a few modern scholars even harbor doubts about it ever truly having happened rather than being the fruit of subsequent pro-Octavian propaganda. He not only has contempt for the queen, the way he would a political rival, but also displays the typical attitude of a Roman man with little respect for a woman. Does he fear her? After all, she was able to ensnare Caesar and Antony . . . In fact, he probably isn't afraid because she no longer has anything to offer.

A few days after the funeral, Octavian pays her a visit. He finds her in pitiful condition, on a modest bed, disheveled and with a ravaged face, voice trembling, and bags under her eyes. You can still see clearly the marks left by the blows on her chest. Everything shows that the body is suffering as much as the spirit, and yet her famous charm and bold beauty have not been extinguished. After Octavian invites her to sit down, Cleopatra begins to justify herself, blaming her past actions on the fear instilled in her by Antony. He responds point by point, however, and in the end she begs him, evidently clinging to life. At this stage Cleopatra hands Octavian the list of all her riches. The two of them are not alone, of course, and when Seleucus, one of her previous administrators, points out that she has left out many valuables, she pounces on him, grabs him by the hair, and starts slapping him. According to Plutarch, when Octavian tries to calm her with a smile, she replies, "Do you not find it unbearable, Octavian, that while you have taken the trouble to call me and speak to me, even though I am reduced to this, my slaves are accusing me because I have put aside a few female ornaments, and not for my wretched self but as a small gift to Octavia and your Livia? Maybe they will

intercede on my behalf and you will be more clement toward me."
Of course, she wouldn't have said this, but some historians, like
Professor Cenerini, believe that this fictionalized reconstruction by
Plutarch might actually conceal a negotiation between Octavian
and Cleopatra, who, although cornered, is trying to find a way out.
However, Octavian infers from her words that she does not wish
to commit suicide or give up on life and leaves, saying to her—
untruthfully—that she will be treated with much more generosity
than she expects. He thinks he's convinced her, but she is the one
who has tricked him, letting him believe that she loves life and
doesn't intend to commit suicide.

The Death of Cleopatra

After this meeting, around August 10 or 12, Cleopatra decides to take
her own life, putting an end to her dynasty and to a kingdom, Egypt,
that has lasted for millennia. Her decision is certainly heavily affected
by the end of a world that can never return and also the prospect
of parading in Rome, in chains, in Octavian's triumph. An intoler-
able affront for a Ptolemaic queen, who still remembers what her
sister Arsinoe suffered when she had been paraded before her (back
in the days when she was Caesar's lover). The last straw, it seems, is
a tip-off. A young friend of Octavian's, called Cornelius Dolabella
(perhaps a son of the famous consul Dolabella, so skilled at jumping
ship), informs her that three days from now, Octavian will be leaving
for Syria, and that he intends to send Cleopatra and her children to
Rome, where they will wait for his return to parade in his triumph.
Her decision is therefore made. But how will she commit suicide?

Here, too, we have two versions that don't fully coincide. A little
like going to the movie theater to see two films on the same topic but
made by two different directors.

Here is what Plutarch says.

Cleopatra allegedly asked to take some libations to Antony's tomb. Having obtained Octavian's permission, she apparently went to the sepulcher with two handmaidens (probably Eiras and Charmion). Plutarch puts in her mouth words that have become famous: we'll never know whether she truly uttered them, but the meaning is plausible.

"Oh, my dear Antony, yesterday I buried you with hands that were still free, but now I offer you libations as a guarded prisoner; they are afraid that by beating my breast and weeping I shall damage this slave body reserved for the triumphs they will celebrate over you. Do not expect to receive further honors or libations: these are the last Cleopatra offers you before being dragged away. When we were alive, nothing could part us, but in death we risk exchanging our places of origin: you, a Roman, lie here, and I, a wretch, am to be buried in Italy, owning nothing from your country but my grave. But if the gods over there have any strength or power, since our own gods here have betrayed us, do not let your woman live and do not allow me to be used as a triumph over you, but instead hide me and bury me with you, because of all my countless woes, none is greater and more dreadful than this short time I have lived without you."

Cleopatra wraps a wreath of flowers over the sarcophagus and embraces it before returning to the palace, where she is living like a prisoner, and ordering her handmaidens to prepare a bath for her. After washing her and sprinkling her with ointments, Eiras and Charmion arrange her hair. Do they know they are taking care of her for the last time? Cleopatra has always trusted them, but could they keep this kind of secret? Could they follow their queen into death, when they might have a chance to save their lives? We will never be sure, but the queen probably confided her plan to them (partly because she needs their help), and while they comb her hair and apply makeup to her face, they may be exchanging worried looks, complicit glances.

Once she has been prepared, Cleopatra orders one last, lavish meal.

Meanwhile, a man arrives from the countryside, a servant of Cleopatra's. He's carrying a basket. The guards eye him as he approaches and stop him, asking where he's going and what he has in the basket. He removes the lid, revealing leaves and, beneath them, figs for the queen. They are huge and ripe. The Roman guards have never seen such large ones and are surprised. Craftily, the man invites them to help themselves but they refuse. Persuaded by the man's affability and the basket's contents, they let him through. Meanwhile, the queen takes a closed, sealed wax tablet on which earlier she wrote a message for Octavian and asks for it to be delivered to him. She then tells everybody, except Eiras and Charmion, to leave the room, and shuts the doors. Outside, unaware of what is about to happen, the Roman guards continue to watch the entrance.

When Octavian receives the tablet, he is probably with friends, discussing the future or the governance of Egypt. He opens it, perhaps absentmindedly, while finishing a sentence or perhaps with a certain amount of curiosity. No doubt the contents make his blood run cold. We can imagine those present see him frown and stare. In those few lines, among other requests, Cleopatra asks him to bury her next to Antony. Octavian immediately understands that she intends to commit suicide. His immediate impulse is to stand up and run to see what's happening, but then he decides to send others to check. When they arrive, they see the guards standing calmly outside the door as though nothing has happened. They open the doors and discover a tragic scene. It must have all happened very quickly. Cleopatra is already dead, lying on a golden bed, dressed like a queen, with her royal ornaments. At her feet, Eiras is breathing her last, while Charmion, staggering drowsily, is arranging the diadem on Cleopatra's head. She's the only one still alive. One of Octavian's men, realizing all is lost now, points at the queen and, according to Plutarch, shouts sarcastically at the handmaiden, "Beautiful work,

Charmion!" referring to Cleopatra's suicide. And she replies, "Of course, very beautiful, worthy of the descendant of such great kings," before collapsing next to the bed on which the lifeless body of her sovereign lies. At that very moment, it's not only the end of Cleopatra's life but that of an entire dynasty, the Ptolemies, which lasted three hundred years; moreover, it's the end of Hellenism, that extraordinary era of cultural blossoming initiated by Alexander the Great and akin to our Renaissance, with as many enlightened minds as our Leonardo da Vinci and Raphael; it's the extinction, effectively, of the whole line of Ancient Egyptian sovereigns who preceded the Ptolemies, sinking into a completely different world made up of dynasties of pharaohs . . . and we're talking of more than three thousand years of history. It's all ended and is there, on that bed, in the pale face of Cleopatra, the last queen of Egypt. Her features are so relaxed, as though she is free now, letting her legendary charm shine through.

Cassius Dio's version is slightly different but tallies in general with Plutarch's story, with a few peculiar additional details.

When she hears of Octavian's imminent departure, Cleopatra manages to convince everybody that she has agreed to the journey to Rome, in chains, and takes out a few jewels she has kept concealed so that she can use them as gifts once she reaches the Eternal City. It's a clever move because it dismisses the notion of a suicide, and her jailers, including Epaphroditus, relax their surveillance. It's to Epaphroditus that she hands the sealed letter in which she asks Octavian to have her buried next to her beloved Antony. In reality, it's a subterfuge for getting Epaphroditus out of the way so that he cannot prevent her suicide. Cassius Dio adds that Cleopatra wears her most beautiful dress and looks her most elegant. Having achieved a perfectly regal appearance, she kills herself. Cassius Dio concludes with a sentence that sounds like an epitaph: thus died the woman who "captured the two greatest Romans of the time, but was destroyed by the third."

Was It Really a Snake?

One of the most famous riddles in ancient history concerns Cleopatra's death. Even now it's still not clear if she used snakes or venom. It was a topic that intrigued and fascinated the ancients. Both Plutarch and Cassius Dio advanced the theory of a snakebite, but also that of a poisoned pin. Here are their versions.

Let's begin with Plutarch and get back to his story about the man who brings the queen the basket of figs. "They say that the asp was brought with the figs, hidden among the leaves: that was what Cleopatra had ordered, so that the snake might attack her without her noticing; but when she removed the figs, she saw it and said, 'So here it was,' and, baring her arm, proffered it for the asp to bite. Others say that the asp was kept in an earthenware pot, and that when Cleopatra provoked it and irritated it with a gold spindle, it leaped out and clung to one of her arms."

Nobody, the ancient biographer claims, knows the truth, however, but he does put forward another interesting theory: that of poison.

"There is also a third version, that Cleopatra kept poison in the hollow of a pin hidden in her hair. And yet there was no mark or any other sign of poison on her body. The snake wasn't seen in the room, of course, but some claimed they had noticed its tracks on the shore, where the room's windows faced; others said they saw two slight, almost invisible punctures on Cleopatra's arm."

Cassius Dio also admits that nobody knows with any certainty how the last queen of Egypt died. He writes that all they found were two small punctures on her arm. "Some say she got herself bitten by an asp brought to her in a pitcher or a pot of flowers. Others claim that she had coated a pin she used to wear in her hair with a special poison, which caused the body no harm but would have brought a swift, pain-free death if it touched a small drop of blood: until then she had kept the pin in her hair, as usual; at that moment, after making a small prick in her arm, she put it in contact with her blood. This way, or in a very similar manner, Cleopatra died with her two handmaidens."

The Roman historian also adds a very interesting detail regarding the treatment of poisons at the time. When Octavian hears the news, as well as being shocked, he wants to see Cleopatra's body. He administers her some medicines, antidotes, perhaps, and appeals to the Psyllians, in the hope of reviving her. The Psyllians were a Libyan people who lived in the Gulf of Great Sirte and were famous for training snakes: "These Psyllians are capable of sucking out snake venom immediately, before the affected person dies, and suffer no harm because they are not stung by any reptile."

If this story is true, then Cleopatra is not yet dead when Octavian or his men arrive, and every attempt is made to resuscitate her, but in vain.

Cassius Dio concludes: "Unable to revive Cleopatra in any way, Octavian felt admiration and pity for her, and felt much regret in his heart because he saw his victory deprived of any glory."

So how do things stand? Cleopatra was killed—all the sources agree on this—by poison. The problem is establishing if it was a natural poison (snake venom, for instance) or an artificial one (i.e., a concoction of various ingredients).

Now scholars tend to exclude the theory of the snake, which in any case would probably have been an Egyptian cobra (*Naja haje*) and not an asp (*Vipera aspis aspis*, a species also common in Italy), as generally believed.

The Egyptian cobra, certainly very dangerous, does not kill instantly; the bite, which is extremely painful, requires several minutes or even hours to cause a terrible death: shivers, sweating, palpitations, partial paralysis, vomiting, diarrhea, etc. Not a very elegant exit for a queen, and not one to be wished on any human being.

Besides, the symptoms of the poison are usually clearly visible: swelling, bruising, skin blisters, and none of these have been mentioned by ancient authors.

In reality, we know that Octavian's men arrive quite promptly and see no sign of severe poisoning on Cleopatra's body. Putting aside the fact that cobras are large snakes (four to five feet long), and would have been seen in the room, because since Eiras and Charmion are also dead, more than one would have been used, for speed's sake if nothing else. According to Plutarch and Cassius Dio, only vague tracks were noticed near the windows overlooking the sea. Finally we need to consider an essential element: a snake is not guaranteed to inject sufficient venom to kill. There is also the chance of a lot of pain and of being left disabled but alive.

It's therefore logical to think that Cleopatra was poisoned another way, and so we come back to a synthetic poison, one deliberately prepared by someone. Could Cleopatra have done it herself? We know from the ancients that she was an expert on poisons, so much so that she may even have written an entire pharmacological treatise. They also say that she had a passion for studying poisons and even took part in experiments on human guinea pigs. Scholars have come to reject this image of Cleopatra as a sadistic vivisectionist who watches the effects of poison on people sentenced to death, but nevertheless concur on her great expertise in the subject. And if she wasn't the one to make up a deadly poison, it could have been her personal physician, Olympos. After all, not far from where she died stood the Musaeum, where there were medical experts also knowledgeable in poisons. In that case, what kind of substance would Cleopatra have used? There are many theories. According to the Greek historian Strabo, Cleopatra spread an unspecified poisonous ointment over her body. Galen, the great physician of Roman times, claims she bit her own wrist, causing a wound, and then poured snake venom into it. But if that had been the case, the wound would have been clearly visible, whereas, thanks to Plutarch, we know that the only marks found on Cleopatra's body were "two faint, practically invisible punctures."

Recently, the German scholars Christoph Schäfer (historian of antiquity) and Dietrich Mebs (toxicologist) have put forward the theory that Cleopatra may have drunk a poisonous liquid containing opium, aconite, and hemlock (we also know that Socrates was killed by a very similar cocktail made from water hemlock, which shows that deadly herb-based concoctions were already known a few centuries before Cleopatra). These ingredients can induce a quick, deadly coma but without causing pain: aconite is a highly poisonous plant, hemlock paralyzes the nervous system and leads to death, making it gradually impossible to breathe, while opium is a painkiller.

However, these natural poisons often leave traces on the body of the victim. Hemlock, for instance, eventually turns the skin pale with a hint of blue, often accompanied by red spots, while aconite brings on a rash. Moreover, the fact that these marks don't always appear, or at least not right away, may tally with the reports of the ancients. In other words, everything points to Cleopatra having used, if not exactly this poison cocktail, then a similar blend, because it would have been quick, definite, not too painful, and without too many side effects. It is furthermore compatible with the short timescale described in connection with her death and the absence of snakes in the room.

For the sake of comprehensive information, let's remember that the American lecturer Alain Touwaide, a historian and expert on ancient medicine, says that in Cleopatra's time, it wasn't customary to mix plant-based poisons: what we know for certain is that the queen was a true expert on the subject.

But then if it wasn't a snake, how come this theory has been so popular until now?

The reason for its success connects back to Cleopatra's desire to identify herself with Isis, a goddess also associated with poison (capable of killing with it but also of curing the effects of poisoning). Moreover, for centuries Egyptian kings had a close link with snakes in general, particularly cobras, as illustrated by the cobra-shaped uraeus on Cleopatra's forehead. Furthermore, Octavian helped to spread this legend. According to Plutarch, during the triumphal procession in Rome, he paraded a painting or statue of Cleopatra with a snake.

So this could be a possible explanation (totally hypothetical since we have no proof): Cleopatra had this poison concealed in the room where she would die, or else had it brought to the court (we could then suppose that the basket contained not snakes but small bottles of concentrated poison, perhaps even hidden inside the figs, described as very large). Before committing suicide, she would have asked her entourage to circulate the story about the snakes, perfectly in line with her identity as Isis and, above all, likely to create a powerful "media" sensation. And she was correct, because the legend of her death was immediately born as we now remember it. Even though, in time, the snakes increased from one to two, and the bite moved from the arm to the breast . . . perhaps because of the sensual, erotic image the queen left behind.

As early as the Roman era, Propertius spreads this notion: "And I could see my arms bitten by the sacred snake and my limbs absorb the poison through secret ways."

12

The Dawn of an Empire

What Happens Next?

Despite his hatred for Cleopatra and his resentment at her death, Octavian respects her wishes almost certainly for one reason only: to avoid antagonizing the Alexandrians, who love their queen very much. He organizes a lavish funeral and agrees that her body be buried next to Antony's.

He does not, however, honor the figure of Mark Antony, which has to endure *damnatio memoriae*, that is, the destruction and deletion of everything that reminds anyone of him, from inscriptions to statues, which are pulled down not only in Alexandria but also in Rome and in all Roman dominions. Moreover, he decides that the date of Antony's birth, January 14, should from then on be considered an inauspicious day. Octavian is also very skillful at destroying incriminating evidence by setting fire to Antony's archive.

As history progresses, Cleopatra comes to a halt, her deeds have ended, and she exits the stage with the same aggressiveness and grit with which she entered it. She has been the one to decide when to enter and exit, and, above all, how . . . Yet more evidence of her great personality and independence.

It's strange to think that while Octavian continues on his journey to success, travels to draw up a series of agreements in Syria, lays the foundations of his principate, and weaves his dominion day by day, Cleopatra is in Alexandria, motionless, embalmed in a sarcophagus.

Most probably, the queen would have been prepared for her long journey to the afterlife according to the Egyptian tradition of embalming. We have no details or descriptions of what happened immediately following her death, but common sense leads us to believe that after the visit of her personal physician and of the Romans (physicians and members of Octavian's entourage; the former to make sure she truly was dead, the latter out of curiosity), her body, lying on a gold bed, would have promptly been sent to be embalmed. Cleopatra is Greek, Macedonian, but has a strong bond with Egyptian traditions. All her ancestors, apart from Ptolemy I, were embalmed, so the same fate most probably awaited her.

Did Octavian come to see the body of the queen he fought so long? We don't know, but he probably did. If anything, seeing her lying there, dead, marks the culmination of his yearslong battle with her. Even so, deep in his heart, he must have felt a degree of disappointment: Cleopatra has deprived him of the satisfaction of seeing her paraded in chains in Rome. In this respect, no doubt he admits to himself with anger that he has been outsmarted by the queen so close to the wire, because she found a way of escaping his power.

He would have agreed to her embalming before leaving. As we said, it's partly a decision made for the sake of public order: Cleopatra is very much loved and her death could trigger rebellion, so it's in Octavian's interest to honor her in Egypt after she dies. It's an entirely different story in Rome, however, where everyone expects to see her defeated and perhaps even executed. Octavian and the other Romans can't have lingered around the queen's body for long, a few hours perhaps, partly because her entourage will have insisted on starting on the embalming rituals immediately, since it's August and heat speeds up the process of decomposition.

Her organs have been removed and placed in canopic vases. Not her brain, which has been taken apart and thrown away, as per custom.

And yet it was Cleopatra's mind that orchestrated and influenced history for years . . . Other hands, not Caesar's or Antony's, have massaged her body, applying protective balms and ointments to prevent decomposition due to bacteria.

For at least thirty days, her body was covered with a salt, natron, to desiccate it. And, petite as she already was, Cleopatra lost even more weight. Even though she was very much altered, her features must still have been recognizable to those who knew her, and one couldn't help but still feel devotion and admiration for her. And then the bandages went around and around, concealing her face from sight and from the world, as well as the hips and lips that drove men like Caesar and Mark Antony—and not only them—crazy.

We do not know what gold items may have adorned her mummy, nor what rites oversaw the closing of her sarcophagus. We do not even have any evidence of her mausoleum. What were the tombs of Antony and Cleopatra like? Nobody knows, because, just like their mummies, they were never found.

And so the tomb of Antony and Cleopatra became a myth for archaeologists. There are frequent reports in the media that it has been unearthed, reports promptly refuted. Like a mirage, the two protagonists of our story make the news again, fascinate everybody, and disappear once again, as confirmation of the mark they left on history. Theirs was, after all, one of the greatest love stories of all time.

But that was already true in antiquity: the myth of Cleopatra lived on vividly for centuries. Thirty years after her death, for instance, a huge temple dedicated to her was still being built, but was never completed. As the archaeologist Duane W. Roller points out, her cult survived for more than four hundred years: we know, for example, that in AD 373, a scribe wrote that he had covered an image of Cleopatra in gold.

A few years later, thanks to the Edict of Thessalonica in 380 and the Theodosian decrees in 391 and 392, which decided that there could

be only one religion in the whole Roman Empire—Christianity—
all pagan temples were attacked and destroyed, obliterating non-
Christian cults, and killing or persecuting anybody who wasn't in
line with this new official creed.

Octavian's Era Begins

Meanwhile, Octavian is launched on his ascent, and begins the celebration of the era that will eventually be identified with his figure. He
founds two cities with the same name, Nikopolis, or "City of Victory,"
one in Actium and the other just outside Alexandria, outside the Gate
of the Sun where he had set up his camp. As years go by, this settlement
would then become a beautiful district of the city, right where Ramla
stands now.

The beginning of his absolute dominion is paved with victims and
bloodshed. Publius Canidius Crassus, Antony's loyal general, is brutally executed despite asking for mercy. A different fate awaits Gaius
Sosius, commander of the left wing of Antony and Cleopatra's fleet at
Actium, who is pardoned.

Then Caesar's last surviving murderer, Gaius Cassius Parmensis, is
also located and eliminated. A poet and the author of vitriolic letters
against Octavian, he is found and murdered in Athens. It's 30 BC:
there's a widespread belief among scholars that at this point, barely
fourteen years after the death of Julius Caesar, none of his assassins is
still alive. They have all been tracked down and killed.

But what became of Cleopatra and Antony's children? Octavian
is merciless with the eldest, starting with the famous Caesarion. Just
before they were finally surrounded, seeing that the end was nigh,
Cleopatra had him flee to India. Plutarch tells us how he died: "He
was sent by his mother with many riches to India, across Europe;
but a tutor called Rodon persuaded him with a trick to turn back,
telling him that Octavian was calling him in order to assign him the

kingdom. While Octavian was deciding what to do with him, they say that Arius said to him, 'It's not good that there be many Caesars.' And so Octavian had him killed." There's a tendency to blame the philosopher Arius, but in truth Octavian knows from the outset that he must kill Caesar's alleged son if he wishes to be his sole and legitimate "heir."

Antyllus, Antony and Fulvia's eldest son, is also brutally murdered. In a self-repeating script, in this case too it's his tutor, called Theodorus, who discloses to Octavian's soldiers where he is hiding. The young man manages to escape but is pursued. During his flight through the streets of Alexandria, he gets into the Caesareum and tries to take shelter next to the statue of Caesar, desperately begging to be saved. Octavian is implacable and has him beheaded by his soldiers. His tutor Theodorus approaches the body and removes a precious stone he's still wearing around his neck. He hides it by sewing it into his belt. Caught red-handed, he tries to refute the evidence but is sentenced and crucified.

Antony and Cleopatra's other children are spared, on the other hand. Antonia of Tralles is probably already dead, but, as we said, her daughter Pythodorida would be used by Octavian in his network of alliances in the east and given in marriage, first to the king of Pontus, Polemon I, and subsequently to Archelaus of Cappadocia, the son of the famous Glaphyra, who had been Antony's lover. This way, Antony and Glaphyra's descendants have been united, thus emulating the secret union between their grandfather and mother.

Iullus Antonius, the second son Antony had with Fulvia, is spared and lovingly raised by Octavia. This woman with a heart of gold would also bring up Antony and Cleopatra's children: the twins Moon (Cleopatra Selene) and Sun (Alexander Helios), as well as the youngest, Ptolemy Philadelphus. Four children that weren't her own would be added to the ones she'd had with Antony: her house in Rome would be crowded with adolescents and history.

This "nursery" is, however, useful to future dynastic unions. Cleopatra Selene would then be married to the king of Numidia and Mauritania, Juba II, under the name of Cleopatra VIII: she would be the last queen in history to carry this name. We've lost track of the two boys, though. According to some scholars, they died of disease at a young age in Rome, while others claim that they joined their sister Cleopatra VIII in Mauritania.

One final noteworthy detail concerning the daughters of Antony and Octavia: Antonia Major and Antonia Minor. No harm would be done to them, since Octavia is Octavian's sister, but their descendants are interesting: Antonia Major would become Nero's grandmother, while Antonia Minor would be the mother of Emperor Claudius and grandmother of Caligula. In other words, Nero, Caligula, and the history of the Roman Empire have Mark Antony's DNA.

Finally, to continue the long trail of blood of young people sacrificed by Octavian, let's remember that he foils a plot against him shortly after Cleopatra's death. It is orchestrated by Lepidus's son Marcus Emilius Lepidus Minor. The conspiracy is discovered in Rome by Maecenas, who has him arrested and taken to Actium, where he is executed by Octavian.

The Birth of the Month of . . . August

The conquest of Egypt represents for Octavian a salient moment in his rise to power. He decides that the day of his entry into Alexandria, August 1, should become a holiday and gives his name, Augustus, to the month (called *Sextilis* until then) when he effectively concludes the civil wars, defeating Cleopatra and Antony and capturing Cleopatra. This is where the word *August*, still used today, comes from.

So once again, Cleopatra is behind the hottest month of the year.

Octavian manages to avert dangerous revolts among the residents of Alexandria as well as in the ranks of his army, which still had to be paid. He persuades the legionaries not to pillage the city and requisitions the enormous riches kept in the royal palace, which include all the assets Cleopatra had carried from the main temples in the city. He moreover seizes the possessions of all the citizens deeply compromised by association with Cleopatra's court. Finally, he imposes a toll not only on the wealthier Alexandrians but on the whole of Egypt. This way, he manages to scrape together a large amount of booty, so much so that when it is taken to Rome, as the historian Michael Grant points out, the normal interest rate on loans goes down from 12 to 4 percent. Thanks to this huge wealth, Octavian finally manages to pay the soldiers with whom he conquered Alexandria, averting looting and satisfying the veterans still waiting in Italy by purchasing for them land on which they can settle.

After solving the soldier issue, he reorganizes all the conquered territories. From this moment, the millennial history of the Egyptian kingdoms, starting with the pharaohs, ends. From now on, and for centuries to come, Egypt will simply be a province of Rome. Like Caesar, Octavian understands perfectly well the risk of letting such a wealthy land be governed by a senator and his inevitable greed. He therefore entrusts Egypt to one of his trusted men originally from the Equites order (so it would be a province different from the others because allocated to a prefect), although in actual fact, Octavian would govern the country as his personal property, forbidding senators by law from going to Egypt: he turns it into a kind of "current account" for his wealth and power. The first of these "viceroys" is Cornelius Gallus, the commander of his troops to the west of Alexandria. The same man who had fallen in love with the actress Licorys. It is clear by now that she missed out on a wonderful opportunity by jilting him.

The Great Triumph

By one of those strange historical coincidences, news of Antony and Cleopatra's death is read in Rome by the consul then in charge: Marcus Cicero, the son of the great orator Antony had assassinated.

The Senate grants Octavian special honors for the victories in Actium and in Egypt. Two arches of triumph are erected in his honor, one in Brindisi and the other in Rome (the Arch of Augustus, next to the Temple of Caesar); moreover, a new tribune is built, the famous Rostra Augustei, decorated with the rostra of the ships sunk at Actium.

On January 11, 29 BC, as a symbol of the newly restored peace, the doors of the Temple of Janus in Rome are closed. The war is over.

Octavian continues his journey to the Middle East to reorganize his alliances, effectively confirming the system created by Antony. Then he returns to Rome. It's August 13, 29 BC, more than a year since his victory over Cleopatra.

By now he is the absolute master and celebrates three great triumphs, the first for his wars in Illyria, the second for his naval battle at Actium, and the third for the conquest of Egypt, in which hippopotamuses and rhinoceroses—animals unknown in Rome—parade (just as Caesar had introduced giraffes).

Among the prisoners there are Cleopatra Selene and Alexander Helios. If their mother, Cleopatra, had not committed suicide, she would have been with them, in chains. And, in a way, she is symbolically present in the large painting carried on a chariot in the parade, which depicts her lying on a couch, dying, with snakes.

At the end of the triumph, the booty is acquired by Rome. Part is put in a few temples to give thanks to the gods. By an irony of fate, also in the Temple of Caesar, who has become a god after death. Part is also placed in the large temple on the Capitoline dedicated to Jupiter, Juno, and Minerva. Of the items coming from Egypt, many had belonged to its queen, Cleopatra. With a subtle hint of irony, Cassius

Dio writes that this way, although vanquished and imprisoned, Cleopatra was paradoxically glorified by Rome, since her ornaments were displayed in some of the most important temples, and she also appears in the form of a gilt bronze statue in the actual Temple of Venus, in Caesar's Forum.

He's right, when it comes down to it. We don't know what this statue looked like, as it has been lost through the centuries. But we can picture it in a Roman dawn, wrapped in the silence of the Temple of Venus, which hasn't yet opened its doors. In the light that is beginning to flood this sacred place, she appears in all her sensuality. The gold seems to give the best kind of luminosity to what used to be her extraordinary desire to live. Her face is gentle and calm, but perhaps also with some veiled sadness.

She is looking at a rather distant horizon, almost as though seeking the embrace of dear, protective sensations and memories.

Cleopatra did not only conquer Rome. Cleopatra conquered eternity.

Conclusion

The story of Cleopatra is that of a woman capable of influencing the course of history like few others can. When we first embarked upon our journey, we wondered just how significant her presence had been during those crucial years of antiquity. Now that we have concluded the story of her life, we can state that her absence would probably have triggered a world quite different from the one we read about in history books. It's thanks to her that Antony chose an eastern solution to his power, a decision that climaxed in an eleven-year relationship, three children, and a gradual detachment from Rome. And it's this very decision that exacerbated the (perhaps inevitable?) conflict with Octavian, ending in Actium, the conquest of Alexandria, and the suicides of Antony and Cleopatra. This itinerary left Octavian alone, without rivals, with the possibility (partly thanks to his exceptional human and political longevity) of laying the foundations of the Roman Empire.

We can therefore wonder what would have happened had Cleopatra not lived. The clash with Mark Antony would have probably been harder without an "enemy" on whom to pin the blame and thereby create consensus. We should also consider the great charisma of his adversary, who, without Cleopatra, would have lived not in Alexandria, but in Rome, where he would have held power. Things would also have turned out differently on the military front. Octavian may not have been able to win and dominate the scene and eventually set up his principate, a preamble to the Empire. Of course, the concept of empire was already in the air: even during Caesar's era there was a feeling that the days of the Republic were numbered, and that the time had come for a single man at the helm, later continued by dozens of emperors throughout the centuries. It would have been a similar history—or perhaps not—but certainly not "the" history we know, and which led to the Roman Empire and, consequently, to the outlines of the current Western world.

Cleopatra was akin to a catalyst in chemical reactions, in that she allowed the acceleration of a process that was by now inevitable in antiquity. However, she did it in a special way, leaving a "product" obtained by a truly extraordinary reaction: Octavian, perhaps the only one capable of founding an empire.

If this viewpoint is correct, then the modern Western world owes a great deal to this woman.

Another aspect is equally clear at the end of our long story about the queen of Egypt. Cleopatra was a modern woman who stood out in antiquity. And it's this modernity of hers that altered history. Hers is the story of a modern woman's victory.

Alone among men, in a world dominated by men, how was she not immediately swept away? We have inherited the image of a sensual woman capable of seducing men of great valor, like Caesar and Antony, with her body and "special" feminine attributes. But this is a male chauvinist cliché derived from a patriarchal Roman culture, ancient writers, and propaganda hostile to her. As we've seen, Cleopatra had a fair amount of charm, but physically was a woman different from the stereotype of the *femme fatale*. It's therefore unlikely that she conquered Roman military leaders with her sensuality alone. Partly because this is a very limited view: it wasn't a matter of luring someone at a banquet; what we're talking about here are very high-level power games on the international chessboard of the time. We cannot talk of love or seduction, but political alliances and financial benefits.

From this perspective, Cleopatra had a different kind of sex appeal. She was the queen of a powerful and above all very wealthy kingdom. Cleopatra's charm was, in a way, that of a rich heiress. All her men, from Caesar to Mark Antony, and even Octavian, are aspiring to the wealth of her kingdom more than to her body. As fortune hunters, they know that her enormous wealth and the power of her fleet are essential for setting up legions, winning battles, and consequently obtaining power and therefore Rome. All three men mentioned had that objective when dealing with her.

And it's at this point that Cleopatra's skill comes in. Not a sensual woman but a woman very capable of managing her "power of attraction" over others, for purposes internal to her kingdom (succeeding in consolidating her throne), as well as on the chessboard of the Mediterranean (extending Egypt's borders in an exceptional way).

The notion that she succeeded because of her body is obviously simplistic and offensive, and the result of Roman propaganda. Of course, there were times when her appearance was an essential touch, like when she suddenly appeared before Caesar after being carried in a sack, or when she first arrived in Tarsus dressed as Aphrodite. But the real ace up her sleeve was her brain, her ideas, her strategic skills, and her plans, rather than her body.

All this is also the result of the place where she was born: Alexandria, at the heart of Hellenism. Cleopatra grew up absorbing a wonderful culture that allowed a woman (especially if of royal blood) to emerge. As we've seen, Cleopatra received a good education, she was erudite, knew languages, learned the art of public speaking and the techniques for conversing effectively, a precious asset in holding her own in diplomatic discussions, when she had before her powerful men who were used to strength, but were not her match when it came to words (one of the few, perhaps, who was able to keep up with her was Octavian).

But everything Alexandria gave Cleopatra cannot alone explain her political and diplomatic success. There's something else behind it: this woman's intelligence. She was different from others, inquisitive, thirsty for knowledge, an expert in various fields of knowledge at the time. In all history there has not been a queen like her; perhaps only Elizabeth I was at her level, but with an entirely different personality.

If Alexandria and Hellenism made a valuable contribution to her talent, so did Cleopatra to them. Through her skill at forming alliances with the most powerful Romans of her time, she succeeded in helping not only Egypt but especially Hellenistic culture to survive. And here we wonder what the ancient Mediterranean would have been like if Cleopatra hadn't lost at Actium, if she had defeated Octavian. Perhaps not Western-Roman, the way it turned out with Octavian, but rather Eastern-Greek with powerful Hellenistic influences, which (and it's just a theory) could perhaps have echoed in the present day in the tone of our way of life.

Hellenism was a moment of grace in the history of mankind, culturally on a par—all due distinctions borne in mind—perhaps only with the Renaissance and the Enlightenment. Hellenism was born with Alexander the Great and ended with Cleopatra. There is much that brings these two protagonists together. Both would go down in history as fascinating young sovereigns, always able to get involved in the game, and with the dream of a great Hellenistic kingdom. Moreover, both were buried in Alexandria, not far from each other. And in both cases their tombs have disappeared.

Cleopatra's true charm was the cultural openness of Hellenism, and certainly not that dark, treacherous, and alluring charm the Romans attributed to her.

Maybe that's where Cleopatra's true meaning in history lies: a queen skilled at the game of alliances, no doubt, but shrewd and even cynical in her management of power, who would otherwise not have been able to survive during that moment in antiquity.

But she was also a woman able to emerge thanks to the cultural sap of her world. A woman with a different, independent, modern mentality. And it's precisely this modernity that changed history. We could say that the mark she left throughout the centuries was founded on the triumph of her culture, Hellenism, and that her success as a queen was founded on her modern mentality, inconceivable to so many of her female contemporaries. Was it this very modern notion that changed ancient history? We'd like to think so.

It's been said that Cleopatra conquered Rome by seducing its military leaders, when in fact she was defeated by Rome. However, she did conquer it in a different way: as a woman. She was defeated as a queen but triumphed as a woman. And so history will remember her forever.

Acknowledgments

Writing this book has been the result of lengthy work, with constant fact-checking and archive research in order to find every ancient text, historical datum, study clue, and archaeological discovery that might illuminate our path.

I must be honest: this book would never have seen the light without the amazing research by Emilio Quinto, an extraordinary investigator of the past. I remember the long conversations and scarce sleep we both got because of a woman: Cleopatra.

A historical journey of more than fourteen years in the heart of antiquity is no easy feat. And it would not have been possible without the advice and corrections of three scholars and great experts on Roman history.

I therefore thank Professor Romolo Augusto Staccioli for his ever-pertinent suggestions and for his extensive knowledge of the Roman world, capable of infecting others with his enthusiasm and his love of history.

I am also indebted to Professor Giovanni Brizzi for having helped me to better understand so many astonishing aspects of Roman history I did not know, particularly on the military front, on which he is the utmost authority in Italy.

Sincere thanks to Professor Francesca Cenerini for her tireless work that helped me get a clear and correct perspective on the figure of Cleopatra, as well as on many ensuing events connected with the complex transition from the end of the Republic to the Augustan era.

I am deeply grateful to Letizia Staccioli, who, with great competence, rigor, and enthusiasm, accompanied this book from its birth. Her help has been essential for crossing one of ancient history's most complex periods.

This journey through history naturally required also a large amount of data and information concerning Cleopatra's everyday life, Alexandria, and Ptolemaic Egypt. In this sense, the collaboration and help provided by a team of Egyptologists have been invaluable, and I sincerely thank them.

I am indebted to my editor, Patrizia Segre, for her professionalism and her tireless patience in waiting for the arrival of my manuscript.

As you can imagine, the book you've just read is the fruit of intense editorial work by a very high-level team. Thanks to Sabrina Annoni, Alessandra Roccato, Frida Sciolla, and obviously Laura Donnini, who is capable of expertly guiding a group of modern women in search of a great woman from antiquity.

Thanks to Studio Leksis for its valuable suggestions.

Finally, I will spare a thought for the woman who has allowed me to take this extraordinary journey to antiquity, and thanks to whom we have all learned so much, including about ourselves. A thought that considers the fact that what we are today is partly thanks to her: Cleopatra.

Maps

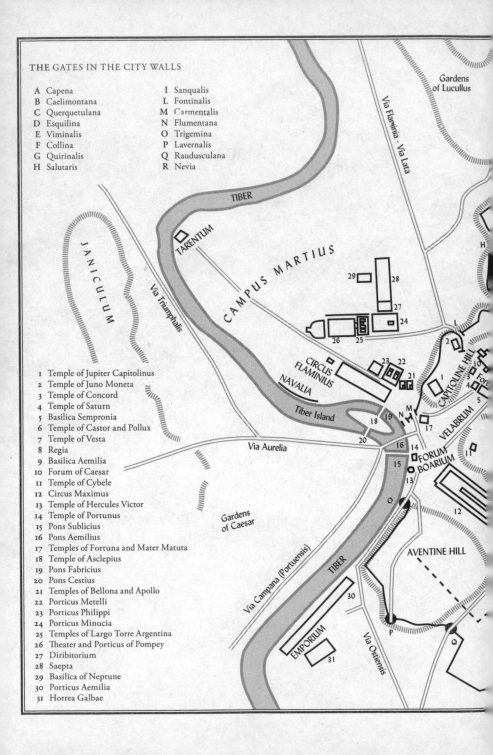

THE GATES IN THE CITY WALLS

A	Capena	I	Sanqualis
B	Caelimontana	L	Fontinalis
C	Querquetulana	M	Carmentalis
D	Esquilina	N	Flumentana
E	Viminalis	O	Trigemina
F	Collina	P	Lavernalis
G	Quirinalis	Q	Raudusculana
H	Salutaris	R	Nevia

1 Temple of Jupiter Capitolinus
2 Temple of Juno Moneta
3 Temple of Concord
4 Temple of Saturn
5 Basilica Sempronia
6 Temple of Castor and Pollux
7 Temple of Vesta
8 Regia
9 Basilica Aemilia
10 Forum of Caesar
11 Temple of Cybele
12 Circus Maximus
13 Temple of Hercules Victor
14 Temple of Portunus
15 Pons Sublicius
16 Pons Aemilius
17 Temples of Fortuna and Mater Matuta
18 Temple of Asclepius
19 Pons Fabricius
20 Pons Cestius
21 Temples of Bellona and Apollo
22 Porticus Metelli
23 Porticus Philippi
24 Porticus Minucia
25 Temples of Largo Torre Argentina
26 Theater and Porticus of Pompey
27 Diribitorium
28 Saepta
29 Basilica of Neptune
30 Porticus Aemilia
31 Horrea Galbae

Gardens of Lucullus

Via Flaminia · Via Lata

TIBER

JANICULUM

Via Triumphalis

TARENTIUM

CAMPUS MARTIUS

29 28

27 24

26 25

CIRCUS FLAMINIANA

NAVALIA

Tiber Island

18 19

20

Via Aurelia

16 14

15

13

O

Gardens of Caesar

Via Campana (Portuensis)

TIBER

Via Ostiensis

EMPORIUM

30

31

H

L

2

Capitoline Hill

For

I

4

5

VELABRUM

M N

17

FORUM BOARIUM

12

AVENTINE HILL

P

Q

Caesar's Rome

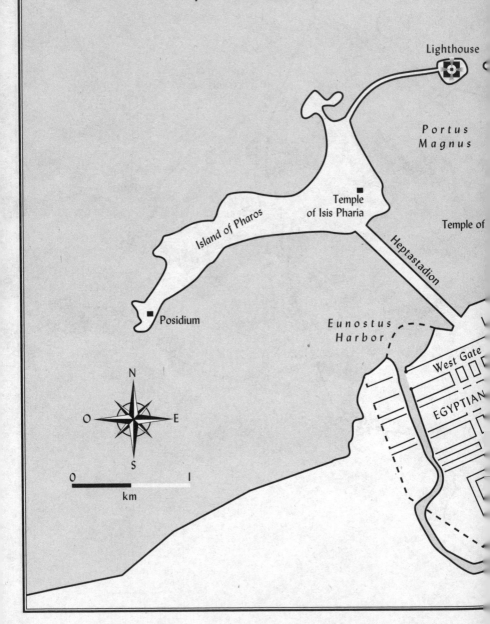

Alexandria in Cleopatra's Time

Lighthouse

Portus Magnus

Island of Pharos

Temple of Isis Pharia

Heptastadion

Temple of

Posidium

Eunostus Harbor

West Gate

EGYPTIAN

N

O — E

S

0 ————— 1
km

GERMANY

GAUL OF

CISALPINE GAUL

NARBONNE

Modena

ADRIATIC SE

Perugia

Rome

Pozzuoli

TYRRHENIAN
SEA

Pompei

Strait
of Messina

SPAIN

Naulochus

SICILY

MAURETANIA

Tripoli

The Mediterranean in Cleopatra's Time

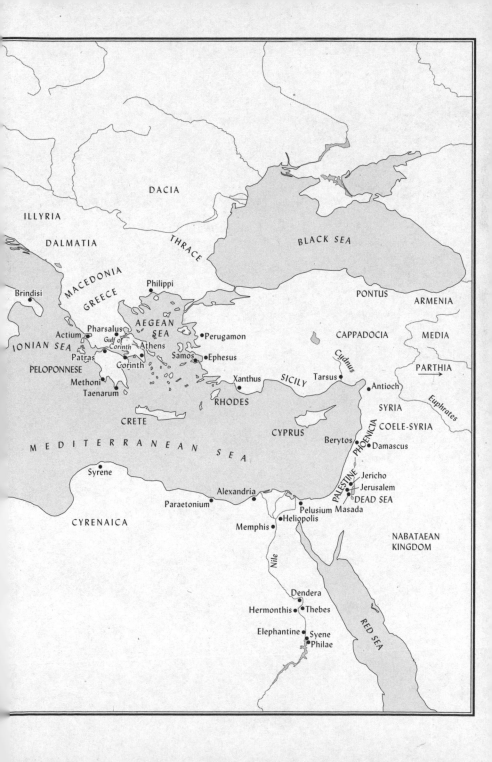

Sources Cited

Editor's note: Passages from the Italian editions listed here have been translated by Katherine Gregor.

Ancient Sources

Appian, *Roman History: The Civil War*, Books XII–XVII, 90, p. 187; II, 117, p. 85; II, 144, p. 119; II, 145, p. 120 (second); II, 145, p. 120 (third); II, 146, p. 120 (first); II, 146, pp. 120–121; II, 146, p. 121; II, 146–47, p. 122; IV, 5, pp. 202–203; IV, 6, p. 203 (first); IV, 11, p. 203 (second); IV, 20, p. 206; IV, 23, p. 205 (second); IV, 30, p. 204 (second); IV, 37, p. 204 (first; IV, 40, p. 205 (first); IV, 63, p. 196; IV, 82, p. 209; IV, 128, p. 225; V, 1, p. 256 (first); V, 8, p. 256 (second); V, 58, p. 232

Athenaeus, *Deipnosophistae, or Banquet of the Learned*, vol. I, edited by Luciano Canfora, V, 204–205, p. 187 (Rome: Salerno Editrice, 2001)

Cassius Dio, *Roman History*, vols. II–IV, edited by Giuseppe Norcio, XLI, 54, 1, p. 50; XLII, 34, 4–5, p. 171 (second); XLII, 34, 6, p. 171 (first); XLII, 35, 1, p. 171 (third); XLII, 35, 2, p. 175 (first); XLII, 35, 2–3, p. 175 (second); XLIV, 11, 2–3, p. 41 (first); XLIV, 11, 2–3, p. 41 (second); XLIV, 17, 1, pp. 56; XLIV, 17, 2, pp. 58; XLIV, 34, 7, p. 111; XLIV, 42, 5, XLIV 43, 1, p. 119; XLIV, 49, 4, p. 120; XLIV, 49, 1–3, pp. 119–120; XLVII, 31, 5, p. 35; XLVII, 43, 3, p. 216; XLVII, 44, 1–4, p. 226; XLVII, 49, p. 229; XLVII, 49, p. 228; XLVIII, 8, 2, p. 286; XLVIII, 10, 4, p. 288; XLVIII, 24, 2, p. 256; XLVIII, 44, 5, p. 299; L, 32, 2, 5–7, pp. 335–336; L, 33, 3, p. 337 (first); L, 33, 4, p. 337 (second); L, 34, 2–5; 35, 2–4, pp. 338–339; LI, 9, 3, p. 348–349; LI, 10, 3, p. 362; LI, 10, 9, p. 374; LI, 14, 1–3, p. 384; LI, 14, 4, p. 385 (first); LI, 14, 6, p. 385 (second); LI, 16, 5, p. 378; LI, 15, 4, p. 384 (Milan: BUR, 2000)

Lucan, *Pharsalia, or The Civil War*, introduced and translated by Luca Canali; foreword and notes by Fabrizio Brena, VIII, 667–91, pp. 166–167; X, 479, p. 178; X, 189–91, p. 186 (first); X, 360, p. 186 (second); X, 107–71, p. 265; X, 107–171, p. 266; X, 107–171, p. 266–267 (Milan: BUR, 1997)

Nicolaus of Damascus, *Life of Augustus*, edited and translated by Giuseppe
　　Turturro, XXIII, p. 74; XXIV, p. 86; XXIV, p. 81; XXVI, p. 102 (Città di
　　Castello-Bari: Macrì, 1945)

Pliny, *Natural History*, Books VIII–XI, introduction, translation, and notes by
　　Francesco Maspero, IX, 58, pp. 267; IX, 5, pp. 268 (Milan: BUR, 2011)

Plutarch, *Parallel Lives—Agesilaus and Pompey*, introduction, translation, and
　　notes for *Agesilaus* by Emma Manes Luppino; introduction, translation,
　　and notes for *Pompey* by Arnaldo Marcone; with contributions from
　　Barbara Scardigli and Mario Manfredini, Mario, *Pompey*: LXXX, 10,
　　p. 167 (Milan: BUR, 1996)

———, *Parallel Lives—Alexander and Caesar*, introduction, translation,
　　and notes for *Alexander* by Domenico Magnino; introduction to *Caesar*
　　by Antonio La Penna; translation and notes for *Caesar* by Domenico
　　Magnino; with contributions from Barbara Scardigli and Mario
　　Manfredini, *Caesar*, XLIV, 6, p. 77; XLIX, 3, p. 171; LXIII, 7, pp. 42;
　　LXIII, 8, p. 45; LXIII, 2, p. 57 (first); LXIII, 3, p. 57 (second); LXIII, 4, p.
　　57–58 (third); LXIII, 6, p. 81; LXVI, 6, p. 85 (first; LXVI, 8, p. 85 (second);
　　LXVI, 9, p. 85–86 (third); LXVI, 10, p. 86 (first); LXVI, 11, p. 86 (second);
　　LXVII, 3, p. 95 (Milan: BUR, 2014)

———, *Parallel Lives—Demetrius and Anthony*, introduction, translation,
　　and notes for *Demetrius* by Osvalda Andrei; introduction, translation,
　　and notes for *Anthony* by Rita Scuderi; with contributions from Barbara
　　Scardigli and Mario Manfredini, *Anthony*, IV, 1–4, p. 128; IV, 4, pp. 128;
　　IV, 5–6, p. 129; X, 5–6, pp. 294–295; XXIV, 1, p. 235 (first); XXIV, 2–3,
　　p. 235 (second); XXV, 2, p. 238; XXV, 3–4, p. 239 (first); XXV, 4–6, pp. 239
　　(second); XXVI, 2, p. 245; XXVI, 6, p. 246; XXVI, 7, p. 248; XXVII, 1–4,
　　p. 251; XXVIII, 1–2, p. 261; XXVIII, 6, p. 265; XXIX, 3–4, p. 263; XXIX,
　　7, p. 270; XXX, 1–3, p. 285; XXXVI, 1, pp. 301; LIII, 5–11, pp. 310; LVII,
　　4–5, p. 320; LXIV, 3–4, p. 330; LXIX, 1, 7, p. 344; LXXIII, 5–6,
　　p. 345; LXXIV, 2–3, pp. 351–352; LXXV, 2, p. 365; LXXV, 3, p. 366 (first);
　　LXXV, 4–6, p. 366 (second); LXXV, 2, p. 368; LXXVI, 3, p. 369; LXXVI,
　　4, p. 370; LXXVI, 5, pp. 370; LXXVI, 6–7, p. 370–371 (first); LXXVI, 9,
　　p. 371 (second); LXXVII, 3–5, p. 373–374 (first); LXXVII, 5, p. 374
　　(second); LXXVII, 5–6, p. 374 (third); LXXVII, 6–7, p. 375; LXXXI, 4–5,
　　LXXXII, 1, pp. 392–393; LXXXII, 3–4, p. 379; LXXXIII, 6–7, p. 380;
　　LXXXIV, 4–8, pp. 381; LXXXV, 8, p. 383; LXXX-VI, 1–3, pp. 384 (first);
　　LXXXVI, 4–5, p. 384 (second); LXXXVI, 5, p. 387 (Milan: BUR, 2015)

———, *Parallel Lives—Demosthenes and Cicero*, introduction, translation,
　　and notes for *Demosthenes* by Chiara Pecorella Longo; introduction to
　　Cicero by Joseph Geiger; translation of *Cicero* by Beatrice Mugelli; notes

for *Cicero* by Lucia Ghilli; with contributions from Barbara Scardigli and
Mario Manfredini, *Cicero*, XLVIII, 4–5, p. 206 (Milan: BUR, 2000)

———, *Parallel Lives—Dio and Brutus*, introduction to *Dio* by Martin
Dreher; translation of *Dio* by Pierangiolo Fabrini; notes for *Dio* by
Federicomaria Muccioli; introduction to *Brutus* by Barbara Scardigli;
translation of *Brutus* by Pierangiolo Fabrini; notes for *Brutus* by Lucia
Ghilli, VIII, 2, p. 44; IX, 7–8, p. 43; XV 2–3, p. 70 (first); XV, 4, p. 70
(second); XV, 9, p. 75; XX, 5–6, p. 122; XXXIII, 4–5, p. 211–212; XLI, 7–8,
p. 216; XLIII, 4–5, p. 217 (first); XLIII, 8, p. 217 (second); XLIV, 2, p. 217
(third); L, 8–9, p. 227 (Milan: BUR, 2000)

Propertius, *Elegies*, introduction by Paolo Fedeli; translation by Luca Canali;
commentary by Riccardo Scarcia, Book III, XI, 53–54, p. 388 (Milan:
BUR, 1987)

Suetonius, *Lives of the Caesars*, vol. I, translation by Felice Dessì (Milan: BUR,
2009). *Caesar*, LII, p. 35; LII, p. 189; LVI, p. 70; LXXXI, pp. 58 (first);
LXXVI, p. 182; LXXXI, p. 63; LXXXI, p. 58 (second); LXXXI, p. 58
(third); LXXXI, p. 56; LXXXII, p. 87; LXXXIII, p. 114; LXXXIV, pp. 119;
LXXXIV, pp. 123 (first); LXXXV, p. 123 (second); *Augustus*, IV, p. 318; XV,
pp. 287; XVIII, p. 378 (first); XVIII, p. 378 (second); LXIX, p. 319

Velleius Paterculus, *Compendium of Roman History*, introduction, translation,
and notes by Renzo Nuti, II, 67, 1–2, p. 204; II, 74, 3, p. 98; II, 79, 5, p. 325
(Milan: BUR, 1997)

Virgil, *Eclogues*, edited by Mario Geymonat, *Eclogue* IV, p. 298–299 (Milan:
Garzanti, 1981)

Modern Studies

Bar Hebraeus, Gregory, *Historia Compendiosa Dynastiarum*, p. 277

Bengtson, Hermann, *Marcus Antonius*, in Joachim Brambach, *Cleopatra*
(Rome: Salerno Editrice, 1997), p. 234

Brambach, Joachim, *Cleopatra* (Rome: Salerno Editrice, 1997), p. 236

Brizzi, Giovanni, *La battaglia di Azio*, nel catalogo della mostra *Cleopatra
Roma e l'incantesimo d'Egitto*, edited by Giovanni Gentili (Milan: SKIRA,
2013), p. 326

Carandini, Andrea, *Le case del potere nell'antica Roma* (Roma-Bari: Laterza,
2010), p. 24

Cardini, Franco, "Romani o musulmani: chi distrusse la biblioteca di
Alessandria?," article from July 27, 2009, p. 277–278

Grant, Michael, *Cleopatra* (New York: Weidenfeld & Nicholson, 1972),
pp. 179, 191, 322, 345

Shakespeare, William. *The Complete Works of William Shakespeare*
(Philadelphia: J. B. Lippincott & Co., 1856), pp. 58

Strauss, Barry, *The Death of Caesar: The Story of History's Most Famous
Assassination* (New York: Simon & Schuster, 2015), pp. 58, 200, 206

Syme, Ronald, *The Roman Revolution* (New York: Oxford University Press,
1960), pp. 219, 287, 322

Traina, Giusto, *Marco Antonio* (Roma-Bari: Laterza, 2003), p. 235

The quotations taken from the BUR Greek and Latin Classics volumes are
under license from Mondadori Libri S.p.A., Milan.

Bibliography

Ancient Sources

Appian, *Roman History: The Civil War*, Books XII–XVII

Athenaeus, *Deipnosophistae, or Banquet of the Learned*, vol. I, edited by Luciano Canfora (Rome: Salerno Editrice, 2001)

Author Unknown, *Bellum Alexandrinum*

———, *Mirabilia Urbis Romae*

Cassius Dio, *Roman History*, vols. II–IV, edited by Giuseppe Norcio (Milan: BUR, 2000)

Cicero, *De Divinatione*, edited and translated by Sebastiano Timpanaro (Milan: Garzanti, 2017)

———, *Epistulae ad Atticum*, vols. I–II

———, *Philippicae*, edited by Giuseppe Bellardi (Milan: BUR, 2003)

———, *Epistulae ad Familiares*, vols. I–II, edited by Alberto Cavarzere (Milan: BUR, 2016)

———, *Epistulae ad Quintum Fratreme*, translated by Carlo Vitali (Bologna: Zanichelli, 1962)

Quintus Curtius Rufus, *Life of Alexander the Great*, introduction, translation, and notes by Giovanna Porti (Milan: BUR, 2011)

Didorus Siculus, *Biblioteca Historica*, vols. I–III, introduced by Luciano Canforia (Palermo: Sellerio, 1988)

Herodotus, *Histories*, introduction, notes, and edited by Luigi Annibaletto (Milan: Mondadori, 2000)

Florus, *Epitome of Roman History*, edited by Eleonora Salomone Gaggero (Milan: Rusconi, 1981)

Julius Caesar, *The Civil Wars*, translated by Antonio La Penna; introduced by Adriano Pennacini; preface by Roberto Andreotti; critical notes by Dionigi Vottero (Turin: Giulio Einaudi Editore, 2008)

———, *The Gallic Wars*, translated and edited by Adriano Pennacini; critical notes by Albino Garzetti (Turin: Giulio Einaudi Editore, 2006)

Josephus Flavius, *The Antiquities of the Jews*, vols. I–II

———, *Against Apion* (Venice: Marsilio, 1993)

Lucan, *Pharsalia, or The Civil Wars*, introduction and translation by Luca
    Canali; foreword and notes by Fabrizio Brena (Milan: BUR 1997)

Martial, *Epigrammata*, edited by Giuseppe Norcio (Turin-Novara: utet-De
    Agostini, 2014)

Nicolaus of Damascus, *Life of Augustus*, edited and translated by Giuseppe
    Turturro (Città di Castello-Bari: Macrì, 1945)

Horace, *Odes and Epodes*, introduction by Alfonso Traina; translation and
    notes by Enzo Mandruzzato (Milan: BUR, 2005)

———, *Satire*, introduction, translation, and notes by Mario Ramous (Milan:
    Garzanti, 2003)

Ovid, *Amores*, introduction by Francesca Lechi; translation by Luca Canali;
    critical apparatus and notes by Riccardo Scarcia (Milan: BUR, 2002)

———, *Fasti*, introduction and translation by Luca Canali; notes by Marco
    Fucecchi (Milan: BUR, 2014)

Philo, *Legatio ad Gaium*

Pliny, *Natural History*, Books VIII–XI, introduction, translation, and notes by
    Francesco Maspero (Milan: BUR, 2011)

Plutarch, *Parallel Lives—Agesilaus and Pompey*, introduction, translation, and
    notes to *Agesilaus* by Emma Manes Luppino; introduction, translation, and
    notes to *Pompey* by Arnaldo Marcone; with contributions from Barbara
    Scardigli and Mario Manfredini (Milan: BUR, 1996)

———, *Parallel Lives—Alexander and Caesar*, introduction, translation, and
    notes to *Alexander* by Domenico Magnino; introduction to *Caesar* by
    Antonio La Penna; translation and notes to *Caesar* by Domenico Magnino;
    with contributions from Barbara Scardigli and Mario Manfredini (Milan:
    BUR, 2014)

———, *Parallel Lives—Demetrius and Antony,* introduction, translation, and
    notes to *Demetrius* by Osvalda Andrei; introduction, translation, and notes
    to *Antony* by Rita Scuderi; with contributions from Barbara Scardigli and
    Mario Manfredini (Milan: BUR, 2015)

———, *Parallel Lives—Demosthenes and Cicero*, introduction, translation,
    and notes for *Demosthenes* by Chiara Pecorella Longo; introduction to
    Cicero by Joseph Geiger; translation of *Cicero* by Beatrice Mugelli; notes
    for *Cicero* by Lucia Ghilli; with contributions from Barbara Scardigli and
    Mario Manfredini (Milan: BUR, 2000)

———, *Parallel Lives—Dio and Brutus*, introduction to *Dio* by Martin
    Dreher; translation of *Dio* by Pierangiolo Fabrini; notes for *Dio* by
    Federicomaria Muccioli; introduction to *Brutus* by Barbara Scardigli;
    translation of *Brutus* by Pierangiolo Fabrini; notes for *Brutus* by Lucia
    Ghilli (Milan: BUR, 2000)

Pomponius Porphyrion, Commentary on Horace

Procopius of Caesarea, *The Gothic Wars*, introduction by Giovannella Cresci Marrone; preface by Elio Bartolini; translation by Domenico Comparetti (Milan: Garzanti, 2005)

Propertius, *Elegies*, introduction by Paolo Fedeli; translation by Luca Canali; commentary by Riccardo Scarcia (Milan: BUR, 1987)

Sallust, *The Conspiracy of Catiline*, edited by Giancarlo Pontiggia (Milan: Mondadori, 2016)

Seneca, *Consolations: To Marcia, his mother, Helvia, to Polybius*, introduction, translation, and notes by Alfonso Traina (Milan: BUR, 2015)

———, *Moral Epistles and Letters from a Stoic,* edited by Fernando Solinas; preface by Carlo Carena (Milan: Mondadori, 2007)

Statius, *The Silvae*, edited by Luca Canali and Maria Pellegrini (Milan: Oscar Mondadori, 2006)

Strabo, *The Geographica* (Milan: BUR, 1993)

Suetonius, *The Lives of the Caesars*, vol. I, translation by Felice Dessì (Milan: BUR, 2009)

Varro, *On the Latin Language*, Book XXV

———, *On Agriculture*, Book III

Velleius Paterculus, *Compendium of Roman History*, introduction, translation, and notes by Renzo Nuti (Milan: BUR, 1997)

Virgil, *Eclogues*, edited by Mario Geymonat (Milan: Garzanti, 1981)

Vitruvius, *The Ten Books of Architecture* (Milan: BUR, 2010)

Modern Studies

Amerio, Maria Luisa, *Storie di proscritti* (Palermo: Sellerio, 1990)

Bar Hebraeus, Gregory, *Historia Compendiosa Dynastiarium*

Bowman, Alan K., *Egypt After the Pharoahs, 332 BC–AD 642: From Alexander to Arab Conquest* (Berkeley: University of California Press, 1986)

Brambach, Joachim, *Cleopatra* (Rome: Salerno Editrice, 1997)

Bradford, Ernle, *Cleopatra* (London: Penguin, 2000)

Brizzi, Giovanni, *Il guerriero, l'oplita, il legionario* (Bologna: il Mulino, 2008)

———, "La battaglia di Azio," nel catalogo della mostra *Cleopatra, Roma e l'incantesimo dell'Egitto*, edited by Giovanni Gentili (Milan: SKIRA, 2013)

Cadario, Matteo, "Il vero volto di Cleopatra," nel catalogo della mostra *Cleopatra, Roma e l'incantesimo dell'Egitto*, edited by Giovanni Gentili (Milan: SKIRA, 2013)

Canfora, Luciano, *Augusto, figlio di Dio* (Rome-Bari: Laterza 2015)

———, *Giulio Cesare, il dittatore democratico* (Rome-Bari: Laterza, 2003)

————, *La biblioteca scomparsa* (Palermo: Sellerio, 2009)

————, *La prima marcia su Roma* (Rome-Bari: Laterza, 2007)

Cantarella, Eva, *L'aspide di Cleopatra* (Milan: Feltrinelli, 2012)

Carandini, Andrea, *Angoli di Roma: guida inconsueta alla città antica* (Rome-Bari: Laterza, 2016)

————, *Le case del potere nell'antica Roma* (Rome-Bari: Laterza, 2010)

Cardini, Franco, "Romani o musulmani: chi distrusse la biblioteca di Alessandria?," July 27, 2009

Casson, Lionel, *Travel in the Ancient World* (Baltimore: Johns Hopkins University Press, 1994)

Cenerini, Francesca, "Cleopatra VII," nel catalogo della mostra *Cleopatra, Roma e l'incantesimo dell'Egitto*, edited by Giovanni Gentili (Milan: SKIRA, 2013)

————, *La donna romana* (Bologna: Il Mulino, 2009)

Chamoux, François, *Marco Antonio: Ultimo principe dell'Oriente greco* (Milan: Rusconi, 1988)

Coarelli, Filippo, *Roma* (Rome-Bari: Laterza, 1997)

Cresci Marrone, Giovannella, *Marco Antonio, la memoria deformata* (Naples: Edises, 2013)

Faoro, Davide, *Praefectus, procurator, praeses. Genesi delle cariche presidiali equestri nell'Alto Impero Romano* (Milan: Le Monnier, 2011)

Fletcher, Joann, *Cleopatra the Great: The Woman Behind the Legend* (New York: Harper Perennial, 2012)

Gentili, Giovanni (ed.), *Cleopatra. Roma e l'incantesimo dell'Egitto* (Milan: SKIRA, 2013)

Giardina, Andrea (ed.), *Roma antica: I luoghi della politica* (Rome-Bari: Laterza, 2014)

————, *Roma antica: Storia di Roma dall'antichità a oggi* (Rome-Bari: Laterza, 2000)

Grant, Michael, *Cleopatra* (New York: Weidenfeld & Nicholson, 1972)

Grimal, Pierre, *Cicerone* (Milan: Garzanti, 2011)

Meadows, Andrew, "Sins of the Fathers: The Inheritance of Cleopatra, Last Queen of Egypt," from *Cleopatra of Egypt: From History to Myth*, edited by Susan Walker and Peter Higgs (London: British Museum Press, 2001)

Paoli, U. E., *Rome: Its People Life and Customs* (London: Longmans, 1963)

Parenti, Michael, *The Assassination of Julius Caesar: A People's History of Ancient Rome* (New York: New Press, 2004)

Pareti, Luigi, *Storia di Roma e del mondo antico*, vol. IV (Torino: utet, 1955)

Pisani Sartorio, Giuseppina, "Mezzi di trasporto e traffico," in *Vita e costume dei romani antichi* 6 (Rome: Quasar, 1988)

Pitassi, Michael, *Le navi da guerra di Roma* (Gorizia: LEG Edizioni, 2013)

Quilici, Lorenzo, "Le strade: Viabilità tra Roma e Lazio," in *Vita e costumi dei romani antichi* 12 (Rome: Quasar, 1991)

Roller, Duane W., *Cleopatra: A Biography* (New York: Oxford University Press, 2010)

Salza Prina Ricotti, Eugenia, *Amori e amanti a Roma: tra Repubblica e Impero* (Rome: L'Erma di Bretschneider, 1992)

Sampoli, Furio, *Le grandi donne di Roma antica* (Rome: Newton Compton, 2011)

Schäfer, Christoph, *Kleopatra: Gestalten der Antiken* (Darmstadt: Wissenschaftliche Buchgesellschaft, 2006)

Sheppard, Si, *Actium 31 BC: Downfall of Antony and Cleopatra* (New York: Bloomsbury USA, 2009)

Schiff, Stacy, *Cleopatra: A Life* (New York: Little, Brown & Co., 2010)

Shakespeare, William, *The Complete Works of William Shakespeare* (Philadelphia: J. B. Lippincott & Co., 1856)

Spinosa, Antonio, *Cesare, il grande giocatore* (Milan: Oscar Mondadori, 1997)

———, *Cleopatra, la regina che ingannò se stessa* (Milan: Oscar Mondadori, 2017)

Strauss, Barry, *The Death of Caesar: The Story of History's Most Famous Assassination* (New York: Simon & Schuster, 2015)

Staccioli, Romolo Augusto, *Roma di ieri, Roma di oggi* (Rome: Roma amor, 1980 and 1990)

———, *Vivere a Roma 2000 anni fa: le opere e i giorni degli antichi* (Rome: Archeoroma, 1991)

Syme, Ronald, *The Roman Revolution* (New York: Oxford University Press, 1960)

Traina, Giusto, *Marco Antonio* (Rome-Bari: Laterza, 2003)

Volkmann, Hans, *Cleopatra: A Study in Politics and Propaganda* (London: Elek Books, 1958)

Walker, Susan, and Sally-Ann Ashton, *Ancients in Action: Cleopatra* (New York: Bloomsbury Academic, 2006)

Walker, Susan, and Peter Higgs (eds.), *Cleopatra of Egypt: From History to Myth* (London: British Museum Press, 2001)

Weill Goudchaux, Guy, "Cleopatra's Subtle Religious Strategy," from *Cleopatra of Egypt: From History to Myth*, edited by Susan Walker and Peter Higgs (London: British Museum Press, 2001)

Wilkinson, Toby, *The Rise and Fall of Ancient Egypt* (New York: Random House, 2011)

A Note from the Translator

Translating *Cleopatra* had a very special meaning for me. I was born in Rome and lived there on and off for several years. It was therefore fascinating for me to read about buildings that stood there and vanished long before those that are now iconic landmarks of the Eternal City. Moreover, although I had already translated a number of historical novels, a nonfiction book of popular history was something new and a welcome challenge. I don't think I have ever translated anything for which I had to do as much research. It's tempting to stick an "*us*" at the end of every name to make it sound Latin, but that's a bet you can't afford to make, so I spent hours entering the names of individuals and places in the original Italian into the search engine and trusting that the ever-useful Wikipedia would provide an immediate mirror image in English. In the majority of cases, it was easy, especially with prominent historical characters and famous locations. However, researching lesser known figures required reading articles and other documents—sometimes trying to locate books in English—hoping to come across the required information. I also had to beware of so-called false friends. For example, wouldn't it be fair to assume that Brutus's wife, in Italian *Porzia*, would be an English *Portia*, just like the heroine in *The Merchant of Venice*? Well, no. In English, Brutus's wife is actually a *Porcia*. Same pronunciation, different spelling: the joy of transliteration into English and its sometimes illogical, inconsistent consequences.

Because of the documented nature of historical nonfiction, you have to be extremely precise as a translator. While in fiction you have to exercise some imagination and reproduce not what the author necessarily writes but what they think, in nonfiction you have to toe the line of literality. You're not required to take residence in the author's thoughts and interpret them as loyally to their essence as you can. You have to convey exactly what they say. There is no shade; everything is out in bright daylight.

In the case of Alberto Angela's *Cleopatra*, the line to toe was clearly defined, therefore easy to follow. The author had a definite sense of direction and this, for a translator, is a most welcome trait.

—*Katherine Gregor*

Here ends Alberto Angela's
Cleopatra.

The first edition of this book was printed
and bound at LSC Communications in
Harrisonburg, Virginia, February 2021.

A NOTE ON THE TYPE

The text of this novel was set in Adobe Garamond Pro, a typeface
designed in 1989 by Robert Slimbach. It was based on two distinctive examples of the French Renaissance style: a Roman type by
Claude Garamond (1499–1561) and an Italic type by Robert Granjon
(1513–1590). The typeface was developed after Slimbach studied
the fifteenth-century equipment at the Plantin-Moretus Museum
in Antwerp, Belgium. Adobe Garamond Pro faithfully captures the
original Garamond's grace and clarity, and it is used extensively in
print for its elegance and readability.

HarperVia

An imprint dedicated to publishing international voices,
offering readers a chance to encounter other lives and other
points of view via the language of the imagination.